NOMADIC THEORY

GENDER AND CULTURE

ROSI BRAIDOTTI

NOMADIC THEORY

THE PORTABLE ROSI BRAIDOTTI

COLUMBIA UNIVERSITY PRESS

NEW YORK

COLUMBIA UNIVERSITY PRESS

Publishers Since 1893

New York Chichester, West Sussex

Copyright © 2011 Columbia University Press

All rights reserved

Library of Congress Cataloging-in-Publication Data

Braidotti, Rosi.

Nomadic theory: the portable Rosi Braidotti / Rosi Braidotti.

p. cm. — (Gender and culture)

Includes bibliographical references (p.) and index.

ISBN 978-0-231-15190-0 (cloth: alk. paper)—ISBN 978-0-231-15191-7 (pbk.:

alk. paper)—ISBN 978-0-231-52542-8 (e-book)

1. Philosophy, Modern—21st century. 2. Continental philosophy.

3. Critical theory. I. Title.

B805.B69 2011

195—dc23

2011040404

Casebound editions of Columbia University Press books are printed
on permanent and durable acid-free paper.

Printed in the United States of America

c 10 9 8 7 6 5 4 3 2 1

p 10 9 8 7 6 5 4 3 2 1

Designed by Lisa Hamm

References to Internet Web sites (URLs) were accurate at the time of writing.
Neither the author nor Columbia University Press is responsible for Web
sites that may have expired or changed since the book was prepared.

CONTENTS

3 NOMADIC CITIZENSHIP

4 POWERS OF AFFIRMATION

5 CONCLUSION

ACKNOWLEDGMENTS

M y heartfelt gratitude goes primarily to Jennifer Crewe, my publisher, who instigated this project and saw it through. Nancy Miller was enthusiastic and supportive as ever; Elizabeth Weed's insightful comments were most welcome. Thanks also to Claire Colebrook for her inspiration and lucid criticism and to Clare Hemmings, Patrick Hanafin, and Lisa Baraiter for their careful reading of my texts. I am very grateful to the dean of my faculty, Wiljan van der Akker, for doing everything in his power to create work conditions conducive to completing this book. I wish to thank many generations of research assistants whose help with bibliographical details and editing was precious: Stephanie Paalvast did an amazing job in the final round, but before her Marleen and Pauline Vincenten, Sandra Solomon, Valeska Hovener, Kristl van Eijk, and Eva Midden provided vital assistance. I also profited enormously from the comments and support of former students and younger colleagues: Bolette Blaagaard and Iris van der Tuin, Maayke Botman, Rutvica Andrijasevic, Cecilia Alsberg, Sarah Bracke, Esther Captain, and Griet Roets were especially supportive. There are too many graduate students I should thank for the inspiration and the vitality, so I acknowledge them all collectively. A special word of thanks and praise for Esther Rinkens, the executive manager of the Centre for the Humanities, whose efficiency management, loyalty, and harmonious disposition created time for my writing and also to Lianne Toussaint. All my gratitude to Natasha Unkart, my favorite photographer, who designed the stunning cover. To my brother Gus, my sister Gio, and to my parents Mario and Bruna for their unfailing enthusiasm.

Special thanks to Anneke Smelik, for an amazing life together.

■■■

"Animals, Anomalies, and Unorganic Others" in *Publications of the Modern Language Association of America* (PMLA) (Modern Language Association, 2009).

"Affirmative Ethics and Bio-Politics" in *New Formations* (Lawrence and Wishart, 2007).

"Biomacht und Nekro-Politik. Überleberungen zu einer Ethik der Nachhaltigkeit" in *Springerin, Hefte fur Gegenwartskunst* (Verein Springerin, 2007).

"Affirmation, Pain, and Empowerment" in *Asian Journal of Women's Studies* (Ewha Womans University Press, 2008).

'Affirmation Versus Vulnerability: On Contemporary Ethical Debates" in *Symposium: Canadian Journal of Continental Philosophy* (Canadian Society for Continental Philosophy, 2006).

"Becoming Woman/Animal/Imperceptible" in Rosi Braidotti, *Transpositions* (Cambridge: Polity, 2006).

"Meta(l)morphoses" in *Theory, Culture, and Society* (Sage, 1997).

"Meta(l)flesh" in Zoe Detsi-Diamanti, Katerina Kitsi-Mitakou, and Effie Yiannopoulou, eds., *The Future of Flesh: Bodily Mutation and Change* (London: Palgrave Macmillan, 2009).

"Towards the Posthuman" in Rosi Braidotti, *la philosophie . . . là où on ne l'attend pas* (Paris: Larousse, 2009).

"Feminist Philosophy" in John Mullarkey and Beth Lord, eds., *The Continuum Companion to Continental Philosophy* (London: Continuum, 2009).

"A Critical Cartography of Feminist Post-postmodernism" in *Australian Feminist Studies* (Taylor and Francis, 2005).

"Intensive Genre and the Demise of Gender" in *Angelaki. Journal of the Theoretical Humanities* (Taylor and Francis, 2008).

"In Spite of the Times: The Postsecular Turn in Feminism" in *Theory, Culture, and Society* (Sage, 2008).

"On Becoming Europeans" in Luisa Passerini, Dawn Lyon, Enrica Capussoti, and Loanna Laliotou, eds., *Women Migrants from East to West. Gender, Mobility and Belonging in Contemporary Europe* (Oxford: Berghahn, 2007).

"Nomadism: Against Methodological Nationalism" in *Diaspora* (Toronto: University of Toronto Press, 2010).

"Elemental Complexity and Relational Vitality: The Relevance of Nomadic Thought for Contemporary Science" in Peter Gaffney, ed., *The Force of the Virtual: Deleuze, Science, and Philosophy* (Minneapolis: University of Minnesota Press, 2010).

"A Secular Prayer" in Bart de Baere, ed., *All That Is Solid Melts Into Air: Five Reflections on Materialist Spirituality in Contemporary Art* (Antwerp: Uitgeverij Lannoo, 2009).

Selected chapters from *Metamorphoses: Towards a Materialist Theory of Becoming* (Cambridge: Polity, 2002).

NOMADIC THEORY

INTRODUCTION

It's not enough simply to say concepts possess movement; you also
have to construct intellectually mobile concepts.

        —GILLES DELEUZE, *NEGOTIATIONS*

This volume of selected essays presents an ongoing project in nomadic
theory, with the aim of analyzing, illustrating, and assessing the relevance of nomadic thought today. It constitutes the companion to *Nomadic Subjects*, which has just been published in a revised and expanded
second edition (Braidotti 2011). The two books are sequential and interlinked, though each is autonomous and stands on its own: *Nomadic Theory*
is in some ways the application of the fundamental principles outlined in
the previous volume. Being single and multiple, independent and interconnected, *Nomadic Subjects* and *Nomadic Theory* form a complex singularity or a nondualistic assemblage. They frame and actualize a nomadology
that instills movement and mobility at the heart of thinking. My aim in this
book is to explore from a variety of locations the method, structure, and the
practical applications of nomadic theory. This volume argues that thinking
today is structurally nomadic. There are at least three ways to illustrate this
principle: conceptually, politically, and contextually. Let me address each one
of these in order, by way of an introduction.

CONCEPT

Conceptually, nomadic thought stresses the idea of embodiment and the embodied and embedded material structure of what we commonly call thinking. It is a materialism of the flesh that unifies mind and body in a new approach that blurs all boundaries. The embodiment of the mind and the embrainment of the body (Marks 1998) are a more apt formulation for nomadic thought than Cartesian or other forms of dualism. Nomadic thought builds on the insights of psychoanalysis by stressing the dynamic and self-organizing structure of thought processes. The space of nomadic thinking is framed by perceptions, concepts, and imaginings that cannot be reduced to human, rational consciousness. In a vitalist materialist way, nomadic thought invests all that lives, even inorganic matter, with the power of consciousness in the sense of self-affection. Not only does consciousness not coincide with mere rationality, but it is not even the prerogative of humans. This emphasis on affect and extended consciousness, however, is not the same as the Freudian unconscious.

Nomadic thought rejects the psychoanalytic idea of repression and the negative definition of desire as lack inherited from Hegelian dialectics. It borrows instead from Spinoza a positive notion of desire as an ontological force of becoming. This achieves an important goal: it makes all thinking into an affirmative activity that aims at the production of concepts, precepts, and affects in the relational motion of approaching multiple others. Thinking is about tracing lines of flight and zigzagging patterns that undo dominant representations. Dynamic and outward bound, nomadic thought undoes the static authority of the past and redefines memory as the faculty that decodes residual traces of half-effaced presences; it retrieves archives of leftover sensations and accesses afterthoughts, flashbacks, and mnemonic traces. Philosophical thought especially is a form of self-reflexivity unfolding in perpetual motion in a continuous present that is project oriented and intrapersonal.

The emphasis nomadic thought places on bodily materialism goes far in dispelling the transcendental assumptions of classical philosophy. It emphasises the machinic yet vibrant quality of the lived body, for instance by stressing how the mind is affected by the dynamic nature of perception and the data inscription relayed by complex neural networks in the brain. Even the loftiest of philosophical dialogues relies on the movements of the vocal chords and lips of speaking subjects engaged in that specific mode of relation. The motions and passions of the cognitive, perceptive, and affective faculties engender creative leaps of the imagination that animate the mind, illuminate the senses, and connect transversally well beyond the frame of the individual self. Nomadic philosophy is the discursive practice with the highest degree of affinity to the mobility of intelligence: it is both physical, material, and yet speculative and ethereal. The dialogue itself is a movement of exchange between two consenting antagonists, such as friends, opponents, or traveling companions. Philosophical thought is the martial art of the mind in that it frames and choreographs the space in between self and other with the aim to figure out, contain, and anticipate each other's reactions. Philosophical thought is structurally nomadic.

This materialist approach to philosophy rests on a monistic vision of matter in opposition to dichotomous and dualistic ways of thought. A nomadic concept offers a strong alternative not only to liberal individualism discourses but also to the branch of poststructurally inflected linguistically based theories that overemphasize melancholia and the work of mourning (Derrida 2001). Nomadic theory foregrounds the force of affirmation as the empowering mode for both critical theory and political praxis. This is a crucial and incisive distinction: whereas the linguistic turn produces a negative form of social constructivism—matter being formatted and regulated by a master code—nomadic thought conceptualizes matter as self-organized and relational in its very structures. This means that each nomadic connection offers at least the possibility of an ethical relation of opening out toward an empowering connection to others. Each relation is therefore an ethical project indexed on affirmation and mutual specification, not on the dialectics of recognition and lack.

POLITICS

Politically, nomadic thought is the expression of a nonunitary vision of the subject, defined by motion in a complex manner that is densely material. It invites us to rethink the structures and boundaries of the self by tackling the deeper conceptual roots of issues of identity. It is particularly important not to confuse the process of nomadic subjectivity with individualism or particularity. Whereas identity is a bounded, ego-indexed habit of fixing and capitalizing on one's selfhood, subjectivity is a socially mediated process of relations and negotiations with multiple others and with multilayered social structures.

Consequently, the emergence of social subjects is always a collective enterprise, "external" to the self, while it also mobilizes the self's in-depth structures. Issues of subjectivity raise questions of entitlement, in terms of power as restrictive (*potestas*) but also as empowering or affirmative (*potentia*). Power relations act simultaneously as the most "external," collective, social phenomenon and also as the most intimate or "internal" one. Or, rather, power is the process that flows incessantly in between the most "internal" and the most "external" forces. As Foucault taught us, power is a situation or a process, not an object or an essence. Subjectivity is the effect of these constant flows of in-between power connections. This produces a methodology that is very important for nomadic thought: the cartographic method. A cartography is a theoretically based and politically informed reading of the process of power relations. It fulfills the function of providing both exegetical tools and creative theoretical alternatives, so as to assess the impact of material and discursive conditions upon our embodied and embedded subjectivity.

As early as the 1970s, Gilles Deleuze (Deleuze and Guattari 1972), while targeting the inertia and structural injustice of the political establishment as a primary concern, also pointed out the limitations of the liberatory potential of Marxism and especially of the violence and authoritarianism of *gauchiste* or left-wing political groups. He was equally suspicious, however, of the humanistic assumptions of the claim to universal human rights or the Kantian idea of the universal and self-correcting validity of human reason. He stressed instead the need to unveil power relations where they are simultaneously most effective and most invisible: in the specific locations of one's own intellectual and social practice. I took this to imply that one has to start from micro-instances of embodied and embedded self and the complex web of social relations that compose subject positions. As feminists say: one has to think global, but act local.

This cartographic approach and the grounded philosophical accountability it entails is more relevant than ever nowadays. Poststructuralist philosophies have produced an array of alternative concepts and practices of nonunitary political subjectivity. From the "split subject" of psychoanalysis to the subject-in-process of Foucault, the "sexed subject which is not one" of Irigaray and the rhizomatic complex of Deleuze and Guattari, multiplicity and complexity have been widely debated in Continental philosophy. After the decline of postmodernism—reductively associated with cognitive and moral relativism—those experimental approaches to the question of the subject raise some skeptical eyebrows. What exactly is the advantage of these alternative notions and practices of the subject? What are the values—ethical and political—they can offer? What good are they to anybody? And how much fun are they? This volume is an attempt to answer these crucial questions by producing an adequate cartography of our historical situation as well as to expose the logic of the new power relations operative today.

CONTEXT

To give the readers of this volume the context for nomadic thought, we need to turn to the philosophies of difference that have emerged in France and the U.S. since the 1980s. Nomadic theory belongs to the branch of poststructuralist philosophy that is less influenced by the "linguistic turn" of semiotics, psychoanalysis, and deconstruction than by a school of political theory, science, and epistemology studies that stretches back to the eighteenth century. It is related to the tradition of "enchanted materialism" that is one of the distinctive traits of French philosophy.

This distinction between different strands of poststructuralist thought is very important, considering that in the U.S. poststructuralism is identified with the linguistic turn. This has led to violent dismissal of the linguistic school on the part of realist Deleuzians like De Landa (2002, 2006). Nomadic thought is more nuanced and less hasty in dismissing others. It is undeniable that the primacy of structures in the process of subject formation is one of the aspects of high structuralism that both Lacan and Derrida retain, albeit in their own original variations. The psychoanalystic emphasis on the role of the symbolic—or the phallologocentric code in Derrida or the heterosexist matrix in Butler—posits a master code, or a single central grid that formats and produces the subject. This social constructivist grid leaves little room for negotiation and instills loss and melancholia at the core of the subject.

Nomadic thought takes a very different route—by positing the primacy of intelligent, sexed, and self-organizing matter, it approaches the process of subject formation in a distributive, dispersed, and multiple manner. Modulations or processes of differing within a common matter rely on a definition of power as both productive and restrictive and strike an affirmative route between empowerment and entrapment. As a consequence, nomadic thought rejects melancholia in favor of the politics of affirmation and mutual specification of self and other in sets of relations or assemblages.

Central to the nomadic subject is the emphasis on the intimate connection between critique and creation. Critique is consequently not only a sterile opposition but also an active engagement of the conceptual imagination in the task of producing sustainable alternatives (see part 4, "Powers of Affirmation," both chapters 10, "Powers of Affirmation," 11, "Sustainable Ethics and the Body in Pain").

Nomadic theory grows from these fundamental assumptions. It critiques the self-interest, the repressive tolerance, and the deeply seated conservatism of the institutions that are officially in charge of knowledge production, especially the university but also the media and the law. Foucault (1975) explicitly singles out for criticism the pretension of classical philosophy to be a master discipline that supervises and organizes other discourses and opposes to this abstract and universalistic mission the idea that philosophy is just a toolbox.

What this means is that the aim of philosophy as nomadic critical theory is the production of pragmatic and localized tools of analysis for the power relations at work in society at large and more specifically within its own practice. The philosopher becomes no more than a provider of analytic services: a technician of knowledge. In the same spirit, Deleuze (1953, 1962) redefines philosophy in the "problematic" mode as the constant questioning of the dominant "image of thought" at work in most of our ideas with the purpose of destabilizing them in the "nomadic" mode. In my own work on nomadic thought I adopt a creative redefinition of thinking that links philosophy to the creation of new forms of subjectivity and collective experiments with ways of actualizing them.

This results in a critique of representational regimes that focus especially on the dominant image of thought as the expression of a white, masculine, adult, heterosexual, urban-dwelling, property-owning subject. Deleuze and Guattari label this dominant subject as the Majority, or the Molar formation; Irigaray calls it the Logic of the Same. For nomadic thought, this replication of sameness is counteracted by creative efforts aimed at activating the positivity of differences as affirmative praxis (see part 1, "Metamorphoses," especially chapters 1, "Transposing Differences," and 2, "Meta(l) morphoses"). Replacing the metaphysics of being with a process ontology bent on becoming, that is to say, subversive moves of detachment from the dominant system of representation. Nomadic theory combines potentially contradictory elements: it is materialist and vitalist, fluid and accountable and it remains resolutely pragmatic throughout. The central tenet of nomadic thought is to reassert the dynamic nature of thinking and the need to reinstate movement at the heart of thought by actualizing a nonunitary vision of the thinking subject.

These genealogical considerations get exacerbated in the present context. Whether as a result of the demise of postmodernist skepticism or as a generalized fatigue of the deconstructive project—a "posttheory" frame of mind has become the doxa of the globalized world. Propped up by the neoliberal ethos that assesses everything—including scientific ideas, philosophical concepts, and human worth—in narrowly economical terms, theory fatigue has merged into a contemporary social landscape that combines populist appeals to neorealism with traditional anti-intellectualism.

The post-1989, post-9/11, postpeace context we inhabit since the official start of perennial warfare against foreign and home-grown "terrorists," and the spread of generalized governance by fear, plays a crucial role. Collectively unable to produce an analysis of globalization that is "worthy" of the present—free of nostalgia but also of tendentious euphoria—advanced liberal societies have replaced critique with acquiescence and doubts with apathy. We are told with no degree of uncertainty that we live in postpostmodern, postsecular, postfeminist, postcommunist, postindustrial times. What all the *posts* point to, however—let alone what they may have in common—is never clarified. One thing is clear, though: all these *posts* are just the pretext for the populist dismissal of high theory.

After the official end of the cold war, all the radical movements of the twentieth century have lost credibility and been discarded, including socialism and feminism. No wonder, then, that the proliferation of *posts* carries on unchallenged and that post-theory is on the social agenda as a necessary prelude to anti-intellectualism. As an antidote to the escalating use of dismissive prefixes—nomadic thought accomplishes a double aim. The first is genealogical or cartographic: it turns to the sources of European critical theory in an inspirational manner. The second is conceptual: it seeks for sustainable alternatives and affirmative modes of engagement in the present by linking the act of thinking to the creation of new concepts and critique to creation. This volume attempts to discuss both these aspects.

Post also evokes the prospect of a looming apocalypse—as if we had indeed reached the end of time (Fukuyama 1989, 2002). Coming after the great theoretical exuberance and sheer genius of the masters and mistresses of poststructuralism, we appear to have entered some sort of afterlife. The spectral dimension of our historicity is felt strongly in Continental philosophy, where disquisitions about mortality and species or environmental extinction have grown into a full-fledged necropolitical field of analysis (see chapter 12, "Forensic Futures"). Nomadic theory strikes its own note in this debate on behalf of the affirmative force of nonhuman life—zoe—and its posthuman potential. I explore especially the ethical implications of affirmation (see chapter 5, "Matter-Realist Feminism," and chapter 6, "Intensive Genre and the Demise of Gender"). In my view, *post* does not spell the end, but the generative start of a new phase of the fundamental idea of nomadic affirmative politics and the empowering feminism, antiracism, and environmentalism it sustains. Nomadic subjects require and produce nonunitary, multiple, and complex politics.

WHY NOMADIC THOUGHT?

In these times of accelerating changes, many traditional points of reference and age-old habits are being recomposed, albeit in contradictory ways. At such a time more conceptual creativity is necessary—a theoretical effort is needed to bring about the conceptual leap across the contemporary social landscape. Nomadic thought is a response to this challenge. This includes the schizoid affective economy of inertia, nostalgia, paranoia, and other forms of critical *stasis,* on the one hand, and overzealous excitement, on the other, that is induced by the contradictory conditions of advanced capitalism. In such a context, we need to learn to think differently about ourselves and the ongoing processes of deep-seated transformation.

A major concern of this book is consequently the deficit in the scale of representation that accompanies the structural transformations of subjectivity in the social, cultural, and political spheres of late postindustrial culture. Accounting adequately for changes is a challenge that shakes up long-established habits of thought. In order to produce grounded accounts and more subtle differentiation in the kind of different nomadic flows at work in our world, we need more conceptual creativity. More ethical courage is also needed and deeper theoretical efforts to sustain the qualitative shift of perspective that may help us confront the complexities of our era (see chapter 7, "Postsecular Paradoxes").

This book aims at providing singular cartographies of some of the political and cultural forces operative in contemporary globalized societies. On that basis, I will present a number of my own variations on nomadic thought, while surveying the state of contemporary feminist philosophies of the subject in general (part 2, "Feminist Transpositions") and of the nomadic subject in particular (part 4 "Powers of Affirmation"), with special focus on the analysis of contemporary culture (part 1, "Metamorphoses"). I will also offer readings of some of the more striking aspects of contemporary political culture, especially the powerful lure of neonationalism and Euro-centric xenophobia (part 3 "Nomadic Citizenship"). The logic of this sequence is partly chronological, building up from earlier to more recent essays, partly conceptual. The book builds up gradually to a political punch line, and the movement flows from more critical pieces to more affirmative ones, as if to demonstrate the necessity of a practice of affirmation. Of course it is my hope that readers may open the book at any one point and be able to start reading it almost at random, in keeping with nomadic habits. Let me briefly introduce each main part of the book.

METAMORPHOSES

Part 1 presents a cartography of the changing social conditions of advanced capitalism. It starts from the acknowledgment that the project of linking thought to movement is centuries-old, and therefore the task of decoding contemporary variations on this theme is quite urgent. Since its pre-Socratic origins, philosophical thought has enjoyed a privileged relationship to movement, mobility, and motion. Closer to physical training than to cerebral ruminations, classical philosophy was conceptualized as gymnastics of the soul, fitness of the wits, robustness of judgment coupled with speculative stamina. From the deliberative steps taken by free men on the Greek agora (women, blacks, non-Europeans, and children need not apply) to the peripatetic pilgrimages of the medieval students across the ancient European universities, most Continental philosophers actually thought on their feet, Emmanuel Kant's punctual daily walk around town being emblematic of this tradition.

European thought, however, is also marked by hostile moves and antagonistic relations. Over the centuries, the scientific and intellectual motions of the European mind have expressed themselves in the violent expulsion of ethnically marked undesirables from the heart of the continent. Since the dawn of modernity, the staunch belief in a "white man's burden" propelled the movement of European colonial expansions across the oceans of the globe. The enforced enslavement of natives, particularly across the transatlantic route, pioneered a new kind of coercive mobility and new levels of brutality in the crossing.

Back in the metropolis, the ponderous yet lazy gaze of the nineteenth-century flaneurs theorized the art of walking as a leisurely literary stroll round town. This endowed the continental urban landscape with the mystery and seduction often reserved for faraway places—a domestic variation on the exotic. Orientalism and Occidentalism proceed hand in hand on the motorways of modernity. A high degree of speeding power is central to the new forms of mobility propelled by technological mediation, all the way to the contemporary information highways. It's on the road again and again for Continental philosophy, yet not all passages are voluntary, freely chosen, or ethically sustainable. Accounting both spatially and temporally or historically for these dramatically different forms of mobility is one of the key ethical challenges of nomadic critical theory today. The aim to construct intellectually mobile concepts requires an ethics of differential coding for the various modes and forms of mobility.

Our historical context has intensified the issue of mobility and multiplied its complexities. The contradictions engendered by globalization confront us in fact with new conceptual, methodological, and political challenges. These are strange times, and strange things are happening. Times of ever expanding, yet spasmodic waves of transformation that engender the simultaneous occurrence of contradictory effects. Times of fast-moving changes that do not wipe out the brutality of power relations, but in many ways intensify them and bring them to the point of implosion (chapter 1, "Transposing Differences"). Living in such times of rapid changes may be alternatively—or simultaneously—exhilarating and exhausting, yet the task of representing these changes to ourselves and engaging productively with the contradictions, paradoxes, and injustices they engender is a perennial challenge. How to account for fast-changing conditions is hard work; how to escape the velocity of change is even harder (chapter 2, "Meta(l)morphoses: Women, Aliens, and Machines"). Unless one likes complexity, one cannot feel at home in the twenty-first century. Transformations, metamorphoses, mutations, processes of change amidst dissonant power relations have become familiar patterns in the lives of most contemporary subjects (chapter 3, "Animals and Other Anomalies"). They are also vital concerns, however, for critical theory and the social and political institutions that are expected to come to terms with them.

A contemporary volume about nomadic theory appearing in a portable edition, moreover, should be able to rejoice in the creative and nonvicious circularity it expresses, since it can hardly avoid it. There is pride in circularity, especially if one is trying to instill movement into thought. Short of abandoning the Gutenberg galaxy altogether and declaring the book form obsolete, a portable book of nomadic critical theory today needs to reflect on its specific forms of mobility and on the material and discursive conditions that support it. More to the point: how can nomadic thought *not* be portable and in what ways can the readers of this specific book expect to be transported into the genre of critical theory and not lose touch with the immediate social-cultural conditions of their lived experience? The desire that sustains this book is to provide ideas that may function as navigational tools to sharpen our understanding of the material conditions of our existence in a fast-changing, technologically mediated world. Nomadic theory rests on politically invested cartographies of the present conditions of mobility in a globalized context. More specifically, it aims at pointing out the various power differences between distinct forms, categories, and practices of movement for both humans and nonhuman mobile units (chapter 4, "The Cosmic Buzz of Insects"). Telling the difference among these different differences is the key question. Language cracks under the strain.

Let us hang on, therefore, to the circular pride of nomadic theory in portable format: what does it tell us about the political economy of meanings and ideas in advanced, globalized, technologically mediated societies? Firstly, it focuses on the paradoxes of dematerialized materiality that lie at the core of our technologically mediated culture, including academic culture. Embracing electronic publishing as the most mobile media and hence the fastest way forward for contemporary thought in some ways begs the question of nomadic theory. Even if all paper-based books were to turn into "Kindles," they would remain just as firmly attached to the material premises that produced them. Kindle, by any other name, is just as bookish as its Gutenberg ancestors. Virtual reality is in fact densely material, and the digital is just the social by another name.

Nomadic theory, especially in a portable format, is mobile because it foregrounds the materialist and vitalist structure of thought. That, however, does not make it any less grounded or ethically accountable. It just relocates the materiality of the technological artifact in a different medium, that is to say, a different social practice, which engenders specific social relations and interactions. The ideas of this book will not be any less portable for those who download it from the Internet or into their Kindles or other electronic readers. It would only become otherwise nomadic in the process. As a consequence, mobility does not necessarily equate digital media or information networks and the electronic Web may not be the most effective means of accessing ideas today. Hence a new set of questions that emerge as central to the concerns of this book: what is the best way to access ideas today? What is the activity of critical thinking like, well into the third millennium?

The social and discursive metamorphoses of our times impose the need to reflect on the perverse temporality at work in the different modes of mobility we experience. We inhabit paradoxical time frames structured by the simultaneity of internally contradictory social effects: the oversaturated (Baudrillard 1993) and the hypervoid (Augé 1995) or the archaic (Gutenberg press) and the hypermodern (electronic books). In this context, contradictory social effects not only coincide and coexist in space and time but also strengthen and support each other. This produces slightly schizophrenic results and locates readers in a permanent state of oscillation between paradoxical options that they seldom had any say in creating in the first place. Moreover, considering the persistence of social—that is to say, genderized, sexualized, racialized, and naturalized—power differences, the fundamental tension that emerges is between spectacular new versions of age-old questions of domination and exclusion.

FEMINIST TRANSPOSITIONS

In part 2 of this volume I will apply some of my key concepts to the production of alternative interventions in the present contextual conditions. Given the complex and internally contradictory nature of the globalized system, feminist critical theory needs to innovate in its very tools of analysis. The current cultural paradoxes: on the one hand, rising conservatism, on the other, fascination with changes and mutant and nonunitary others, express both a deep anxiety about the fast rate of transformation of identities and also the poverty of our social imaginary to cope creatively with the ongoing transformations. In rising to this challenge, feminist theory engages with contemporary scientific advances and new understandings of the structure of bodies and matter (see chapter 5, "Matter-Realist Feminism").

Feminism is the social and theoretical movement that, more than any other, expressed a double-edged vision that combined creativity with critique. Although it is critical in political orientation, feminist nomadic thought is never negative; on the contrary, it makes an explicit case for affirmative politics. The ongoing processes of transformation require alternative figurations to express the kind of internally contradictory multifaceted subjects we have become. There is a noticeable gap between how we live—in emancipated or postfeminist, multiethnic global societies, with high technologies and telecommunication, allegedly free borders, and increased security controls as well as a state of warfare—and how we represent to ourselves this lived familiarity. This belies an imaginative poverty that can be partly read as the "jet lag" problem of living simultaneously in different time zones. The schizophrenic mode that is characteristic of our historical era creates methodological difficulties of representation. I propose transdisciplinarity and the method of transpositions and nonlinearity as ways of addressing these challenges (see especially chapter 8).

It is urgent to both explore the need and to provide illustrations for new figurations, i.e., alternative representations and social locations for the kind of hybrid, sexualized nomadic subjects we are becoming. Figurations are not figurative ways of thinking, but rather more materialistic mappings of situated, embedded, and embodied positions. They derive from the feminist method of the "politics of location" and build it into a discursive strategy.

Figurations are ways of expressing different situated subject positions. A figuration renders the nonunitary image of a multilayered subject. Feminist theories since postmodernism demonstrated that the definition of identities takes place between the polarized duality of: nature/technology; male/female; black/white—in the spaces that flow and connect in between. We live in permanent processes of transition, hybridization, and nomadization (see chapter 6, "Intensive Genre and the Politics of Gender"). And these in-between states and stages defy established modes of theoretical representation. The figuration of nomadic subjects, however, should never be taken as a new universal metaphor for the human or posthuman condition. As I argued in the companion volume, *Nomadic Subjects* (Braidotti, 2011), we need to provide, instead, accurate cartographies of the different politics of location for subjects-in-becoming.

A figuration is a living map, a transformative account of the self—it's no metaphor. It fulfills the purpose of finding suitable situated locations to make the difference between different locations. Being nomadic, home-less, a migrant, an exile, a refugee, a tourist, a rape-in-war victim, an itinerant migrant, an illegal immigrant, an expatriate, a mail-order bride, a foreign caretaker of the young or the elderly of the economically developed world, a global venture financial expert, a humanitarian relief worker in the UN global system, a citizen of a country that no longer exists (Yugoslavia, Czechoslovakia, the Soviet Union)—these are no metaphors, but social locations.

Having no passport or having too many of them is neither equivalent nor is it merely metaphorical, as some feminist critics of nomadic subjectivity have suggested. These are highly specific geopolitical and historical locations—it's history tattooed on your body. One may be empowered or beautified by it, but most people are not; some just die of it. Figurations attempt to draw a cartography of the power relations that define these respective positions. They don't just embellish or metaphorize: they rather express different socioeconomic and symbolic locations. Situated locations draw a cartographic map of power relations and thus can also help identify possible sites and strategies of resistance. In other words, the project of finding adequate representations, which was raised to new heights by the poststructuralist generation, is neither a retreat into self-referential textuality, nor is it a form of apolitical resignation. Nonlinearity and a nonunitary vision of the subject do not necessarily result in either cognitive or moral relativism, let alone social anarchy. I rather see them as significant sites for reconfiguring feminist political practice and redefining political subjectivity.

If the only constant in the third millennium is change, then the challenge lies in how to think about processes rather than concepts. This is neither a simple nor a particularly welcome task in the theoretical language and conventions that have become the norm in social and political theory as well as cultural critique. In spite of the sustained efforts of many radical critics, the mental habit of linearity and objectivity persists in its hegemonic hold over our thinking. Thus, it is by far simpler to think about the concept A or B or of B as non A, rather than the process of what goes on in between A and B. Thinking through flows and interconnections remains a difficult challenge. The fact that theoretical reason is concept bound and fastened upon essential notions makes it difficult to find adequate representations for processes, fluid in-between flows of data, experience, and information. They tend to get frozen in spatial, metaphorical modes of representation that itemize them as "problems."

How to represent mutations, changes, transformations, rather than Being in its classical modes, is the challenge for those who are committed to engendering and enjoying changes and the great source of anxiety for those who are not. This is one of the issues that the feminist philosopher Luce Irigaray (1985) addresses, notably in her praise of the "mechanic of fluids" against the fixity and lethal inertia of conceptual thinking (also known as the phallocentric logic of masculine self-representation). Gilles Deleuze (1962, 1968) also takes up this challenge by loosening the conceptual ties that have kept philosophy fastened on some semireligiously held beliefs about reason, logos, the metaphysics of presence, and the logic of the Same (also known as molar, sedentary, majority).

The relocation of difference and of the self-other relation constitutes one of the main themes of this book. The perverse spin of globalized capitalism has altered the status and interrelation of the anthropological differences that preoccupied high poststructuralism back in the 1980s. The sexualized, racialized, and naturalized difference embodied in the "constitutive others" of modernity has entered into the spinning effects of global proliferation and commodification. The deterritorialization process results in the relocation of what used to be called difference and of the dialectical relationship between self and others. These have shifted along the axes of contemporary biogenetic capitalism. What emerges today as a result of these transformations, both social and scientific, is the biopolitical relevance of Life itself as a nonhuman force. This posthuman horizon is one of the great paradoxes of our times—caught as we are in the schizophrenic mode of overdevelopment and underexperimentation, euphoria and melancholia, scientific revolutions and political restoration. My code name for the posthuman dimension is zoe—nonhuman life, which will play a major role in this book (see especially chapter 7, "Postsecular Paradoxes").

NOMADIC CITIZENSHIP

In part 3 I will explore more specifically the consequences of the ongoing changes for the theory and practice of active citizenship. The contemporary world has changed considerably since the days when the poststructuralist philosophers put "difference" on the theoretical and political agenda. The ideological climate has turned to new forms of essentialism with a vengeance. The return of biological naturalism, under the cover of genetics, molecular biology, evolutionary theories, and the despotic authority of the DNA has caused both an inflation and a reification of the notion of "difference" and a reductive view of matter. In scientific culture, on the other hand, the understanding of "matter" has evolved dramatically since the days of historical materialism: a new brand of "materialism" is current in our scientific practices, which reinstates the vital, self-organizing capacities of what was previously seen as inert matter (see especially chapter 5, "Matter-Realist Feminism"). As a result, the dualistic mode of thinking supported by social constructivism is no longer sufficient, though it remains a necessary hermeneutical key to the analysis of the present. The process-oriented structure of vital materialism is one of the strengths of nomadic thought, supported by its Spinozist monistic philosophy. Vital materialism is both in tune with the great scientific discovery of our age—biogenetics, new evolutionary theories, neural and cognitive sciences—and with the ethical imperative to engage with the present and be worthy of it (see chapter 10, "Powers of Affirmation").

The political repercussions, however, are often problematic. After the official end of the cold war in 1989, rhetorical celebrations of the superiority of capitalism as the optimal form of human evolution (Fukuyama 1989) have become a new master-narrative. Rising right-wing populism across the

European Union promotes cultural essentialism, racism, and Islamophobia. Resting on fixed notions of one's cultural parameters and territory, their ideas of "cultural difference" are deterministic, oppositional, and hence exclusive as well as both intrinsically and explicitly xenophobic. The deportation of unwanted people is a reality in most Western societies today. The Berlin Wall may have come down, but new ones have gone up just as speedily: on the U.S.-Mexican border, in the occupied territories in Palestine, and all around the edges of "Fortress Europe."

In the contemporary political context, *difference* functions as a negative term indexed on a hierarchy of values governed by binary oppositions: it conveys power relations and structural patterns of exclusion at the national, regional, provincial, or even more local level. Like a historical process of sedimentation, or a progressive accumulation of toxins, the concept of difference has been poisoned and has become the equivalent of inferiority: to be different from means to be worth less than. How can difference be cleansed of this negative charge? Is the positivity of difference, sometimes called "pure difference," thinkable? What are the conditions that may facilitate the thinkability of positive difference? What is the specific contribution of nomadic theory to these questions? It is precisely because of what I consider the political and social regression of this essentialist notion of difference that I find it important to reset the concept of difference in the direction of a nomadic, nonhierarchical, multidirectional social and discursive practice of multiplicity (see chapter 8, "Against Methodological Nationalism").

Again, the complexities multiply: advanced capitalism has mutated into a "difference engine" (Ansell-Pearson 1999) that functions through a proliferation of quantitative differences for the sake of commodification and profit. What seems to surface amidst the quantitative proliferation of differences, moreover, is the distinct absence of a qualitative shift of perspectives that may alter the rules of the game and challenge the master code, that is to say, the dominant axiom. Theoretical care is needed here because advanced capitalism is the great nomad par excellence in that it is propelled by the mobility of goods, data, and finances for the sake of profit and commodification. This profit-oriented, perverse nomadism translates into socioeconomic terms in the so-called flexibility of the working force: interim, untenured, substandard, underpaid work has become the norm in most advanced liberal economies. This negative and exploitative form of social mobility engenders transnational flows of migration and precariousness of actual working conditions, which produce categories of transitory citizens, temporary settlers, and resident foreigners. A global ideology of allegedly free mobility coexists alongside frozen borders and increasing discrimination and exclusion of multiple "disposable" others. In another paradoxical twist, therefore, the deterritorializations induced by the hypermobility of capitalism and the forms of migration and human mobility they entail, instead of challenging the hegemony of nation-states, strengthen their hold not only over territory and social space but also over identity and cultural memory. European racism today targets these alien others, migrants, and postcolonial subjects, as well as refuges and asylum seekers, for discriminatory practices and socioeconomic marginalization. Reductive reterritorializations form an integral part of the resurgence of nationalism as a knee-jerk reaction against globalized mobility. Centerless, but highly controlled in its all-pervasive global surveillance system, advanced capitalism installs a political economy of fear and suspicion, not only among the new geopolitical blocks that have emerged at the end of the cold war but also within them.

The analysis of this perverse political economy was already provided by Deleuze and Guattari (1972, 1980) and is still extraordinarily apt, accurate, and to the point today. So much so, that nomadic practices are still extremely popular nowadays in organizational management, corporate dynamics, and business administration. What might appear as a congruence of capitalism with nomadic theory verging on complicity, however, is also the means to identify ways of exceeding this system by setting it in motion from within. My practice of nomadic theory aims at cartographic accuracy, at providing qualitative analyses of the present that are in tune with the times but also adequately account for the brutality and the violence of our times as well as for their creative potential.

By extension, social and cultural critique is neither a matter of opposition in a dialectical and confrontational mode, nor just the lame quest for angles of resistance. It requires a robust praxis of collective engagement with the specific conditions of our times—for instance, the proliferation of quantitative differences and the erasure of qualitative shifts in ethical and political accountability. Furthermore, nomadic thought engages with the present not oppositionally but rather affirmatively and does so not out of acquiescence but rather out of the pragmatic conviction that the conditions that engender qualitative shifts will not emerge dialectically from a direct and violent confrontation with the present. They can only be actualized as praxis from conditions that are not there yet: they are virtual, that is to say, they need to be counteractualized, created, and brought about in a collective effort. The productive engagement with the present engenders sustainable futures (as I argue in chapters 11 and 12).

More specifically, in this volume I will explore possible models of nomadic citizenship (chapter 9, "Nomadic European Citizenship"). These are based on delinking the three basic components of the liberal view of citizenship: ethnic origin, national identity, and political agency. They also recompose them in new packages of rights and entitlements that require flexibility and hence multiple ecologies of belonging.

Thus, while being critically aware of the fact that nomadism is very much the thought of our age—in a way that had Foucault admitting that "one day our century will be Deleuzian"—I see this parallelism as a way of synchronizing critical theory with the present, which offers optimal conditions for the production of social alternatives. It is precisely because of the sharpness of the navigational tools provided by nomadic thought that we can assert the necessity of engaging with the present—being worthy of all that happens to us—in order to affect qualitative changes. What I propose is to work critically from within in order to exceed the present frame, while resisting nostalgic calls from worn-out formulae about "overthrowing the system." These dialectical formulations are both conceptually and politically inadequate to the perverse political economy of schizoid repetitions, internal contradictions, and ruthless executions of human and nonhuman disposable others that is the core of advanced, biogenetic capitalism.

As a consequence, I want to resist both the gravitational pull of a self-perpetuating replication of sameness on the part of the center and its dominant subject positions and also the reduction of the center to mere inertia and incurable melancholia. I am convinced that a new vital political role needs to be devised for the many "centers" punctuating the global economy and that this should aim at instilling processes of qualitative change at the very heart of the system. Margins and centers are relocated so as to destabilize each other in parallel, albeit dissymmetrical ways. The main objective is, through nomadic interventions, to deterritorialize dogmatic and hegemonic exclusionary power structures at the heart of the scattered hegemonic centers of the contemporary global world.

Considering the extent of the mutations taking place in our globalized world, it is clear that these transformations don't affect only the pole of the "others" but also dislocate the position and the prerogatives of the same, the dominant subject. The customary standard-bearers of Eurocentric phallocentrism no longer hold in a civil society that has become sexed female, male, and in between, multicultural and not inevitably or exclusively Christian. New emerging subject positions not only challenge this normative view of what counts as the subject but also trace alternative processes of becoming in an affirmative manner. Nomadic theory therefore addresses the issue of what may be the specific political and ethical initiative of the former center in order to rebalance and counteract contemporary power differentials.

In other words, the center needs to be set in motion toward a becoming-minoritarian that requires qualitative changes in the very structures of its subjectivity, but so do the margins. For there is no uncontaminated location free of power. Nor is there a subject—collective or individual—that can rightfully pretend to be the motor of the development of world history—in spite of unwarranted claims by self-appointed champions of leftist nostalgia. We need more humility and more pragmatism, if we are to invent a left-wing politics worthy of the third millennium. Much could be learned from political movements such as those espousing feminism, against racism, for gay rights, against war, and for the environmental. These movements made the critique of metadiscourse into a political priority and resisted the siren calls of overarching discourses about world revolution. Situated politics of locations is the best way to proceed: we need to think global but act local, in the situated here and now of our lived experience.

POWERS OF AFFIRMATION

In part 4 I will expose the vision of nomadic politics as affirmation and the construction of robust alternatives. Against the various liberal discourses on rights, but also in opposition to the aporias of a poststructuralist stance that wallows in melancholic self-pity and nostalgic longings, nomadic theory posits the politics of affirmation as a significant alternative for both critical theory and political praxis (chapter 10, "Powers of Affirmation"). Hence one of my key concerns in his book: how can qualitative shifts be framed and actualised, in clear dissonance from the pluralistic proliferation of quantified and commodified differences, which is the axiom of advanced capitalism? What forms of ethical and political practices of subjectivity are best suited to the task?

In opposition to the dominant practice of aporetic politics or reactive melancholia, this volume pleads for a more joyful perspective that stresses the role of thought as the creation of new concepts and the importance of politics in making such transmutations of values possible. It is only fitting, therefore, that this collection centers around essays on the forces of affirmation, inspired by Spinoza's ontological theories of desire. In opposition to the entropic and negative theory of desire in Hegel, Freud, and Lacan, I want to draw on a notion of desire that is not built on lack but rather constitutes a powerful force in itself: vitalism as "the politics of life itself" (Rose 2001). This is not a naive position of avoidance of pain or negativity (see chapter 11, "Sustainable Ethics and the Body in Pain") but rather the conviction that ethics is about the transformation of negative into affirmative passions. The aim of the ethical transmutations of values is to construct social horizons of hope and sustainable futures (chapter 12, "Forensic Futures").

My emphasis on zoe rather than bios also aims at discarding old, phallologocentric modes of thinking about life. Becoming-nomadic, therefore, is not a one-way street, but a multifaceted circuit. The subject is stripped of its old genderized, racialized, normalized straitjacket and relocated into patterns of different becomings: becoming-minoritarian, becoming-woman, becoming-insect, becoming-cyborg (see chapters 1–4). Never orthodox in any of my allegiances, in spite of a fundamental sense of loyalty to my sources, I do not conform to the rather oedipalized track of many contemporary Deleuzians, who either repeat or repudiate his master's voice. Truly nomadic, I paid my former teacher the utmost compliment of not agreeing with everything he taught me (chapter 13, "A Secular Prayer"). What matters is the itinerary of thought he inspired and in which I actively and creatively embed my own work. Thus my theories are strictly nomadic in a unique way, in that I use this nomadic dictum not only in a strictly philosophical sense but also to criticize socioeconomic issues such as capitalism and neoliberalism and to contemplate current developments in globalization, the EU, feminism, citizenship, and ethics. Critical but always close to the American school of gender, I insist on focusing on the European school of sexual difference as that which constitutes a subject in the process of differing from others and within itself. As a nomadic thinker however, I never link this difference to established normative heterosexual modes of thought and thus engage with queer theory as an important aspect of my nomadic work. This volume aims to illustrate the importance of using critical theory as a tool to develop all the *posts* not as an end, but into the seeds of new paths of thought here and now, in an affirmative engagement with the present that is neither acquiescent nor resigned, but rather pragmatic and praxis oriented.

I dedicated *Patterns of Dissonance* to the figuration of the acrobat walking a tightrope across the academic and political postmodern skeptical void. In *Nomadic Subjects* I ventured across a set of conceptual variations and territorial excursions. *Metamorphoses* ended up on the rope of a bungee jumper, dangling in a tantalizing way in the void, making quick excursions into it, but always bouncing back to safety. *Transpositions* enacted a number of musical and theoretical mutations across the boundaries of complexity and diversity, ending in a firm commitment to sustainable futures. This portable collection is neither a tightrope nor a web, but it does read like a navigation route across the idiosyncratic itineraries and paradoxical twists and turns of contemporary culture and politics. It is a map that draws the trajectory of changes, transformations, and becomings. This is a book of explorations and risks, of convictions and desires. For these are strange times, and strange things are happening.

METAMORPHOSES

PART ONE

1

TRANSPOSING DIFFERENCES

Advanced capitalism is a difference engine in that it promotes the marketing of pluralistic differences and the commodification of the existence, the culture, the discourses of "others," for the purpose of consumerism. As a consequence, the global system of the postindustrial world produces scattered and polycentered, profit-oriented power relations. In our post–cold war era, power functions not so much by binary oppositions but in a fragmented and all-pervasive manner. This rhizomic or weblike structure of contemporary power and its change of scale, however, do not fundamentally alter its terms of application. If anything, power relations in globalization are more ruthless than ever, as I will show in the course of this and the next three chapters.

Late postindustrial societies have proved far more flexible and adaptable toward the proliferation of differences than the classical left expected. These "differences" have been turned, however, into and constructed as marketable, consumable, and often disposable "others." Popular culture—from music to cinema, new media, fashion, and gastronomy—is a reliable indicator of this trend, which sells "world music" or a savvy mixture of the exotic and the domestic, often in the mode of neocolonial appropriation of multicultural others.

An important implication of this situation is that advanced capitalism functions as the great nomad, the organizer of the mobility of commodified products. A generalized practice of "free circulation" pertains, however, almost exclusively to the domain of goods and commodities, regardless of their place of origin, provided they guarantee maximum profit. People do not circulate nearly as freely (Virno 2004; Lazzarato 1996). It is therefore crucial to expose the perverse nomadism of a logic of economic exploitation that equates capitalist flows and flux with profit-minded circulation of commodities. Given that technologies—more specifically the convergence of information and biotechnologies—are intrinsic to the social and discursive structures of postindustrial societies, they deserve special attention. The most critical aspect of the technological apparatus is the issue of access and participation. Considering the inequalities in the availability of electricity supplies, let alone telephone lines and modems, well may one wonder about the "democratic" or "revolutionary" potential of the new electronic and biogenetic frontiers. Like all colonial expansion, moreover, frontiers are never free of struggle or violence. Thus, access and participation to the new high-tech world is unevenly distributed worldwide, with gender, age, and ethnicity acting as major axes of negative differentiation (Eisenstein 1998).

Globalization is primarily about structural injustices in "post-industrial/colonial/communist" societies. It is about the becoming–third world of the first world, while continuing the exploitation of developing countries. It is about the decline of "legal" economies and the rise of structural illegality as a factor in the world economy—also known as "capital as cocaine" (Land 1995). It is about the militarization of the technological and also of the social space. It is also about the globalization of pornography and the trafficking and prostitution of women and children, in a ruthless trade in human life. It is about the feminization of poverty and the rising rates of female illiteracy as well as the structural unemployability of large sectors of the population, especially the youth. This social order is also about the difficulty of the law in coping with phenomena such as the new reproductive rights, ranging from copyright laws in the use of photocopiers, video recorders, and the Internet, to the regulation of surrogate motherhood and artificial procreation. Not to mention the problem of environmental control, this extensive web of microrelations of power is at the heart of what Foucault calls biopower, that is to say, a centerless system of diffuse and hence perniciously effective surveillance and overregulation that takes "life itself" as its target.

Brian Massumi, in his political analysis of the historical condition of postmodernity (1998), describes global capitalism as a profit-oriented mix-

and-match system that vampirizes everything. Contemporary capitalism functions by "circulatory stratification": "It sucks value from pre-existing formations but in killing them endows them with eternal after-life" (Massumi 1998:53). The media industry is an integral part of this circular and spectral logic of commodification. Images constitute a serious, never-ending, forever-dead source of capital: a spectral economy of the eternal return. To be a recognizable icon—the kind of face that launches a thousand identifications—is capital value in our economic system. I would argue that in terms of power this system rests on the paradox of the simultaneous occurrence of contradictory trends. On the one hand, the globalization of economic and cultural processes: this engenders increasing conformity in lifestyle, telecommunications, and consumerism. On the other hand, the fragmentation of these processes, with the concomitant effects of increased structural injustices, marginalization of large sections of the population, and resurgence of regional, local, ethnic, and cultural differences not only between geopolitical blocks but also within them (Eisenstein 1998).

Given that the political economy of global capitalism consists in multiplying and distributing differences for the sake of profit, it produces ever-shifting waves of genderization and sexualization, racialization and naturalization of multiple "others." It has thus effectively disrupted the traditional dialectical relationship between the empirical referents of Otherness—women, natives, and animal or earth's others—and the processes of discursive formation of genderization/racialization/naturalization. Once this dialectical bond is unhinged, advanced capitalism looks like a system that promotes feminism without women, racism without races, natural laws without nature, reproduction without sex, sexuality without genders, multiculturalism without ending racism, economic growth without development, and cash flow without money. Late capitalism also produces fat-free ice creams and alcohol-free beer next to genetically modified health food, companion species alongside computer viruses, new animal and human immunity breakdowns and deficiencies, and the increased longevity of these who inhabit the advanced world. Welcome to capitalism as schizophrenia! (Deleuze and Guattari 1972, 1980).

The spasmodic concurrence of these phenomena is the distinctive trait of our age. The commodification of differences turned the "others" into objects of consumption, alternately granting them a familiar and threatening quality that bypasses the dialectics' revolving door. We have entered instead into a zigzagging pattern of dissonant nomadic subjects. Expressing the positivity of difference in the age of its commodified proliferation is a conceptual task that, however, keeps on bumping against the walls of dialectical habits of thought. How to overcome the dualistic mode that has become so entrenched to our way of thinking remains the main challenge.

On a conceptual level, our historical moment marks the decline of some of the fundamental premises of the Enlightenment, namely, the ideal of the progress of mankind through a self-regulatory and teleologically ordained use of scientific rationality aimed at the "perfectibility" of Man. The emancipatory project of modernity entails a view of "the knowing subject" (Lloyd 1985), which excludes several "boundary markers" also known as "constitutive others." These are sexualized others, also known as women, ethnic or racialized others, and the natural environment. They constitute the three interconnected facets of structural otherness or difference as pejoration, which simultaneously construct and are excluded in modernity (Beauvoir 1973; Irigaray 1974; Deleuze and Guattari 1980). As such, they play an important—albeit specular—role in the definition of the norm, the normal, the normative view of the subject. More specifically, they have been instrumental to the institution of masculine self-assertion (Woolf 1938).

The dominant power structures in our system work by organizing differences according to a hierarchical scale that is governed by the standardized mainstream subject. Deleuze calls it "The Majority subject" or the Molar center of Being; Derrida calls it "phallologocentrism"; Irigaray opts for "the hyperinflated, falsely universal logic of the Same." In such a scheme normality, as Canguilhem presciently put it, equals the zero degree of deviancy or monstrosity. Deleuze echoes this in stating that racism functions by assigning the Norm to White Man and distributing differences negatively across a multitude of marginalized others (Deleuze and Guattari 1980). Difference as pejoration is the term that indexes power according to the metaphysical arrogance of a subject that feeds structurally upon the bodies of devalorized others. Also known as "metaphysical cannibalism" (Atkinson 1974) this dualistic use of violence helps us illuminate the complex and dissymmetrical power relations at work within the dominant subject position.

To say that the structural others of the modern subject reemerge in postmodernity amounts to making them into a paradoxical and polyvalent site. They are simultaneously the symptom of the crisis of the subject, and for conservatives even its "cause," but they also express positive, i.e., nonreactive alternatives. It is a historical fact that the great emancipatory movements of postmodernity are driven and fueled by the resurgent "others": the women's and gay rights movement, the antiracism and decolonization movements, the antinuclear and pro-environment movements are the voices of the structural Others of modernity. They also inevitably mark the crisis of the former "center" or dominant subject position. In the language of philosophical nomadology, they express both the crisis of the majority and the patterns of becoming of the minorities. In this section and in the next three chapters I will analyze this phenomenon in terms of the displacement of the main axes of "becoming." The process of becoming-woman refers to the differential axis of sexualization: the becoming-other of racialization and the becoming-animal/insect/earth of naturalization. The whole point about a critical theory of becoming consists in providing both the methodological navigational tools and an ethical compass to allow us to tell the difference between these different flows of mutation. More specifically, we need normative distinctions between reactive, profit-oriented differences, on the one hand, and affirmative empowerment of alternative differences, on the other. The criterion by which such difference can be established is ethical and its implications political and cultural, as I will argue in chapter 11.

I BECOME, THEREFORE I WILL HAVE BEEN

Nomadic theory's central figuration expresses a process ontology that privileges change and motion over stability. This is also rendered in terms of a general becoming-minority or becoming-nomad or becoming-molecular/woman/animal, etc. The minority is the dynamic or intensive principle of change in nomadic theory, whereas the heart of the (phallogocentric) Majority is dead. Insofar as man represents the majority, there is no creative or affirmative "becoming-man": the dominant subject is stuck with the burden of self-perpetuating Being and the flat repetition of existing patterns. As I argued at the start of this chapter, this logic of quantitative proliferation of multiples of One constitutes the core of the political economy of advanced capitalism. Nomadic thought opposes to this an ethics of qualitative transformation and a politics of complexity and affirmation (see also chapters 11 and 12).

By extension, this scheme also implies that the various empirical minorities (women, children, blacks, natives, animals, plants, seeds, and molecules, etc.) are the privileged starting point for active and empowering processes of becoming. In my own terms, this means that the multiple locations of devalued difference are also, though not at the same time, positive sites for the redefinition of subjectivity. All becoming takes place in a space of affinity and in symbiosis with positive forces and dynamic relations of proximity. This transversal interconnection frames the space of common actualization of alternative modes of relations and affective connection. Boundas (1994:99–118) suggests that the most effective way to think about Deleuze's becoming is as a serialized notion, removed from the dualistic scheme of transcendental philosophy, which inevitably indexes the process of becoming onto a notion of the self, the individual, or the ego.

The process of becoming, which aims at decolonizing the thinking subject from the dualistic grip, also requires the dissolution of all sexed identities based on gendered opposition. Thus the becoming-woman is the necessary starting point for the deconstruction of phallogocentric identities precisely because sexuality as an institution structured around sexual dualism and its corollary—the positioning of women and sexual "deviants" as figure of otherness—are constitutive of Western thought. In a feminist twist, however, Deleuze, just like Derrida and other poststructuralists, opposes to the "majority/sedentary/molar" vision of woman as a structural operator of the phallogocentric system the affirmative or transformative vision of woman as "becoming/minority/molecular/nomadic."

Thus an asymmetrical starting position between minority and majority—center and margins—needs to be strongly emphasized here, whether this is in keeping with orthodox readings of Deleuze or not (Braidotti 2011). This means that the process of deterritorialization is dual and the quantitative minorities can undergo the process of becoming only by disengaging themselves from a unitary identity as others, which is imposed by their opposition to the majority. It is in this sense that Woman (as "the second sex" or "the other of the Same," as Luce Irigaray put it) needs to "become-woman" in the molecular sense of the process (or "the other of the Other," as Irigaray put it). This is an internally differentiated movement that overthrows the oppositional dialectics in a parallel yet asymmetrical move: "There is no subject of the becoming except as a deterritorialized variable of the majority; there is no medium of becoming except as a deterritorialized variable of a minority" (Deleuze and Guattari 1980:292).

Thus, the suggestion is of a block of common, albeit asymmetrical becoming, which turns the former dialectical opponents (men and women, old and young, white and black, human and animal or machine, etc., etc.) into allies in a process of becoming that aims at undoing the common grounds for their former unitarian—and dualistically opposed—identity. In this respect, as Burger pointed out, " an argumentational strategy characteristic of rhizome-thinking is: that it again and again reproduces the categories that it negates" (1985:33–44). I would like to add, however, that this repetition of the very terms one takes one's departure from, far from being the reiteration of a system of domination, constitutes the necessary anchoring point for the cartography of becoming Deleuze and Guattari are sketching. Whereas in Derridean deconstruction this structural pattern of repetition of the very terms one is rejecting results in a productive relationship to the aporetic and the recognition of a fundamental double bind that ties the self to the radical alterity of others, nomadic theory takes another path. This path moves toward a politics of affirmation, which aims at "active counter-actualization of the current state of affairs" (Boundas 2007a:187) through the project of transforming negative into positive relations, encounters, and passions (I will explore this more fully in chapter 11).

One must indeed start from somewhere specific: a grounded and accountable location and the process of becoming is a time bomb placed at the very heart of the social and symbolic system that has welded together being, subjectivity, masculinity, compulsory heterosexuality, and (western) ethnocentrism. The different becomings are lines cutting open this space and demanding from us constant remapping: it is a question, every time, of finding new coordinates. This is not only a spatial but also a temporal phenomenon. Crucial to this entire process of becoming-molecular is the question of memory (la mémoire). The Majority: white, heterosexual, property-owning, and male—is a huge data bank of centralized knowledge, which is relayed through every aspect of his activities. The Majority Subject holds the keys to the central memory of the system and has reduced to the rank of insignificant practices, the alternative or subjugated memories of the many minorities. The line of becoming for the majority is consequently an anti-memory, which, instead of bringing back in a linear order specific memories (les souvenirs), functions as a deterritorializing agency that dislodges the subject from his/her sense of unified and consolidated identity.

A nomadic, nonlinear philosophy of time as a zigzagging line of internally fractured coalitions of dynamic subjects-in-becoming supports a very creative reading of memory and of its close relationship to the imagination.

This is especially important in the case of negative or traumatic memories of pain, wound or abuse. This sort of negative capital is an integral component of the consciousness of historically marginalized or oppressed subjects. The pain and negativity that structure the oppositional consciousness of the "minorities" are a crucial concern for nomadic political theory and practice. While acknowledging this particular location—as a wounded memory of pain as well as a historically grounded space—nomadic political subjectivity defines the political as the gesture that aims at transcending the present state of affairs and empowering creative "counteractualizations" or transformative alternatives.

The corollary of this notion of time and of the political is that the specifically grounded memories of the minorities are not just static splinters of negativity forever inscribed in the flesh of the victims of history. Molecular or nomadic memories are also, and more especially, a creative force that gives the "wretched of the earth," as Fanon put it, a head start toward the world-historical task of envisaging alternative world orders and more humane and sustainable social systems. It comes down to a double consciousness of both the multiple axes of oppression, and hence of hurt, humiliation, and pain, as well as the creative force they can generate as motors of transversal and collective transformation. (I shall return to this in chapters 11 and 12.)

Please note, however, that, whereas in classical dialectics empirical minorities are automatically positioned as the motor of historical developments and the guiding principle of revolutionary action and ethical agency, in nomadic politics this is not the case. The negative capital of oppression is just a privileged starting point for a process of the transmutation of values—to use Nietzsche's rather more heroic rendition of the same idea—that encompasses the minorities themselves: they have to become-minoritarian as well. The essentialized vision of identities is challenged all the way by nomadic theory—and it does not leave unscathed the minorities: they also need to activate their memories against the black hole of counteridentity claims as well as against the grain of the dominant vision of the subject.

So what does one do when one remembers nomadically, and what kind of temporal allocation is a nomadic memory? Molecular, minoritarian, or nomadic memories are affirmative, destabilizing forces that propel subjects actively toward change. They are the kind of memories that are linked to ethical and political consciousness and concern events one simply forgot to forget. In Deleuze's language, these memories pertain to the realm of the virtual and hence are abstract in the positive sense of leaning toward actualization. They are just as "real," however, as anything else in our memory data banks—both the majority-bound one indexing on the dominant time line of Chronos and the minoritarian one that orbits around Aion—the time of becoming.

What matters ultimately about the job of remembering is the capacity to engender the kind of conditions and relations that can empower creative alternatives. The process of actualization is like a composition of passions, intensities, and visions that coalesce in an adequate frame of composition. What is "adequate" about it is a purely pragmatic matter, not a normative measure or an ideological injunction. It is whatever works to create sustainable lines and productive planes of transversal interconnection among entities and subjects that are related by empathy and affective affinity, not by some generic moral model or idealized paradigm.

This type of remembrance is not identity bound or ego indexed, but rather impersonal or postidentitarian. It is linked to a radical process of defamiliarization or disidentification from dominant representational and even self-representational practices. Remembering nomadically amounts to reinventing a self as other—as the expression of a nomadic subject's structural ability to actualize selfhood as a process of transformation and transversality. Remembering is consequently *not* about being equal to yourself, but rather in differing as much as possible from all you had been before. This process is analogous to the overthrowing of the simulacrum in Deleuze's critique of Platonic representation. It is not about being what I was like before (before what? and like whom?), in a relationship of spatiotemporal sameness between present and past self-representations, i.e., between me now and myself then. It is rather about differing from myself as much and as often as possible. Insofar as this process requires the overthrowing of the dialectics that separates self from other, I would argue that Deleuze's critique of Platonism begins at home, especially in the relative familiarity of the spatiotemporal continuum of one's bodily self. Remembering is less about forgetting to forget than about retaking, as in refilming a sequence: it is about differing from oneself.

Following Foucault, Deleuze does not fail to stress that the elements composing Sameness—i.e., self-identity, continuity of self-interests, and attachment to the ego—index negative passions of narcissism and paranoia and are all part of the molar or majority system. They suit perfectly the requirements of a social order that is so constructed as to extract from its subjects the pound of flesh (both real and symbolic) that makes these subjects both docile and functional. The primary function of molar elements is to ensure the governability of the very subjects they engender. It is in this sense that a nomadic political theory of becoming is also a theory of desire: the only possible way to undertake this process is to actually be attracted to change, to *want* it, the way one wants a lover—in the flesh. Nomadic becoming is a theory of ontological and nonfigurative desire. Thus defined, desire is political because it entails the social construction of different desiring subjects, that is to say, subjects who desire differently. Breaking out of the official mold of oedipalized, socially productive libidinal economies, nomadic becoming paves the way for all kind of other economies and apparati of desire. They cannot be dissociated, however, from the singular desire to construct oneself "as" different. In conclusion, nomadic "remembering" is not indexed on the authority of the past. It rather occurs in relation to creative imagination in the future anterior: "you will have changed," "they will have fought for justice," "we will have been free."

This point is crucial to feminist and antiracist democratic politics, in that the nomadic subjects-in-becoming develop alongside the discourses and practices of the "others" of postmodernity and engage with them in a creative manner. Nomadic theory requires, however, a high degree of self-reflexivity precisely because it does *not* engage with discourses and practices of otherness in a mimetic or consumerist manner. It rather cuts a more creative path through these discourses in a nondialectical manner. It does so by giving priority to the undoing of the dominant model of subjectivity and thus putting on the spot the discourse of the Same, the One. This is what is at stake in the nomadic theory of becoming: a critique of the center from the center. All becomings are minoritarian, that is to say, they inevitably and necessarily move in the direction of the "others" of classical dualism—dis-placing them and reterritorializing them in the process, but always and only on a temporal basis. The nomadic subject thus engages with his/her external others in a constructive, "symbiotic" (Ansell-Pearson 1999) block of becoming, which bypasses dialectical interaction. This rhizomic mode is a persistent challenge and an opposition to Molar, steady identities: it functions along an anti-Hegelian, antidevelopmental, antiteleological model.

"Becoming" works on a time sequence that is neither linear nor sequential because processes of becoming are not predicated upon a stable, centralized Self who supervises their unfolding. These processes rather rest on a nonunitary, multilayered, dynamic subject attached to multiple communities. Becoming woman/animal/insect is an affect that flows, like writing; it is a composition, a location that needs to be constructed together with, that is to say, in the encounter with others. They push the subject to his/her limits, in a constant encounter with external, different others. The nomadic subject as a nonunitary entity is simultaneously self-propelling and heterodefined, i.e., outward bound.

The different stages or levels of becoming trace an itinerary that consists in erasing and recomposing the former boundaries between self and others. In a different philosophical tradition one could say that the becoming woman/animal/insect/imperceptible consists of deconstructive steps across the boundaries that used to separate qualitatively Self/same from others. In philosophical nomadology, on the other hand, these are not deconstructive steps, as they do not feed upon themselves, in the way that Irigaray's strategic mimesis does. As Tamsin Lorraine put it: "one lesson of Deleuze & Guattari's anti-psychoanalytic stance, however, is that destratification does not necessarily have to retrace the route of one's personal history" (1999:202). They are postidentitarian grounded instantiations of the general principle of transcendental empiricism and the force of the virtual.

Therefore, it is in the worst possible conceptual taste to even think of being able to separate out the becoming-woman from the other unfolding and deploying of multiple becomings. The process of becoming-nomadic is rather a zigzagging itinerary of successive but not linear steps that, starting from "becoming-woman," marks different thresholds or patterns of "becoming-minoritarian" that cross through the animal and go into the "becoming-imperceptible" and beyond.

Nonetheless, for the sake of the argument, but also to facilitate the linearity of the process of reading/writing, I will distinguish and address the specific instances of becoming separately. In so doing, I want to defend a multilayered argument: firstly, that the concept of becoming is crucial to Deleuze's philosophy of immanence. Secondly, that the "becoming-woman" is both integral to the concept and process of becoming and also uncomfortably written into it as a constitutive contradiction of Deleuze's nomadic subjectivity. Thirdly, that there are no systematic, linear, or teleological stages or phases of becoming; each plateau marks a framed and sustainable block or moment of immanently actualized transformations. Thinking across these processes remains the central challenge.

MINORITIES AND BECOMING-MINORITARIAN

There is a positive and creative tension between the identitarian claims of political movements that are grounded in the historical experience of oppression and the empirical transcendental aspirations of nomadic theory to postulate a new collective transversal bond through multiple processes of becoming.

In identifying the points of exit from phallocentric modes of thought toward a new, intensive image of philosophy, nomadic theory stresses the need for new images for these subject positions. This results in the elaboration of a set of postmetaphysical figurations of the subject. Figurations such as rhizomes, becomings, lines of escape, flows, relays, and bodies without organs release and express active states of being, which break through the conventional schemes of theoretical representation. Alternative figurations of the subject, including different feminine, masculine, and in-between subject positions, are figural modes of expression that displace the vision of consciousness away from the dominant premises. Deleuze's central figuration is a general becoming-minority or becoming-nomad or becoming-molecular. The minority marks a crossing or a trajectory; nothing happens at the center, for Deleuze, but at the periphery there roam the youthful gangs of the new nomads.

As I asserted earlier, in so far as Man, the male, is the main referent for thinking subjectivity, the standard-bearer of the Norm, the Law, the Logos, Woman is dualistically, i.e., oppositionally positioned as his "other." The consequence is that there is no possible becoming-minority of man and that the becoming-woman is a privileged position for the minority consciousness of all. Man as the privileged referent of subjectivity, the standard-bearer of the norm/law/logos, represents the majority, i.e., the dead heart of the system. The consequences are, on the one hand, that masculinity is antithetical to the process of becoming and can only be the site of deconstruction or critique. On the other hand, the becoming-woman is a fundamental step in the process of becoming for both and for all sexes.

Deleuze states that all the lines of deterritorialization go necessarily through the stage of "becoming-woman," which is the key, the precondition, and the necessary starting point for the whole process. The reference to "woman" in the process of "becoming-woman," however, does not refer to empirical females, but rather to topological positions, degrees, and levels of intensity, affective states. The becoming woman is the marker for a general process of transformation: it affirms positive forces and levels of nomadic, rhizomatic consciousness.

> There is a becoming-woman, a becoming-child that does not resemble the woman or the child as clearly distinct entities. . . . What we term a molecular entity is, for example, the woman as defined by her form, endowed with organs and functions and assigned as a subject. Becoming-woman is not imitating this entity or even transforming oneself into it. . . . Not imitating or assuming the female form, but emitting particles that enter the relation of movement and rest, or the zone of proximity, of a micro femininity, in other words, that produce in us a molecular woman, create the molecular woman.
>
> (DELEUZE AND GUATTARI 1980:275)

There is consequently an unresolved knot in Deleuze's relation to the becoming-woman and the feminine, which I have analysed extensively elsewhere (Braidotti 1991, 1994b, 2002a, 2006, 2011) . It has to do with a double pull, between, on the one hand, empowering a generalized "becoming-woman" as the prerequisite for all other becomings and, on the other hand, calling for its transcendence. On the one hand, the becoming-minority/nomad/molecular/bodies-without-organs/woman starts from the feminine, on the other hand, it is posited as the general figuration for the kind of subjectivity Deleuze advocates. Deleuzian becomings emphasize the generative powers of complex and multiple states of transition between, beneath, and beyond the metaphysical anchoring points that are the masculine and feminine. But they do not quite solve the issue of their interaction. Deleuze's work displays a great empathy with the feminist assumption that we have to start from the critique of phallocentrism. Insofar as woman is positioned dualistically—as the other—in this system, she is annexed to the phallus, albeit by negation. In this sense, and in this sense only, can it be said that sexual difference is the primary axis of differentiation and therefore must be given priority. On the other hand, nomadic theory aims at the tendency to dilute metaphysical difference into a multiple and undifferentiated becoming. Which prompts my question: what feminist politics follow from nomadic theory's emphasis on sexuality without genders (see also chapters 7 and 8)?

For instance, in her defense of sexual difference against its hasty dismissal as part of the deconstruction of the subject, Luce Irigaray refers negatively to the Deleuzian diagram of the desiring machines (Irigaray 1974, 1977, 1980, 1984, 1987, 1989, 1990). The notion of "the body without organs" is for Irigaray reminiscent of a condition of dis-possession of the bodily self, a structurally splintered position that is historically associated with femininity as a symbolic mark of absence and with women as its empirical referent. She points out that the emphasis on the machinic, the inorganic, as well as the notion of loss of self, dispersion, and fluidity are all too familiar to women: is not the "body without organs" women's own historical condition? (Irigaray 1977:140) Irigaray's critique of Deleuze is radical: she points out that the dispersal of sexuality into a generalized "becoming" results in undermining the feminist claims to a redefinition of the female subject.

Deleuze comes down on the side of the basic feminist epistemological distinction between Woman as representation and women as concrete agents of experience and ends up making analogous distinctions internal to the category of woman herself. Hence also Deleuze's explicit support for a feminist political position: "It is, of course, indispensable for women to conduct a molar politics, with a view to winning back their own organism, their own history, their own subjectivity. . . . But it is dangerous to confine oneself to such a subject, which does not function without drying up a spring or stopping a flow" (Deleuze and Guattari 1980: 276).

In spite of such evident support for women's uphill struggle toward achieving full subjectivity, with human and citizenship rights, Deleuze opposes to the "majority/sedentary/molar" vision of woman as the structural operator of the phallogocentric system the woman as "becoming/minority/molecular/nomadic."

This is understandable in view of the crucial importance of sexuality as the dominant discourse of power in the West, as Foucault taught us (Foucault 1975, 1976, 1984a, 1984b). By virtue of the economic, cultural, and symbolic importance that Western culture has attributed to sexuality, it follows that gender and sexual difference have historically evolved as a primary—though by no means unique—site of the constitution of subjectivity. Sexuality is a major element in the complex technologies of the self and the complex networks of power to which they connect.

Insofar as the male/female dichotomy has moreover become the prototype of Western individualism, the process of decolonizing the subject from this dualistic grip requires as its starting point the dissolution of all sexed identities based on this gendered opposition. In this framework, sexual polarizations and gender dichotomy are rejected as the prototype of the dualistic reduction of difference to a subcategory of Being. This does not alter the fact, however, that for nomadic theory sexuality is never reducible to or contained—let alone constructed—within the gender system. Deleuze's ultimate aim with respect to sexual difference is to move toward its final overcoming. The nomadic or intensive horizon is a sexuality "beyond gender" in the sense of being dispersed, not binary, multiple, not dualistic, interconnected, not dialectical and in a constant flux, not fixed. This idea is expressed in figurations like "polysexuality," the "molecular woman," and the "bodies without organs" to which Deleuze's dephallic style actively contributes. This is nomadic queer theory to which I shall return in chapter 12.

Thus the becoming-woman is necessarily the starting point insofar as the overemphasis on masculine sexuality, compulsory reproductive heterosexuality, the persistence of sexual dualism, and the positioning of woman as the privileged figure of otherness are constitutive of Western subject positions. In other words, "becoming-woman" triggers off the deconstruction of phallic identity through a set of deconstructive steps that retrace backward, so as to undo them, different stages of the social-symbolic construction of this difference and other differences.

Deleuze also uses his theory of the becoming-woman of women as the basis for a critique of identity-based feminist politics. All transformative politics should be about becoming-minoritarian, to dissolve the subject "woman" into a series of processes geared toward a generalized and "gender-free" becoming. In other words, it is important to keep in mind the broader picture in order to avoid microdespotisms and the repetition of power concentrations within the minorities. Feminists, in other words, are conceptually mistaken, though their political heart may be in the right place, when they argue for a specifically feminine sexuality: exclusive emphasis on the feminine is restrictive. Deleuze suggests that feminists should instead draw on the multisexed structure of the subject and reclaim all the sexes of which women have been deprived. "For us . . . there are as many sexes as there are terms in symbiosis, as many differences as elements contributing to a process of contagion. We know that many beings pass between a man and a woman; they come from different worlds, are born on the wind, form rhizomes around roots; they cannot be understood in terms of production, only in terms of becoming" (Deleuze and Guattari 1980:242). These different degrees of becoming are diagrams of subject positions, typologies of ideas, politically informed maps, variations on intensive states. Multiplicity does not reproduce one single model—as in the Platonic mode—but rather creates and multiplies differences.

Ultimately, what Deleuze finds objectionable in feminist theory is that it perpetuates flat repetitions of dominant values or identities, which it claims to have repossessed dialectically. This amounts to perpetuating reactive, molar, or majority thinking: in Nietzsche's scale of values, feminists have a slave morality. As an ICA artist put it recently: "ironic mimesis is not a critique, it is the mentality of a slave."[1] For Deleuze, feminists would be subversive if, in their becoming, they contributed both socially and theoretically to constructing a nonoedipal woman by freeing the multiple possibilities of desire meant as positivity and affirmation. This new general configuration of the feminine as the post- or, rather, unoedipal subject of becoming, is explicitly opposed to what Deleuze constructs as the feminist configuration of a new universal based on female specificity or, rather, an exacerbation of the sexual dichotomy. The former aims at deessentialized forms of radical embodiment, the latter to strategically reessentialized embodiment.

As a nomadic philosopher, I am all for the politics of becoming minoritarian; this position, however, in not unproblematic theoretically, because it suggests symmetry between the sexes. This results in attributing the same psychic, conceptual, and deconstructive itineraries to both and to all sexes. I would challenge this alleged symmetry between the sexes. Undoing difference is not a task that can be dissolved easily without causing psychic and social damage. This perspective is shared not only with an older generation of feminists like Irigaray, but also with younger ones. As Claire Colebrook asks: "Just what are Deleuze and Guattari doing when they take Woolf and the women's movement away from the concepts of identity, recognition, emancipation and the subject towards a new plane of becoming?" (Colebrook 2000b:3) Resisting the flat equivalence in the speaking positions of the two or of all other sexes, I would reassert difference as the nomadic principle of non-one and not as a sexuate universal. Nomadic difference is a

TRANSPOSING DIFFERENCES 41

productive asymmetry that functions as a permanent fracture, not as a static given—it is a constant becoming, not a quest for counteridentity sacralized by the pain of a wounded historical memory.

A nomadic becoming-woman starts from the recognition of the dissymmetry between the sexes and the emphasis on female specificity as the starting point for the process of redefining subjectivity. It does not, however, stop there—it moves toward a broadening of the traditional feminist political agenda to include, on top of issue of women's social rights, also a larger spectrum of options. These range from global political issues of social justice to cultural concerns related to writing and creativity, to issues that, at first sight, seem to have nothing to do with women specifically. That is precisely the point: the coexistence of feminine specificity with larger, less sex-specific concerns. Nomadic feminism is about tracing a zigzagging path between them.

As an illustration of the general principle of becoming minoritarian, I would paraphrase Griggers (1997), who in turn paraphrases the Chiapas movement, and argue that nomadic subjects could be any of the following: gays in Cuba, blacks in South Africa, a Palestinian in Israel, an illegal migrant in the EU, a gang member in any slum of the world's metropolises, a communist in the post–cold war era, an artist without gallery or portfolio, a pacifist in Bosnia, a housewife alone on Saturday night in any neighborhood in any city of any country, a single woman on the metro at 10 P.M., a peasant without land, an unemployed worker, a dissident among free-market fetishists, a writer without books or readers. In other words, the nomadic subject signifies both vulnerability and affirmation. My emphasis falls on the potential becoming, the opening out—the transformative power of all the exploited, marginalized, oppressed minorities. Just being a minority, however, is not enough: it is only the starting point. Crucial to becoming-nomad is the undoing of the oppositional dualism majority/minority and arousing an affirmative passion for the transformative flows that destabilize all identities.

Becoming-minority is a task also for the minorities, who too often tend to be caught in the paralyzing gaze of the master—hating and envying him at the same time. To shift from this dialectically binding location, she needs to activate different countermemories and actualize multiple ecologies of belonging. Becoming nomadic means that one learns to reinvent oneself, and one desires the self as a process of transformation. It's about the desire for qualitative transformations, for flows and shifts of multiple desires. Nomadic theory rests on a nonunitary yet politically engaged and ethically accountable vision of nomadic subject. Nomadic thought stresses the need for a change of conceptual schemes altogether, an overcoming of the dialectic of Majority/Minority or Master/Slave. Both the majority and the minorities need to untie the knots of envy (negative desire) and domination (dialectics) that bind them so tightly. In this process they will necessarily follow asymmetrical lines of becoming, given that their starting positions are so different. For the majority, there is no possible becoming—other than in the undoing of its central position altogether. The center is void; all the action is on the margins.

For the real-life minorities, however, the pattern is different: women, blacks, youth, postcolonial subjects, migrants, exiled, and homeless may first need to go through a phase of "identity politics"—of claiming a fixed location. This is both inevitable and necessary because, as I have often argued, you cannot give up something you have never had (Braidotti 1991). Nor can you dispose nomadically of a subject position that you have never controlled to begin with. I think, consequently, that the process of becoming-nomad (-minority, -woman) is internally differentiated, and it depends largely on where one starts off from. The politics of location is crucial. In other words, heterogeneity is injected into both poles of the dialectical opposition, which gets undone accordingly. The "Molar" line—that of Being, identity, fixity, and potestas, and the "Molecular" line—that of becoming, nomadic subjectivity, and potentia—are absolutely not the same. They are two dissymmetrical "others." Within phallogocentrism they have been captured in a dualistic mold. They are differentiated by structural inequalities that impose Sameness in a set of hierarchical relations. Deleuze defines the Molar/Majority as the standard and the Molecular/Minority as the other in the sense of "the other of the same." The central challenge of nomadic philosophy, however, is how to undo this dualistic mode and redistribute the power relations of the two terms. More important than either of them, therefore, is the Line of Flight or of becoming. This is always and only a becoming-minoritarian as in woman/child/animal/imperceptible.

The differences in the starting positions are important in that they mark different qualitative levels of relation. Thus, if one starts from the Majority position (the Same), there is only one possible path: through the Minority (the Other)—hence the imperative to become woman as the first move in the deterritorialization of the dominant subject (also known as the feminization of Man). For those who start from the position of empirical minorities, on the other hand, more options are open. If the pull toward assimilation or integration into the majority is strong for the minorities (hence the phenomenon of phallic women), so is the appeal of the lines of escape toward minoritarian becomings. In other words, you can have a becoming-woman that produces Lady Thatcher and one that produces Lady Gaga: neither of whom is "feminine" in any conventional sense of the term, and yet they are as different from each other as the workhorse is from the racehorse.

What matters here is to keep open the process of becoming-minoritarian and not to stop at the dialectical role reversal that usually sees the former slaves in the position of new masters or the former mistress in the position of dominatrix. The point is to go beyond the logic of reversibility. This is especially important for those social subjects—women, blacks, postcolonial and other "others"—who are the carriers of the hopes of the minorities. The process of becoming nomadic is not merely antiessentialist, but asubjective, beyond received notions of individuality. It is a transpersonal mode, ultimately collective. You can never be a nomad; you can only go on trying to become nomadic.

THE DESPOTIC AND PATHETIC FACE OF (WHITE) FEMININITY

In a nomadic perspective, the "feminine" is neither one essentialized entity, nor an immediately accessible one: it is rather both an embodied and embedded location and a virtual reality. It is the effect of a project, a political and conceptual project of transcending the traditional ("Molar") subject position of Woman. This transcendence, however, occurs through the flesh into embodied locations and not in a flight away from them.

If I were to think in figurations and locate the issues of embodiment in a contemporary cartography, so as to stress some of the paradoxes of political sensibilities of this millennium in Europe, I would pick two contradictory ones: the first is the public's schizoid reaction to the death of Diana, Princess of Wales. The second is the nameless bodies of thousands of asylum seekers in the European Union today.

Alternatively labeled—depending on one's politics—"a phenomenon of mass hysteria" or "the floral revolution"—analogous to the Eastern Europeans' "velvet revolution"—the events around Diana's death have already entered the realm of political mythology. They constitute one of the biggest media events focused on a single individual ever. What is most extraordinary about the com/passionate reaction of the British public is the fact that it consisted to an overwhelming degree of young women, gays, and people of color. The excluded or marginal social subjects, those whom neoliberalism had forgotten or swept aside, bounced back onto the political and media arena with a vengeance. It was the return of the repressed, not with a bang but a whimper. It formed a suitable complement to the landslide that had brought Tony Blair's "New Labour" to power in the UK a few months before and to a renewal of respect for emotions, affectivity, and the role they can and should play in public and political life. It was also a powerful expression of the continuing potency of the white goddess as an object of collective worship (Davies and Smith 1999). That it was subsequently denied and repressed as a ritual of collective bonding and outpour of emotions merely confirms the symptomatic value of the event.

One of the things I find relevant about Princess Diana is the fact that she was a woman in full transformation. In other words, she was more interesting for what she was becoming than for what she actually was. I think this dynamic and transformative dimension is crucial to understanding Diana's charisma. As Julie Burchill put it: "She was never a plaything: she was always a work in progress" (Burchill 1998:44). This was not deprived of opportunism, as Rushdie suggested, in a less charitable vein: "Diana was not given to using words like 'semiotics,' but she was a capable semiotician of herself. With increasing confidence, she gave us the signs by which we might know her as she wished to be known" (Rushdie 1997:68). In this respect, Diana personifies the combination of high visibility with intense self-definition.

By way of counterpoint and in order not to confine the cartography of the body within the parameters of the dominant cultural code, I want to turn to another significant case. The second image therefore is that of nameless women, men, child refugees, or asylum seekers who have been uprooted from their homes and countries in the many micro-wars that are festering across the globe, including in Europe, at the dawn of the Third Millennium. The century-old virus of nationalism combines, in contemporary Europe, with the destabilizing effects created by the postcommunist world order as well as the globalization process. The end result is an influx of refugees and a rise in violence, exclusion, racism, and human misery that has no equivalent in postwar Europe. These two examples represent for me two sides of the same coin, which is the saturation of our social space by media images and representations.

This results in positioning embodied subjects, and especially the female ones, at the intersection of some formidable locations of power: visibility and media representations produced a consumerist approach to images in a dissonant or internally differentiated manner. Female-embodied subjects-in-process today include interchangeably the highly groomed body of Princess Diana (like Marilyn Monroe before her) *and* the highly disposable bodies of women, men, and children in war-torn lands.

At both the macro and the micro levels the body is caught in a network of power effects mostly induced by technology. This is the driving force of the globalization system and the transnational economy which engender continuous constitutive contradictions at the "g-local" level. Manuel Castells, in his seminal work on network societies, argues that postindustrial societies are operating under the acceleration of digitally driven "new" cybereconomies. Capital-flow undeterred by topological or territorial constraints has achieved a double goal. It has simultaneously "dematerialized" social reality and hardened it. Suffice it to think of media events such as Princess Diana's burial or the latest update from Baghdad—which are experienced in the relative quiet of one's living room television set as virtual happenings. The "virtual" reality of the migrants, asylum seekers, or refugees is qualitatively different: not high tech, but rather approaching an overexposed kind of anonymity or social invisibility. The virtual reality of hypermedia and cyberspace, however "immaterial," constitutes a highly contested social space or, rather, a set of dense social relations mediated by the technological flow of information.

By extension, cyberspace and the "cyborg" subjectivity it offers are no longer the stuff science fiction is made of but are concretely embedded social relations, as I will argue in the next chapter. On the contrary, the blurring of the boundaries between humans and machines is socially enacted at all levels: from medicine, to telecommunication, finance, and modern warfare, cyber-relations define our social framework or interaction in very grounded and concrete ways.

Femininity is caught in the double bind of late postmodernity by being simultaneously "Other" (of the same) and fully mainstream and integrated in the Majority. In late postindustrial societies, this dominant femininity functions as the site of proliferating and commodified differences. Like Princess Diana: she is both the pathetic and despotic face of white femininity and the scapegoat sacrificial victim of a political ontology that requires her symbolic absence. As Salman Rushdie pointed out in his commentary on Princess Diana's death (1997), even her atrocious end became eroticized and glamorized by consumers in two major ways. The first is in the cyborglike lethal mingling of her body with the metal of the car that crushed her. The second is in the equally murderous power of visualization by the photographers who chased her and contributed to her demise. Diana's death by car crash was "a cathartic event for millions" (Becker 1999:282), related both to and by the media. As such, it brings out some of the central paradoxes of contemporary technoculture, almost like a cruel illustration of everything Ballard and Cronenberg are trying to demonstrate in their film *Crash*. Princess Diana's crushed body acquires semireligious significance, like a collective ritual on wheels, relayed cathodically all over the globe. Rushdie argues that Ballard's novel blends together under the sign of a powerful new technosexuality the two dominant fetishes of our culture: consumers' commodities (the car) and celebrity (the star). The two get combined with almost obscene self-evidence in Princess Diana's death. The third party in the plot, crucial to the whole story, is the camera's eye—in Diana's case, the flashing lights of the paparazzi (Rushdie 1997:68).

"In Diana's fatal crash, the camera (as both Reporter and Lover) is joined to the Automobile and the Star, and the cocktail of death and desire becomes even more powerful than the one in Ballard's book. . . . The object of desire, in the moment of her death, sees the phallic lenses advancing upon her, snapping, snapping. Think of it this way, and the pornography of Diana Spencer's death becomes apparent. She died in a sublimated sexual assault."

Rushdie reads Diana's desperate last drive as her attempt to exercise some control over her status as collective object of desire, to emancipate herself from commodity to humanity, i.e., to acquire some subjectivity. In vain: she was not in the driver's seat. Becoming-cyborgs may be virtual, but it is nonetheless socially enacted, materially grounded—embodied and embedded. To the end, enfleshed. And yet, all this information comes to us through the camera eye—it is technologically transmitted. Their power of visualization has saturated the social sphere (Braidotti 2011).

The iconic value of Princess Diana's face as white, imperial, and sacrificial at the same time is a relevant figuration for the paradoxes of one brand of contemporary femininity. This is one of the reasons why Diana has received global iconic status and renewed critical attention of late, especially the light of the powers of identification that Diana triggers in many marginal people. Valerie Walkerdine (1999) sees another pattern of identification with Diana on a broader, "mass" level. Diana's struggle for survival reflects and represents the ordinary struggle for self-definition that most human beings have to go through in order to become psychological subjects. Diana embodies the dynamic, pain-drenched nature of becoming-a-subject. Johnson (1999), for instance, argues that Diana was a gay icon, because of the tale of oppression and redemption which marked her existence. Her spectacularly pathetic "coming out" as a bulimic—a condition that is closeted per definition—also contributes to her gay appeal, as does Diana's undeniable affinity for the glamour and attractiveness of gay men in show business. The AIDS activism and her unhappy quest for emotional and erotic fulfillment are part of the same configuration: she is abject and glorious at the same time.

Equally important to Diana's evocative, queer power, as Spurlin argues (1999), is her brave and desperate denunciation of gender politics within the British royal family (Campbell 1998): her refusal to "go away quietly," her stepping out of the codified conventions of loveless upper-class marriage, and her defiance of heterosexual normativity in the realm of male infidelities and female subservience and passivity. Diana transgresses and exceeds the heterosexual matrix and thus joins forces with queer politics, though she's clearly not gay herself.

Diana as a sociosymbolic event is a subversive subject insofar as she grows increasingly aware of the ways in which she simultaneously inhabits and challenges or disrupts the many facets of her social identity as princess/mother/wife/celebrity/sexualized female flesh/bulimic/desiring subject/single woman/philanthropist/victim, etc., etc. It's a multiplicity at odds with itself that makes her strike out on her own, but as a dissonant, fragmented, and rather messy subject—a leaky body, a less-than-perfect image. I think the mix of pathos and privilege is an integral part of her appeal and also of her enduring charisma. Millions identified with this, partly because it is a less-than-perfect whole, a partial success only.

In this respect, it is essential to racialize the process and think of the white despotic and pathetic face of Princess Diana—as the contested and contradictory site where transformation must occur. The iconic value of Princess Diana's face prompts a number of comments about the political economy of late postmodernity and the location of whiteness within it. In their analysis of "faciality," Deleuze and Guattari (1980) stress the iconic and despotic powers of *the* face (that launched a thousand ships) as the master signifier. Commenting extensively on the racialization and sexualization of the master's face, especially in relation to the face of Christ, they connect the process of becoming to delinking the face from these powers of masterful signification and escaping the black hole of molar subjectivity. The alternative, nomadic path also moves toward discovering and experimenting with the many possible other faces one might be capable of inhabiting: "Free your faces! Know your faces!" (Deleuze and Guattari 1980:190).

Possessing the "right" face is a social process of subjectivization that functions by binary exclusions: "Is she black or white? Straight or lesbian? The face will tell" (Griggers 1997:3). Griggers analyzes the production of White Femininity as the site of schizoid contradictory trends: privilege and commodification. This takes place, as I argued earlier, in the global contest of the dissolution of imperial entities and the generalized spreading of diasporic identities in postmodernity. According to Jatinder Verma, Princess Diana stood out from within the generalized "bleaching" (Verma 1999:121) or whitening processes (Frankenberg 1993) that go on in the constitution of contemporary identities. I shall return to a critical evaluation of whiteness in chapter 10.

I want to juxtapose the white iconicity of Princess Diana's body to the anonymous faces of endless female victims that stare at us from the back streets and television screens in quest of aid for survival. These are two sides of the same coin of hyperinflated femininity in the era of postmodernity. They are also opposite in terms of power locations, entitlement, and privilege. The case of Princess Diana is significant in that she at times manages to combine elements of both sacrifice and triumph, thus causing great turmoil in the register of representation. We have to apply a differential treatment to the production of white femininity on white women and of the many "others" or minorities. The despotic white face on a white woman is the sign of her Molarity and Normality; on a black woman it is a measure of racism, an attempt to integrate difference into the logic of sameness. Michael Jackson's whitening effects come to mind here, as the widespread use of bleaching/whitening products on black bodies, hair and faces especially, throughout most of the globe today. There are several ongoing attempts at situating and relocating whiteness, and not all of them go in the direction of the Molar: some entail antiracist processes of becoming-minoritarian. Thus, a white face imposed on a drag queen, as in the fashion of lesbian radical chic, can be an act of subversion. These point to asymmetrical and differentiated paths of becoming, which unfold from dissymmetrical and ultimately irreconcilable starting-off subject positions. The dissymmetry needs to be kept in mind in order to make sense of the patterns of both negative and affirmative deconstruction, undoing or becoming that flow from it. Sexual difference today is a nomadic process of sexual differing that acts as a permanent fracture within the quantitative proliferation of consumable differences in advanced capitalism.

DISSYMMETRICAL BECOMINGS

The political stance consists in becoming-minoritarian or molecular in a radical materialist, pragmatic philosophy of multilayered transformations. The becoming-woman is subversive in that it works actively toward the transformation of the signs, the social practices, and the embodied histories of white institutionalized femininity. A Deleuzian approach calls to relinquish this quest for identity modeled on the Molar/sedentary subject, to activate instead multiple becomings, beyond identity. Some of these transitions are happening already as demonstrated in the fact that so many bodies are malfunctioning or ceasing to produce the programmed codes, of which the use of Prozac, the spreading of anorexia and bulimia are clear symptoms. These breakdowns are not enough, however, to disrupt the machine. A proliferation of gay, queer, and lesbian identities is no exception to the paradoxical rule of globalized fragmentation and proliferation of differences.

As the events around the photos of the Abu Ghraib prison painfully indicate, at a time in history where right-wing politicians like Bush and opportunists like Tony Blair appeal to feminism as an alleged justification for their wars of conquest, we need to be more vigilant than ever. Sexual nationalism is as pernicious as all other forms of nationalism. Feminism—women's and gay rights—is situated at the crucible of some of the most dramatic geopolitical questions as an issue of the highest degree of turbulence. Feminists and gay activists are caught in the same historical contradictions as everyone else: they are simultaneously within and without the majority. The emphasis falls on the pursuit of qualitative transformations and changes. Nomadic feminism thus enlarges the definition of female sexuality and the subject to encompass more global power relations than the ones determined by gender alone, with special concerns for issues of military violence, war, and lethal technologies of death. The only way to resist this death-bound machinery is to elaborate hybrid, transformative identities working inside and outside, on the majority and the minoritarian front simultaneously.

In one of those double binds that occur so often in the mainstream representation of difference, women are simultaneously portrayed as the unruly element that needs to be straightened out—natives to be subjugated or cyberamazons in need of some governance—and as already complicitous with and integrated into the industrial reproductive complex. Sofia Zoe puts it admirably: "Superman has incorporated and taken over female functions to become a high-tech Supermom, who feeds and fertilizes us with junk food, spermatic images and silicon chips, and who tempts us with terminal apples" (Zoe 1984:51).

Translated into the Deleuzian language of the becoming-woman, the maternal/material feminine is simultaneously the despotic face of the Majority and the pathetic face of its minorities. On her increasingly contaminated body, postindustrial culture fights the battle of its own renewal. To survive, advanced capitalism must incorporate the mother, the better to metabolize her offspring. This is also known as the "feminization" of advanced cultures, in the sense of what I would call the becoming-woman of men.

The classic 1990s *Alien* film series operates a welcome and often feminist intervention in this area. It turns the "new female monsters" engineered by late postindustrial technosocieties into the heroic subjects who are most likely to save humanity form its techno-activated annihilation: the feminist as the last of the humans or the becoming-woman of humanity. J. H. Kavanagh (1990) argues that *Alien* in fact celebrates the rebirth of humanism in the shape of progressive sociosymbolic institution of femininity. The struggle is internal to the feminine, and it takes place between an archaic monstrous feminine represented by the alien and the postfeminist, emancipated woman represented by Ripley/Sigourney Weaver. The alien is a *phallus dentatus* born from a man's stomach, grotesquely erect most of the time and prone to oral rapes with its phallic tail. Ripley emerges by contrast as the life-giving postfeminist principle. A warrior with a heart of gold, rescuing pets and little girls as well as life in the galaxy as a whole, she is the new humanist hero: woman as the savior of mankind.

I think it would be far too predictable an ending, however, were an intergalactic Joan of Arc bearing Sigourney Weaver's ghostly white face to represent all feminism can do for a species in advanced state of crisis. Not that saving humanity is an unworthy cause, but it is a role that historically women have been called upon to play often—especially in times of war, invasion, liberation struggles, or other forms of daily resistance. They have, however, seldom drawn any real benefits for their status in society from these episodes of heroism. Moreover, as Barbara Kruger put it: "we don't need another hero." To have the dialectics of the sexes merely reversed to the benefit of women—mostly white, highly educated women—would be a defeat, since the power structures are left practically unchanged. By the third millennium, women's participation in ensuring the future of humanity needs consequently to be negotiated and not to be taken for granted. I think it would be more beneficial to all concerned if the tensions that are built into the end-of-century crisis of values were allowed to explode also within feminism, bringing its paradoxes to the fore. Because feminism is definitely not about a quest for final authenticity, for the golden fleece of truth, in the new millennium we need to acquire a flair for complicating the issues, so as to live up to the complexities of our age. I would like feminists to avoid repetitions without difference and the flat-out recomposition of genderized and racialized power differences, on the one hand, or, on the other, the equally unsatisfactory assumption of a morally superior triumphant feminine showing the one-way road to the future.

CONCLUSION: SEXUAL DIFFERENCE AS THE PRINCIPLE OF NOT ONE

One of the key points in this chapter is not so much that sexualized, racialized, and naturalized differences don't matter, but rather that they no longer coincide with sexually, racially, and naturally differentiated bodies. Advanced capitalism has delinked the empirical referents of otherness (woman/native/earth other) from the imaginary institutions of sexuality/race/nature, which traditionally framed them. Genetic engineering and biotechnologies have seen to it that a qualitative dislocation has taken place. The sexualized, racialized, and naturalized others are no longer the boundary markers of categorical distinctions. Genetic engineering and contemporary molecular biology have located the markers for the organization and distribution of differences in micro-instances like the cells of living organisms. We have come a long way from the gross system that used to mark difference on the basis of visually verifiable anatomical differences between the empirical sexes, the races, and the species. We have moved from the biopower that Foucault exemplified by comparative anatomy to a society based on the governance of molecular bios-zoe power today. From disciplinary to control societies. In postmodernity, under the impact of the technological revolution, the political economy of the Panopticon is no longer adequate and has been replaced by the molecular informatics of domination. Regimes of discipline have metamorphosed into modulations of power that land on the living matter that composes the individual. By extension, it follows that the classical others are no longer the necessary point of reference for the organization of a symbolic division of labor between the sexes, the races, and the species. Today they have been transformed in the spectral economy of dematerialization of difference.

This is not to say, however, that the classical power relations have improved or that the function that difference was called to perform is over. The collapse of the former system of marking difference makes it all the more urgent to reassert sexual difference as the privileged principle of alterity, of not-One as constitutive of the subject, and to elaborate nomadic forms of ethical accountability to match it. What is needed is an ethics of embodied differences that can sustain this challenge: an undifferentiated grammar of becoming simply will not do. To critique the content of the sociosymbolic myth of difference, therefore, is not the same as dismantling or even displacing its structural function. Difference, understood as the principle of Not-One, in Levi Strauss's sense of "zero institution," fulfills the function of marking a fundamental break at the site of origin of the subject. What needs to be broken is the fantasy of unity, totality, and oneness. This is what the psychoanalytic idea of the original loss stands for: it is the pound of flesh one needs to hand over in order to enter the sociosymbolic contract. What is knocked out from the subject's psychic landscape is the delusion of Oneness, the fantasy of omnipotence. To recognize this basic, ego-deflating principle is ground zero of subject formation. The recognition of alterity in the sense of incommensurable loss and an unpayable outstanding debt to others entails the awareness that one is the effect of irrepressible flows of encounters, interactions, affectivity, and desire, which one is not in charge of. This humbling experience of not-Oneness, which is constitutive of the nonunitary subject, far from opening the doors to relativism, anchors the subject in an ethical bond to alterity, to the multiple and external others that are constitutive of that entity which, out of laziness and habit, we call the "self." The split, or nonunitary, nature of the subject entails the recognition of a prediscursive structure of the "self," of a necessary loss of that which is always already there—an affective, interactive entity endowed with intelligent flesh and an embodied mind. Whereas Lacanian psychoanalytic theory ontologizes this loss and Derrida, with some help from Lévinas, institutionalizes it as the constitutive interdependence of self to other—nomadic theory builds on the productive aspects of the condition of not-One.

We have to learn to endure the principle of not-one at the in-depth structures of our subjectivity. Becoming nomadic, by constructing communities where the notion of transience, of passing is acknowledged in a sober secular manner that binds us to multiple "others" in a vital web of complex interrelations. Kinships systems and social bonding, like flexible citizenship, can be rethought differently and differentially, moving away from the blood, earth, and origin of the classical social contract. Given the extent of the transpositions brought about by advanced capitalism and the dislocations of traditional values and social bonding they have triggered, the conditions for a renegotiation of our being in *this* together are timely.

A nomadic politics of becoming-minoritarian is a posthumanist, vitalist, nonunitarian and yet accountable recomposition of a missing people. A community not bound together by the guilt of shared violence or by unpayable ontological debts, but rather by the compassionate acknowledgment of our shared need to negotiate processes of sustainable transformations with multiple others in the flow of monstrous energy of a "Life" that does not respond to our names. (More on this in chapter 11.)

Faithful to my initial promise that politics begins with our desires, and that desires escape us, are always ahead of us, in that they are the driving force that propels us, I want to argue that we need to express political passions in ways that are adequate to our paradoxical historical condition. Being a child of my times, I am in love with changes and transformations and very excited about the pathbreaking developments I have witnessed in my lifetime. Neither nostalgia nor utopia will do. We rather need a leap forward toward a creative reinvention of life conditions, affectivity, and figurations for the new kind of subjects we have already become. In the meantime, we need to live with transitions and processes, in-between states and transformations. In terms of theoretical practice, I would recommend that we do not rush forward to hasty resolutions of complexities we can hardly account for. Let us instead linger a little longer within complexities and paradoxes, resisting fear of the imminent catastrophe. Let us take the Time to go through with these processes.

There is consequently little time or space for nostalgia. Deleuze's hybrid nomadic selves, the multiple feminist-operated becoming-woman of women, Irigaray's woman as not-one, Haraway's cyborgs, the overexposed faces of celebrities and the anonymous faceless masses of migrants and asylum seekers, not unlike Cixous's new Medusa, express the transposed differences that constitute our era. They are often rendered in the old-fashioned social imaginary as monstrous, hybrid, scary deviants. What if what was at fault here, however, were the very social imaginary that can only register changes of this magnitude on the panic-stricken moralistic register of deviancy? What if these unprogrammed-for others were forms of subjectivity that have simply shrugged off the shadow of binary logic and negativity and moved on? Through met(r)amorphoses and meta(l)morphoses, the process of transformation of the subject goes on. So what if this new nomadic subject looks, feels, and sounds unusual? S/he is monstrous, mixed, hybrid, beautiful, and, guess what . . . ? S/he is laughing!

2

META(L)MORPHOSES

Women, Aliens, and Machines

BECOMING-MACHINES

In the case of the technological "other," or machine, even more than the becoming-woman, animal, insect, or alien others (about which more in the next two chapters), processes of hybrid transformation show the same trend I outlined in the previous chapter. Namely, a systematic displacement of the boundaries of difference or structural "otherness"; secondly, the un-hinging of difference from the "others" who traditionally acted as its empirical referents—women, natives, animals, and earth others; thirdly, the free-floating expansion of differences in the spinning machine of advanced capitalism—a quantitative proliferation that, paradoxically, makes no qualitative shift in the power relations between the sovereign or dominant subject and his "others." Last, but not least, I also stressed the shortcomings of our social imaginary,which seems unable to represent these social mutations in productively positive ways and opts instead for a schizoid alternation of euphoria and melancholia. Excitement about the changes is coupled with political and social conservatism, nostalgia, and a social climate of anxiety and fear. Equally striking is the persistence of the negative trend to represent transformations of the relations between humans and machines in the mode of hyped-up neogothic horror. I have labeled this narrow and negative social imaginary techno-teratological (Braidotti 2002a). That is to say, an object of simultaneous admiration and aberration, exactly like the organically mal-formed human monster (Braidotti 2011).

Both machines and monsters are hybrids—that is to say, they blur funda-mental distinctions or constitutive boundaries between different ontologi-cal categories—the human/the nonhuman, the organic other/the inorganic other, flesh/metal, the born/the manufactured. Technology is at the heart of the process that recombines all these categories into a powerfully posthuman mix transforming what we used to call "the living being." The dis-enchanted clinical gaze of classical anatomy—which Foucault positions at the heart of the modern political economy of subjectivity—has by now extended into the very genetic core of life itself, both human and nonhuman.

This is something other than the traditional metaphorical relation to machines and their representational function. For instance, during the first industrial revolution, the steam engine, in keeping with nineteenth-century mechanics and the laws of thermodynamics, provided Freud with the fun-damental metaphor for the splitting of the humanistic subject through un-conscious sources. Wiener (1948), in his influential classification of tech-nological artifacts, defines the nineteenth century as a whole as the age of the steam engine. The psychoanalytic discourse on the libido as the hidden motor of the subject relies on the same imagery and connects desire to the machine, or technology, in both internal and external ways. Internally, the libido acts as the built-in sort of energy and source of motion of the subject. Externally, it points instead to an increasing standardization of human dis-tress, which translates into the tensions and neuroses that Freud's patients bring into psychoanalysis. In both cases the technological factor acts as a powerful bridge maker or in-between player in framing the crisis of moder-nity and its subjects.

As I argued elsewhere (Braidotti 2011), there is a materialist tradition in French philosophy of science that runs through Bachelard and Canguilhem into Foucault and Deleuze's systems of thought. This tradition construes technology halfway between mind and body, reason and the imagination. More importantly, it stresses the anthropocentric dimension of the techno-logical universe: the machine imitates the embodied human, and vice versa, in a relationship of mutual receptivity that defies binary polarization. This cybernetic imaginary, machine friendly and evolution minded, is very fitting for the contemporary context.

The metamorphic function of machines that simulate the human also ex-tends to sexual organs and erotic energies. Machines question the boundary between the functional and the gratuitous, productivity and waste, moderation and excess. The machine as a connector and distributor of energy is a transformation engine: it transmits and produces connections and relations with fierce and mindless energy. From Eisenstein to Cronenberg, the erotic power of the machine has not failed to impress filmmakers, artists, and activists. Some of them have not hesitated to stress the theatricality of the machines, their pure, unproductive representational value as "bachelor machines," that is to say, pure objects of play and pleasure, utterly deprived of functionalism. This gratuitousness is central to the ludic power of the machine and was both explored and exploited in anthropomorphic machines, automata since the seventeenth century.

This metaphoric function is suspended today by a more complex political economy that connects bodies to machines more intimately, through simulation and mutual modification. As Andreas Huyssen (1986) has argued, in the electronic era, wires and circuitry exercise another kind of seduction than the pistons and grinding engines of industrial machinery. The main thrust of micro-electronic seduction is actually neural, in that it foregrounds the fusion of one's consciousness and nervous system with the general electronic network. Nomadic theory argues that, far from abolishing or replacing the body, new technologies strengthen the corporeal structure of both humans and machines and their interconnection. The body-machine or cyborg is a culturally dominant icon whose effects go well beyond cinema or media. They also affect the corporeal behavior of "real" humans the world over and, as we saw in the previous chapter, enact a series of mutations that affect all species.

Let's take for example Dolly the sheep as the main figuration for the perverse temporalities and contradictions that structure our technological culture. Dolly is that sex which is not one—a collective entity repackaged as a bounded self. She/it is simultaneously the last specimen of her species— descended from the lineage of sheep that were conceived and reproduced as such—and the first specimen of a new species: the electronic and biogenetic sheep that Phillip K. Dick dreamed of, the forerunner of the androids society of *Blade Runner*. Cloned, not conceived sexually, heterogeneous mix of organism and machine, Dolly simply changes the name of the game. Severed from reproduction and hence divorced from descent, both the gender and the kinship, Dolly is no daughter of any member of her/its old species— simultaneously orphan and mother of her/itself. First of a new gender, she/ it is also beyond gender dichotomies.

Copy made in the absence of one single original, Dolly pushes the logic of the postmodern simulacrum to its ultimate perversion. She/it brings Immaculate Conception into a biogenetic third-century version. The irony reaches a convulsive peak when we remember that Dolly died of a banal and all too familiar disease: rheumatism. After which, to add insult to injury, she suffered a last indignity: taxidermy. She was embalmed and exhibited in a science museum as a scientific rarity (shades of the nineteenth century) and a media celebrity (very twentieth century!). Dolly is simultaneously archaic and hypermodern; she/it is a compound of multiple anachronisms situated across different chronological axes; she/it inhabits different and self-contradictory time zones. Like other contemporary technoteratological animals or entities, (OncoMouse comes to mind), Dolly shatters the linearity of time and exists in a continuous present. This techno-electronic timeless time is saturated with asynchronicity, that is to say, it is structurally unhinged.

Thinking about Dolly blurs the categories of thought we have inherited from the past—she/it stretches the longitude and latitude of thought itself, adding depth, intensity, and contradiction. Because she/it embodies complexity, this entity, which is no longer an animal but not yet fully a machine, is THE philosophical problem of today.

THE NOMADIC MACHINE

A new productive link is thus established between the human, science, the natural environment, and the evolutionary traits of humanity, enhanced and challenged by the new technologies. Our historical era is marked by a new and perversely fruitful alliance with technology. This produces relations of proximity, familiarity, and increased intimacy between the human and the technological universe. At such a time of important relocations for cultural and political practices of interaction with the technological universe, nomadic cultural theory pleads for resistance to both the fatal attraction of nostalgia and the fantasy of techno-utopias. .

Nomadic theory about the new body-machine starts from the resistance to the negative or reactive passions that surround the public debate on the technologies and builds affirmatively upon it. Practicing the radical empiricism of the feminist politics of location, let us start from the assumption that cyborg-entities are the now dominant social and cultural formations active throughout the social fabric and hence rich in economic and political implications. It would therefore be a mistake to restrict or—even worse— to dismiss them as merely cultural trends. In fact, the discourse celebrating the union of humans and electronics, thus the equation between neural and digital networks, is very popular in the scientific community and among the technological elite as well as in many aspects of popular culture. To take the case of cinema—one just has to compare that masterpiece of high modernism that is Fritz Lang's *Metropolis* (1927) to the posthuman redemptive saga of James Cameron's *Avatar* (2009) to get a measure of the distance our culture has covered in reconceptualizing the relationship between the organic human body and its mechanic or technologically mediated body-other.

As Huyssen pointed out in his seminal analysis (1986), the cyborg of Fritz Lang's film is a female robot that holds the key to the industrial future of her people, with predictable powers of destruction. The ambivalence about technology is cast in the mode of the ancestral suspicion our culture feels toward powerful women, women in positions of power. Sexual difference is thus structurally present in this vision of Western modernity. The progressive promise and the destructive potential are held in close and calculated balance. Both "machine-vamp" and praying mantis, both virgin mother and pregnant suicide bomber, Fritz Lang's Maria in the masterful *Metropolis* expresses unequivocally the highly sexualized and deeply gendered nature of the early twentieth century's relationship to its industrial machinery and technical body-doubles.

Now shift from this predigital world to the environmental postapocalypse world of *Avatar* and the shock could not be greater. Electronic technology has disrupted, in a creative manner, the century-old distinction between human and machines or humans and nonhumans, terrestrials and extraterrestrials. Electronic machines are, from this angle, quite emblematic, as they are immaterial: plastic boxes and metal wires that convey information. They do not "represent" anything, but rather carry clear instructions and can reproduce clear information patterns. They work and in so doing sum up to perfection the genealogy of machines as industrial slaves. Contemporary information and communication technologies, however, go even further in that they exteriorize and duplicate electronically the human nervous system. Which has prompted a shift in our field of perception: the visual modes of representation have been replaced by sensorial-neuronal modes of simulation. Images can be shot into the cortex and not merely projected into the retina. This shift is not without implications for human consciousness and its relations to sensorial data perception.

Scott Bukatman argues (1993:259) that "the computer alone is narrated as a prosthetic extension, as an addictive substance, as a space to enter, as a technological intrusion into human genetic structures and finally as a replacement for the human in a posthuman world." The escalation of the interface and the intimacy between the human and the electronic machine is telling: from juxtaposition to superimposition until finally the technology supersedes the human. Bukatman argues that this projection of the physical self into an artificial environment feeds into a dream of terminal identity outside the body, a sort of "cybersubject" (Bukatman 1993:187). This exemplifies the most conservative tendencies of postmodern disembodiment and new age fantasies of cosmic redemption via technology. Ultimately, these different ways of escaping form the body tend to suggest or yearn for the abolition of death in an evolutionary perspective of more-than-the human. This is precisely the plot, as well as the fantasy, visualized with spectacular technological means and equally striking absence of creativity in Cameron's *Avatar*: a perfect example of images without imagination (Braidotti 2011).

The sexual politics of representation and hence the location of sexual difference have shifted accordingly. In the electronic frontier, the future is not female and the original sin does not cast a lingering shadow over the female of the species. Advanced capitalism is a postgender system capable of accommodating a high degree of androgyny and a significant blurring of the categorical divide between the sexes, as I argued in the previous chapter. This does not make it, however, any more egalitarian or less heterosexist in this vehement commitment to uphold family values, albeit—in the case of *Avatar*—of the intergalactic and alien kind. What is really eroticized, in contemporary technoculture, is precisely the power our technologies have reached in destabilizing the categorical axes of difference that used to structure our culture. Techno-transcendence is the true object of desire, especially when coupled to a consumers-oriented brand of liberal individualism: this is the transsexual social imaginary of advanced capitalism.

Technological body doubles and other cyborgs are therefore no longer feminized, but rather neutralized as figures of mixity, hybridity, interconnectiveness, and in-between states that make transsexuality into a dominant topos. If the machine is both prosthetic and transgender, the old organic human body needs to be relocated somehow. I want to argue that it is in free fall, outside the gender system, in a sort of sexually undifferentiated becoming-other. In this context a feminist appropriation of Deleuze's becoming-machine can act not only as an analytic tool but also as a powerful reminder of alternative forms of reembodiment. As such it constitutes a significant intervention in the paradoxical social imaginary of late postindustrial societies.

It is precisely the schizoid nature of advanced capitalism that provides it with its multiple lethal charges. To assume that it works according to rational laws of logic would be really to do it too much honor. A nomadic neomaterialist philosophy of the enfleshed self keeps the technohype in check by a sustainable ethics of transformations. This position juxtaposes the rhetoric of "the desire to be wired" to a more radical sense of the materialism of "proud to be flesh." Nomadic radical immanence, reworked with feminist politics, allows us to respect the bond of mutual dependence between bodies and technological others, while avoiding the contempt for the flesh and the subsequent fantasy of escape from the finite materiality of the enfleshed self. The issue of death and mortality will be raised by necessity (see chapter 13).

Philosophical nomadism acknowledges the technocultural status of contemporary corporeality, but it also challenges some of its self-destructive or nihilistic tendencies with reference to the key concepts of bodily materialism and immanence. Deleuze's emphasis on antiessentialist vitalism and complexity is not a recipe for cybernetic fantasies of escape from the body, but rather a rigorous call for rethinking human embodiment in a manner that is coextensive with our technological habitat. Deleuze shows that both the established ideas of the Organic and those of the mechanical world are equally Molar and sedentary—or Majority—based. In terms of technology, they result in the humanistic vision of assembled parts working together to create a harmonious and well-functioning whole. In opposition to this holistic view of the mechanical world, Deleuze will defend a molecular, machinic one, which is about becoming and transformation without ultimate purpose or finality. A kind of generalized "becoming—bachelor—machine," which is also known as "body without organs" or organized afunctionalism. The greatest misunderstanding about Deleuze and Guattari's body-machines is that they are often taken literally, as actual pieces of wires, silicon, metal, and circuitry. Or else they are taken metaphorically, as if automata and cyborgs best exemplified the philosophical concept of body-machines. That in turn generates wild and wide associative readings of cyborgs, terminators, and the like as expressions of nomadic becoming-machines. Nomadic machines, however, are no metaphors: they are engines or devices that both capture and process forces and energies, facilitating interrelations, multiple connections, and assemblages.

The "machine," understood in the abstract sense proposed by Deleuze, bears a privileged bond with the becoming-insects and becoming-imperceptible, in the sense of an empirical transcendental yearning for dissolution into and merging with one's planetary environment (more of this in chapter 4). The merger of the human with the technological, or the machinic, not unlike the symbiotic relationship between the animal and its habitat, results in a new compound, a new kind of ecosophical unity. In the perspective of the philosophical nomadism that I defend, this is neither holistic fusion nor Christian transcendence—it rather marks the highlight of radical immanence. It's not biology, but an ethology of forces—an ethics of mutual interdependence.

SEXUAL DIFFERENCE IN CYBERTIMES

In keeping with the nomadic redefinition of bodily materialism as vital processes of becoming, I want to focus on the paradox of the simultaneous overexposure and disappearance of the body in the age of advanced capitalism. This results in a proliferation of discourses about and practices of knowledge over the body. Anne Balsamo (1996:5): "A range of new visualization techniques contributes to the fragmentation of the body into organs, fluids and gene codes, which in turn promotes a self-conscious self-surveillance, whereby the body becomes an object of intense vigilance and control."

In my previous work (Braidotti 2011), I have commented, in a Foucauldian framework, on the paradox of the visual overexposure of the body and the loss of any substantial consensus about bodily unity. In fact, scientific and biotechnological developments accomplish a progressive fragmentation of bodily integrity and a dematerialization of corporeal matter. Whether for the sake of biogenetic exploitation, or for that of scientific experimentation, we have entered the era of "organs without bodies" (Braidotti 1994a). No longer Cartesian *res extensa*, the body fragments into a multiplicity of discourses and practices that take living matter as their target. Foucault (1963) refers to this process as an empirical-transcendental doubling up: the body is transformed, on the one hand, into an assemblage of detachable parts, on the other, a threshold of transcendence of the subject. This paradoxical mixture of loss of unity and multiplication of discourses constitutes the core of contemporary body politics.

This engenders the simultaneous explosion of the body into a network of social practices (dieting, medical control, and pharmaceutical interventions) as well as an implosion of the body as the fetishized and obsessive object of individual concern and collective care. Biopower constructs the body as a multilayered entity that is situated over a multiple and potentially contradictory set of variables. The contemporary body is ultimately an embodied memory, best understood in light of the increasingly complex amount of information that contemporary science has been able to provide about it. With reference to molecular biology, genetics, and neural sciences—to mention just a few—the body today can and should be described adequately and with credibility as a sensor as well, an integrated site of information networks. It is also a messenger carrying thousands of communication systems: cardiovascular, respiratory, visual, acoustic, tactile, olfactory, hormonal, psychic, emotional, erotic, etc., etc. Coordinated by an inimitable circuit of information transmission, the body is a living recording system, capable of storing and then retrieving the necessary information to process it at such speed that it can react "instinctively." Fundamentally prone to pleasure, the embodied subject tends toward the recollection and repetition of experiences that pleasure has "fixed" psychically and sensually upon the subject (to re-member, after all, is to re-peat, and repetition tends to favor that which gave joy and not that which gave pain). The body is not only multifunctional but also in some ways multilingual: it speaks through temperature, motion, speed, emotions, excitement that affects the cardiac rhythm and the like.

The political line of questioning has to start from here, to raise some key questions. For instances, Hayles: "What do gendered bodies have to do with the erasure of embodiment and the subsequent merging of machine and human intelligence in the figure of the cyborg?" (1999:xii). In a similar vein, Balsamo, who believes that bodies are always and already marked by gender and race, asks (1996:6): "When the human body is fractured into organs, fluids and genetic codes, what happens to gender identity? When the body is fractured into functional parts and molecular codes, where is gender located?"

In advanced capitalism, femininity, i.e., the sociosymbolic institution that used to be the referent for nature and nurture, the flesh and the emotions, sexuality and procreation, has undergone a significant set of mutations. Propped up by major networks of technological mediation, the feminine has metamorphosed into a mother-machine, on the one hand, and a gender-bending machinic interface on the other (Braidotti 2011). This means that the woman's body is fractured, accordingly, along internally contradictory axes: as the privileged site of reinscription of the natural, insofar as it is generative, "wetware" is feminine. Hence phenomena such as technologically assisted reproduction, the artificial uterus, and the mother-machine. On the other hand, the female body has evolved into the site of inscription of the artificial or technological gender-bending other and as such it continues to function as the projection of fantasies and desires.

The strategic position of the maternal/material feminine inscribes it at the heart of schizoid lines of development in postindustrial technosciences. Susan Squier (1995) sums it up in three key figurations: the extra-uterine fetus, the surrogate mother, and the pregnant man. Inspired by Foucault, Squier focuses on the dislocation of the means and modes of reproduction and the extent to which they have redefined the link between the material body and its offspring's. The metaphorical break between mother and fetus is both the effect and also a mode of production of contemporary biotechnological power. These images embody powerful social and economic interests, but also fulfill different functions depending on the politics of location, that is to say, on the institutional and other power relations of those who practice them. The extra-uterine fetus, the surrogate mother, and the pregnant man, in other words, are not linear images, but complex, contradictory, and often overlapping figurations that point to different locations. Here we need to return to the feminist politics of location in order to provide adequate cartographies as politically informed accounts of these paradoxes (Braidotti 2011).

The trend toward a blurring if not a downright erasure of sexual difference, due to the impact of cyborgs, or techno-bodies, is also evident in the tendency of mainstream postmodern philosophies to use the feminine as the means of expressing the anxieties and fears of the hystericized, male subject-in-crisis. Bukatman (1993:247) has commented on the notion of "body panic" and on feminization as the signifier of the dominant subject's identity crisis. "As with Baudrillard, all meanings are imploded; "all social practices are equal and equally dispersed throughout the techno cultural system. . . . It has fallen to feminist and gay forces to confront the politics of reproductive technologies and viral containment, while postmodern meta-phors and discourses madly multiply around them." I think Bukatman is pointing out something very important here: on the issue of techno-bodies and the marvel of technologically enhanced bodies, our culture has gone into such a spin that a sober account of the state of the arts is difficult. Significantly, it is up to the minorities to try to ground, i.e., to provide an accountable location, for a subject that has entered terminal hysteria about his technologically supported potentialities. As in the best of the modernist tradition, women, gays, antiracist, and other alternative forces, with their historically "leaky bodies" (Grosz 1994a), are ideally placed to reassert the powers, prerogatives, and beauty of the embodied flesh, also known as "wet-ware." This proves once again that a process of becoming woman is the necessary stepping-stone for nomadic becomings.

CYBORGS AND NOMADS

Donna Haraway pursues the debate about bodily materiality in the lan-guage of science and technology through a redefinition of materialism. She is a non-nostalgic posthuman thinker: her conceptual universe is the high-technology world of informatics and telecommunications and a post-anthropocentric universe of companion species. In this respect, she is con-ceptually part of the same epistemological tradition as Bachelard and—her former teacher—Canguilhem, for whom the scientific ratio is not necessar-ily hostile to humanistic approaches and cultural values. Moreover, in this line of thinking the practice of science is not seen as narrowly rationalistic, but it rather allows for a broadened definition of the term to include the play of the unconscious, dreams, and the imagination. Following Foucault (1977a), Haraway draws our attention to the construction and manipulation of docile, knowable bodies in our present social system. She invites us to think of what new kinds of bodies and gender system are being constructed right now.

Haraway proposes the figuration of the cyborg as a hybrid or body-machine. The cyborg is a connection-making entity, a figure of interrela-tionality, receptivity, and global communication that deliberately blurs cate-gorical distinctions (human/machine, nature/culture, male/female, oedipal/nonoedipal). It allows Haraway to think specificity without falling into relativism. The cyborg is Haraway's representation of a generic feminist humanity, thus answering the question of how feminists reconcile the radical historical specificity of their embodied experience with the insistence on constructing new values that can benefit humanity as a whole. Moreover, the body in the cyborg model is neither physical nor mechanical—nor is it only textual. As a new powerful replacement of the mind/body debate—the cyborg is both a postanthropocentric and postmetaphysical construct that redefines the interaction between bodies and machines. Figuration of the cyborg reminds us of the need for a new political ontology that may enable us to rethink the unity of the human being.

In a productive paradox, which is beginning to look quite familiar, the cyborg bears a privileged bond to the female body. Woman as the "other of the same" is in fact the primary artifact, produced through a whole social web of "technologies of gender" (De Lauretis 1987). Translated into nomadic language, Haraway's figuration of the cyborg is a sort of feminist becoming-woman that bypasses the feminine only in order to open up toward broader and considerably less anthropo-centric horizons. In this respect it is significant, as Pisters has astutely noted (1998) that Haraway describes the cyborg as a girl. A girl, that is to say, not a fully grown woman, already caught in the Molar line of stratification. This emphasizes the anti-oedipal function of the cyborg, and it stresses that Deleuze and Guattari (Battersby 1998) single out the little girl, Alice, as the marker of the moment of oscillation of identity, prior to entry into the Phallic symbolic. In this respect, Pisters goes onto argue that Haraway's cyborg can be compared to Deleuze's body without organs, and that Alice/the little girl's body can provide an illuminating lead into the discussion of techno-bodies in contemporary media and multi-information societies (1998).

Cyborgs and nomads are traveling companions: they are productive figurations that stress the impact of creativity in the thinking process. Both exemplify the notion that we need new forms of literacy to decode today's world. Adequate figurations also entail a discursive ethics: that one cannot know properly, or even begin to understand, that towards which one has no affinity. Critical intelligence for Haraway is a form of sympathy. One should never criticize that which one is not complicitous with: criticism must be conjugated in a nonreactive mode, a creative gesture, so as to avoid the oedipal plot of phallologocentric theory. Both nomadic subjects and cyborgs as embodied and socially embedded assemblages structurally interconnected to technological *apparati*, however, are determined *not* to recompose a unitary subject position. The cyborg is rather a multilayered, complex, and internally differentiated subject. Cyborgs today would include for me as much the underpaid, exploitative labor of women and children on offshore production plants (Sandoval 1999) as the sleek and highly trained physiques of jet fighter war pilots who interface with computer technologies at posthuman levels of speed and simultaneity. Both the highly groomed body of Princess Diana and the highly disposable bodies of women in war-torn, ethnic-cleansing lands. As a political cartography, or figuration, the cyborg evokes simultaneously the triumphant charge of Schwarzenegger's *Terminator* and the frail bodies of those workers whose bodily juices—mostly blood, sweat, and tears—fuel the technological revolution. One does not stir without the other. Once this complexity is respected, the cyborg can act as an empowering political myth of resistance to contemporary power formations.

However postgender it may claim to be, the cyborg also challenges the androcentrism of the poststructuralists' corporeal materialism. Thus, while sharing a great deal of Foucault's premises about the modern regime of truth as "biopower," Haraway also challenges his redefinition of power. Haraway notes that contemporary power does not work by normalized heterogeneity any more, but rather by networking, communication redesigns, and multiple interconnections. She concludes that Foucault "names a form of power at its moment of implosion. The discourse of bio-politics gives way to techno babble" (Haraway 1991:245, note 4). In other words, Haraway raises a point that Deleuze also noted in his analysis of Foucault, namely, that the Foucauldian diagrams of power describe what we have already ceased to be. Like all cartography, they act a posteriori and therefore fail to account for the situation here and now. In this respect, Haraway opposes to Foucault's biopower a deconstructive genealogy of the embodied subjectivities of women. Whereas Foucault's analysis rests on a nineteenth-century view of the production system, Haraway inscribes her analysis of the condition of women into an up-to-date analysis of the postindustrial system of production. Arguing that white capitalist patriarchy has turned into the "informatics of domination" (1990a:162), Haraway argues that the bodies of women and other minorities have been cannibalized by the new technologies; they have undergone a significant mutation, as I indicated in the previous chapter. The simultaneous overexposure and loss of substantial unity of bodily matter is the central feature of our times. The globalized industrial system makes oppositional mass politics redundant. A new politics must be invented, on the basis of a more adequate understanding of how the contemporary subject functions.

Chela Sandoval expands Haraway's insight into a full analysis of the political economy of "cyborgs," focusing on the human elements of exploitation of those underpaid workers who: "know the pain of the union of machine and bodily tissue, the robotic conditions and, in the late twentieth century, the cyborg conditions under which the notion of human agency must take on new meanings" (Sandoval 1999:248). As the majority of this new underclass is composed of women, ethnic others, immigrants or refugees, Sandoval stresses the gender and ethnicity aspects of the cyborgs' social space, which are significantly neglected in most theories of globalization. "Cyborg life: life of a worker who flips burgers, who speaks the cyborg speech of McDonalds, is a life the workers of the future must prepare themselves for in small, everyday ways" (1999:408).

Haraway's cyborg inserts an oppositional consciousness at the heart of the debate on the new technological societies currently being shaped, in such a way as to highlight issues of gender and sexual difference within a much broader discussion about survival and social justice. Stressing an antirelativistic acceptance of differences, nomads and cyborgs are embedded and embodied entities that seek for connections and articulations not only in a nongender-centered and nonethnocentric perspective but also in a postanthropocentric one.

Haraway's distinctive and idiosyncratic writing style expresses the force of the decentering she operates at the conceptual level, forcing readers to readjust or perish. Nowhere is the empowering force more visible than in Haraway's treatments of animals, machines, and the monstrous, hybrid "others." Deeply immersed in contemporary culture, science fiction and cyberpunk included, Haraway is fascinated by the difference embodied by reconstructed, mutant, or altered others. Her techno-monsters contain enthralling promises of possible reembodiments and actualized differences. Complex, heterogeneous, uncivilized, they show the way to multiple virtual possibilities. The cyborg, the monster, the animal—the classical "other than" the human—are thus emancipated from the category of pejorative difference and shown forth in an altogether more positive light. Haraway rejects the dialectics of otherness within which these others are constructed as simultaneously necessary and as indigestible, inappropriate/d, thus, alien. The strength of Haraway's position is that she has already leapt over to the other side of the great divide and is perfectly at home in a posthuman world. Haraway's intimate knowledge of technology is the tool that facilitates this qualitative leap; in this respect, she is a true cyberteratologist.

TECHNOBODIES IN THE SOCIAL-CYBERSPACE

In a nomadic perspective, all cyborgs, the majority as well as the minoritarian ones, inhabit a posthuman body, that is to say, an artificially reconstructed body (Balsamo 1996), which, as Francis Barker puts it (1984), marks the apex of the historical process of denaturalization. Foucault reformulates this in terms of the paradox of simultaneous disappearance and overexposure of the body (Braidotti 2011). Embodied subjectivity is thus a paradox that rests simultaneously on the historical decline of mind/body distinctions and the proliferation of discourses about the body. The problem that lingers on is how to readjust our ethics and politics to this shift. Let me sum up the key ideas here: firstly, the hyperreality of the cyborg or posthuman predicament does not wipe out politics or the need for political resistance: it just makes it more necessary than ever to work towards a radical redefinition of political action. The challenge is rather how to combine the recognition of postmodern embodied subjects with resistance to power but also the rejection of relativism and cynicism.

Secondly, posthuman embodiment is written into the cash nexus, as Chela Sandoval also pointed out. As Bukatman notes (1993), cyberspace is a highly contested social space that exists parallel to increasingly complex social realities. The clearest exemplification of the social powers of these technologies is the flow of money through computer-governed stock exchanges that always work and never sleep the world over. Capital functions through these immaterial flows of pure data traveling in cyberspace. Their alleged immateriality, however, does not conceal their heavy material relations of power and exclusion. This new political economy spells the decline of the master narratives of modernism, but, as Bukatman astutely observes, it also constitutes a sort of master narrative of its own, which spells the dawn of the age of posthumanity (Bukatman 1993).

Bukatman stresses the positive and potentially empowering impact of the new virtual, artificial environments and the extent to which they simultaneously dislocate and reground the bodily human subject. The point of origin of the subject is shifted from meaningful interiority and consciousness-driven stability to a complex and shifty technoculturally mediated process ontology. However, capital harps on and trades in body fluids: the cheap sweat and blood of the disposable workforce throughout the third world, but also the wetness of desire of first world consumers as they commodify their existence into an oversaturated stupor. Hyperreality does not wipe out class relations: it just intensifies them. Postmodernity rests on the paradox of simultaneous commodification and conformism of cultures, while intensifying disparities among them as well as structural inequalities.

Another example of the new political economy of cyberbodies is the extent to which contemporary capital takes over living matter as the analysis of labor and economic politics in terms of global migration, growing statelessness, and the rise of "the emerging digital proletariat that underpins the new world economy" (Raqs Media Collective 2003:85). The case I want to evoke is that of workers in call centers that cater to the information society by processing phone inquiries from selected locations miles away from the callers' home. Strongly denounced by Arundati Roy (2001), these "call centers," or data outsourcing agencies, are a multibillion dollar industry that has attracted a great deal of critical attention both in mainstream and in alternative media.[1] Workers in these centers answer queries on a wide range of subjects; crucial to the success of the work of these ethnic, indigenous workers is their ability to simulate the Westerns consumers' accents, attitudes, and interests. The heart of this business is never to let the caller as much as suspect that his/her call is being processed in Delhi: reproducing a simulacrum of proximity and familiarity is what one is paid for.

This kind of labor presents a number of features that innovate on exploitation of what a body can do. The strategy is not mere impersonation, for there is no visual or physical contact between the parties involved. Nor can it be seen as a form of identification, as the worker need not feel or experience herself as being from a different culture/nation in order to fulfill her contractual obligations. It rather resembles the logistics of carefully orchestrated simulation. As such, it requires a radical "Othering" of oneself, or a mild form of schizophrenia, which is not a masquerade, in the ironic sense of self-exploration, but reification of the worker's own life-world (Lazzarato 2004). Not unlike characters in a chat room, the call center worker performs her labor market persona—at one-tenth of her Western counterpart's wages.

Another significant example of the same phenomenon is the extensive reliance of the computer games industry on test players drawn from mostly male youth in former Eastern Europe. Playing computer games up to fifteen hours a day at a time—in an industry that operates continuously, twenty-four hours a day, seven days a week—for wages of about 130 U.S. dollars a month, these digital workers have invented the virtual sweatshop.[2]

This is today's variation on the theme of physical exploitation, which fits into the global marketing of both material commodities and of immaterial Western life-styles, cultures and accents. Hardt and Negri (2000) stress the immaterial and affective nature of this labor force, which trades phonetic skills, linguistic ability, and proper accent services as well as requiring attention, concentration, and great care. This tour de force by the digital workers of the new global economy rests on an acute awareness of one's location in space and time, and yet it functions through border crossings, nomadic shifts, and paths of deterritorialization. It exposes the material foundations of a cyberculture that prides itself in its allegedly ethereal nature. It foregrounds the collapse of the binary opposition of center-periphery in a new fluctuating continuum between discrete spaces in the global economy. But it also emphasizes the growing power dissymmetry between those locations and the disturbing racialized and sexualized structure of the new digital proletariat.

The underlying aspect of this situation is the omnipotence of the visual media. Our era has turned visualization into the ultimate form of control. As I argued elsewhere (Braidotti 2011), the techniques of visualization of the body and of living matter discipline not only the corporeal material and the individualized subject that inhabits it, but also the eye, mind, and mental structure of the scientists themselves. Daston and Galison (2007) have provided brilliant analyses of the structural connections between scientific practices, visual instruments and practices, and the pursuit of the self-styling by the scientist. The rule of self-mastery being of primary importance, it follows that no genuine neutrality can be attached to the golden rule of scientific objectivity. What this rule does uphold, however, is a specific normative vision of what the subject ought to be like. The claim of objectivity as the neutralization of individual differences simultaneously produces the idealized norm of value-free scientific rationality and of the scientist as the prototype of responsible citizenship. In other words, visualization in science finds an immediate counterpart in both individual and social processes of self-formation.

This marks not only the final stage in the commodification of the scopic but also the triumph of vision over all the other senses. It is also something of special concern from a feminist perspective, because it tends to reinstate a hierarchy of bodily perception that over-privileges vision over other senses, especially touch and sound. The primacy of vision has been challenged by feminist theories, which have inspiring things to say about scopophilia, that is to say, a vision-centered approach to thought, knowledge, and science (Braidotti 2001I). In a psychoanalytic perspective, this takes the form of a critique of the phallogocentric bias that is built into vision. Thus Irigaray (1974) links it to the pervasive powers of the masculine symbolic. Keller (1983) reads it instead as a rapacious drive towards cognitive penetration of the "secrets of nature" which bears a direct link to the social and psychic construction of masculinity. In a more sociopolitical framework, Haraway (1991) attacks the priority our culture gives to the logocentric hold of disembodied vision, which is best exemplified by the satellite/eye in the sky. She opposes to it an embodied and therefore accountable redefinition of the act of seeing as a form of connection to the object of vision, which she defines in terms of "passionate detachment."

Thirdly, the cyberbodies that simultaneously gain visibility and high-definition identity or singularity are prevalently white. Whiteness here does not designate any specific racial entity; it is rather a way of indexing access to power, entitlement, and visibility with—identity. In his perverse wit, hyperreal con artist Jeff Koons (ex-husband of the posthuman Italian porno star Cicciolina) depicted Michael Jackson in a ceramic piece, as a lily-white god holding a monkey in his arms. With great panache, Koons announced that this was a tribute to Michael Jackson's pursuit of the perfectibility of his body. The many cosmetic surgery operations he has undergone testify to Jackson's willful sculpting and crafting of the self. In the posthuman worldview deliberate attempts to pursue perfection are seen as a complement to evolution, bringing the embodied self to a higher stage of accomplishment. Whiteness being, in Koons's sublime simplicity, the undisputed and utterly final standards of beauty, Jackson's superstardom could only be depicted in white. Hyperreality does not wipe out racism: it intensifies it and it brings it to implosion.

Another aspect of the racialization of posthuman bodies concerns the ethnic-specific values it conveys. Many have questioned the extent to which we are all being recolonized by an American and more specifically a Californian "body-beautiful" ideology. Insofar as U.S. corporations own the technology, they leave their cultural imprints upon the contemporary imaginary.

This leaves little room to any other cultural alternatives. The recolonization of the social cyberimaginary whitens out all diversity.

One of the great contradictions of digital images is therefore that they titillate our imagination, promising the marvels and wonders of a gender-free world while they simultaneously reproduce some of the most banal, flat images of gender identity, but also class and race relations. Virtual Reality images also titillate our imagination, as is characteristic of the pornographic regime of representation. As if the imaginative misery were not enough, postmodernity is marked by a widespread impact and a qualitative shift of pornography in every sphere of cultural activity. Pornography is more and more about power relations and less and less about sex. In classical pornography, sex was a vehicle by which to convey power relations. Nowadays anything can become such a vehicle: the becoming-culture of pornography means that any cultural activity or product can become a commodity and through that process express inequalities, patterns of exclusion, fantasies of domination, desires for power and control (Kappelar 1987).

In this context Deleuze and Guattari's body-machines provide an empowering figuration for the nonunitary structure of the contemporary subject. The "machinic" part merely refers to the subject's capacity for multiple, outward-bound interrelations with a number of external forces or others. As I suggested previously, the machine stands for networks of interconnections, arranged along lines of flight or of becoming. These do not follow a linear path; they are not teleological, but rather zigzag across multiple, unexpected, and often contradictory variables. The selection and dosages of the forces that are intermingled is essential to the whole exercise. The rational model is the same as the animal's proximity, intimacy and possession of its territory. It's about symbiotic alliances and fusion; it's more about viral or parasitic interdependence than dialectical oppositions. Deleuze uses images like the swarms of insects, the interdependence of the wasp and the orchid, the mutual dependence on territorial frames of reference to express the notion of "desiring machines." A desiring machine is a productive assemblage of selected forces that assemble for the sake of becoming-minoritarian: it is a nomadic subject.

As Goodchild points out (1996), the Deleuzian machines are planes of immanence or connecting devices that anchor the subject to a territory, a set of assemblages and encounters. They are not about signification, human intention, or the Heideggerian meaning of being. They are assemblages that create patterns through repetition; they express certain forces and infuse them through the assemblage. As such, the Deleuzian subjects are desiring machines, but not because they are the objects of (consumerist) desires. They rather express impersonal forces and intensive resonances across transversal formations that express a subject's fundamental desire to relate, connect, and endure in the bond of others.

The implications for sexual politics are not less significant, considering that, with electronic technology, the intimacy between bodies and machines reaches higher levels of complexity. Insofar as contemporary technologies blur the boundaries between humans and others, they are transgressive. As such, they are often taken as a symbol for all kinds of other transgressions, including sexual ones. For instance in a piece pointedly called "Birth of the Cyberqueer," Morton (1999:370) takes Deleuze and Guattari's body-machines as framing a space of "sexual deregulation" where sexuality can be oedipalized and return to its primary, ludic, and polymorphous flows. As such, Morton argues that Deleuzian bodies share in the queer movement. In a similar mode, Jordan (1995) adapts Deleuze's theory of desire to his interpretation of rave parties and the culture of house music and ecstasy. The machinic assemblage of these events is crucial (1995:130): "This undifferentiated state is a collective delirium produced by thousands of people making the connections of drugs to dance, dance to drugs, drugs to time, time to music and so on, and thereby gradually constructing the state of raving and so the Bodies-without Organs of raving."

I always find myself resisting these pop interpretations of Deleuze's concepts, while I admire the creativity of those who so freely kidnap these complex notions and adapt them to their own ends. In the case of the drug culture, I doubt very much that one needs or particularly gains anything by attempting to frame it within a nomadic theory of desire. I remain skeptical of "narco-philosophers" of all kinds. In an analogous manner, Richard Barbrook has written angrily against the sixties rhetoric of many Internet gurus. Some of them embrace Deleuze and Guattari and link them with digital elitism in the name of sixties libertarianism. They thus end up with a form of aristocratic anarchism that is eerily similar to Californian neo-liberalism. In the post-1989 context of decline of revolutionary ideologies the Internet prophets are the only ones still pursuing dreams of change and social transformation. Barbrook argues that the aesthetization of the sixties' is central to the European approach to Internet experiments, in opposition to the corporate ideology dominant in California. "Deleuze and Guattari seem to provide theoretical metaphors which describe the non-theoretical aspects of the net. For instance, the rhizome captures how cyberspace is organized as an open-ended, spontaneous and horizontal network. Their Bodies-without-organs phase can be used to romanticize cyber-sex. Deleuze and Guattari's nomad myth reflects the mobility of contemporary net users as workers and tourists."

The techno-nomads control the Internet and have reinvented avant-gardism with techno-music spearheading the revolution. For Barbrook, the alliance between liberal individualism, corporate ideology, and this techno-primitivism is the worst possible connection. He argues that Deleuze's philosophy does not belong with such absurd bedfellows and that a more rigorous approach is needed to theorize positively and not sentimentally the unique brand of electronic vitalism that is running through contemporary cyberculture.

Bukatman agrees that the most serious problems arise from the unholy alliance of cyberideology to individualism, i.e., the liberal market economy and the sentimental attachment to a humanist definition of the subject as "conscience and a heart." Bukatman goes on to praise Deleuze as a techno-anarchist who can lead us to neotranscendence through technology. "Deleuze and Guattari are cyberpunks, too, constructing fictions of terminal identity in the nearly familiar language of a techno-surrealism (1993:326). Without going that far, I take Deleuze and Guattari's notion of "bodies without organs"—a sort of organic bachelor machine—aims to deconstruct the myth of wholeness and organicism, but also to refuse the technocratic takeover of the human body. The political resistance suggested by philosophical nomadism consists in working within the belly of the beast, situating the human as coextensive and intimately connected to the technological, but also stressing the way in which the human occupies the threshold between technology and narration. Hayles (1999:286) also makes a powerful intervention in favor of a more sober and balanced account of contemporary techno-bodies: "But the posthuman does not really mean the end of humanity. It signals instead the end of a certain conception of the human. . . . What is lethal is not the posthuman as such but the grafting of the posthuman onto a liberal humanist view of the self. . . . Located within the dialectic of pattern/randomness and grounded in embodied actuality rather than disembodied information, the posthuman offers resources for rethinking the articulation of humans with intelligent machines."

Resting on Deleuze and on feminist epistemology, Hayles attacks the classical humanistic notion that subjectivity must coincide with conscious agency and takes a firm stand in favor of a radical redefinition of the subject in such a way as to avoid some of the mistakes of the humanist past, notably the liberal vision of an autonomous subject whose "manifest destiny is to dominate and control nature" (Hayles 1999:288).

■ ■ ■

The becoming-machine or meta(l)morphoses need not be cast in the apocalyptic mode or mood. I would recommend that we approach them nomadically—because we are indeed rooted, even though we go with the flow. In relation to cyberculture, I think it important to take distance equally from two related pitfalls. On the one hand, the euphoria of professional optimists who advocate proliferation of differences and the promises of electronic democracy for net citizens or the optimism of the techno-nerds who grab advanced technology and especially cyberspace as the possibility for multiple fantasies of escape. On the other hand, critical distance is needed from the many prophets of doom who mourn the decline of the classical world and transform nostalgia into a political platform, not to speak of those, like the Unabomber, who fall into eschatological violence.

I would therefore rather keep a sober perspective on what I consider to be the great challenge of contemporary social theory and cultural practice, namely, how to make the new technologies enhance the embodied subject. Which does not mean, however, that I will not also be critical of the cyberteratological imaginary itself. My specific target in this regard is the tendency, which I consider nihilistic, that consists in declaring the superfluity of the body, its alleged irrelevance. Or else to reduce it to "meat" or to the status of a familiar parasite and the liquid insubstantiality of "wetware." These result, paradoxically, in both accelerating and denying its mortality, rendering bodily pain and suffering both more ubiquitous and more irrelevant in the process. Against such denials, I want to reassert my bodily brand of materialism and remain to the end proud to be flesh!

Technology has become a challenge—it is the chance we have given ourselves, as a culture, to reinvent ourselves and display some creativity. Technology should assist human evolution. If the question is not "what we are?"
but "who do we want to become?" then the next step is "how can technoculture help us achieve this?" I would consequently reset the question of technology in the framework of the challenge of evolutionary change or transformation, which I see as central to both mapping the present and working
toward a constructive future. We need, instead, to learn to think differently,
more self-critically. The "we" in question here refers to those who occupy
a center—any of the poly-located centers that situate most inhabitants of
the North of the world in a position of structural advantage. Some more
than others, of course—but all more than most of the other dwellers of
this planet. Acknowledging one's participation in and sharing of locations
of power is the starting point for the cartographic method, also known in
feminism as the politics of location.

To sum up: while criticizing the imaginative deficit of our culture—that is
to say, our collective inability to find adequate representations of the kind of
embodied nomadic subjects we have already become—multiple, complex,
and multilayered selves—I want to explore the conceptual and representational shifts of perspective needed in order for transformations to be enacted
at the depth of subjectivity and thus make a lasting impact on the social and
cultural spheres. I have quarreled with the nostalgic tendency that accounts
for changes, especially technological ones, in a paranoid mode that renders
them as "monstrous," pathological, decadent, or threatening and with the
euphoric approach that turns them into easy *panacea*. I will also offer, in
chapters 5 and 6, counterreadings of these changes in such a way as to highlight their positivity and force.

One of the risks of the "hype" that surrounds the meta(l)morphoses
of the cyberculture of body-machines is that of re-creating a hard-core,
unitary vision of the subject, under the cover of pluralistic fragmentation
to reassert transcendence via technological meditation and to propose a
neouniversal machinic ethos. In the language of philosophical nomadism,
this would produce the deception of a quantitative multiplicity that does
not entail any qualitative shifts. To avoid this pitfall, which fits in with the
neoliberal euphoria of much contemporary politics, and in order to enact
qualitative transformations instead, I think it important to critique the assimilation of cyborgs who defend the classical bourgeois notion of indi-

vidualism and the corollaries of commodification and consumerism that it entails.

A strong sense of embodied and embedded materialism is very relevant to the task of rethinking the symbiotic relationship between humans and machines while avoiding the hype. I have taken a clear position that wants to be equally distanced from both hyped-up disembodiment and fantasies of escape as well as a reessentialized, centralized notion of liberal individualism, providing my own reading of techno-bodies and the web of power relations and effects in which they navigate. I have concluded that the consumerminded techno-hype neither wipes out nor solves traditional patterns of exclusion and domination, but rather confirms the traditional entitlements of a subject position that is made to coincide with masculine, white, heterosexual, European identity. Nor does it help to reconfigure either femininity as the classical Other of Man or whiteness as a position of naturalized structural privilege. In some ways technocultures even reenforce some of the worst traits of the traditional regimes of power, using the management of the insecurities triggered by the changes as the pre-text to the restoration of traditional hierarchies.

In my analysis of the social imaginary of late postindustrial societies, I singled out some trends about the identification of women with machines. In modernity the machine often acts as a substitute for social functions usually fulfilled by women. That goes as much for household appliances as for the eroticized body-double of the film *Metropolis*. Because of this socially induced association, which is activated by popular culture and especially cinema, women and machines are presented as competitive with each other. What they compete for is, mostly, male attention, be it the father's or the (hetero)sexual partner.

This changes with the coming of postmodern machinery and electronics. The increasing degree of incorporation of technology by humans also shifts the grounds for the interaction between women and technology. I argued earlier in this chapter that whereas in modernity woman was associated with technology, and sexual difference was integral to modernist discourses and practices, in postmodernity the maternal/material feminine is represented as already incorporated into the technological complex. This incorporation has the effect of assimilating it—and sexual difference along with it—into the techno-industrial machinery. This also implies that the technological field has evolved into a space of sexual indeterminacy, which I rendered in terms of a transsexual imaginary. Advanced capitalism has consumed and subsumed the old gender system.

At first sight, in fact, the sexual undecidability of these new technologies, and the promises of endless restructuring and redefinitions of sexual identity that it entails, may appear attractive. Hence the tone of euphoria that marks a great many cyberfeminists. On closer scrutiny, however, I would argue that there is ample room for concern. As often is the case with promises of transsexual "openness," in fact, the evacuation of the feminine is not far off. That would not be a problem in itself, as I for one long for the bypassing of the dialectics of sexual difference understood as pejoration. The problem is that these shifts of perspective, changes, and transformations do not take place in a vacuum. Nor are they the mere effects of textual or deconstructive discursive strategies. These transformations are rather embedded and embodied in the specific power relations of a social context that constructs technologies as liberating while using them for the most confining, profit-making, war-seeking, and sexually conservative ends—a system that declares gender redundant, while reconfirming social hierarchies and their white supremacist, ethnocentric component as the culturally dominant road to proper, civilized human behavior. Hence my commitment to a materialist approach to the analysis of contemporary culture, which I defend in terms of the need for cartographic accounts of the paradoxical changes that are occurring in postindustrial societies and in their imaginary. I have reasserted the need for a philosophical brand of embodied and embedded nomadism. This implies that attention be given to the simultaneity and mutual implication of issues of culture and power, political economies and structures of signification. Nomadic subjects combine qualitative shifts with a firm rejection of liberal individualism and connect a distinct sense of singularity with respect for complexities and interconnections. This is a collectively oriented, externally bound, multiple subject whose singularity is the result of constant renegotiations with a variety of forces.

Such a vision of the subject requires readjustments also in terms of patterns of desire. Sexualities are also being renegotiated and reconfigured along multiple, nomadic, and hence potentially contradictory axes. Across such multiplicities, however, I have reasserted the recurrence of a process of "feminization" of the sensibility of nomadic subjects in terms of affectivity, fluidity, porosity of boundaries, and constant interrelations. Sexual difference, from being a boundary marker, has to be relocated along the idea of "the sensible transcendental" proposed by Irigaray and of Deleuze's notion of the empirical transcendental, so as to become a threshold for the elaboration and the expression of multiple differences, which extend beyond gender but also beyond the human. The emergence of the earth, and of "earth-others" as political subjects, is the surest indicator of this shift of perspective. I will turn to them in the next two chapters, treating the ecophilosophy of nomadism, as an attempt to rethink in a materialist manner the intricate web of interrelations that mark the contemporary subjects' relationship to their multiple e-ecologies of belonging.

Such new political subjects move in the background of the postindustrial worldview and in the ruins of the cold war in a postnuclear condition. They dwell in the political economy of terror or fear for the imminent and immanent accident, of the impending catastrophe of the disaster within and without. Technology is a powerful mediator for these fears and a major factor in actualizing them. The nuclear accomplished historically the improbable task of turning technology away from the Enlightenment promise of liberation through rationality. The contemporary predicament is marked by the fear of contamination, of viral attacks that result in an evolutionary catastrophe, a devolutionary crisis, a metabolic breakdown. They consequently actualize the social imaginary of disaster and enact the aesthetics of "traumatic realism," the enfleshed point of no return, the fatal impact of bodies against machines in the lethal realm of pure speed. Like Princess Diana's metal-flesh in the contorted ruins of an automobile driven by a junkie and surrounded by media jackals. To account for these meta(l)morphoses, we need an ethics of neorealist appraisals of risks and fears, which in turn expresses skepticism toward more grandiose metadiscourses such as Marxism and psychoanalysis. Fully immersed in these meta(l)morphoses, nomadic theory keeps us moving toward a colder and slightly more posthuman political sensibility.

3

ANIMALS AND OTHER ANOMALIES

DE-OEDIPALIZING THE ANIMAL-OTHER

This chapter looks at the process of becoming-animal as a way of de-stabilizing the axis of naturalized difference. I will speak of a generic becoming-animal also as a figuration for the humanoid hybrids we are in the process of becoming.

The animal today has lost its metaphysical substantial presence and the magical aura that surrounded it. As a result, it has ceased to be one of the privileged terms that index the European subject's relationship to otherness. Writing in that tradition, Borges argued that animals come in three main categories: those we Euro-humans eat; those we watch television with, and those we are frightened of (wild, exotic, or untamed ones). This mock-taxonomy highlights the peculiar and rather perverse familiarity that characterizes Westerners' interaction with organic animal-others.

These varying degrees of familiarity mark the parameters of an essentially oedipal relationship. That is to say, an intimate and inner-looking relationship, framed nonetheless by the dominant human and structurally masculine habit of taking for granted free access to and consumption of the bodies of others, animals included. As a mode of relation, it is structurally violent and saturated accordingly with projections, identifications, and fantasies. These are centered on the dyad fear and desire, which is the trademark of the Western subject's relationship to the phallic law, the lack and the power of the master signifier, as Lacan astutely noted. It is also a token of this same subject's sense of supreme ontological entitlement. Derrida also referred to this human power over animals in terms of: "carnophallogocentrism" (Derrida 2006).

Desire and fear for the animal outside but also the animal within. This thick affective and libidinal layering, in fact, simultaneous unveils and disavows the "beast within" the human. The wild and passionate animal in us may be cheered as the trace of a primordial evolutionary trajectory or cherished as a repository of unconscious drives, but it also calls for containment and control for exactly the same reasons. The technologies to discipline these wild passions are both genderized and racialized to a very high degree. They tend to harp with distressing regularity on the disposable bodies of "others."

The ancient metaphysics of otherness rests on an assumed political anatomy, according to which the counterpart of the "power of reason" is the notion of Man as "rational animal." The latter is expected to inhabit a perfectly functional physical body, implicitly modeled upon ideals of white masculinity, normality, youth, and health. All other modes of embodiment, both in the sense of dialectical otherness (nonwhite, nonmasculine, nonnormal, nonyoung, nonhealthy) and also of categorical otherness (zoomorphic, disabled, or malformed) are pathologized and cast on the other side of normality, that is to say anomaly, deviance, and monstrosity. This process is inherently anthropocentric, genderized, and racialized in that it upholds aesthetic and moral ideals based on white, masculine European civilization. The morphological normativity at work in these standardized habits is best exemplified in Leonardo's figure of the naked, male, white body that represents the Renaissance ideal of Man as the measure of all things. This image of thought as a standard by which all others are indeed measured sets the frame for a self-congratulating relationship of Man to himself, which confirms the dominant subject as much in what he includes as his core characteristics as in what he excludes as "other."

My argument is that this mode of relation is currently being restructured. A bioegalitarian turn is taking place that encourages us to engage in an animal relationship with animals—the ways hunters do and anthropologists can only dream of. I want to argue that the challenge today is how to deterritorialize or nomadize, the human-animal interaction so as to bypass the metaphysics of substance and its corollary, the dialectics of otherness, secularizing accordingly the concept of human nature and the life that animates it. What we are dealing with today is anti-oedipal animality at work within a fast-changing technoculture that engenders mutations at all levels.

On the methodological front, de-oedipalizing the relationship to animals is a form of estrangement that entails a radical repositioning on the part of the subject. Critical theory over the last twenty years has provided ample evidence of the productive nature of the strategy of defamiliarization or estrangement. In poststructuralist feminism this discursive strategy has also been discussed in terms of disidentifying ourselves from familiar and hence comforting values and identities, such as the dominant institutions and representations of femininity and masculinity, so as to move sexual difference toward the process of becoming-minoritarian (Braidotti 1994a, b, 2006). Disidentification involves the loss of familiar habits of thought and representation in order to pave the way for the creation of creative alternatives. Spinozist feminist political thinkers like Moira Gatens and Genevieve Lloyd (1999) argue that socially embedded and historically grounded changes require a qualitative shift of our "collective imaginings" or a shared desire for transformations. Feminist, race, and postcolonial theories have made important contributions to the methodology and the political strategy of disidentification or defamiliarization. I shall return to an in-depth analysis of this notion in chapter 9.

Nomadic thought rests on the practice of estrangement as a way to free the process of subject formation from the normative vision of the self. The frame of reference becomes the open-ended, interrelational, multisexed, and transspecies flows of becoming by interaction with multiple others. A subject thus constituted explodes the boundaries of humanism at skin level; thus the Deleuzian unorganic body (Deleuze and Guattari 1972, 1980) is unlinked from the codes of phallologocentric functional identity. The "body without organs" is a body freed from efficiency-indexed organization. As such, it rejects the political regime of discipline and punishment (Foucault 1975), singing the praise of anomalies, and it also introduces a sort of joyful insurrection of the senses, a vitalist and pan-erotic approach to the flesh. It is recomposed so as to induce creative disjunctions in this system, freeing organs from their indexing to certain prerequisite functions. This calls for a generalized recoding of the normative political anatomy and its assigned bodily functions, as a way of scrambling the old metaphysical master code and loosening its power over the constitution of subjectivity. The subject is recast in the nomadic mode of collective assemblages. The aim of deterritorializing the norm also supports the process of becoming-animal/woman/minoritarian/nomadic.

The postmetaphysical figurations of both the "becoming-woman" and even more the "becoming-animal" express the rejection of the principle of adequation to and identification with a normative image of thought. This conceptual project has another important methodological implication. The project of the becoming-animal as posthuman subjectivity in Deleuze and Guattari foregrounds the idea that the activity of thinking cannot and must not be reduced to reactive ("sedentary") critique, but must also involve significant doses of creativity. Thinking can be critical, if by critical we mean the active, assertive process of inventing new images of thought. Thinking is life lived at the highest possible power, both creative and critical, enfleshed, erotic, and pleasure driven. It is essentially about change and transformations and it is a perversion of sorts, like an unprogrammed mutation. More clinical than critical, it cuts to the core of classical visions of subjectivity. In keeping with the radical immanence of nomadic thought, posthuman subjectivity implies an expanded vision of a mind-body interaction. The embodiment of the mind and the embrainment of matter are the key intertwined ideas.

AGAINST METAPHORS

Animals have long acted as boundary makers between fundamental categories and have spelled out the social grammar of categorical distinctions between the species. This ontological function resulted in the metaphorical habit of composing a sort of moral and cognitive bestiary that uses animals as referents for values, norms, and morals. Instead of waxing lyrical about the nobleness of the eagle, the deceit of foxes, or the humility of lambs, I propose that we acknowledge the century-old history and subtlety of this animal glossary. Let us also go on to admire the illustrious literary pedigree it has engendered, which ranges from Livy to Dante, from Molière to Melville and Kafka. The main point, however, is for us to move on, beyond the empire of the sign, toward a neoliteral relationship to animals, anomalies, and unorganic others. The old metaphorical dimension has in fact been overridden by a new mode of relation. Animals are no longer the signifying system that props up humans' self-projections and moral aspirations. Nor are they the gatekeepers that trace the liminal positions in between species. They have rather started to function quite literally, as a code system of their own.

This neoliteral approach begins to appear with the masters of modernity. With Freud and Darwin's insights about the structures of subjectivity, a profound inhumanity is opened up at the heart of the subject. Unconscious memories drill out time lines that stretch across generations and store the traces of events that may not have happened to any one single individual and yet endure in the generic imaginary of the community. Evolutionary theory acknowledges the cumulative and embodied memory of the species. It thus installs a time line that connects us intergenerationally to the prehuman and prepersonal layers of our existence. From the angle of critical theory, psychoanalysis propels the instance of the unconscious into a critique of rationality and logocentrism. Evolutionary theory, on the other hand, pushes the line of inquiry outside the frame of anthropocentrism into a fast-moving field of sciences and technologies of "life." The politics of life itself (Rose 2001) is the end result of in-depth criticism of the subject of humanism. Pushed even further with philosophical nomadology (Braidotti 2006), the metaphorical dimension of the human interaction with others is replaced by a literal approach based on the neo-vitalist immanence of life.

This deeply materialist approach has important ethical implications. In terms of the human-animal interaction, the ego-saturated familiarity of the past is replaced by the recognition of a deep bioegalitarianism, namely, that "we" are in this together. The bond between "us" is a vital connection based on sharing this territory or environment on terms that are no longer hierarchical or self-evident. They are, rather, fast evolving and need to be renegotiated accordingly. Gilles Deleuze and Felix Guattari's theory of "becoming animal" expresses this profound and vital interconnection by positing a qualitative shift of the relationship away from speciesism and toward an ethical appreciation of what bodies (human, animal, others) can do. An ethology of forces emerges as the ethical code that can reconnect humans and animals. As Deleuze put it: the workhorse is more different from the racehorse than it is from the ox. The animal is not classified according to scientific taxonomies, nor is it interpreted metaphorically. It is rather taken in its radical immanence as a body that can do a great deal, as a field of forces, a quantity of speed and intensity and as a cluster of capabilities. This is posthuman bodily materialism laying the grounds for bioegalitarian ethics.

THE CASH NEXUS

There are, of course, historical precedents that approached animals as materialist, energetic entities. These tended to be posited, however, in a rather functional technological-industrial mode. Since antiquity, animals have constituted a sort of zoo proletariat. They have been associated with and used for hard labor, as mechanical slaves and logistical supports for humans prior to the age of the machines. This ruthless exploitation was due not only to the species hierarchy upheld by the old metaphysical system, namely, their alleged lack of an innate rational soul and consequently a will and sovereign subjectivity of their own. It was also due to the fact that they constitute an industrial resource in themselves. Animals' bodies are primary material products: think of the tusks of elephants, the hides of most creatures, the sheep of wool, the oil and fat of whales, the silk of caterpillars, and then, of course, milk and edible meat. The bodies of animals are classified like industrial production plants, especially insects, which are taken nowadays as prototypes for advanced robotics and electronics, as I will argue in the next chapter.

This political economy on full-scale exploitation continues, with animals providing living material for scientific experiment, for our biotechnological agriculture, the cosmetics industry, drugs and pharmaceutical industries, and other sectors of the economy. In advanced capitalism, animals have turned into tradable disposable bodies of all categories and species, which are inscribed in a global market of posthuman exploitation. Traffic in animals constitutes the third largest illegal trade in the world today, after drugs and arms but ahead of women. Brazil provides the majority of the imports, stolen from the fast-disappearing Amazon forest. The Mariatee butterfly, the Amazon turtle, the black tamarin (a tiny primate smaller than the palm of a hand), and the pink river dolphin are the most sought-after items, with prices ranging from $4,000 to $70,000; RENCTAS, the Portuguese acronym for the National Network to Fight Traffic in Wild Animals, estimates the industry to be worth $15 billion a year.[1] Animals like pigs and mice are genetically modified to produce organs for humans in xeno-transplantation experiments. Cloning animals is now an established scientific practice: OncoMouse and Dolly the sheep are already part of history; the first cloned horse was born in Italy on May 28, 2003. It took more than 800 embryos and 9 would-be surrogate mother mares to produce just one foal, and now here it is.[2]

These developments are in keeping with the complex and dynamic logic of contemporary genetics. They confront us in ways that cannot be adequately described as dialectical opposites, but are better rendered as nonlinear transpositions. Globalization means the commercialization of planet earth in all its forms through a series of interrelated modes of appropriation. According to Haraway (1997), these are the technomilitary proliferation of microconflicts on a global scale: the hypercapitalist accumulation of wealth, the turning of the ecosystem into a planetary apparatus of production, and the global infotainment apparatus of the new multimedia environment.

Whereas mainstream culture reacts to these innovations with the mix of euphoria and panic, overoptimism and nostalgia, I want to strike a more affirmative note, both affectively and conceptually. Accepting full accountability for the science and technology we have collectively invented seems the start of realism and sanity as well as the basic premise for a morally relevant position. Furthermore, the mutual contaminations and intraspecies crossbreeding that mark our historical era are also breeding grounds for rich new alliances.

Part of the reason for my joyful engagement with the posthuman predicament is due to the political practice of accountability for one's situated perspectives, which I learned through feminist activism. I situate myself at the tail end of biopolitical regimes, that is to say, amidst the relentless consumption of all that lives. I am committed to start my critical work from there, not from a nostalgic reinvention of an all-inclusive holistic ideal. Considering the extent of this posthumanist turn, it seems correct to suggest that, to enact a process of becoming-animal/minoritarian, you are better off cultivating "your inner housefly or cockroach, instead of your inner child" (Shaviro 1995:53)—that is to say, anomalous and unorganic alliances, not oedipal and hierarchical relationships.

BEYOND ANIMAL RIGHTS

A critique of human arrogance as an epistemological and moral assumption is explicitly stated in mainstream discussions about animal rights, as it is in most environmental thinking. Within the tradition of liberal feminism, for instance, Mary Midgley (1996) argues that, since the Enlightenment, social contract theory has privileged the human to the detriment of all nonhuman agents such as animals and plants. She warns us that social contract thinking must not be taken as the ultimate guide, but only as a provisional tool to protect basic forms of liberty that should be updated whenever necessary.

In this vein, Midgley is careful to point out the very destructive side of that individualism which lies at the heart of contract thinking and entails selfishness and individualistic ideologies leading to moral cowardice. She also acknowledges that the opposite approach, the organic model, has been discredited through association with tyranny. Midgley argues that "a new environmental consciousness may lift the taboo on organic ways of thinking. It may even become possible for our species to admit that it is not really some supernatural variety of Lego, but a kind of an animal. This ought to make it easier to admit that we are not self-contained and self-sufficient, either as a species or as individuals, but live naturally in deep mutual dependence" (1996:9–10).

In keeping with the classical liberal tradition that she espouses, Midgley warns us not to take any models for granted but to keep a healthy dose of skepticism. Unfortunately, skepticism becomes only the pretext for a series of digs against the postmodernist treatment of ethics. Yet Midgley agrees that the notion of liberal individualism has always been biased in favor of men and is a masculine ideal, which entails not only the exclusion of many others but also a very deceptive picture of what counts as independence and autonomy: "the supposed independence of the male was a lie, which concealed its parasitic dependence on the love and the service of non-autonomous females. A false universal" (1996:76).

Species politics, on the other hand, has militated in favor of anthropocentrism since Greek antiquity. Midgley does not like the term *anthropocentrism* and prefers to it "human chauvinism; narrowness of sympathy, comparable to national, or race or gender—chauvinism. It could also be called exclusive humanism, as opposed to the hospitable, friendly, inclusive kind" (1996:105). Because of this critical approach to human chauvinism, Midgley defends the end of "anthropolatry" and calls for more respect and priority to be given to the interests of other species and life-forms: less ego, both individually and collectively.

The question is not the Kantian one: "can animals think?" but rather the empathic one: "can they suffer?" Because they clearly do, concludes

The ethical part of the project concerns the creation of a new kinship system: a new social nexus and new forms of social connection with these techno-others. What kinds of bonds can be established, and how can they be sustained? Here the notion of the "patent," which was so crucial to Shiva's analysis of globalization, returns with a vengeance. Haraway, however, is like Franklin, Lury, and Stacey (2000) in stressing the productive potential of patents. They challenge established categories of ownership in the name of that very mixity and impurity which technological culture is now capable of producing. Both kinship and ownership need to be redefined in such a way as to rethink links of affectivity and responsibility for these newly patented creatures—they are our offspring, much as Frankenstein is Mary Shelley's "hideous progeny."

In this framework, Haraway draws an analogy between OncoMouse and Irigaray's "hysteria" or matrix—it is the site of procreation or the womb-passage. Western science answers the masculine fantasy of self-birth through rational acquisition—the mind replacing the womb as site of creation (Braidotti 2011). Natural offspring being replaced by corporate brands and manufactured and patented bio-products, the ethical imperative to bind to them and be accountable for their well-being remains as strong as ever. We just need new genealogies, alternative theoretical and legal representations of the new kinship system and adequate narratives to live up to this challenge.

The minimum requirement is that the dualism human-nonhuman/animal has to be relinquished, in favour of a more dynamic notion of relation or relationality. In her recent work on "companion species" (2003), Donna Haraway draws a direct line between the early figurations of the cyborg and of OncoMouse, on the one hand, and companion species like dogs on the other. They mark the shifting boundaries of very affective and dynamic kinship relations. For Haraway this needs to be redefined in the context of a technoscientific world that has replaced the traditional natural order with a nature-culture compound. An epistemological question therefore generates a new ethical dimension. Accordingly, the human-animal relation needs be lifted out of the oedipal and infantilizing narrative within which it has historically been confined. The most dominant spin-off of this narrative is the sentimental discourse about dogs' devotion and unconditional loyalty, which Haraway argues against with all her mighty passion. As a nature cultural compound, a dog—not unlike other products of technoscience—is a radical other, albeit a significant other. We need to devise a symbolic kinship system that matches its complexity. This is not a reference to the literary bestiary as an established genre, with its own grammar and a metaphorical reference to animals like letters in an alternative alphabet (Braidotti 2002a:158).

The question then becomes: how can we respect animals' otherness? How can we address this issue in its immanent and material specificity, without falling into the worn-out rhetoric of human dignity defined as the denial of our shared animality? How can we disengage this discussion from the platitudes and nostalgia that marks the discussion of "animal rights"—also, especially in the neoliberal political context alone, the future of our own species? My answer is by stepping beyond anthropocentrism to try and look at the world from a dramatically different perspective, which does not assume a passive nature and a consciousness that must be, per definition, human.

In my own language, the same point needs to be made about the ethics of becoming-animal as about those of becoming-woman, namely: we need a qualitative shift of perspective. Which is made all the more difficult, but also more necessary, by the extent to which advanced capitalism has already erased the classical metaphysical distinctions between humans and animals on at least three grounds: firstly in their commercial value as objects of exchange for the sake of profit; secondly in terms of genetic engineering and the circulation of cellular and other matter among different species; thirdly in the timid attempts to include animals in the logic of "human" rights. Nomadic theory tries to move beyond these three obstacles.

Becoming-animal consequently is a process of redefining one's sense of attachment and connection to a shared world, a territorial space. It expresses multiple ecologies of belonging, while it enacts the transformation of one's sensorial and perceptual coordinates in order to acknowledge the collective nature and outward-bound direction of what we call the self. This is in fact a movable assemblage within a common life-space that the subject never masters or possesses, but merely inhabits, crosses, always in a community, a pack, a group, or a cluster. Becoming-animal marks the frame of an embodied subject, which is by no means suspended in an essential distance from the habitat/environment/territory, but is rather radically immanent to it. For philosophical nomadism, the subject is fully immersed in and immanent to a network of nonhuman (animal, vegetable, viral) relations. The zoe-centered embodied subject is shot through with relational linkages of the symbiotic contaminating/viral kind that interconnect it to a variety of others, starting with environmental or eco-others.

This nonessentialist brand of vitalism reduces the hubris of rational consciousness, which, far from being an act of vertical transcendence, is rather recast as a downward push, a grounding exercise. It is an act of unfolding of the self onto the world and the enfolding within of the world. What if consciousness were, in fact, just another cognitive mode of relating to one's own environment and to others? What if, by comparison with the immanent know-how of animals, conscious self-representation were blighted by narcissistic delusions of transcendence and consequently blinded by its own aspirations to self-transparency? What if consciousness were ultimately incapable of finding a remedy for its obscure disease, this life, this zoe, an impersonal force that moves us without asking for our permission to do so?

The process ontology centered on life confronts this possibility lucidly, without making concessions to either moral panic or melancholia. It asserts an ethical drive to enter into modes of relation that enhance and sustain one's ability to renew and expand what consciousness can become. The ethical ideal is to actualize the cognitive, affective, and sensorial means to cultivate higher degrees of empowerment and affirmation of one's interconnections to others in their complexity. As I will argue in chapter 5, Spinoza's lesson is crucial for Deleuze's ethical project. The selection of the affective forces that propel the process of becoming-animal/minoritarian is regulated by an ethics of joy and affirmation that functions through the transformation of negative into positive passions.

In order to grasp this process, it is important to depsychologize it. What is positive about positive passions is not a "feel-good" sort of sentimentality, but rather a rigorous composition of forces and relations that converge upon the enhancement of one's conatus/potentia. That is, the ability to express one's freedom as the ability to take in and sustain connectedness to others. An expansion, acceleration, or intensification of interrelation. What is negative about negative passions is a decrease, a dimming or slowing-down effect, a dampening of the intensity, which results in a loss of the capacity for interrelations with others (and hence a decrease in the expression of conatus/potentia). Ethics is consequently about cultivating the kind of relations that compose and empower positive passions and avoid the negative ones. I will elaborate on this point in the following chapters.

Thus, the ethical relation is essentially a matter of affinity: being able to enter a relation with another entity whose elements encourage positive encounters. They express one's potentia and increase the subject's capacity to enter into further relations, grow, and expand. This expansion is eco-logically grounded and time bound: by expressing and increasing its positive passions, the subject-in-becoming empowers itself to last, to endure, to continue through and in time. By entering into affirmative ethical relations, the processes of becoming-animal/minoritarian engender possible futures. They construct possible worlds through a web of sustainable interconnections. This is the point of becoming: a collective assemblage of forces that coalesce around commonly shared elements and empower them to grow and to endure.

The biological egalitarianism of zoe is likely to attract those who have become disenchanted with and disengaged from the anthropocentrism that is built into humanistic thought, even in what is left of the political left and of feminism. That which, in one's structure, no longer identifies with the dominant categories of subjectivity, but is not yet completely out of the cage of identity runs with zoe. These rebellious components for me are related to the feminist consciousness of what it means to be embodied female. As such, I am a she-wolf, a breeder that multiplies cells in all directions; I am an incubator and a carrier of vital and lethal viruses. I am mother earth, the generator of the future. In the political economy of phallogocentrism and of anthropocentric humanism, which predicates the sovereignty of Same-ness in a falsely universalistic mode, my sex fell on the side of "Otherness," understood as pejorative difference or as being-worth-less-than. The becom-ing-animal/minoritarian world speaks to my feminist self, partly because my sex, historically speaking, never quite made it into full humanity, so my allegiance to that category is at best negotiable and never to be taken for granted.

Very much a philosophy of the outside, of open spaces and embodied enactments, nomadic thought encourages us not to think in terms of within/ without established categories, but rather as encounters with anomalous and unfamiliar forces, drives, yearnings, or sensations. A sort of spiritual and sensorial stretching of the boundaries of what one's body can do. In other words, a qualitative leap is needed, and it is neither a suicidal jump into the void nor a fall into moral relativism, but rather an immanent sort of happening. I see it as a way of making the contemporary subject slightly more familiar with and consequently less anxious about the yet untapped possibilities that are opened by his/her historical location in the technologically mediated, gene-centered world of today. Becoming-animal/minoritarian/anomalous/unorganic is a way to potentiate what embodied and embedded subjects are capable of doing. It is a way of living more intensely, by increasing one's potentia and, with it, one's freedom and understanding of the complexities one inhabits in a world that is neither anthropocentric nor anthropomorphic, but rather geopolitical, ecophilosophical, and proudly biocentered.

4

THE COSMIC BUZZ OF INSECTS

TOWARD THE POSTHUMAN

Of the three fundamental axes of difference I mentioned in the previous chapters—sexualization, racialization, and naturalization—the most difficult to account for is the nonanthropocentric one: the kind of becoming-other that concerns the naturalized or "earths" others. Whereas the dislocation of the status and location of sexualized and racialized differences can be accommodated to the sociopolitical critique of advanced capitalism, as they are integral to it, the transposition of nature poses a number of conceptual, methodological, and practical complications that lean toward a critique of anthropocentrism. This is due to the pragmatic fact that, as embodied and embedded entities, we are all part of nature, "we" being humans, nonhumans, and others, even though philosophy continues to claim transcendental grounds for human consciousness. As a brand of "enchanted materialism," philosophical nomadism contests the arrogance of anthropocentrism and strikes an alliance with the productive force of zoe—or life in its nonhuman aspects. Nomadic philosophies also challenge the new perverse dualism that is surreptitiously introduced by technoeuphoria "when nature is unhumanized and mankind is artificialized," as Keith Ansell-Pearson so aptly put it (1997:161).

Consequently, the human is called into question. I have argued throughout this book that the historical imperative for critical theory is to rethink the embodied structure of contemporary subjectivity in terms of the convergence of biotechnologies and information technologies. This task is complicated by the socioeconomic proliferation of commodified differences that advanced capitalism engenders for the sake of profit. These social practices converge into a new subject compound, which is nomadic and hence not unitary, hybrid and thus impure and denaturalized through technological mediation and hence posthumanist. This insight stresses the extent to which the management of Life in a posthuman mode has taken center stage in the political economy of advanced capitalism. This includes the proliferation of practices, both scientific and social, that extend beyond human life. Contemporary genetics and biotechnologies are central to this shift toward posthuman ideas of "Life" or zoe, the nonhuman, in a new, mutual interdependence of bodies and technologies that creates a symbiotic relationship between them. This inaugurates an ecophilosophical approach to subjectivity and hence also new ecologies of belonging. They both rest on a radical critique of anthropocentrism in favor of the recognition of the entanglement of material, biocultural, and symbolic forces in the making of the subject.

In other words, what "returns" with the return of Life as zoe and of "real bodies" or neomaterialism, under the impact of advanced technologies, is not only the others of the classical subject of modernity, woman/native/nature. What returns now is the "other" of the living body in its humanistic definition: the other face of bios, that is to say zoe, the generative vitality of the non- or prehuman (Braidotti 2006). Zoe stands for the mindless vitality of Life carrying on independently, regardless of rational control. This vital energy is the dubious privilege attributed to nonhumans and to all the "others" of Man, whereas bios refers to the specific human capacity to construct a social nexus. That these two competing notions of "life" coincide on the human body turns the issue of embodiment into a contested space and a political arena.

Mind-body dualism has historically functioned as a shortcut through the complexities of this question by introducing a criterion of hierarchical distinction that is sexualized, racialized, and naturalized. Given that this concept of "the human" was colonized by phallogocentrism, it has come to be identified with male, white, heterosexual, Christian, property-owning, standard language–speaking citizens. Zoe marks the outside of this vision of the subject, supported by the efforts of evolutionary theory to strike a new relationship with the nonhuman. Along with the genetic revolution, we can speak of a generalized "becoming infrahuman" of bios. Contemporary scientific practices have forced us to touch the bottom of some inhumanity that connects to the human precisely in the immanence of its bodily materialism. The category of "life" has, accordingly, cracked under the strain.

Thus, affinity for zoe is a good starting point for what may constitute the last act of the critique of dominant subject positions, namely, the return of animal, insect, or earth life in all its potency. The breakdown of species distinction (human/nonhuman) and the explosion of zoe power, therefore, shifts the grounds of the problem of the breakdown of categories of individuation (gender and sexuality; ethnicity and race). This introduces the issue of becoming to a planetary or worldwide dimension, the earth being not one element among others, but rather that which brings them all together in a notion of the "milieu" as our habitat or territory. In this chapter I will consequently explore the relevance of nomadic philosophy for political ecology and hence for rethinking the shifting boundaries between the human and his nonanthropomorphic others.

THE INSECT PARADIGM

Most of the discussions about the interface between the human and the nonhuman take the technological artifact as the point of reference, as if manufactured entities and cultivated artificiality necessarily belonged to a nonhuman world. For nomadic theory, on the other hand, the boundaries of the nonhuman are much closer to home, so to speak: they are ecological and focus on zoe and hence cut into the core of the most familiar and daily relations to a large variety of "others." The nomadic becoming-insect offers a materialist framework that emphasizes the proximity of zoe—stressing both immanence and vitality—and of "life"-centred perspectives—and situating them both outside the boundaries of anthropocentrism.

The essential premise for this discussion was already stated in the previous chapters: technologically mediated advanced capitalism progresses by blurring fundamental categorical divides between self and other. This produces a colossal hybridization that combines animals, monsters, insects, aliens, and machines into a powerfully posthuman approach to what we used to call "the embodied subject." Steven Shaviro (1995) describes this in terms of a new paradigm: we have entered the rhizomatic, "viral," or "parasitic" mode of relations. This is a graphic way of explaining the extent to which today's body is immersed in a set of technologically mediated practices of prosthetic and nonanthropomorphic extension. This stresses, in fact, the coextensivity of the body with its environment or territory, which is one of the salient features of the nomadic notion of "becoming-animal." A body is a portion of forces life bound to the environment that feeds it; all organisms are collective and interdependent. Insects, parasites, and viruses are heterodirected: they need other organisms. Admittedly, they relate to them as incubators or hosts, releasing their genetically encoded message as a matter of necessity. Nonetheless, the key point here is that the insects/virus/parasite constitutes a model of a symbiotic relationship that defeats binary oppositions. As such it is an inspiring model for a nomadic ecophilosophy.

A second critical concept to keep in mind is that the intensive or nomadic subject is transgenerational and environmentally bound. As a living organism, it partakes of the shared time sequence of the genetic code, which makes it a collective entity that moves across species and beyond anthropocentrism. The human organism is an in-between that is plugged into and connected to a variety of possible sources, time lines, and forces. It may be useful to define it as a machine, which does not mean an appliance or anything with a specifically utilitarian aim, but rather something that is simultaneously more abstract and more materially embedded. As I indicated in chapter 2, my minimalist definition of a nomadic body-machine is an embodied, affective, and intelligent entity that captures processes and transforms energies and forces. A nomadic entity therefore feeds upon, incorporates, and transforms its environment (be it "natural," "social," "human," or whatever) constantly. Being embodied in this high-tech ecological manner means being immersed in fields of constant flows and transformations. Not all of them are positive, of course, some are downright agonistic, although in such a dynamic system this cannot be known or judged a priori. The core of the matter is the relentless generative force of bios|zoe and the specific brand of transspecies egalitarianism they establish between human and nonhuman others.

As we saw in the previous chapter, for philosophical nomadology, the strength of animals lies precisely in their not being-one, which is expressed in their attachment to and interdependence on a territory, an environment, or a "milieu." A living entity is situated in between a multitude of others. They rely on small and highly defined slices of environment to which they relate sensorially and perceptively. Insects, especially spiders and parasites like ticks, are among Deleuze's favorites. Like artists, animals mark their territory physically, by color, sound, or marking and framing. In order to mark|code|possess|frame their territory, animals produce signals and signs constantly; insects buzz and make all sort of sounds; upper primates practically talk; cats, wolves, and dogs mark the lands with bodily fluids of their own production, dogs bark and howl in pain and need. They are immanent to their gestures aimed at coping with needs and environments. In the process of recognizing, coding, and coping, they transcend their sheer animality, joining up with the human in the effort to express, inhabit, and protect their territory. Orienting oneself in a strange territory; finding food and water, let alone a mate, expressing all this so that the others in the collective pack or group can get the idea—this is a model of radical immanence that needs to be revalued. It is nonverbal communication at its best. In this respect, humans may have more in common with their multiple genetic neighbors than they may care to admit. In philosophical nomadism the proximity is transspecies and transgenic, material in the sense of matter|*mater*. It has to do with a chain of connections that can best be described as an ecological philosophy of nonunitary, embodied, self-organized organisms.

BECOMING-INSECT

Let me illustrate the ecophilosophical dimension of nomadic theory by turning to one of the many possible nonhuman worlds with which we share our planet: insects. They are neither technological artifacts nor trendy innovations: they have been here far longer than we have, although invisible to our scopic apparatus, impenetrable to our gross senses, and inaudible by our damaged ears. Insects signal their ecology of belonging in clear and unequivocal—albeit nonlinguistic—codes. They are actualized slices of alternative living matter, which expresses the multiplicity of possible worlds and their copresence within our humanized universe. They are a radical form of otherness we cannot perceive, wrapped up as we are in our habits, which are the locus of our structural limitations.

Insects also have a very respectable literary pedigree in European culture and are very much coded culturally. In the postnuclear historical context, they have become the sign of a widespread repertoire of angst-ridden fears and deep anxiety as phobic objects. Creepy mutants, vermin emerging from the sewerage, resilient survivors, tentacular leftover from a previous evolutionary era, one of the ten plagues of Egypt in Saint John's Apocalypse, signs of the wrath of God as the biblical locusts, insects cover a staggering number of signifying practices. On the positive side, from Aesop to La Fontaine to contemporary Hollywood animation films, ants are the prototype of the industrial robot or the industrious factory worker. Capable of lifting fifty times their own bodily weight, they are resistant to pesticides and enjoy fast reproductive cycles. Crickets may be lazy hedonists lying in the sun, however, they have amazing destructive powers. Louis-Vincent Thomas (1979) estimates that crickets can reach a density of 2,000 square meters, they can also cover 10 kilometers a day and thus can destroy something like 4,000 tons of greens every 24 hours. With maniacal precision Thomas also adds that there are five million different species of insects. At the average weight of 2.5 mg, they sure make their presence on the earth felt! After all, they have lived on it for more than 300 million years. Bees are, historically, sophisticated industrial engineers. Pliny, in his *Natural History*, marvels at them as real-life factories. In a model form of social organizations that has inspired every possible political theorist, insects run perfect social systems. They produce honey, make wax, and serve a thousand practical purposes; they work hard, follow their leaders, and respect their collective organization. Collective minded, they are ideal members of the polity, though, like ants, they tend to get obsessive. Jacques Derrida (1997) resorts to the metaphor of bees to express his disapproval of academic feminists and to condemn our allegedly regimented and authoritarian ways of thinking. Bees also, however, believe in collective assemblages and in productive enterprise; they produce their own medicine—propolis—and one perfectly integrated with their own environment and life cycle. Great leaders, military minds, businessmen and engineers, the bees leave Pliny gasping for air and Derrida wishing for more.

Other qualities that make insects paradigmatic are the fast rate of metamorphosis, the talents for parasitism, the power of mimetism or blending with their territory and environment, and the speed of movement. They defy gravity and embody a specific temporality of their own, with fast rates of genetic recombination. Their hyperactive sexuality, with highly accelerated rhythms, travels via many rhizome transspecies copulations with plants and flowers as well as entities of the same species.

Shaviro argues that "insect life is an alien presence that we can neither assimilate nor expel" (1995:47). As such it dwells between different states of in-betweenness, arousing the same spasmodic reactions in humans as the monstrous, the sacred, or the alien (Braidotti 2011). This is a reaction of simultaneous attraction and repulsion, disgust and desire. They pose the question of radical otherness not in metaphorical but in biomorphic terms, that is to say as a metamorphosis of the sensory, cognitive, and perceptual human apparatus. In that regard, the insect provides a new paradigm for discontinuous transmutations within a stable entity. The key elements of this paradigm are larval metamorphoses, the speed of their reproductive system (a full life cycle can be completed in twenty-four hours), the propensity to generate mutations, the faster rate of genetic recombination. Moreover, not having any major neuronal reservoir, insects are free from the hold of memory and the socially enforced forms of sedimented memory known as institutions. In Deleuze's terminology, they are multiple singularities without fixed identities, mostly because of the specificity of their bodily coordinates and the speed of their lifespan. The significant traits of the insect as bodily entity in terms of a Deleuzian mapping of forces are dryness, hairiness, metal-like body frames, great resilience, mimicry, and lightness. They are environment bound, thus elemental, either because linked to the earth and to its underground|crust (chthonic forces) or because of their ability to defy gravity thanks to aircraftlike body frames (recall the exhilaration of Kafka's Gregor when he discovers that he can actually crawl upon the ceiling and hang upside down on it).

Moreover, insects are technological artifacts, or entities, that stand in between the organic and the inorganic. Bukatman, in his analysis of Bruce Sterling's cyberpunk novels, argues that "insects are only the most evident metaphorical process conflating a number of irreconcilable terms such as life/nonlife, biology/technology, human/machine" (Bukatman 2003:277). As such, insects signal a high degree of imbrication of the organic with the technological; this can be evidenced in the insectoid and arachnoid terminology so often used to describe advanced technologies, especially robots and virtual reality artifacts. This kind of imagery stresses the interdependence of technology on other social and environmental forces. Cyberfeminists like

Helene van Oldenburg argue that the Internet, or the computer-mediated Web, can only be arachnoidic or spiderlike. The World Wide Web functions via lines, knots, connections, relations in a manner that is also analogous to the human brain. Thus the discourse of arachnomancy can be used to explore possible evolutions of information technologies: weaving a quilt with the synapses of our brains and the sinews of our nerves.

Haraway also hints at an "insect paradigm" in contemporary molecular biology, which has moved beyond the classical opposition of "vitalistic" to "mechanistic" principles to evolve instead in the direction of serial repetitions. Haraway takes this as a serious indication that we have already left the era of "bio-politics" to enter that of "the informatics of domination" (Haraway 1991:161). In biology it's the speed and efficiency of its molecular structure, and more especially of its reproductive cycle, that has made the fruit-fly into the most important experimental site in modern molecular research (Keller 1983).

Insects are powerful indicators of the decentering of anthropocentrism and point to posthuman sensibilities and sexualities. They have also gained widespread prominence and star billing in contemporary media culture. An evident insect and also a spider paradigm is on full display in recent cinematic exploits in the genre of computer games, cyberpunk, and science fiction. Gigantic metal-framed imitation insects crawl all over the surface of films such as *Star Wars VI: The Return of the Jedi* (1983), *Robocop* (1987), as well as in the digital nightmare-worlds of *The Matrix* (1999). Insect aesthetics reaches its apotheosis in the digital images of *Antz* (1998) and *A Bug's Life* (1998), which make official a topos that is firmly instilled in the contemporary imaginary: the posthuman mix of the organic and the inorganic.

ACOUSTIC ENVIRONMENTS

In all these regards, the insects are a perfect machinic organism as different from mammals and therefore humans as biologically possible. What interests Deleuze particularly about the speed of the insects' body, however, is their technological performativity. Insects are fantastic music makers. Deleuze distinctly warns us that he does not mean the usual bodily noises that one makes in moving about the planet, but rather the specific capacity to produce sounds that have speeds, variations, and intensities worthy of and even superior to human compositions. Insects—as well as other animals—offer convincing examples of nonlinguistic communication and modes of thought, ranging from visual apprehension to sonar and other acoustic technologies, including an acute sense of internal time. It is probably on that score that insects constitute a real challenge for humanity; they deprive the human of his/her alleged monopoly over music making. They also replace the songs of birds and other species by actualizing instead sounds of the quasi-inaudible molecular kind: "The reign of birds seems to have been replaced by the age of insects, with its much more molecular vibrations, chirring, rustling, buzzing, clicking, scratching and scraping. Birds are vocal, but insects are instrumental" (Deleuze and Guattari 1987:308). The molecular quality of becoming insect consists in "the capacity to make the elementary communicate with the cosmic" (Deleuze and Guattari 1987:308).

In music, time can be heard. It is a pure form of time through the mediation of rhythm. This, in a nutshell, is its relevance for nomadic subjectivity. Technologically mediated music denaturalizes and dehumanizes the time sequence. It can push speed and pitch to posthuman heights, but it can also fade them to prehuman depths of inaudibility. How to make us hear the inaudible, the imperceptible, that roar which lies on the other side of silence, the cosmic buzz, is what is at stake in this process. How to impose an audible form upon the amorphous mass of sounds we inhabit is, for Deleuzian composers, the challenge. The method of composition is in keeping with Deleuze's criteria of selection, process, and in-between transitions. In music one can hear the transitions in the form of intervals. In nomadic music the interval marks the proximity but also the singularity of each sound, so as to avoid synthesis, harmony, or melodic resolution. It is a way of pursuing dissonance by returning it to the external world, where sounds belong, always in transit, like radio waves moving ineluctably to outer spaces, chatting on, with nobody to listen.

Most dwellers of the postindustrial urban space have developed a paradoxical relationship to their own acoustic space. Technology has endowed us with the capacity to create and carry around on our embodied selves our own musical habitat. This may or may not coincide with the mass-produced saturation of commercial sounds or the gothic pastiche of the MTV scene. Of all technologies we inhabit, the musical, acoustic, or sound ones are the most pervasive and intimate, yet also the most collective. They thus summarize the paradoxes of nomadic subjectivity as simultaneously external and singular.

The interconnection sounds/technology/insects/music, however, prompts another observation. Namely, how rare it is to encounter music or sound that reflects the acoustic quality of the urban environment most of us inhabit. That is to say, a very crowded, noisy, highly resonant urban environment where stillness and silence are practically unknown. I think that a great deal of music or sound production of the alternative kind today precisely aims at capturing the intense sonority of our lived-in spaces and yet emptying it of its representational value. Technosounds, and the technological performances of Deleuze-inspired music colorists like Robin Rimbaud, also known as Scanner, or D.J. Spooky, or of contemporary artists like Soundlab, Cultural Alchemy, is a gamble with this apparently contradictory aim: to map out the acoustic environments of here and now while undoing the classical function of music as the incarnation of the most sublime transcendent ideals of the humanist European subject.

There is also a political side to this. Considering the epistemological privileges granted to vision—the King of the senses—in our concept of subject formation: think, for instance, of the importance of the gaze for phenomenology and psychoanalysis. And, given that visualization techniques and the invention of appropriate visual technologies are the fundamental motor of Western science (Galison and Daston 2007), we can only conclude that vision is a hegemonic aspect of our culture's self-understanding. This point was radicalized by Foucault in his analysis of biopolitical regimes of surveillance and control in the technologically mediated globalized world. As such, it is saturated with power relations, which is less prominent in the case of sounds or the acoustic regime. Sound is more abstract, less prone to immediate commodification because less codified by power. Since the youth revolution of the 1960s, the counterculture has invested in experimentation with and production of alternative acoustic environments and forms of sound transmission as central elements of cultural and political activism, from the free radio stations of the 1970s to the digital means of today. The coming of the new information technologies, mobile phones, and iPods have merely intensified this trend.

Whereas most musical genres and traditions, including pop, rock, and their offshoots, aim at resonances, and the constitution of alternative resisting countercultural subjectivities, nomadic or rhizomatic musicology attempts to make us hear the inaudible. It aims at a virtual sound space: this is a space of deterritorialization of our acoustic habits through the production of unexpected, speedy, unfamiliar sounds that facilitate unexpected connections and surprising encounters. In fact, the example of insects suggests that we inhabit uncoded, posthuman acoustic environments all the time: we just call it "nature" and mostly ignore it. We just do not hear them—we are not used to "taking them in" or to tuning into them. Rhizo-music forces this encounter by re-creating technologically, in the best musical tradition, different frequencies. As such, it represents a space of becoming. The process of becoming-insect in rhizo-musicology aims at composing an environment, an acoustic territory, a plane of composition of spatiotemporal coordinates where possible worlds are produced. Hence the connection to animals and insects, territories, or habitats that are constituted through the composition and the organization of refrains or rhythms. These are understood as patterns of repetition, marking a space of intensive connection to impersonal and often indiscernible others. Invisible signatures of the virtual, so to speak.

Deleuze's vision of the becoming-minoritarian of music is the core of becoming-insect. It offers a way of reconstructing the subject's relationship to his environment, earthly and cosmic, in a nonrepresentational mode. Deleuze's "abstract machines," best expressed in his becoming-insect, are rhythmic and abstract. Deleuze challenges the representational function of music as expressing the harmony of the spheres, in opposition to the dark chaos of unaccounted-for space. The rational accountability of space is ensured by mathematical ordering; in Plato's philosophy this results in a time-honored connection between music, mathematics, and cosmology. It is this cosmic quality of music that makes it relevant for philosophical nomadism, in that it points to the infinite in a very grounded, embedded fashion.

In their committed anti-Platonic mode, Deleuze and Guattari want to delink the representation of the cosmos from its reliance on the rationality of a mathematical order and the transcendent vision of reason it entails. They approach it instead as an open system, uncontainable and incommensurable with the human faculty of reason or the capacity to count. Music is accordingly liberated from its human constraints and turned into a transversal space of molecular becomings. Rhythms acquire a singularity and autonomy of their own. The sheer materiality of the human body and its fleshy contents (lungs, nerves, brains, intestines, etc.) are as many sound-making acoustic chambers. Enhanced technologically, these internal sounds can confront the listener with as shocking a sensation of unfamiliarity as the external rumbles of the cosmos. The embodied materiality of a living organism is such as to enable a folding inward of the world and an unfolding outward of the specific world one inhabits. Multiple possible worlds are already here, copresent in the complexity of bodies that are freed from a strictly functional organization bounded by the dominant system based on phallologocentric premises. Time, or rather the multiple temporalities that structure a living organism (genetic, genealogical, transgenerational, affective, etc.), is split accordingly along a variety of axes. This complex level of organization is such as to make synchronization into a lifelong project and harmony into a permanent challenge. We just do not seem able to extend our perception, cognition, and empathy far enough to actually inhabit all these possible worlds and do justice to their multiplicity.

The becoming-animal or insect has nothing to do with imitating the sounds of animals or insects. That mimetic capacity has been amply used in classical music (Saint-Saens, for example). It has produced entertaining and often banal renditions of animal sounds that make a mockery of themselves. As Deleuze suggests, art should not imitate: it should rather steal and run away. The painter does not imitate the bird: it captures it as line, speed, and color. This is a process of becoming that deterritorializes both the artist and his/her object. Against imitation, rhizomatic music aims at deterritorializing our acoustic habits, making us aware that the human is not the ruling principle in the harmony of the spheres. Most of all, it makes it possible for us to hear the multiplicity of frequencies that structure our possible worlds and the infinite generative force of the cosmos as a whole. Deleuze famously said that chaos is not chaotic—but rather points to infinity as the nth power of becoming. Rhizo-music, or nomadic sounds, evoke this dimension. Listening to it, so as to be able to hear that particular frequency, requires a transformation of our perceptual apparatus: we need to develop new faculties by recording the organs in our bodies. We have to become-insect in order to be tuned into the nonhuman temporality of our cosmic world.

Lawrence Grossberg sees acoustic refrains as a crucial element in framing space and creating sound walls that encircle and contain the subject. Sonic bricks that allow for stability, albeit temporarily. Under the impact of molecular becomings, however, sounds can also split all boundaries open, tear down the walls, and rejoin the cosmos. It is a case of mobility versus the "disciplined mobilization" (Grossberg 1997:97) of social space. The becoming-minoritarian of music produces a practice of expression without a monolithic or unitary subject that supervises the operations and capitalizes upon them. It literally brings the cosmos home.

Music increases the intensity of becoming: it is about crossing as many thresholds of intensity as the subject can sustain. All becoming is transgressive; it also aims at approaching the imperceptible, the unthinkable, and the inaudible. Just as intensive writing for Deleuze can engender becoming by being intransitive, so music can express affectivity, immanence, and the dissolution of boundaries. Music is constant becoming, its refrains and rhythmic narrations. It makes audible the irreducibility of in-between spaces, polyphonic hybridization, and multiple sonic interferences.

IN-SECTS/SEX

The significant thing about insect bodies of all species is therefore their dense materiality. They are surprisingly generative, in that they stubbornly and relentlessly reproduce themselves. The terms of their reproduction are slightly offbeat by good old humanist and anthropocentric standards in that they involve insect models of both sexual and asexual reproduction. In fact, insects display a whole array of possible alternative morphologies and "other" sexual and reproductive systems. Queer critics like Judith Halberstam and Ira Livingston are quick to point out how this generative diversity in contemporary molecular biology and genetics is echoed by the evolution of sexed identities and sexualities in contemporary societies towards a state of flux, indeterminacy, and generalized "gender trouble" (Butler 1991). In other words, it has become historically, scientifically, and culturally impossible to hold sexed bodies in a rational reproductive order. Halberstam and Livingston conclude: "Queer, cyborg, metametazoan, hybrid, PWA; bodies-without-organs, bodies-in-process, virtual bodies: in unvisualizable amniotic indeterminacy, and unfazed by the hype of their always premature and redundant annunciation, posthuman bodies thrive in the mutual deformations of totem and taxonomy" (1995:19). The deviant reproductive system, transformative speed, as well as immense powers of adaptation combined make insects the entity most closely attuned to the becoming molecular and becoming imperceptible. The fact that most of their life cycle is made of metamorphoses through different stadium of development is a manifestation of the same principles, but strikes a distinctly queerer note.

For Aristotle, insects have no specific sex; for Pliny, their sexuality is undecidable as their sex is invisible. Tiny miniatures, they exercise the same immense sense of estrangement as dinosaurs, dragons, or other gigantic monsters. Improbable morphological constructs, they challenge and titillate; nonmammals that lay eggs, they are hybrid par excellence. Insects carry life in their cross-species pollinating encounters with plants and flowers. They also carry death, through their own bodily reserves of poison, stings, bites, and burns, but also by carrying around powerful viruses, malaria being the best known.

Grosz (1995) focuses on the fascination of humans with insect sexuality. Grosz sees the insect as a highly sexualized "queer" entity, capable of titillating the collective imagination especially on the issue of sex and death. She concentrates on two insects particularly: the black widow spider and the praying mantis, especially in the work of Roger Caillois and Alphonso Lingis. She finds in these the prototype of a posthuman philosophy. In their mimicry and camouflage abilities, insects enact the psychoanalytic phenomenon of psychasthenia, that is to say, a disintegration of the bounds of consciousness and the relinquishing of its ties to the body so that the distinction between the inside and the outside becomes difficult to hold. Accordingly, the sexual connotation of this orgiastic dissolution of the boundaries of decency in insects leads Caillois to a semidelirious set of associations between the praying mantis-religion-food-orality-vampires-vagina-dentata-automatism-female android. What emerges loud and clear from the series of associations is the insect paradigm as a model for polymorphous antiphallic sexuality. Lingis argues that the orgasmic body cannot be reduced to the organic body but to an organic assemblage of forces that exceeds and challenges the boundaries of morphology and finds an interesting resonance in the sexuality of insects.

In terms of their reproduction, insects have perfected hybridity. They point to a disturbingly diverse sexual cycle, when compared to the mammals; in fact, insects are nonmammals that lay eggs. As such, they are likely to feed into the most insidious anxieties about unnatural copulations and births, especially in a "posthumanist" culture obsessed with artificial reproduction. Moreover, because of their speedy organism, there is no question of caring for their infants, mostly because they are not born prematurely (unlike humans). In a Deleuzian vein, these relatively obvious differences from the human lay out the grid of a new set of spatiotemporal coordinates that translate into territorial typologies and speed or rhythms.

Disruption, rather than the unfolding of the predictable old scenario of heterosexual seduction, is the key to trigger off the sexual scenarios in these posthuman times. Transformations of intimacy and metamorphoses of the gender relations are the true object of desire. Insect sexuality stresses the longing for asymmetrically embodied ecstasy in and of difference, through the construction of unprogrammed surfaces of pleasure and not the articulation of the libidinal economy of the same. Lust and pleasure in the nomadic mode melt down the cohesion and unity of the body, allowing for the cricket in you to sing and the cockroach in you to endure. Insect sexuality is enough to make pure mockery of any Christian eulogy of "nature": bisexuality, same-sex sex, hermaphrodites, incest, and all other kinds of unnatural sexual practices are part of the animal kingdom. This is enough to shatter any romantic of essentialist assumptions about a natural sexual order. It's a queer natural world out there!

THE ETHICS OF BIOCENTERED EGALITARIANISM

I described (Braidotti 2002a) zoe as the affirmative power of Life, as a vector of transformation, a conveyor or a carrier that enacts in-depth transformations. As such, it actualizes a set of both social and symbolic interactions that inscribe the human-nonhuman bond, also known as biocentered egalitarianism, at the heart of our concerns. The notion of the relation is central to this discussion. Ecological theories and practice reflect an idea of interconnectedness that is quite relevant, in spite of its holistic connotations. Relations and interactions within philosophical nomadism are posited along the more materialist lines of becoming as deep transformations of self and society. I thus want to resist the sacralization of "Life" while addressing the issue of limits and values in terms of thresholds of sustainability. I propose such a position as a possible alliance with moral and social philosophers from other theoretical traditions.

"Life" is a slippery concept, especially animal or insect life in the vitalist mode of zoe; it is far too often assimilated to the abject in the sense of the monstrous object of horror (Kristeva 1980; Creed 1993). It is thus represented as the unassimilated, the unpresentable, the unrepresented and even the unthinkable. Philosophical nomadism allows us to think of it instead as an integral part of ourselves and, as such, not as an alien other. To think this way, I reconfigure the subject as embodied materiality: the analogy between woman, animal, mother, and earth is neither about identification nor about the logic of rights and claims. It is about the primacy of life as production or zoe as generative power. Zoe needs to be activated through living matter as a virtual path of becoming that leads outward, outside the human. An integral part of this process is to confront and go through those unrepresentable, unthinkable, and abject elements of our bound selves and very embodiment that is being activated and transformed. Zoe needs to be put center stage. Although, for the purposes of my ethical project, the human still gets preferential treatment, I consider this a matter of habit, not of value.

The human body and especially the female body are both bios and zoe, and, as such, it is a highly contested social and physical sphere. Zoe is not value free or neutral, but a highly sexualized, racialized, and "species-field" concept. The change of scale from macro- to microprocesses in itself is no guarantee of a qualitative shift. Thus the issue of power does not miraculously evaporate in this admittedly momentous transition, it merely shifts its grounds. Relentlessly vital, zoe is endowed with endurance and resilience— qualities I will discuss more extensively in the next chapter. Zoe carries on regardless: it is radically immanent. Consciousness attempts to contain it, but actually lives in fear of it. Such a life force is experienced as threatening by a mind that fears the loss of control. This is the dominant view of consciousness as feeding on negative passions: a clearinghouse of the kind of neuroses (such as narcissism and paranoia) that are rewarded in the socialized, civilized West. Civilization and its discontents extol their pound of flesh as the price to pay for not being a pack of werewolves howling, mating, and killing in the moonlight. Thus the self is politics by another name and the dominant vision of the self we have institutionalized in the West, which lies at the heart of liberal individualism, serves the purpose of a vampirelike economic system based on the axiomatic of stock and exchange, common standards and unjust distribution; accumulation and profit.

An ethical approach based on posthumanist values, or on biocentered egalitarianism, on the other hand, critiques individualism and attempts to think the interconnection of human and nonhuman agents. Biocentered egalitarianism is a philosophy of affirmative becoming that activates a no-madic subject into sustainable processes of transformation. The political and theoretical values I want to defend in relation to this include the principle of nonprofit, which means a stand against individualism and exploitation, in favor of self-expression and communally held property rights over both biological and cultural artifacts. This calls for the respect of diversity, in both its biological and cultural dimension, as well as a firm commitment to collective ownership and open access to technological "products." My position aims at rethinking the ethical and political implications of a non-unitary subject. This involves negotiating the tension between complexities, on the one hand, and a sustained commitment to social justice and emancipatory politics, on the other. This balancing act takes us to another dimension of this epistemological but also ethical shift away from anthropocentrism. To argue for the recognition of animal, insect, planetary, and machinic "otherness" breaks many an established taboo, not the least of which is the established expectation of reciprocity. The latter can almost be considered the trademark of liberal individualism and its idea of moral responsibility: reciprocal respect is a foundational principle. In opposition to this, biocentric ethics of sustainable relations posits a different expectation: that of an approach to the other that assumes the impossibility of mutual recognition—for instance between humans and animals—and replaces it with a relation of mutual specification.

CHAOSMOSIS: BECOMING-WORLD

The ecological ethics for Guattari and Deleuze is something more than a problem of the environment; it aims at producing a virtual social ecology. It includes social, political, ethical, and aesthetic dimensions as well. To address it adequately, we need a qualitative leap of our ethical imagination so as to reconstitute ethics, politics, and new process aesthetics. The method is to create transversal links between the categories, while facing the ethical relation as the sign of change. Intellectuals should devote themselves to creating conditions for the implementation of transversality. The fundamental political desire is for an individual and collective reappropriation of the production of subjectivity, along the lines of "ontological heterogenesis" or chaosmic desegregation of the different categories. We need to actively desire to reinvent subjectivity as a set of mutant values and to draw our pleasure from that, not from the static contemplation of the perpetuation of the regime of the same. Chaosmos (*chaos* plus *cosmos*, borrowed from James Joyce) is the universe of reference for becomings in the sense of the unfolding of virtualities or mutant values.

The work of Francisco Varela is of the greatest importance in redesigning this type of environmentally bound, postanthropocentric, and anti-Cartesian ethics of codetermination between self and other. The notion of codependence replaces that of recognition, much as the ethics of sustainability replaces the moral philosophy of rights. Within the frame of biocentered egalitarianism, the codependence of different species not only challenges liberal humanism but also reiterates the importance of grounded, situated, and very specific and hence accountable perspectives. This amounts to accepting a strong sense of limits in the kind of ethical relations we can engage in— and also in those we are able to sustain.

Shiva (1997), resting on a distinction proposed by Maturana and Varela (1972), distinguishes between, on the one hand, "autopoietic systems," which are mostly biological organisms, self-organizing and capable of self-renewal, and, on the other, "allopoietic systems." The latter are mostly technical artifacts that need input from the outside in order to function. In the mechanistic world order imposed by the Western idea of science, argues Shiva, the former is often coined as "chaos," whereas the latter enjoys the privilege of "order": one is organic, the other machinic. According to Shiva, the autopoietic systems are dynamic structures that, being endogenously driven, constitute the sheer essence of health and ecological stability for living systems. They are structurally opposed to genetic engineering and the mechanistic way of life. This has particular relevance to the status of women and the takeover of the maternal function in biotechnologies and human genetic engineering. The theft of the regenerative powers of women may well be the last act in this ultimate colonization of living organisms by predatory Western science.

Felix Guattari, in his analysis of the "collective existential mutations" (1995:2) currently taking place, also refers to the same distinction between autopoietic and allopoietic systems as Vandana Shiva does. Guattari's use of the distinction (autopoietic/allopoietic), however, goes further than Shiva's. He relates it firstly to the quest for redefinitions of subjectivity, which he considers the main challenge for contemporary philosophy. Secondly, he ex-tends the principle of autopoiesis, which for Varela as for Shiva is reserved for the biological organisms, to cover also the machines or technological ones. Another name for chaosmosis is autopoietic subjectivation: "poiesis," in other words, refers to the process of resingularized universes of subjectivation or self-styling.

Guattari's machinic autopoiesis establishes a qualitative link between organic matter and technological or machinic artifacts. This results in a radical redefinition of the generative power of "life." The failure to recognize the autopoietic nature of machines helps the hegemony of scientific reductionism in Western thought. Machines have their own temporality and develop through "generations": they contain their own virtuality and futurity. Consequently, they entertain their own forms of alterity not only toward humans but also among themselves. Whereas organic structures are inhabited by the desire for eternity, machines are driven by the desire for abolition. Through this shift of perspective, Guattari moves beyond the distinction proposed by Varela and proposes a transversal definition of the technological elements as "others" or "a more collective machinism without delimited unity, whose autonomy accommodates diverse mediums of alterity" (1995:42). Heterogeneity is the key idea. It is this nonhuman model of enunciation that constitutes the specific enunciative consistency of machines.

As for Deleuze, the problem then becomes how to relate these collective approaches to processes of subjectivation. Guattari defines the collective as a transversalist notion, "the sense of a multiplicity that deploys itself as much beyond the individual, on the side of the socius, as before the person, on the side of preverbal intensities, indicating a logic of affects rather than a logic of delimited sets" (1995:9). Whether subjectivity becomes individualized or collectivized depends on the historical contexts. The paradox of subjectivation and individualization raises the question of how to reconcile the need to redefine subjectivity nomadically, yet in an accountable manner, against the forces that tend to reterritorialize it or essentialize it. The answer to these paradoxes, according to Guattari, is a "transversalist conception of subjectivity" that cuts across and therefore recombines these opposite trends. As a schizo-analyst, Guattari stresses the "non-human" parts of human subjectivity, which is not an antihumanist position but merely the acknowledgment that subjectivity does not and need not coincide with either the notion of the individual or that of person. It is rather the case that these are historical manifestations of the subject. This leads us to a very dynamic vision of the subject as a self-organizing or "autopoietic system," which is Guattari's aesthetic and political paradigm.

Autopoiesis is the maintenance of a machinic system, through the mediation of potential energy into organized and distributed matter. Disparate orders of magnitude are thus brought into communication to create the metastability, which is the precondition of individuation. The system achieves stability while avoiding closure: it engenders self-organization with high levels of creativity or autonomy from the flow of forces. Ansell-Pearson puts it as follows: "An autopoietic machine is one which continuously generates and specifies its own organization through its operation as a system of production of its own components. . . . An autopoietic machine is defined not in terms of the components or their static relations, but by the particular network of processes (relations) of production. The relations of production of components are given only as processes; if the processes "stop," then the relations vanish. Therefore machines require regeneration by the components they produce" (1997:140–141). This autopoietic system accounts both for living organisms, humans as self-organizing systems, and also for inorganic matter, challenging the prejudice that only humans can manufacture a living and self-organizing system. Although Maturana and Varela's dualistic scheme opposes the inert to the living and is thus more oppositional than nomadic, it has proved of great inspirational force in rethinking the "Life" force of inorganic matter.

The biocentered egalitarianism I want to defend pursues the same project of coming to terms with the generative power of nonhuman and nonorganic entities. This line is pursued with great lucidity by Keith Ansell-Pearson, who starts from the assumption that the biotechnical revolution of today entails a redefinition of evolution in a distinctly less anthropocentric manner than most would expect. In his critique of the rhetoric of biotechnological vitalism (1997), Ansell-Pearson warns us against the pernicious fantasy of a renaturalized evolution led by biotechnological capitalism. He sees this as one of the master narratives of neoliberalism and as a serious error in the assessment of our historical condition. The paranoid mode of presentation of a totalizing technofuture perpetuates the split between "Life" and the human, pitching one against the other and expressing the fear of loss of mastery by the latter. The point is to rethink evolution in a nondeterministic but also a nonanthropocentric manner. In a response to the divinely ordained evolutionary teleology of Teilhard de Chardin (1959), the emphasis falls instead on the quest for a more adequate understanding of the topology and the ethology of forces involved in chaosmosis, defined as the radical immanence of life as a complex system. Central to this nonessentialist vision of vitalism is the idea of affinity among different forces, in a set of connective disjunctions that is not a synthesis but a recomposition. Resting on Guattari's concept of "chaosmosis," Ansell-Pearson wants to think the vital autonomy of evolution in terms of the specific enunciative practices of machinic phylogenesis. Machinic autopoiesis means that the machine is a site of becoming or the threshold to many possible worlds. Humans, therefore, need to review our schemes of representation of the machinic processes.

Autopoiesis is processual creativity, which I would locate in an enlarged ontology of gratuitousness or nonprofit. The subjects' fundamental aspiration is neither to "make sense," that is to say, to emit meaningful utterances within a signifying system—nor is it about conforming to ideal models of behavior. The subject merely aims at self-completion, which is to say at achieving singularity: it is an enduring, affective entity capable of affecting and of being affected by a multiplicity of others. As subject-in-becoming, she or he is a vector of subjectivation. Subjectivity for Guattari is "pathetic" in the sense of empathic, affective, multiply–mediated, and complex. Like Deleuze, Guattari investigates the paradox of this affectivity, which is constantly evacuated from discourse, although, or maybe because, it is that which makes it possible in the first instance.

To understand such a subject, we need to approach it through his three fundamental ecologies: that of the environment, of the socius, and of the psyche. And, more importantly, we need to create transversal lines through all three of them. It is crucial to see the interconnections between the greenhouse effect, the status of women, racism and xenophobia, and frantic consumerism. We must not stop at any fragmented portions of these realities, but rather trace transversal interconnections among them. The subject is a plane of consistency that includes "territorialized existential territories" and "deterritorialized incorporeal universes" (1995:26). Under phallogocentrism, this complexity is misread and reduced to a logic of discourse where capital becomes the referent for labor, the signifier for semiotic expression, and being the great principle of reduction of that very ontological polyvocality Guattari locates at the heart of the matter of subjectivity.

Psychoanalytic theory is of no great assistance, being equally subjected to the rule of the signifier. Freudian metapsychology, moreover, opposes two antagonistic drives, of life and death, complexity and chaos. By contrast, the idea of chaosmosis establishes a common background, which is not indifferentiation, but the vital energy of virtual ways and modes of becoming: positive alterity as complexity.

Guattari proposes an analysis of complexity in four dimensions: instead of the libido, the notion of material and semiotic fluxes of energy. Instead of the realm of the linguistic signifier, the concrete and abstract machinic entities (or phylum); instead of the unconscious, virtual universes of value; and in place of the self, finite existential territories. Again, the point of such a distinction is to create transversal connections across the lines in a creative process of transversality.

Guattari stresses that our world is incapable of absorbing the technomutations that are currently shaking it. As the terms of reference break down one by one, a vertiginous race toward radical renewal is the only positive alternative: "An ecology of the virtual is just as pressing as ecologies of the visible world" (1995:91).

How to deal with this ontological intensity in a secular and creative manner is the challenge. Guattari expresses it in terms of registers of coexistence and crystallization of intensity. It is literally a question of synchronizing the ontological intensity with machinic arrangements of the structure of affectivity that would allow it to resonate freely. This refers to the parallelism of mind and body defended by Spinoza, to which I will return in the next chapter.

How to reconstitute the subject? By empowering processes of becoming, in the chaosmic deterritorializations within it. This includes high levels of intensity and a state of flux or oscillation between the "no longer" and the "not yet," i.e., between a proliferation of possibilities and a degree zero of self-presence. This is akin to a schizoid state. Not only is it the case that the existence of chaosmic stases is not the privilege of psychopathology, but without it there would be no creativity of any kind.

This qualitative step forward is necessary if we want subjectivity to escape the regime of self-withdrawal, infantilization through the media, and denial of alterity that are the traits of our historical era. "Virtual ecology" aims at engendering the conditions for the creation and development of unprecedented formations of subjectivity. It is a generalized ecology, also known as ecosophy, that aims at crossing transversally the multiple layers of the subject, from interiority to exteriority and everything in between. These are Deleuze's and Guattari's becomings defined as nuclei of differentiation and singularization.

The emphasis falls on the micropolitics of relations as a posthumanist ethics that traces transversal connections among material and symbolic, ·concrete and discursive lines or forces. Transversality actualizes biocentered egalitarianism as an ethics and also as a method to account for both material and immaterial forms of labor subjectivity in the age of bios-zoe power, which trades in all that lives and breeds. An ethics based on the primacy of the relation, of interdependence, values zoe in itself.

Loyal to the method and the political practice of locations, however, I also want to situate this discussion in terms of more general geopolitical power relations within advanced societies. "We" are in this together, but we are not all the same. Dolly the sheep and I share a structural proximity in terms of our inscription in genetic engineering, but this cannot be adequately accounted for within the logic of rights. I therefore want to defend the qualitative process of becoming-animal as a creative transformation that stresses the productivity of biopower in terms of zoe, or generative, non-logocentric life. A micropolitics of affective becomings.

CONCLUSION: BECOMING-IMPERCEPTIBLE

In the case of the becoming-woman/animal, which are classical cases of minoritarian or oppositional politics, it can be argued that such a position incurs a rather high risk of colluding with the strategies of advanced capitalism, insofar as this system can be described as a force that deterritorializes, pluralizes, and complexifies for the purpose of profit. The great vampire incorporates and displaces all that lives in a series of successive waves of consumption. Nomadic theory therefore argues that resistance has to be generated from within this system. Processes of becoming are such forms of resistance, in that they aim at empowerment and the enhancement of what subjects can do (their potentia) for the sake of nonprofit. This nonrapacious production of empowering and affirmative differences is a qualitative change of gears within the system of advanced capitalism. Becoming woman/animal, etc. trace the same patterns as minority formations, but disrupt them and qualitatively shift their aims and forces.

What looks from one angle to be a potential threat of contamination of the minorities by the dominant norm or standard, from another appears instead to be active resistance and innovation. This is not relativism, but a politics of location. What keeps the danger of homologation or vampiristic absorption at bay is the strategy of inserting motion, acceleration, and hence disruption within the processes of successive de- and reterritorializa- ton that are induced by the flows of capital. This dynamic process of mo- tion ensures that the processes keep on going and never stop. In the mode of emancipatory politics, this means that they do not stop at the mere assertion of counteridentities, but rather go further and push toward qualitatively stronger deterritorializations. Even identity politics and feminist strategic essentialism can open paths of becoming, so long as they do not stop at the mere reassertions of identities they taught us to despise.

It is important to stress the difference, however, between minoritarian becomings and the third case I examined, namely, the becoming-world or merging with the environment or the earth. This does not fit in with this pat- tern because it is a pure form of becoming that is immanent to all the oth- ers: it is planetary. It is the only form of becoming that is not minoritarian but qualitatively at a distance from the standard or norm of the dominant subject position or Majority. As such, it has the power to deterritorialize the Majority and its main categories and classifications. The becoming- imperceptible is the most forceful expression of this positive or qualitative shift or deterritorialization. It concerns the movement of the totality of all that lives, of that great animal/machine that is the cosmos itself. It concerns the planet as a whole. In this sense the becoming-imperceptible traces a gen- eral ecophilosophy of becoming that produces positive interconnections on a planetary scale. The phrase "we are in this together" accurately sums up the global dimension of the problems we are facing when we take the power relations around bios/zoe as the defining feature of our historicity.

An important reason for needing a new grounded, embodied, and em- bedded subject has to do with the second half of that crucial sentence: "we" are in this together. What this refers to is the cartography as a cluster of interconnected problems that touches the structure of subjectivity and the very possibility of the future as a sustainable option. "We" are in this to- gether, in fact, enlarges the sense of collectively bound subjectivity to non- human agents, from our genetic neighbors the animals to the earth as biosphere. "We," therefore, is a nonanthropocentric construct, which refers to a commonly shared territory or habitat ("this"). How to do justice to this relatively simple yet highly problematic reality requires a shift of perspective. As Haraway suggests, we need to work toward "a new techno-scientific democracy" (1997:95). This is indeed a totality, finite and confined. The implications of this fact are multiple, and they concern the issue of the limits of social constructivism with which I opened this chapter. Because of the kind of complexities "we" are facing, we need to review methodologies that have tended to underplay the role of biological or genetic factors. This calls for a new set of alliances of a more transversal and transdisciplinary nature with different communities of scholars and activists.

What nomadic ethics stands for, therefore, is a regrounding of the subject in a materially embedded sense of responsibility and ethical accountability for the environments s/he inhabits. What is at stake is the very possibility of the future, of duration or continuity. Becomings are the sustainable shifts or changes undergone by nomadic subjects in their active resistance against being subsumed in the commodification of their own diversity. Becomings are unprogrammed as mutations, disruptions, and points of resistance. Their time frame is always the future anterior, that is to say, a linkage across present and past in the act of constructing and actualizing possible futures.

My concern is, as always, to make sure that dissymmetry and hence power differences are not leveled out. The times and modes of women's and other marginal groups becoming can be respected while we engage in the process of negotiations and constructive dialogue with the technocratic cultures of our days. The bare fact of human embodiment, of that corporeal materiality which is definitional of the subject, remains central. Embodiment, however, has to be thought of in the nomadic mode of a sexualized, racialized, and enfleshed complexity, not as a unity. However technologically mediated and in spite of electronic fantasies, we are still mortal (not-forever), enfleshed (not-immaterial), made of language (interactive) and hence of alterity (interconnective). At both the organic and the symbolic level we are made of the encounter of different cells and genetic codes (principle of not-One). The raw materiality of life and death, which I refer to as the bios/zoe principle, is staring us in the face, requiring urgent new forms of configuration. The very thinkability of zoe, its relentless and in some ways careless generative powers, is the heart of the matter. Zoe has a monstrously strong capacity for becoming and for upsetting established categorical distinctions of thought. Given this potentia and the technological means we have at our disposals, all sorts of alternative worlds have become possible.

Before we can get there, however, we need to elaborate narratives that match the complexity of our age and resist both the lure of euphoria and the temptation of nostalgic regression. The issue of how far we can push the ongoing changes and what we can collectively hope for needs to be grounded in a more inclusive and materialist analysis of how much "we" can take of this.

FEMINIST TRANSPOSITIONS

PART TWO

5

MATTER-REALIST FEMINISM

A t the start of the third millennium, feminist philosophy is going through an astonishing period of renewal and growth. The diversification and expansion of feminist philosophies, fueled by a brand new generation of post-postfeminists, is both supported by and productive of a significant growth of institutional practices, some of which happen outside the strict confines of academic philosophy, mostly in new transdisciplinary areas like women's gender, race, and postcolonial studies, social theories of globalization and migration, and philosophies of new media science and biotechnology. This theoretical vitality raises a range of methodological questions about the uses and limitations of interdisciplinarity in feminist theory and more specifically about the criteria of classification, the use of analytic categories, and the canonization processes. As a result, the need for a systematic metadiscursive approach to the interdisciplinary methods of feminist philosophy is among the top priorities for philosophy today (Alcoff 2000) as well as women's, gender, and feminist studies as an established discipline (Wiegman 2002). If it is the case that what was once subversive is now mainstream, it follows that the challenge for feminist philosophers today is how to hold their position while striving to achieve more conceptual creativity (Deleuze and Guattari 1991).

In a globally connected and technologically mediated world that is marked by the sort of mutations, structural inequalities, and increased militarization I have described in the previous chapters, feminist scholarship has intensified theoretical and methodological efforts to come to grips with the complexities of the present, while resisting the moral and cognitive panic that marks so much of contemporary social theories of globalization (Fukuyama 2002; Habermas 2003). With the demise of postmodernism, which has gone down in history as a form of radical skepticism and moral and cognitive relativism, feminist philosophers tend to move beyond the linguistic mediation paradigm of deconstructive theory and to work instead toward the production of robust alternatives. Issues of embodiment and accountability, positionality and location have become both more relevant and more diverse. My main argument in this chapter is that feminist philosophy is currently finding a new course between posthumanism, on the one hand, and postanthropocentric theories, on the other. The convergence between these two approaches, multiplied across the many interdisciplinary lines that structure feminist theory, ends up radicalizing the very premises of feminist philosophy. It especially results in a reconsideration of the priority of sexuality and the relevance of the sex/gender distinction. I will analyze the different aspects of this convergence and attempt to work out some of its implications.

THE LEGACY OF FEMINIST POSTHUMANISM

As starting premises, let me add a few remarks: feminist philosophy builds on the embodied and embedded brand of materialism that was pioneered in the last century by Simone de Beauvoir. It combines, in a complex and groundbreaking manner, phenomenological theory of embodiment with Marxist—and, later on, poststructuralist—reelaborations of the intersection between bodies and power. This rich legacy has two long-lasting theoretical consequences. The first is that feminist philosophy goes even further than mainstream Continental philosophy in rejecting dualistic partitions of minds from bodies or nature from culture. Whereas the chasm between the binary oppositions is bridged by Anglo-American gender theorists through dynamic schemes of social constructivism (Butler and Scott 1992), Continental feminist perspectives move toward either theories of sexual difference or a monistic political ontology that makes the sex/gender distinction redundant. I shall return later to this crucial aspect of my argument.

The second consequence of this specific brand of materialism is that oppositional consciousness combines critique with creativity, in a "double-edged vision" (Kelly 1979) that does not stop at critical deconstruction but moves on to the active production of alternatives. Thus feminist philosophers have introduced a new brand of materialism of the embodied and embedded kind. The cornerstone of this theoretical innovation is a specific brand of situated epistemology (Haraway 1988), which evolves from the practice of "the politics of locations" (Rich 1985) and infuses standpoint feminist theory and the debates with postmodernist feminism (Harding 1991) throughout the 1990s.

As a metamethodological innovation, the embodied and embedded brand of feminist materialist philosophy of the subject introduces a break from both universalism and dualism. As to the former, universalized claims to a subject position that allegedly transcends spatiotemporal and geopolitical specificities are criticized as being disembodied and disembedded, i.e., abstract. Universalism, best exemplified in the notion of "abstract masculinity" (Hartsock 1987) and triumphant whiteness (Ware 1992), is objectionable not only on epistemological but also on ethical grounds. Situated perspectives lay the preconditions for ethical accountability for one's own implications with the very structures one is analyzing and opposing politically. The key concept in feminist "enchanted" materialism is the sexualized nature and radical immanence of power relations and their effects on the world. In this Foucauldian perspective, power is not only negative or confining (potestas), but also affirmative (potentia) or productive of alternative subject positions and social relations.

Feminist antihumanism, also known as postmodern feminism, expanded on the basic critique of one-side universalism, while pointing out the dangers implicit in a flat application of equal opportunities policies. Contrary to "standpoint theory" (Harding 1986), posthumanist feminist philosophers do not unquestionably rely on the notion of "difference" as the dialectical motor of social change. They rather add more complexity to this debate by analyzing the ways in which "otherness" and "sameness" interact in an asymmetrical set of power relations. The fundamental axes of difference—which I analyzed in an earlier chapter of this book—namely, sexualization, racialization, and naturalization—are analyzed as dynamic variables and not as unitary categories. As a consequence, their interaction and their shifting relations emerge as more significant than any identity they may actually engender. The complexity of the interaction or sameness with otherness results in calling into question accepted ideas about what constitutes the boundaries of our common humanity.

Posthumanist feminist epistemologies propose radical new ways to look at the "human" from a more inclusive and diverse angle. As a result, the dominant vision of the subject in politics, law, and science is abandoned in favor of renewed attention to complexities and inner contradictions. Closer to the phenomenological tradition of the intelligence of the flesh and more and more compatible with neural sciences, materialist feminism rests on a complex and articulate notion of "embodiment." This refers to a know-how immanent to the living and lived body, as well as the idea of a transgenerational, nonlinear memory of one's belonging to one's species and community. We are subjected to, as well as being the subjects of, forces that cut across us, splitting us open, but also—and by the same gesture—connecting us in powerful and often obscure ways.

Throughout the 1990s the recognition of the normative structure of science and of the partiality of scientific statements, as well as the rejection of universalism and the recognition of the necessarily contingent nature of all utterances, involved two polemics, which retrospectively appear symptomatic of great anxiety. One concerned essentialism, and the other relativism. One of the worst lasting effects of the politically conservative backlash of that period was that the affirmative and progressive potential of feminist critiques of the dominant subject position were reduced to and dismissed as being merely relativistic. What I value in those radical feminist positions is precisely the extent to which they allow for a productive critique of falsely universal pretensions. As a consequence, they enact the desire to pluralize the options, paradigms, and practices of subjectivity within Western philosophical reason. The recognition of the necessarily situated and hence partial and contingent nature of our utterances and discursive practices has nothing to do with relativism and all to do with accountability or situated perspectives.

For example, whereas the deconstruction of masculinity and whiteness is an end in itself, the nonessentialist reconstruction of black perspectives as well as the feminist reconstruction of multiple ways of being women also has new alternatives to offer. In other words, some notions need to be deconstructed so as to be laid to rest once and for all: masculinity, whiteness, heterosexism, classism, and ageism. Others need to be deconstructed only as a prelude to offering positive new values and effective ways of asserting the political presence of newly empowered subjects: feminism, diversity, multiculturalism, environmentalism. All claims to authenticity need to be subjected to serious critical inquiry, but not left hanging in some sort of theoretical "undecidability," as Butler would have it (Butler 2004a). The affirmation of robust alternatives is what feminist philosophies of the subject are all about.

Antihumanism is crucial for nomadic theory and for poststructuralist feminism, and it rests on a number of key concepts: embodied materialism versus universalism and monism instead of dualism. The antihumanism of the "high" poststructuralists unfolds from their deeply seated anti-Cartesianism. It rests on a very innovative definition of bodily materialism. Both the corporeal elements and the concept of matter are carefully repositioned as a radical critique of the two major strands of twentieth-century social constructivism: Marxism and psychoanalysis.

Feminist antihumanism rejects the unitary identities indexed on phallocentric, Eurocentric, and normative standardized views of what constitutes the humanist ideal of "Man." Unconscious memories as well as collective channels of neural and genetic information bind us more strongly than any moral imperative. They make our identities into collective, outward-bound, and retrospective entities—not at all the measure of all things, but more like a sedimented accumulation of leftovers.

After all is said and done, at the remains of the day of reason, where the Cartesian "I" once ruled in his truculent self-confidence, the oblique but all-pervasive force of nonunitary but ethically sustainable nomadic subjectivity comes center stage. Nomadic bodily materialism is communitarian, in its own exquisitely perverse way. It consequently resonates with analogous but other (wise) situated postcolonial and race perspectives that critique humanism or its racist connotations and racialized bias and oppose to the biased Western brand many other cultural and ethnic traditions of non-Western humanism (Hill Collins 1991; Shiva 1997; Gilroy 2000). This alliance between Western posthumanist and non-Western antihumanist positions converges on the impossibility of speaking in one unified voice about women and other marginal subjects, thus stressing issues of diversity and differences among them.

As a result of this inclusive, transversal, and diverse angle, the dominant vision of the subject in politics, law, and science is abandoned in favor of renewed attention to complexities and inner contradictions. Antihumanist philosophies are committed both to a radical politics of resistance and to the critique of the simultaneity of potentially contradictory social and textual effects (Braidotti 1994a). This simultaneity is not to be confused with easy parallels or arguments by analogy. That gender, race, class, and sexual choice may be equally effective power variables does not amount to flattening out any differences between them (Crenshaw 1995). By extension, the claim to universality by scientific rationality is challenged on both epistemological and political grounds (Spivak 1987), all knowledge claims being expressions of Western culture and of its drive to mastery.

THE POSTANTHROPOCENTRIC TURN

The legacy of antihumanism sets the backdrop for the shifts currently taking place in the work of a new generation of feminist scholars (Fraser 2002; Bennett 2001, 2010). A range of positions has emerged that bridge the gap between the classical opposition "materialism/idealism" and move toward a nonessentialist brand of contemporary vitalism or thought on "life itself" (Rose 2001). They converge on discourses about "life" and living matter/bodies: be it under the guise of political reflections on "biopower," or in the form of analyses of science and technology, they bring us back to the organic reality of "real bodies." After so much emphasis on the linguistic and cultural turn, an ontology of presence replaces textual or other deconstruction.

I refer to these neorealist practices of bodily materialism as "matter-realism," radical neomaterialism, or posthuman feminism. One of the main reasons to explain them concerns the changing conceptual structure of materialism itself, under the impact of contemporary biogenetics and information technologies. The switch to a monistic political ontology stresses processes, vital politics, and nondeterministic evolutionary theories—as prophesied by Keith Ansell-Pearson a decade ago. The most striking feature is the dislocation of difference from binaries to rhizomatics. Post-poststructuralist critical theory looks carefully at the dislocation of the dialectical relationships between the traditional axes of difference, sexualization/racialization/naturalization, and attempts to come to terms with this challenge. It can also be described as a sort of "anthropological exodus" from the dominant configurations of the human (Hardt and Negri

2000:215)—a massive hybridization of the species that topples the anthro-pocentric Human from the sovereign position it has enjoyed for so long. This standard is posited in a universal mode as Man, but this pseudo universal has been widely criticized (Lloyd 1985) precisely because of its partiality. Universal Man, in fact, is implicitly assumed to be masculine, white, urbanized, speaking a standard language, heterosexually inscribed in a reproductive unit, and a full citizen of a recognized polity.

Massumi refers to this phenomenon as "Ex-Man," "a genetic matrix embedded in the materiality of the human" and as such undergoing significant mutations: "species integrity is lost in a bio-chemical mode expressing the mutability of human matter" (Massumi 1998:60). Haraway puts it most lu-cidly: "this is Man the taxonomic type become Man the brand" (1997:74). Posthuman times force us to confront the challenges of the postanthropocentric turn and the different degrees of inhumanity it encompasses. What emerges from the posthumanist convergence with postanthropocentrism is the vital politics of life, which in turn raises the question of the possible modes of critique of advanced, globalized capitalism.

Considering the extent to which contemporary capitalist economies depend on the commodification of life itself, there is a perverse form of post-human condition emerging form the very postanthropocentric opportunism of advanced capitalism. The biogenetic structure of advanced capitalism is such that it is not only genocentric (Fausto-Sterling 2000:235), but also ruthlessly and structurally unjust. Deleuze and Guattari (1991) analyzed this in terms of capitalism as a conflict between, on the one hand, the rising demands for subjective singularities and, on the other hand, the conservative reterritorialization of desires for the purpose of commercial profit. This achieves the doubly disastrous effect of reasserting liberal individualism as the unquestionable standard for subject formation while reducing it to consumerism.

Furthermore, as Keith Ansell-Pearson argued, some grand narratives have come back into fashion through "the dynamics of contemporary hyper-colonialist capitalism" (Ansell-Pearson 1997:303). They tend to be deterministic and evolutionary in a naive and oddly old-fashioned way: "A new mythology of the machine is emerging and finds expression in current claims that technology is simply the pursuit of life by means other than life" (Ansell-Pearson 1997:202). This simplistic and reductive reading of the transformations currently at work in our global system reveal a conceptual poverty that most critical thinkers have complained about. A hierarchical fantasy of vertical perfectibility, a technologically mediated quest for immortality and for disciplined and acquiescent subjects has gained widespread currency, which betrays the nomadic potential of contemporary science (Stengers 1997). In opposition to this master narrative, which corresponds to what Donna Haraway calls "the informatics of domination," feminist and nomadic matter-realist philosophers stress the relevance of materialist, vital, and complex philosophies of becoming as an alternative conceptual framework in the service of a sustainable future.

The epistemological analysis intersects with the political one: because the self-replicating vitality of living matter is targeted for consumption and commercial exploitation of biogenetic culture, environmentally based political struggles have evolved into a new global alliance for sustainable futures. Haraway recognizes this trend and pays tribute to the martyrized body of OncoMouse (Haraway 1997) as the farming ground for the new genetic revolution and manufacturer of spare parts for other species. Vandana Shiva (1997) also stresses the extent to which the bodies of the empirical subjects who signify difference (woman/native/earth or natural others) have become the disposable bodies of the global economy. Contemporary capitalism is "biopolitical" in that it aims at controlling all that lives: it has already turned into a form of biopiracy in that it aims at exploiting the generative powers of women, animals, plants, genes, and cells. This means that human and anthropomorphic others are relocated in a continuum with nonanthropomorphic or "earth" others. The categorical distinction that separated the Human from his naturalized others has shifted, taking the humanist assumptions about what constitutes the basic unit of reference for the "human" into a spin.

Matter-realist feminist thought gathers the remains of poststructuralist antihumanism and joins them with feminist reappraisals of contemporary technoculture in a nondeterministic frame (Haraway 1997, 2003; Hayles 1999). Feminist scholarship here falls neatly in two interconnected areas: new feminist science studies and epistemology, on the one hand, and political critiques of globalization and its economic and military violence, on the other. They converge on the notion that what matters about materialism today is the concept of "matter" itself (Bennett 2001, 2010; De Landa 2002). The switch to a monistic political ontology stresses processes, vital politics, and nondeterministic evolutionary theories (Grosz 2004; Irigaray 1992).

Pheng Cheah refers to this as "non-dialectical materialism" (2008b:143), based on speeds, flows of differentiations, and particles. Cheah compares it to classical dialectical materialism with its specific kind of "organistic vitalism" (2008b:155). That is to say, a dynamism generated by processes of organization or a dialectical scheme of organization. Nomadic vitalism is thus virtual, or incorporeal: an impersonal ontology of bodies without organs. Another term proposed for this new kind of materialism is "mattering" (Cheah 1996:108). "The process where history and nature become uncannily indistinguishable in a manner that is both enabling and disabling for political transformation, its condition of (un)possibility." This vision is indebted, among others, to Louis Althusser's notion of "materialisme aléatoire" (2005), nondialectical and hence nonoppositional.

For instance, Karen Barad's work on "agential realism" (Barad 2003, 2007) stresses the onto-epistemological aspect of feminist knowledge claims today. Barad's agential realism builds on but also radically expands the redefinitions of objectivity and embodiment that took place in high-feminist poststructuralism and thus also reshapes the forms of ethical and political accountability that rest upon them. By choosing to privilege neither the material nor the cultural, agential realism focuses instead on the process of their interaction. It accordingly redefines the apparatus of bodily production as material-cultural in order to foster the interrogation of the boundaries between them. This results also in specifically feminist formulations of critical reflexivity and a renewed call for the necessity of an ethics of knowing that reflects and respects complexity.

One of Karen Barad's most astute commentators, Iris van der Tuin (2008), claims that this materialist reconfiguration of the process of interaction between the material and the semiotic, also known as the onto-epistemological shift, constitutes a new paradigm that ends up displacing both its poles of reference. What gets redefined in the process is the process-oriented, relational, and fundamentally affective structure of subjectivity and knowledge production. According to van der Tuin, this approach encourages the constitution of a transdisciplinary perspective that combines feminist science studies, postcolonial studies, and Deleuzian feminism in a new brand of third wave feminist materialism.

Luciana Parisi also emphasizes (Parisi 2004) that the great advantage of Spinozist monism is that it defines nature/culture as a continuum that evolves through variations or differentiations. Deleuze and Guattari theorize them in terms of transversal assemblages or transversal lines of interconnection. At the core of the "chaosmosis" proposed by Guattari lies a mixed semiotics that combines the virtual (indeterminate) and the actual domains. The nonsemiotic codes (the DNA or all genetic material) intersect with complex assemblages of affects, embodied practices, and other performances that include but are not confined to the linguistic realm. Parisi strengthens this case by cross-referencing the new epistemology of Margulis (Margulis and Sagan 1995), through the concept of endosymbiosis, which, like autopoiesis, indicates a creative form of evolution. It defines the vitality of matter as an ecology of differentiation, which means that the genetic material is exposed to processes of becoming. This questions any ontological foundation for difference, while avoiding social constructivism.

The implications of this argument are twofold: the first point is that difference emerges as pure production of becoming-molecular and that the transitions or stratifications are internal to the single process of formation or of assemblage. They are intensive or affective variations that produce semiotic and asemiotic practices. This is not just about dismissing semiotics or the linguistic turn, but rather an attempt at using it more rigorously, within the domains of its strict application (Massumi 2002). It is also important to connect it transversally to other discourses. The second key point is that primacy is given to the relation over the terms. Parisi expresses this in Guattari's language as "schizogenesis"—or the affective being of the middle, the interconnection, the relation. This is the space-time where the differentiation occurs and with it the modifications. The emphasis falls, accordingly, on the micropolitics of relations, as a posthumanist ethics that traces transversal connections among material and symbolic concrete and discursive lines or forces. Transversality actualizes an ethics based on the primacy of the relation, of interdependence, which values nonhuman or apersonal Life. This is what I call zoe itself (Braidotti 2006). Feminist theory looks carefully at the dislocation of the dialectical relationships between the traditional axes of difference, sexualization/racialization/naturalization, and attempts to come to terms with this challenge. A further methodological issue arises as a result: the advanced, biogenetic structure of capitalism as a schizophrenic global economy does not function in a linear manner, but is weblike, scattered, and polycentered. It is not monolithic, but an internally contradictory process, the effects of which are differentiated geopolitically and along gender and ethnicity lines, to name only the main ones. This creates a few methodological difficulties for the social critic, because it translates into a heteroglossia of data that makes both classical and modernist social theories inadequate to cope with the complexities. We need to adopt nonlinearity as a major principle and to develop cartographies of power that account for the paradoxes and contradictions of the era of globalization and do not take shortcuts through its complexities. This call for new "figurations" of the subjects we are in the process of becoming resonates positively with the radical feminist call for the elaboration of empowering alternatives to the dominant vision of the subject.

Feminist politics, as outlined in the previous section, is pragmatic: we need schemes of thought and figurations that enable us to account in empowering and positive terms for the changes and transformations currently on the way. We already live in emancipated (postfeminist), multiethnic societies with high degrees of technological intervention. These are neither simple nor linear events, but rather multilayered and internally contradictory phenomena. They combine elements of ultramodernity with splinters of neoarchaism, high-tech advances and neoprimitivism, which defy the logic of excluded middle. Contemporary culture and institutional philosophy are unable to represent these realities adequately. The unitary vision of the subject cannot provide an effective antidote to the processes of fragmentation, flows, and mutations that mark our era. As Deleuze predicted, we need to learn to think differently about ourselves, starting with adequate cartographies of our embedded and embodied positions.

One of the areas in which contemporary feminist philosophy is attempting to actualize this political project is social theory and globalization studies. The consensual discursive strategy attempts to account for the speed and simultaneity of the contradictory social effects induced by advanced capitalism, including the structural inequalities that emerge in the age of globalization—also known as "scattered hegemonies" (Grewal and Kaplan 1994)—and stresses the need to safeguard women's interests, dignity, and well-being amidst the dissemination of hybrid and fast-changing ethnic, racial, national, and religious identities. Others follow on from classical deconstructive methodologies in attempting to map out processes of knowledge transfer and by adopting dynamic and nonlinear methods of analysis. The field known as "traveling theories" is significant (Hemmings 2006). Feminist social theory tries to do justice to both complexity and processes of change as operational concepts in the constitution of social subjects. It stresses the productive aspects of the dislocation and recasting of identities under advanced capitalism, in either a conservative mode of rational and moral universalism (Nussbaum 2006; MacKinnon 2006) or in more innovative ways.

The theoretical advantage of this monistic and vital approach is the ability to account for the fluid workings of power in advanced capitalism by grounding them in immanent relations and hence to resist them by the same means. This philosophical position is exemplified by the notion of nonhierarchical or horizontal transcendence (Irigaray 1984) and by the idea of radical immanence in Deleuzian feminism (Braidotti 1991; Colebrook 2000a, 2004; Grosz 2004).

Third wave feminism (Henry 2004; Tuin 2008) has embraced nonlinearity by voicing anti-oedipal philosophical and methodological claims about feminist time lines that redesign possible futures in affirmative ways. This transversal convergence between philosophical antifoundationalism and feminist epistemology results in a posthuman wave that radicalizes the premises of science studies beyond anything envisaged by classical postmodernist feminism (Wilson 1998; Bryld and Lykke 1999; Franklin, Lury, and Stacy 2000). Interest in Darwin and evolutionary theory has grown considerably (Grosz 2004), as have feminist interests in nonteleological and antideterministic evolutionary theory. Feminist cultural studies of science attempt to disengage biology from the structural functionalism of DNA-driven linearity and to move it toward more creative patterns of evolutionary development (Halberstam and Livingston 1995). The result is a nonessentialist brand of vital neo-holistic thought that points explicitly to a spiritual evolutionary dimension, best exemplified by the growing number of references to Bergson (Fraser, Ember, and Lury 2006; Grosz 2004).

POSTHUMAN FEMINISM

The emergence of vitalist politics causes a considerable amount of epistemological disarray. This is due to the redistribution of the self-other relation along a rhizomatic, or multilayered axis, in contrast to a binary or dualistic axis of opposition, as I argued in chapters 2 and 3. As a result of the eruption of complexity at the heart of what used to be dialectics, the self-other relation is shifting, as we saw in the analysis of the changing status of animals and nonhuman "others." The classical dialectics of Otherness, and the varying degrees of interaction between the center and the margins, which was simultaneously intimate and public, inner-looking and framed nonetheless by clear relations of power, is currently being restructured. A bioegalitarian turn is taking place that encourages us to engage in a radically other relationship with others; the time is ripe for a social and political ecology of things, as Bennett so eloquently puts it (Bennett 2010). I want to argue that the challenge today is how to deterritorialize or nomadize the human-other interaction so as to bypass the metaphysics of substance and its corollary, the dialectics of otherness, thus secularizing the concept of human nature and the life that animates it. Nomadic processes of becoming are of great assistance in this project.

As I argued previously, the three dialectical axes in the constitution of otherness according to the unitary subject of classical humanism—sexualization/racialization/naturalization—and the hierarchical scale of pejorative differences they uphold have shifted. They no longer correspond to a dialectical model of opposition, but rather follow a more dynamic, nonlinear, and hence less predictable pattern that composes a zigzagging line of internally contradictory options. The "others" are not merely the markers of exclusion or marginality but also the sites of powerful and alternative subject-positions. Thus the bodies of others become simultaneously disposable commodities and also decisive agents for political and ethical transformation (Braidotti 2002a). This relocation of otherness along a rhizomatic web, however, seems to leave miraculously unscathed the centuries-old forms of sexism, racism, and anthropocentric arrogance that have marked our culture. The transformation of the axes of sexualized, racialized, and naturalized difference form intersecting patterns of becoming. They compose a new complex political economy of otherness and are therefore of great ethical and political relevance.

As I argued previously, there is a qualitative difference between the dislocation of sexualized and racialized differences and the transposition of naturalized differences. The conceptual, methodological, and practical implications of the critique of anthropocentrism go much further in questioning the structures of subjectivity. As a brand of "enchanted materialism," philosophical nomadism contests the arrogance of anthropocentrism and strikes an alliance with the productive force of zoe or life in its inhuman aspects.

Thus, affinity for zoe is a good starting point for what may constitute the last act of the critique of dominant subject positions, namely, the return of animal or earth life in all its potency, as I have argued in chapter 4. The breakdown of species distinction (human/nonhuman) and the explosion of zoe power, therefore, shifts the grounds of the problem of the breakdown of categories of individuation or subject formation (gender and sexuality; ethnicity and race). This introduces the issue of becoming into a planetary or worldwide dimension, the earth or natural other being not one element among others, but rather that which brings them all together.

Social theory since poststructuralism has emphasized the materially grounded transformative processes of becoming, reappraised the relevance of complexity in network societies, and shifted the political analyses from biopower to vital politics. Classical vitalism is a problematic notion, considering its dramatic history of holism and complicity with fascism. Contemporary neovitalism as a philosophy of flows of complex information systems and flux of data in the continuum of "timeless time" (Castells 1996), however, presupposes and benefits from the philosophical monism that is central to a materialist and nonunitary vision of subjectivity.

SEXUALITY BEYOND GENDER

This matter-realist turn has important implications for the discussion of sexuality and gender, which has been central to feminist philosophy since the change of paradigm toward queer theory, introduced by de Lauretis (1990) and developed by Butler in the 1990s. As I have argued elsewhere (Braidotti 2002a), Butler's claim to undo gender (2004b) is flatly contradicted by the binary structure of queer thinking, which locates the heterosexual matrix at the core of its analyses and opposes to it queer melancholia. The related criticism is that queer theory has avoided the main lesson of psychoanalysis about the polymorphous and perverse structure of human sexuality. It has accordingly narrowed down the scope of the original loss of unity of the subject, placing all the emphasis on the loss of the homosexual component. By contrast, Deleuze and Guattari broaden the scope of the discussion by stressing the theft of the complexity, polymorphousness, and perversity of sexuality and its reduction through the capture of a majoritarian scheme of sexuality that privileges heterosexual reproductive sex.

Irigaray shifts the emphasis on the original and foundational act that is the theft of the little girl's sexuality—according to the sacrificial ontology of a phallocentric system that requires the exchange of women to fuel its sociosymbolic structures. The emphasis thus falls on the specificity of women's own sexual economy. It is in this spirit that Irigaray praises the instance of feminine homosexuality as a moment of high symbolic significance in confirming a woman's sense of self-worth.

Both Irigaray and Deleuze challenge queer theory's reductive rendition of the original foreclosure of the first love object—the mother—and of the sexual complexity that marks the polymorphous and perverse structure of human sexuality. Both engage, in different but powerful ways, with the unconscious or transhistorical and transpersonal carnal elements that are involved in the process of capture or theft of the primordial sexual body. What is emerging more clearly in current discussions about sexuality is that, whereas queer theory is solidly ensconced in social constructivist methods and political strategies, matter-realist thinkers affirm and explore the ontological aspects of sexuality and sexual difference and not only its constructed elements.

As a consequence, matter-realist or vitalist feminism, resting on a dynamic monistic political ontology, shifts the focus away from the sex/gender distinction, bringing sexuality as process into full focus. The first concerns the irrelevance of the category "same sex" to account for the complex and multiple affects generated in the relation between two beings. The redundancy of the sex/gender distinction for feminist philosophies of the subject had been noted by English-speaking feminists working in Continental philosophy, like Gatens (1991), Grosz (1999a), and Braidotti (1991, 1994b), before it was recast in a new paradigm by Butler's performative turn (1991). Contemporary feminist philosophers argue the same case on different grounds. For instance, Patricia MacCormack (2008) draws attention to the need to return to sexuality as a polymorphous and complex force and to disengage it from both identity issues and all dualistic oppositions. She looks for subversion not in counteridentity formations but rather in pure dislocations of identities via perversion of standardized patterns of interaction.

MacCormack's emphasis on visceral subjects rests on Deleuze and Guattari's idea of radical empiricism and on Irigaray's emphasis on the sensible transcendental, to stress that becomings or transformations are open-ended and not necessarily contained by sociosymbolic forms, such as phallogocentrism, or categories, such as the anthropocentric idea of the human. The ethics of becoming is rather an ethology of the forces that propel the subject to overcome both forms and categories, deterritorializing all identities on its line of flight. This means, by extension, that sexuality is a force, or constitutive element, that is capable of deterritorializing gender identity and institutions.

A renewed emphasis on sexuality, as opposed to classical or queer theories of sex and gender, emerges form the shift of perspective introduced by matter-realist feminism. In a recent contribution to this debate, Benjamin Noys (2008) argues forcefully for the need to reconsider the by now canonical reception of Foucault's theses on sexuality. Emphasizing Foucault's earlier work, Noys reappraises the radical critique Foucault developed of the overemphasis our culture places on sex-gender as an indicator of identities and inner truths about ourselves. As an operator of power, a conveyor of major social regulations, and a tool for consumerism, sex is a trap from which we need to liberate ourselves. Foucault's notorious criticism of feminist theories of sexual liberation, in the first volume of his history of sexuality, reiterates the point that there is no possible liberation through but only from sex-gender. By extension, the idea that sexual liberation is central to a political project of liberation or emancipation—which is constitutive of Western feminism and central to its secular bias—paradoxically reiterates the Christian notion that desire is central to the constitution of subjectivity.

Foucault's project challenges this bias by proclaiming the "end of the monarchy of sex" as being in congruence with the deregulation of sexual repression and the commercial exploitation of marginal or dissident sexualities. The only credible subversive move, according to Foucault, is the refusal of all identities based on sex-gender, and not only of a dominant heterosexual model or of its binary homosexual counterpart. Even more crucial is the effort to undertake serious experimentations with alternative modes of relation that are not mediated via sex and therefore escape both commercial commodification and the social normativity that accompanies it. This experimental sexual pragmatics also accomplishes the creative task of returning sexuality to its original complexity as a force of intensity, intimacy, and relationality. The centrality of desire is accordingly displaced by experimenting with modes of ethical subjectivity (for the later Foucault) and transversal collective assemblages (for Deleuze and Guattari) that free the subject from the dictatorship of sex as a term that indexes access to identity formations and their respective power entitlements. Neoasceticism (Braidotti 2006) emerges as a resource, with renewed emphasis on a political spirituality that labors to free the subject from constituted identities and experiment with new modes of relation.

This element is crucial to the postsecular turn, which I come back to in chapter 7. Both Irigaray and Deleuze embody and embed the universal, according to the principle of carnal materialism. They also conceptualize the space of the relation, the interconnection among forces and entities. The universal therefore is located transversally, in the specific singularity of immanent interrelations among subjects collectively engaged in the expression and actualization of potentia. The intersubjective space is a laboratory of becoming. Deleuze's antiessentialist, high-tech vitalism echoes the ideas of Irigaray about the subject as a bodily human entity, sensitive flesh framed by the skin. Irigaray turns to non-Christian religions, notably Judaism, Buddhism, and the philosophy of Lévinas. The model of alternative ethics proposed by philosophies of nomadism implies a nonhierarchical idea of transcendence and a nonbinary model of interrelation. They propose immanent concepts of the subject as dynamic becoming, where the bodily self is analyzed according to the concrete forces or material variables that compose it and sustain it.

SEXUAL DIFFERENCE REVISITED

The ontological status of sexuality in contemporary matter-realist discussions combines realism about essences with vitalism in ethical interrelations. Relationality and affirmative experimentations with other modes of ethical interaction are the rule. They imply that sexual difference is the starting point for transformative practice: a robust and essential starting point, not a burden to be cast away at the earliest opportunity.

All the Deleuzian radical empiricists share this point and stress the ontological dimension of both sexuality and sexual difference. Other voices, however, are emerging in the discussion, arguing that sexual difference is simply not a problem at all. This statement can be construed in several different ways, and the lines of differentiation are quite significant. For instance, in what could be described as a classical exposition of Deleuzian feminism, Gatens and Lloyd (1999) argue that the political ontology of monism, which Deleuze adapts from Spinoza, offers some relevant opportunities for feminist theory. Mind-body parallelism, as opposed to Cartesian dualism, can be rendered in terms of simultaneous effects. These entail the embodiment of mind as much as the "embrainment of matter," to use an expression coined by John Marks (1998:203). There is only one substance: an intelligent flesh-mind-matter compound. This implies that bodily differences are both a banality and a cornerstone in the process of differentiation of variation. The resonances between this feminist project and Deleuze's nomadism are many and manyfold.

Lloyd argues that the parallelism between mind and body and the intrinsically affective or conatus-driven vision of the subject implies that different bodies have different degrees and levels of power and force of understanding. This has clear implications for sexual difference. Given that, on a Spinozist account, the mind is nothing more than the actual idea of the body, sexual difference can reach into the mind, as the mind is not independent of the body in which it is situated. If bodies are differently sexed, so are minds. Lloyd emphasizes the extent to which Spinoza recognizes that there are distinctive powers and pleasures associated with different kinds of bodies, which then are enacted in different minds. Thus, a female body cannot fail to affect a female mind. Spinoza's mind is not neutral, and this, according to Lloyd, has great potential for a feminist theory of female subjectivity that aims at avoiding the essentialist trap of a genuine female nature, while rejecting the idea of the neutrality of the mind. Although Spinoza gives in to the traditionally subordinate vision of women of his times, and thus excludes women from the polity, Lloyd is careful in pointing out the liberatory potential of Spinoza's monistic vision of the embodied nature of the mind. Its worth can be measured most effectively in comparison with the Cartesian dualistic vision of the mind-body dichotomy, which historically proved more damaging for women than his idea of the sex-neutrality of the mind. What a female nature is must consequently be determined in each case and cannot be spelled out a priori, because each embodied compound has its own specificity. This is due to the fact that, in a neo-Spinozist perspective, embodied subjects are constituted by encounters with other forces in patterns of affinity or dissonance, which gives them very clear configurations that cannot be known in advance.

In a monistic perspective, difference need not be rendered in essentialist terms, be it biological, psychic, or any other type. The fact that for Spinoza the body is intelligent matter and the mind is embodied sensibility has the advantage of bypassing the pitfalls of essentialism altogether. This offers a way out of the essentialism-constructivism impasse. Accordingly, Lloyd, even more than Gatens, contemplates a nonpsychoanalytic theory of sexual difference that rests on Spinoza's monism and reaches out for what I have called the "enchanted materialism" of immanence.

Lloyd (1994) stresses the continuing relevance of sexual difference, against the theoretical illusions of an infinitely malleable, free-floating gender. Grounded and situated, sexual difference as a mode of embodied and embedded actualization of difference shapes the space-time continuum of nomadic subjectivity. Lloyd and Gatens explicitly take aim at the dualism of the sex-gender distinction, which posits a transcendent gender as the matrix that formats sex. By extension, they also expose the absurdity of any political project that would aim at "undoing gender" (Butler 2004b). To undo gender would mean to unmake bodies, and much as this aspiration fits in with the consumerist logic of advanced biocapitalism, it makes very little sense politically.

Thus Lloyd argues that sexually differentiated bodies mark sexually differentiated spatio-temporal segments of subjectivity. In other words, sexual difference speaks through or is expressed in every cognitive, moral, political, or other activity of the subject. Whereas Irigaray and the feminism of sexual difference attribute a (positive) normative value to this statement, Lloyd keeps it neutral. It is a factual statement: it is just the way things are. What does become important for both Lloyd and Gatens, however, is the extent to which this monistic vision of the subject, and its built-in assertion of sexual difference, allows for an enlargement of both the notion of moral agency and that of political subjectivity and more particularly of citizenship. Insofar as all subjects partake of the same essence, and are therefore part of nature, their common features can be located precisely in this shared capacity for affecting and being affected. This transversality lays the grounds for a postindividualistic understanding of the subject and a radical redefinition of common humanity. The latter is an embedded and embodied collection of singularities that are endowed with common features: qualitative complexities, not quantitative pluralities.

If for Lloyd and Gatens sexual difference is not a problematic issue, in that it remains of great relevance, for Claire Colebrook it is no longer a problem, because the political and theoretical terms of the feminist debate have shifted since the days of high, or early, feminist poststructuralism. Colebrook (2000a) suggests that a younger feminist wave is looking at the question of sexual difference as not only or primarily a question that concerns the subject or the subject's body. She is very vocal in wanting to move beyond the phenomenological legacy of feminist theory and enlists Deleuze's philosophy in the attempt to bypass the quasi-transcendentalist mode of feminist theory. Colebrook stresses that for Irigaray sexual difference is clearly a metaphysical question, but in the foundational sense that it determines metaphysics as such. Sexual difference poses the question of the conditions of possibility for thought as a self-originating system of representation of itself as the ultimate presence. Thus, sexual difference produces subjectivity in general. The conceptual tool by which Irigaray shows up this peculiar logic is the notion of "the sensible transcendental." By showing that what are erased in the process of erection of the transcendental subject are the maternal grounds of origin, Irigaray simultaneously demystifies the vertical transcendence of the subject and calls for an alternative metaphysics. Irigaray's transcendental is sensible and grounded in the very particular fact that all human life is, for the time being, still "of woman born" (Rich 1977).

According to Colebrook, Deleuze's emphasis on the productive and positive force of difference is troublesome for feminist theory insofar as it challenges the foundational value of sexual difference. For Irigaray, the metaphysical question of sexual difference is the horizon of feminist theory; for Grosz (1994) it is its precondition; for Butler (1993) it is the limit of the discourse of embodiment; for Braidotti (1994b) it is a negotiable, transversal, affective space. The advantage of a Deleuzian approach is that the emphasis shifts from the metaphysics to the ethics of sexual difference. Deleuze's brand of philosophical pragmatism questions whether sexual difference demands a metaphysics at all. This, for Colebrook, translates into a crucial question: "Is feminism a critical inhabitation of metaphysical closure, or the task of thinking a new metaphysics?" (Colebrook 2000a:112). Following Deleuze's empiricism, Colebrook wants to shift the grounds of the debate away from metaphysical foundations to a philosophy of immanence that stresses the need to create new concepts. This creative gesture is a way of responding to the given, to experience, and is thus linked to the notion of the event. The creation of concepts is itself experience or experimentation. There is a double implication here: firstly that philosophy need not be seen as the master discourse or the unavoidable horizon of thought: artistic and scientific practices have their role to play as well. Secondly, given that ethical questions do not require a metaphysics, the feminist engagement with concepts need not be critical but can be inventive and creative. In other words, experimenting with thinking is what we all need to learn.

Colebrook struggles with the idea of what kind of problem sexual difference could be, if it were not defined as a question of truth, recognition, self-representation, or radical anteriority. She does not come to a convincing conclusion, but this does not detract from the relevance of her project. In order to answer the question of sexual difference, one would simply have to redefine the function or status of philosophy altogether. This is a classical radical feminist statement, which situates Colebrook's third wave feminism in a continuum with previous generations. Feminist theory does indeed challenge what we have come to recognize as thinking. Calling for an embodied philosophy of radical immanence marks the start of a bodily philosophy of relations. The body is for Colebrook an incorporeal complex assemblage of virtualities: "The body is a relation to what is not itself, a movement or an activity from a point of difference to other points of difference. And so difference is neither an imposed scheme, nor an otherwise uniform substance, nor is difference the relation between already differentiated self-identical entities. What something is, is given through the activity of differentiation" (Colebrook 2000b:87).

This is the basic meaning of the positivity of difference, and it is linked to corporeality through the notion of virtual becomings. Loyal to her Deleuzian premises, Colebrook defines the ethics of sexual difference "not as the telos of some universal law, but as the responsibility and recognition of the self-formation of the body" (Colebrook 2000b:88). In other words, as the becoming of bodies occurs within a single substance, the question is no longer "how are the sexes differentiated?" but rather "how are different modalities of sexual differentiation due to the specificity of different bodies?" (Colebrook 2000b:90). Once this question is raised, the whole issue of essentialism simply collapses.

The point of consensus among these different positions is that sexual difference is not a problem that needs to be explained in relation to an epistemological paradigm that assumes a priori sameness and a dialectical frame of pejorative difference. It is rather the case that sexual difference is just an embodied and embedded point of departure that signals simultaneously the ontological priority of difference and its self-organizing and self-transforming force. The ontology of becoming allows difference to emerge as radical immanence, i.e., as creative evolution. Chrysanthi Nigianni (2008) argues that this position moves political thought beyond both emancipationist historicism and liberal progressivism, allowing instead for a politics of becomings that posits transversal subjectivity as machinic assemblages that embrace the openness but also the materiality of the virtual (Massumi 2002).

■ ■ ■

This emphasis on the productive nature of desire and the view of sexuality as the vital force that deterritorializes gender and its binary system is the signature of nomadic feminism. Sexuality as the complex, multilayered force that produces encounters, resonances, and relations of all sorts cannot be contained in the power (potestas) structures of the dialectics masculine/feminine. It is rather an active space of empowerment (potentia) and becoming that is capable of producing spaces of intimacy, experimentation, and relation to others. Sexual difference no longer coincides with the rather narrow field of anatomical and sociological differences between the sexes. This is what I analyzed elsewhere (Braidotti 2011) as the first level of difference. Nor does it stop at level two of the differentiation process—the differences between different categories of women—and three, the differences *within* each singular woman.

A nomadic process of sexual differing is a permanent fracture, and it's a block of becoming positioned outside the gender system, which mobilizes untapped forces and energies and sets them to the task of sustaining processes of deterritorialization. Given that the only ethical question is the activation of affirmative and sustainable alternatives—as I will argue in chapters 11 and 12—then the force of an ethical relation consists in supporting the actualization of virtual possibilities geared to the empowerment of higher and larger forms of interrelation with multiple others. If "empower us to act" is the ethical injunction of nomadic subjectivity, then sexuality as one of the strongest modes of encounters is the necessary premise to the enlargement of one's fields of perception and capacity to encounter and sustain the impact with others. The vitalist force of matter-realist feminism locates sexuality as a concrete and vital resource to both decenter the individual ego and unlink desire from the restrictions of a gender system that is instrumental to the biopolitical management and disciplining of bodies.

The wager is how to bring sexuality to allow the unfolding of ever-intensifying affects and thus to construct sustainable futures of and as becoming-other. Desire as the productive, deterritorializing force of radical encounters is postidentitarian and impersonal. It designs new landscapes of relationality around the face of the beloved, and thus it cannot be restricted to the mere human *persona* that enacts it. What is needed as the end result of the shift of perspective is a postindividual and nonanthropocentric theory of desire that may do justice to the complexity of materialist and vital nomadic subjects of becoming.

6

INTENSIVE GENRE AND THE DEMISE OF GENDER

We leave a great blank here, which must be taken to indicate that
the space is filled to repletion.

—VIRGINIA WOOLF, QUOTED IN LEE, *VIRGINIA WOOLF*

You have the individuality of a day, a season, a year, *a life* . . . a
climate, a wind, a fog, a swarm, a pack. . . . A cloud of locusts carried in by the wind at 5 in the evening; a vampire who goes out at
night, a werewolf at full moon. . . . It is the entire assemblage in its
individuated aggregate that is a haecceity. . . . It is the wolf itself,
and the horse, and the child that cease to be subjects to become
events, in assemblages that are inseparable from an hour, a season,
an atmosphere, an air, a life.

—DELEUZE AND GUATTARI, *A THOUSAND PLATEAUS*

In this chapter I want to argue that Virginia Woolf's extensive corpus is
a singular example of an intensive genre that cuts transversally across a
number of established literary forms to constitute a qualitative mode of its
own. I will connect this intensive genre to the process of nomadic becoming,
with special emphasis on the concepts of creativity and desire. I will argue

that Woolf's work exemplifies not only the becoming-woman/animal/world in the minoritarian mode theorized by Gilles Deleuze and Felix Guattari but also the process that is immanent to all others and hence more powerful (in the sense of potentia), namely, the becoming-imperceptible.[1] In this respect, Woolf's stream-of-consciousness style expresses with uncanny precision the seriality as well as the radical immanence and structural contingency of the patterns of repetition by which qualitative processes of transformation can be actualized. Thus Woolf invents a genre of her own—the intensive genre of becoming.

NOMADIC BECOMINGS AND WOOLF'S INTENSIVE GENRE

Creativity is a nomadic process in that it entails the active displacement of dominant formations of identity, memory, and identification. Becoming-nomadic as a variation on the theme of becoming-minoritarian is neither the swinging of the pendulum of dialectical opposition nor the unfolding of an essence in a teleologically ordained process supervised by a transcendent consciousness. Nomadic becomings are rather the process of affirmation of the unalterably positive structure of difference, unhinged from the binary system that traditionally opposed it to Sameness. Difference as positivity entails a multiple process of transformation, a play of complexity that expresses the principle of not-One. Accordingly, the thinking subject is not the expression of in-depth interiority; neither is it the enactment of transcendental models of reflexive consciousness. It is a collective assemblage, a relay point for a web of complex relations that displace the centrality of ego-indexed notions of identity. Deleuze argues that, considering the deterritorializing force of processes of becoming, they gather force from some energetic core or vibrating hub of activity, which is the creative pole of power as potentia. This is opposed to the restrictive pole of institutionalized power as potestas, which can only replicate and perpetuate it. Only potential or joyful affirmation had the power to generate qualitative shifts in the processes of becoming, hence the axiom that there is becoming other than minoritarian/nomadic/woman/animal/other. According to Gatens and Lloyd (1999), this nomadic becoming is an ethology, that is to say, a process of expression, composition, selection, and incorporation of forces aimed at positive transformation of the subject. As such, it is also crucial to the project of a creative redefinition of philosophical reason and of its relation to conceptual creativity, imagination, and affectivity.

Becoming has to do with emptying out the self, opening it out to possible encounters with the "outside." Virgina Woolf's intensive genre is exemplary here, in that the artist's "eye" captures the outside world by making itself receptive to the totality of perception. What gets activated is a seemingly absent-minded floating attention or a fluid sensibility that is porous to the outside and which our culture has coded as "feminine." This sensibility is central to the creative process. It combines the accuracy of the cartographer with the hypersensitivity of the sensualist in apprehending the precise quality of an assemblage of elements, like the shade of the light at dusk or the curve of the wind just before the rain falls. In those moments of floating awareness, when rational control releases its hold, "Life" rushes on toward the sensorial/perceptive apparatus with exceptional vigor and higher degrees of definition. This onrush of data, information, and affectivity is the relational bond that simultaneously propels the self out of the black hole of its atomized isolation and disperses it into a myriad bits and pieces of data imprinting or impressions. Conceptualized by Deleuze as the folding in and out of perception, it also confirms the singularity of that particular entity which both receives and recomposes itself around the onrush of data and affects.

One needs to be able to sustain the impact with the onrushing affectivity, to "hold" it, without being completely overwhelmed by it. But "holding" it or capturing it does not occur on the paranoid or rapacious model of a dominant, dialectically driven consciousness. It rather takes the form of a sustainable model of an affective, depersonalized, highly receptive subject, which, quite simply, is not one, not there, not that. As Virginia Woolf put it: "I am rooted, but I flow" (1977b:69). The singularity of this nomadic, floating subjectivity rests on the spatiotemporal coordinates that make it possible for him/her to coincide with nothing more than the degrees, levels, expansion, and extension of the head-on rush of the "outside" folding inward. What is mobilized is one's capacity to feel, sense, process, and sustain the impact with the complex materiality of the outside.

The processes and flows of becoming and the heightened states of perception and receptivity they both assume and engender defy canonical genre classifications and install a sort of parallelism between the arts, sciences, and conceptual thinking. The point of convergence is the quest for creativity in the form of experimenting with the immersion of one's sensibility in the field of forces—formatted as by music, color, sound, light, speed, temperature, intensity. Deleuze and Guattari (1991) argue, for instance, that writers speak the unsayable; painters make visible forces that previously were not, much as composers make us hear sounds that were unheard of. Similarly, philosophers can make thinkable concepts that did not exist before. Artistic genres are variables coexisting along a continuum. It comes down to a question of style, but style here is no mere rhetorical device; it is rather a navigational tool. It negotiates our path across sets of material coordinates that, assembled and composed in a sustainable and enduring manner, allow for the qualitative transformation of the affects and the forces involved. They thus trigger the process of becoming.

The imagination plays a crucial role in enabling the whole process of becoming-minoritarian and hence of conceptual creativity and ethical empowerment. It is connected to memory: the affective force of remembrance is the propelling of becoming-intensive. When you remember in the intensive or minority-mode, you open up spaces of movement and of deterritorialization that actualize virtual possibilities that had been frozen in the image of the past. Opening up these virtual spaces is a creative effort. When you remember to become what you are—a subject-in-becoming—you actually reinvent yourself on the basis of what you hope you could become with a little help from your friends.

It is crucial, in fact, to see to what extent processes of becoming are collective, intersubjective, and not individual or isolated: it is always a matter of blocks of becoming. "Others" are the integral element of one's successive becomings. A Deleuzian approach favors the destitution of the liberal notion of the sovereign subject altogether and consequently overcomes the dualism Self/Other, Sameness/Difference intrinsic to that vision of the subject. Subjects are collective assemblages, that is to say, they are dynamic, but framed: fields of forces that aim at duration and affirmative self-realization. In order to fulfill them, they need to be drawn together along a line of composition. This is rather like pitching a musical tone.

Remembering in this nomadic mode is a key element of this process. Woolf's work reflects the dual structure of time: the linear one—*Chronos*— and the undifferentiated one—*Aion*. Being and Becoming confront each other in an unsteady balance. Aion is the "pure empty form of time," free of content, which is shot through with vibrations of becoming. If this be chaos, it is not chaotic, but generative (Ansell-Pearson 1999). It produces assemblages that organize space and time around them. The "haecceity," or individuated aggregate, is the specific and highly contingent actualization of a field of forces stable enough and consolidated by their structural affinity so as to be able to constitute a plane of immanence.

Remembering in the nomadic mode as I argued in chapter 1, is the active reinvention of a self that is joyfully discontinuous, as opposed to being mournfully consistent as programmed by phallogocentric culture. It destabilizes the sanctity of the past and the authority of experience. The tense that best expresses the power of the imagination is the future perfect: "I will have been free." Quoting Virginia Woolf, Deleuze also says: "This will be childhood, but it must not be my childhood" (Deleuze and Guattari 1977:294). "Shifting away from the reassuring platitudes of the past to the openings hinted at by the future perfect. This is the tense of a virtual sense of potential. Memories need the imagination to empower the actualization of virtual possibilities in the subject. They allow the subject to differ from oneself as much as possible while remaining faithful to oneself, or in other words: enduring."

The "plane of immanence" composes and sustains the actualization of processes of becoming as relational, external, and collective. This process of composition and assemblage of forces is what desire is all about, as an ontological layer of affinity and sympathy between different enfleshed subjects.

This intensive approach to processes of becoming does not pursue a Hegelian project of recognition of consciousness and hence does not posit desire as lack or rationality as implicitly linked to the violent struggle for autonomy (Benjamin 1988). Desire as plenitude rather challenges the matrix of having and lacking access to recognition by Self and Other as transcendent categories. Becoming is molecular, in that it requires singular overthrowing of the internalized simulacra of the self consolidated by habits and flat repetitions. The dynamic vision of the subject as assemblage is central to a vitalist, yet antiessentialist theory of desire, which also prompts a new practice of sustainable ethics.

Desire is the propelling and compelling force that is driven by self-affirmation or the transformation of negative into positive passions. This is a desire not to preserve, but to change: it is a deep yearning for transformation or a process of affirmation. Empathy and compassion are key features of this nomadic yearning for in-depth transformation. The space of becoming is a space of affinity and correlation of elements between compatible and mutually attractive forces and the constitutive elements of the process. Proximity, attraction, or intellectual sympathy is both a topological and qualitative notion: it is a question of ethical temperature. It is an affective framing for the becoming of subjects as sensible or intelligent matter. The affectivity of the imagination is the motor for these encounters and of the conceptual creativity they trigger off. It is a transformative force that propels multiple, heterogeneous "becomings" of the subject.

The sheer genius of Virginia Woolf rests in her ability to present her life as a gesture of passing through, i.e., of writing "as if already gone" in a vitalist and productive relationship to mortality. In *The Waves*, for instance, Woolf captures the concrete multiplicity—as well as the shimmering intensity—of becoming. She is the writer of multiple and intransitive becomings, in-between ages, sexes, elements, characters. Woolf's texts enact a flow of positions, a crossing of boundaries, and an overflowing into a plenitude of affects where life is asserted to its highest degree. She is an intensive multiplier of affects. Woolf also provides Deleuze with a model for the "plane of immanence," where different elements can encounter one another, producing those assemblages of forces without which there is no becoming. She expresses with stark intensity the pain involved in trying to synchronize the heterogeneity of life as zoe, as positive vitality.

Although Deleuze recognizes the extraordinary position of Woolf as a conveyor or relay point for this passionate process of becoming in both *Dialogues* and *A Thousand Plateaus*, he is very careful to disengage Woolf's work from her being-a-woman and even more from the *écriture féminine* style made popular by sexual difference feminism since the 1980s. Woolf's language expresses the free indirect speech that is central to the nomadic vision of the subject as heterogeneous assemblage. Yet something in what feminists of sexual difference call the "feminine libidinal economy" of excess without self-destruction, and desire as plenitude without lack, is central to the whole Deleuzian project of becoming (Colebrook 2000b). This is why he positions the "becoming-woman" so prominently as a necessary moment of transition in his scheme of things, not only in his philosophy of the subject but also in the related theories of aesthetics and art. Nonetheless, as I argued at length elsewhere (Braidotti 1991, 2002a, 2006), Deleuze cannot resolve his ambivalence toward it.

Woolf's intensive genre and her flair for affirming positive passions provide not only a significant illustration of the functions of writing and desire but also project an ethics of sustainability. The intensive text is an experimental site, a laboratory for the new in the sense of the actualizations of experiments in becoming. The literary text—as an experiment in sustainable models of change—is a laboratory grounded in accurate knowledge and subjected to the same rigorous rules of verification as science or philosophy. This fundamental parallelism cuts across different areas, disciplines, and textual genres. Life, science, and art are equally enlisted to the project of experimenting with transformations. The author, writer, or agent is a complex multiplicity, a factor of empowerment of potentia, that is to say, multiplier of virtual possibilities, through the rigorous application of the rules of composition of assemblages. Life as zoe is approached as a splendid complexity—cosmic or, rather, "chaosmic" (Guattari 1995) and vitalist in essence.

FREE INDIRECT SPEECH; OR, WRITING WITH AN ACCENT

Throughout Woolf's corpus of free indirect speech (in her letters and diaries as well as in her fictional works), the figure of Vita Sackville-West—her friend, lover, and real-life model for *Orlando*—looms large. What is particularly striking is the highly defined field of perception that Woolf enacts and, in some ways, organizes. From their very first encounter in 1923, which was dutifully recorded in Woolf's diaries, through to the end of her life, Vita stands for a life force of mythical proportions. Clearly magnified through the lens of erotic desire, but stretching beyond the whimsical tricks of Eros, that cruel god, Vita endures in a field of her own, which is one of perpetual becomings. Spatiotemporal coordinates gather around Vita, carried by her statuesque legs, the arch of her shoulders, the specific hue of her complexion: she organizes Virginia's cosmos around her. There's a specific quality of light around her, which is recorded and repeated in the diaries with mathematical precision. It has to do with the porpoise radiance and the luster of pink and of pearls. There's an acceleration of life about Vita, due to the speed of desire but also to the more bearable lightness of becoming. The space gets filled with warmth, with that shimmering intensity which we also find in Woolf's novels. There's a heightening of sensorial perception, the flowing of deep-seated affinity, of immense compassion, to the very end: "Vita was here: and when she went, I began to feel the quality of the evening—how it was spring coming; a silver light; mixing with the early lamps; the cabs all rushing through the streets; I had a tremendous sense of life beginning; mixed with that emotion, which is the essence of my feeling, but escapes description. . . . I felt the spring beginning and Vita's life so full and flush; and all the doors opening; and this is I believe the moth shaking its wings in me" (Woolf 1930:287).

Virginia will remember these affects, and be able to retrieve their spatio-temporal coordinates throughout her life, even when the actual relationship with Vita has lost its brilliance. These spatiotemporal, geographical, historical, and meteorological features are Vita—as a vector for zoe—and constitute the plane of immanence where she and Virginia activate a process of becoming that goes beyond their psychological, amorous, and sexual relationship. Something much more elemental, rawer, is at stake: desire draws its own affective landscapes.

The polymorphous vitalism of the Vita-Virginia encounter enacts a block of becoming and the conditions for what we commonly would call desire. What I want to stress is the impersonal or rather apersonal nature of the interaction that is enacted in this encounter, however, and which makes it sustainable. This means that authors, characters, texts, friends, and lovers are blocks of becoming actualizing the virtuality that is activated by their relation or interconnection. The space between us is active with intensity—it is fertile, generative. The affects, concepts, and perceptions mobilized by art, science, or literature are multiple, infinitesimal, and located in a myriad of possible combinations, which form that which mobilizes yet unactualized real-life potentials.

There is a sort of geometry, geology, and meteorology of forces that gather round the actors—V & V—but do not fully coincide with them. The reader can map out these forces, in an exercise that is an ethology of affects or a cartography of their effects. First and foremost among these effects, the sheer pleasure, the joy, even the *jouissance,* which is but a sort of acceleration, a becoming-intense of existence: "life so full & flush," as Woolf admirably puts it. Secondly, and in some ways more importantly, it produces writing, "the moth shaking its wings" in Woolf's highly sensitive inner sensors. Becoming woman, animal, and writing machine proceed at equal speed, framing a space of perfect stillness.

The best way to measure the intensity mobilized in this encounter and to assess the scale of its magnitude—and hence of the possible becomings it activates—is by turning to the literature itself: the letters and diaries as well as the fictional work. All of Virginia Woolf's relationships mixed work and play, life and writing, starting with Leonard himself. Vita with her looks, intensity, and unconventional manners provided more fuel, and of a higher quality, than most. This is not to say that the affects and the passions are functional to the production of written work. Desire is a nonprofit mechanism and its contribution to meaningful production is simply the form it takes to express itself: desire is always the desire to express and to make things happen. As Elspeth Probyn put it: "desire here is no metaphor; it is a method of doing things, of getting places. Desire here is the mode of connection and communication between things, inevitably giving way to the literalness of things" (1996:40). The immanent and intensive approach makes for an absence of metaphoricity and renewed emphasis on concrete, literal actualizations.

Desire is, nonetheless, a surplus value that does ensue from the expression of affectivity and its successful encounter with other forces. It is a gift in some ways, but one that is disengaged from the political economy of exchanges regulated by lack and negativity. Virginia and Vita simply cannot help but write to, of, and through each other: it is a case of addiction. Addiction to what? An addiction to "Life," a seduction into "Life," to the adrenalin charge, the intensification of existence, the rush of energy that occurs in the spatiotemporal zone of their encounter. The space between us is creative and generative, it frames a network of becoming, a spider web of potentials. Together, we become other than what we were before we came close. Sexuality is not the "cause" or the driving force of this (these two women were only accidental lovers), but a mere consequence of some more fundamental shift of perspective that they operate for each other: potentia is activated (Grosz 1994).

Let us look at the specific genre that is their correspondence. This is neither a biography nor a love letter; it is the unfolding, with meticulous regularity, of the virtual layers of potentia contained in the encounter between Virginia & Vita. The actualization of multiple and virtual realities, possibilities such as they are perceived, recognized, and amplified by that writer of genius who was Woolf. In her study of Woolf's correspondence, Kate Stimpson (1988) argues that the epistolary genre is very specific and can best be defined as an in-between space, bringing together the public and the private. As such, the letters possess a fluid quality that allows the readers to catch a glimpse of the fleeting state of the writer's mind. They transcribe free indirect speech with increased intensity. Moreover, the letters are inter-active exchanges that construct an intersubjective space with her (privileged) interlocutor. The space of the letters is an in-between; a third party that does not fully coincide with either Virginia or Vita, but rather frames the space of their relationship. Read with Deleuze, it is a space of becoming. Read with Irigaray (1991), it is a space of mediation of the love between them. Read with Glissant (1990), it is a poetics of relation. As a mediating factor, it organizes space and time, thus allowing each partner to take care of the rela-tionship as a space of transition. Virginia and Vita "write" one another into their life, and they also produce a relationship as a space of transition. They draw a space of flow and becoming, a spider web and rhizome, through a set of epistolary relations that are enacted in a communal, albeit volatile, com-municative space. Today's equivalent would be e-mail exchanges.

Hermione Lee argues that in the relationship between Virginia and Vita "more was asked (on both sides) than could be given" (Lee 1996:485) and that, in their intense interchange, they made each other up imaginatively. They cast each other in dramatic roles which fed their respective writing, whereby "Virginia was the will of the wisp, the invalid, the frail virgin, the 'ragamuffin' or 'scallywag,' the puritan.... Vita was the rich, supple, luxuri-ous, high-coloured, glowing, dusky, fruity, fiery, winy, passionate, striding, adventuring traveller, also dumb, dense, a 'donkey.' Virginia was the one with the head; Vita was the one with the legs" (Lee 1996:485).

These imaginary constructions were their route to intimacy. This is no metaphor, but rather a vital form of literalness: conceptual personae acti-vated and intensified. The intense and deep affectivity that is expressed in these letters opens a space of freedom that allows simultaneously for experi-ments with different writing techniques and for experimenting with residual spirituality and complex emotions. These letters, as Stimpson argues, "oc-cupy a psychological and rhetorical middle space between what she wrote for herself and what she produced for a general audience. They are a bril-liant, glittering encyclopaedia of the partially-said ... the materials or a full autobiography of consciousness, mediation between life and work.... They concern social worlds that she needed and wanted. They form an autobiog-raphy of the self with others, a citizen/denizen of relationships" (Stimpson 1988:130). It is the link, the affinity, the bond of potentia and recognition between each of them as a complex multiplicity that results in setting the frame for the affirmation of the joyful potency of desire.

This high degree of intensity is all the more remarkable if you consider that, in real life, the actual V & V were far from the life forces that they happened to become together. Virginia could hardly sustain, in her frail body and even more vulnerable psychic balance, the intensity of the forces that she registered, evoked, and recorded: she lived on the crack. As for Vita, Virginia put her finger on it, with the disarming cruelty of her superior intelligence: "The thing I call central transparency sometimes fails you there too." And again: "There's something that doesn't vibrate in you; it may be purposely—you don't let it: but I see it with other people as well as with me: something reserved, muted" (Nicholson and Trautman 1977:302). That she hit the mark is testified by Vita's comments in her correspondence to her husband Harold Nicholson: "Damn the woman! She has put her finger on it. There is something that . . . doesn't come alive . . . it makes everything I do (i.e.: write) a little unreal; it gives the effect of having been drawn from the outside. It is the thing which spoils me as a writer; destroys me as a poet. . . . It is what spoils my human relationships too" (Nicholson 1992:173).

But this fundamental opacity of Vita's soul is compensated and sustained by a feminine magnificence about her: "Vita very free & easy, always giving me great pleasure to watch & recalling some image of a ship breasting a sea, nobly, magnificently, with all sails spread & the gold sunlight on them" (Woolf 1980:146).

A Deleuzian feminist reader could draw a cartography of the affective forces that frame the encounters between Virginia and Vita, such as they are reported in the diaries and the letters (literature and work of remembrance) as well as in the fiction (literature and work of the imagination). Again, I want to stress the apersonal nature of the desire at work here: it does not coincide at all with the individual biographies of the protagonists. On the contrary, that desire actively reinvents itself as they rewrite each other's lives, intervening energetically in its course. There is an enormous investment of the memory and the imagination at work in the space of the encounter between V & V; something that mobilizes the roots of their embodied genealogy, but transcends it: a becoming-other.

The most recurrent affect that Woolf gathers from her geometrical-geological and cosmic appreciation of Vita are images of radiance and vitality, such as the porpoise, the pink light, the pearls, which occur systematically throughout her writings. Vita produces a diagram that contains forces of the utmost intensity: a quality of the light coupled with a degree of intensity that may alternatively generate desire or trigger an outburst of comic laughter. Vita becomes a factor that introduces acceleration in the pulse of life, the opening up of possibilities, like the fluttering of wings before one takes flight. Vita not merely re-presents but actually enacts and organizes physically as well as in writing the becoming-woman of Virginia Woolf. A becoming-woman, becoming-animal that has a distinctly marine quality about it, so ubiquitous are the images of fluidity, flowing, waves, and sea animals. It does mark a fundamental moment in Woolf's race against time, the "becoming-imperceptible," which is the space where she could finally write. Hence the importance of the nonfunctional, apersonal space of writing as a sort of launching pad, a legal addiction that brings on a much-needed acceleration of life, something that propels the writer onward and forward. It is this "push" that simultaneously constructs the field of becoming and also the space for the corpus of writing. Accordingly, the assemblage of forces that activate the becoming-Orlando of Vita requires a careful phase of composition of forces that go through the becoming-woman of Virginia and the becoming-lesbian of both Vita and Virginia, but only in order to move on, to keep on becoming until that last recognition of the bond to Vita as an imperceptible and all-encompassing life force. A pattern of deterritorialization takes place between them, which runs parallel to and in and out of their respective and mutual existences, but certainly does not stop there.

It will have been a joyful and towering passion, though not entirely Virginia's or Vita's or my own, or yours. You cannot have your own "plane of immanence" and still hold onto it. You can only share in the composition of one, in the company of others. One does not run with Woolf alone: women, even Virginia Woolf herself, must learn to run with other (s/he)-wolves. How much of it she could or could not take raises the issue of sustainability, but such a question can never be settled in isolation. It is a matter for negotiations, dosages, and adjustments that can only take place interactively. They mark the place of the encounter. "Too much-ness" and hence the question of limits is as crucial in pleasure as it is in pain. Learning to dose and time is the alchemy of a successful relationship, the stakes of which include the successful outcome of respective lives and life projects as well as the mutual fulfillment of the participants. A whole world is always implicated when a plane of immanent becoming is composed. Two is quite a crowd, when one is a multiple, complex, and depersonalized entity to begin with.

The real-life Vita recognizes this interdependence, much as she had acknowledged from the start her friend's superior literary genius. After reading Orlando, for which she is the model, she actually fails to cope with the shock: "How could you hang so splendid a garment on so poor a peg? . . . Also, you have invented a new form of narcissism—I confess—I am in love with Orlando—this is a complication I had not foreseen" (Salvo and Leaska 1984:305–6).

The life that Virginia sees in her is something that Vita herself deeply aspires to. This has nothing to do with narcissistic delight—it is actually a sort of yearning on Vita's part for the potential that lays not so much in her as in the encounter between herself and Virginia. It is simultaneously the slightly ashamed recognition of her own limitations ("I'm not that good, really!") and the grateful recognition of what she owes to her lover's passionate enhancement of the life that is in her ("Thank God you saw that in me!").

In other words, the relation between what in psychoanalysis is called the empirical level (the real-life Vita) and its symbolic representation (the leading character in *Orlando*) is no longer adequate to make sense of the intense transformation that takes place around the field of forces that is activated by Virginia & Vita. The empirical psychology of the two women has nothing to do with this; the psychoanalytic notion of identifications is equally inadequate to account for the magnitude of the exchange that takes place between these two high-powered subjects. This becoming is not about being faithful to the authority of past experience and the solidity of foundations. It is about inventing it together in the space that is framed by the encounter between the two of them out of the transitory flows of multiple and incoherent experiences of all kinds, speeds and intensity, spaces where transformation can occur. The life that flowed between Vita and Virginia certainly was an intensified and accelerated space of becoming.

ETHICS OF SUSTAINABILITY, EROS OF AFFIRMATION

Flesh is only the thermometer of becoming. The flesh is too tender. The second element is not so much bone or skeletal structure, as house or framework. The body blossoms in the house.
—DELEUZE AND GUATTARI, *WHAT IS PHILOSOPHY?*

In the framework of an ethics of joyful affirmation, the dilemma is clear. One oscillates between positive and negative passions, gratification and resentment, gratitude and envy. Ultimately I find that Vita settles for the more ethical option because she transforms negative into positive passions and consents to go along with the process of alchemical transformation of her own life and image, which Virginia has actualized. Vita, too, goes running with Woolves. A transcendence of negative into positive passions is needed here, a qualitative transformation of potentially destructive emotions such as competition, jealousy, and envy. Without such alchemical shift, no affect is sustainable. Potentia can endure only if it receives the feedback of positive and life-enhancing charges. And both V & V want their passion to endure because it provides intensity and added meaning to their lives. It also does engender, in a nonprofit manner, written work that will in turn endure.

In other words, one's affirmation of the life that one is shot through with is materially embodied and embedded in the singularity that is one's enfleshed self. But this singular entity is collectively defined, interrelational, and external: it is impersonal but highly singular because it is crossed over with all sorts of "encounters" with others and with multiple cultural codes, bits, and pieces of the sticky social imaginary that constitutes the subject by literally gluing it together, for a while at least. This is not an atomized individual, but a moment in a chain of being that passes on, goes through the instance of individuation, but does not stop there; it moves on nomadically, by multiple becomings: zoe as relentless vitality.

If instead of conceptualizing fluid identities spatially, one also projects them temporally as moments of being (following Virginia Woolf), the coherence and the unity of the self appear as the result of repetition, of orchestrated returns. Virginia Woolf knows this not only intuitively but also because her own psychopathology opens her eyes to the fragility of Life. It also made it imperative for her to find some balance, some stability within the exhausting roller coaster of her embodied fluctuating self. Relationships, especially her lifelong love for Vita, were simultaneously stimulants and stabilizers: points of impact that could cause internal catastrophes (strong passions, unfulfilled desires, jealousy, etc.), but also points of harmony that could engender the bliss of sustainable intensity.

Moments: spatiotemporal zones, chronotropes, fleeting and contingent. They are just enough, however, to get her through the day, through to the next book, the second-last diary entry, the last letter to Vita. Just enough, till Virginia could not take it anymore and decided to walk back into her liquid element; death by water. For someone who had made fluency and fluidity into more than a style, they were her mode of relation. This partiality, this fluid interactivity is the stuff coherence can be made of, if by coherence we do not mean the despotic solidity of a relational self or the hierarchically ordained implementation of a moral agency. Coherence is a matter for a posteriori, external, relational, and momentary synchronizations. One's ability to remember it and reconstruct it as a unified block is the necessary, albeit delusional, expression of a yearning for a unity, a self-presence, that is not within reach of the humans of today—if ever it was. Molar memory tricks us into believing that the self is a linear, self-present entity. A molecular nomadic countermemory knows, however, that this is not the case. "It will have been me" is the mode that best expresses the impersonality and yet also, paradoxically, the deep faithfulness of the self—a self that endures, that painfully and joyfully goes on. That capacity to endure is collective; it is to be shared. It is held together by narratives, stories, exchanges, shared emotions, and affects. It is neither equal to itself nor does it guarantee self-perpetuation. It is a moment in a process of becoming; as Virginia Woolf puts it: "But when we sit together, close . . . we melt into each other with phrases. We are edged with mist. We make an unsubstantial territory" (Woolf 1977a:11).

There is something extremely familiar and almost self-evident about these processes of transformation of the self through an other who triggers processes of metamorphosis of the self. That is precisely the point. What happens is really a relocation of the function of the subject through the joining of memory and the imagination into propelling a vital force that aims · at transformation.

As the case of Virginia and Vita shows, however, the ethical moment is not so much the ascetic withdrawal from the world of negativity; of potestas with its quick, short-term, hit-and-run successes. It rather rests in the act of transcending the negativity itself, transforming it into something positive. This transformation is only possible if one does not sit in judgment either upon oneself or upon others, but rather recognizes within oneself the difficulties involved in not giving into the paranoid-narcissistic self-nexus. In fact, it is only at the point of utter destitution of one's "self" that the activity of transformation of negativity can actually be undertaken.

This effort requires endurance—some pain and some time—but it also calls for creativity, insofar as one needs to provide precisely what one does not immediately dispose of: positive passions. They have to be created in a process of patient cultivation of and efforts toward the kind of interaction with others that is likely to generate productive ethical relations. Affirmation, the result of a process of transformation of negative into positive passions, is essentially and intrinsically the expression of joy and positivity. This is constitutive of the potentia of the subject. Such potency, however, is a virtuality, which needs to be materialized in very concrete, embodied conditions of expression. Bringing about such movements or a mass of affectivity is crucial to the process of becoming as actualization. The ethical moment consists in overcoming the slight sense of shame, the ethical nausea that marks the recognition of the intrinsically negative structure of one's passions. In other words, the ethical act consists in relinquishing the paranoid-narcissistic ego and installing instead an open ended, interrelational self.

It is the empowerment of the positive side that marks the ethical moment of transformation, the reversal of the negative dialectic and its eternal repetitions, the transcendence of one's starving ego. What matters most is the process by which the transformation takes place, which is neither painless nor self-evident. Hence the importance of literature, the arts, theater, music, and film. They do not fulfill merely an illustrative function, but they are the privileged field of application for the kind of conceptual creativity that Deleuze would like to make operative also within philosophy. What is expressed as a result of this process is a force of affirmation, the potency of a joy that goes beyond the metaphysical divide of sexual or other forms of differentiation. And yet the affirmation of that life force requires as its inalienable and inevitable starting point, the process of becoming-woman. It requires it of Virginia & Vita, as it does of Deleuze, indeed, of any reader.

Paradoxically, this requires also the recognition of the impersonality of the many forces that compose us. Sustaining them, so as to endure positive changes, is the key political and ethical concern of an era of transition like ours. Finding adequate representation for these processes is a challenge for all thinking beings. One that is best met not by critique, but by taking the risk of creativity. A risk that may involve the kind of cognitive and affective stutter that shatters all uncertainties and opens the doors of perception to multiple lines of unexpected possibilities. Changes of this magnitude mark qualitative shifts and internal forms of mobility. They can happen anytime, anywhere, and whenever subjects become events or assemblages. Then Virginia Woolf's moth flutters its wings and "Life" rushes onto you with intensive, untimely, and unending vitality.

POSTGENDER: INTENSIVE GENRE

Life (bios-zoe) has no brandname on it, nor does it have a price-tag attached to it. It does not flow within the constraints of a phallogocentric scheme of signification that imposes its old narrative: desire as lack, alterity and/as negativity, the burden of Being that coincides with consciousness. None of this applies any longer. Psychoanalysis cannot do justice to these kinds of concrete and highly singular processes of becoming. We are better off seeing Virginia & Vita as a transversal block of becoming, a plane for the realization of forces that transcend them both and yet require their presence and affinity in order to become actualized. Forces that are concentrated, focused, and activated in the space between them and aim at the fulfillment of their own potentia. These forces are the accelerations of pure becoming.

Three concepts are crucial here. The first concerns the irrelevance of the category "same sex" to account for the complex and multiple affects generated in the relation between two beings. Virginia and Vita may happen to be two morphological empirical embodied subjects, and yet the space of becoming that connects them is complex, multiple, and multilayered. A polymorphous and highly sexual text such as *Orlando* is the perfect manifesto for it. The homophobic assumption that same-sex relationships cause fusion and confusion insofar as they fail to establish sufficiently strong boundaries of alterity is flatly rejected by the experience of high singularity and intense definition that emerges from the encounter of Virginia with Vita. The fact that Virginia and Vita meet within this category of sexual "sameness" encourages them to look beyond the delusional aspects of the identity ("women") they supposedly share. This proliferation of differences between women, and within each one of them, is evident in the outcomes and products of their relationship, be it in the literature Virginia and Vita produced or in the many social, cultural, and political projects they were engaged in. These included marriages, motherhood and child rearing, political activism, socializing, campaigning, publishing and working as a publisher, gardening and the pursuit of friendships, of pleasures, and of hard work.

Virginia and Vita propose an ethical model where the play of sameness-difference is not modeled on the dialectics of masculinity and femininity; it is rather an active space of becoming, which is productive of new meanings and definitions. It is in this spirit that Irigaray praises the specific instance of feminine homosexuality as a moment of high symbolic significance in confirming a woman's sense of self-worth. This primary narcissism, this love of one-self as reflected in the eyes of another who is morphologically "the same," is, according to the early Irigaray, a necessary precondition to the affirmation of a positive difference that repairs the symbolic damage suffered by women in a phallogocentric system. This is no essentialism, but rather a molecular, transversal space of formation of collectively sustained microsingularities.

In other words, sexuality deterritorializes and undoes the actual gender of the people it involves in the process of becoming. The assemblage composed by Virginia & Vita as blocks of becoming is postgender but not beyond sex—it is actually deeply embedded in sexuality and can be best understood in relation to neovital politics. An important question that can be raised here is: what happens to gender if sexuality is not based on oppositional terms? what happens when there is sexuality without the possibility of heterosexual or homosexual union? (MacCormack 2008). What happens is vitalist erotics, which includes intensive deterritorializations, unhealthy alliances, hybrid cross-fertilizations, productive anomalies, and generative encounters.

The second remark is that the disappearance of firm boundaries between self and other, in the love encounter, in intense friendship, in the spiritual experience, as in more everyday interpersonal connections, is the necessary premise to the enlargement of one's fields of perception and capacity to experience. In pleasure as in pain, in a secular, spiritual, erotic mode that combines at once elements from all these, the decentering and opening up of the individual ego coincides not only with communication with other fellow human beings but also with a heightening of the intensity of such communication. This shows the advantages of a nonunitary vision of the subject. A depersonalization of the self, in a gesture of everyday transcendence of the ego, is a connecting force, a binding force that links the self to larger internal and external relations. An isolated vision of the individual is a hindrance to such a process.

The third comment is that such sets of interconnections or encounters constitute a project, which requires active involvement and work. Desire is never a given. Rather, like a long shadow projected from the past, it is a forward-moving horizon that lies ahead and toward which one moves. Between the no longer and the not yet, desire traces the possible patterns of becoming. These intersect with and mobilize sexuality, but never stop there as they construct space and time and thus design possible worlds by allowing the unfolding of ever-intensified affects. Desire sketches the conditions for the future by bringing into focus the present, through the unavoidable accident of an encounter, a flush (Woolf 1993), a sudden acceleration that marks a point of nonreturn. Call it falling in love, if you wish, but only if you can rescue the notion from the sentimental banality into which it has sunk in commercial culture. Moreover, if falling in love it is, it is disengaged from the human subject that is wrongly held responsible for the event. Here love is an intensive encounter that mobilizes the sheer quality of the light and the shape of the landscape. Deleuze's remark on the grasshoppers flying in at five P.M. on the back of the evening wind also evokes nonhuman cosmic elements in the creation of a space of becoming. This indicates that desire designs a whole territory, and thus it cannot be restricted to the mere human persona that enacts it. We need a postanthropocentric theory of both desire and love in order to do justice to the complexity of subjects of becoming.

The final point concerns the specificity of the intensive genre and its relevance as an analytical tool by which we can assess the ethical impact of texts, regardless of their formal characteristics and categorizations as either scientific/artistic/philosophical or otherwise. As Deleuze and Guattari argue in their analysis of Woolf, it is the expressive potency of the text that counts, that is, the transversal force of an intensive genre that displaces such categories and demands instead an ethology of forces as system of indexation of what a text is capable of mobilizing and actualizing in the ways of affects, concepts, and percepts.

Vita herself does justice to this process of intensive deterritorialization by accepting to become other than she is, engaging with great generosity with her own reflected image. Fulfilling the nomadic prophecy, she ends up becoming her conceptual persona: thus she becomes a mere reader and not the main star of the process of becoming-Orlando. Being an aristocrat, and a much celebrated author in her own right, this displacement required some humility and flexibility on Vita's part. Qualities of which we know she was notoriously deficient. Yet she displays surprising skills of adaptation by letting her narcissism be gratified: "I love myself as Orlando!" but simultaneously blown to smithereens, not only in the sense of "I will never have been as fascinating and complex as Orlando" but also "Orlando is the literary creation of a woman who is a much greater writer than I will ever be!"

Thus it is Vita's shameful recognition of her failing, not the jubilant assertion of her triumph, which opens the gates through which flows the intensity that shapes the encounter between Virginia & Vita. The moment of negative passion (envy, resentment, feeling of dispossession) is the prelude to the ethical gesture that involves transcending the negativity and accepting the displacement of the self through the impact of an other that is so very close. This is a case of destitution of the ego, not of its triumphant apotheosis. This is also the ethical moment in their interaction, which rescued *Orlando* from being an act of cannibalistic consumption of the other and turns it into one of the greatest love stories of all times. Similarly, Virginia's self-effacement is crucial to the whole process of being able to sustain, provoke, record, and return the life that is in Vita, amplified to the nth power. Such is the task of potentia and such is the genius of Virginia Woolf's writing.

7

POSTSECULAR PARADOXES

n this chapter I will explore the posthumanist predicament from the so-called postsecular angle and from different but intersecting perspectives. The theme is wide-ranging and includes the impact of extremism on all monotheistic religions in a global context of neoconservative politics and perpetual war, the proliferation of new or alternative religions, and the quest for ethical values in ways that are attuned to the complexities and contradictions of our era. The first part of the chapter offers a sort of cartography of postsecular discourses and practices, with special emphasis on feminist issues. The second develops a theoretical argument that the postsecular predicament stands for a vision of consciousness that links critique to affirmation, instead of negativity, and that it shows traces of residual spirituality as well as a distinctly planetary dimension.

INTRODUCTION: THE RETURN OF MASTER NARRATIVES

The common trait of the new contemporary master narratives is the return of different forms of determinism, be it the neoliberal or the genetic brand: the former defends the superiority of capitalism, the latter the total authority of the DNA. As we saw in the earlier sections of this book, advanced capitalism thrives at the convergence between the two, investing in "Life itself"

POSTSECULAR PARADOXES 171

(Rose 2001) and spinning quantitative differences into a consumerist mode. The same opportunistic emphasis on difference is also discursively produced in the dominant political ideologies of today. Both neoliberalism and resurgent nationalism are differential value systems that celebrate, rather than denigrate, the power of difference. In these conservative discourses, however, difference is essentialized and reattached to unitary identities and consolidated traditions. In the xenophobic social climate of contemporary Europe, these traditional values once again produce hierarchies of identities, cultures, and even civilizational belongings. In other words, the deterministic reassertion of differences introduces structural patterns of mutual exclusion at the national, regional, provincial, or even more local level. These master narratives are not "new" in any historical or theoretical sense, but they have gained a renewal of interest and a new momentum in the present context, under the combined impact of the new technologies and the triumphant, post–cold war neoliberal belief in the capitalist market economy as the allegedly highest form of human evolution.

Alain Touraine describes this phenomenon as *la pensée unique,* that is to say a de facto hegemony of a neoliberal orthodoxy, which denies "the existence of autonomous social actors capable of influencing political decision-making" (Touraine 2001:1). Arguing forcefully that globalization has not dissolved our collective capacity for political action, Touraine calls for renewed social activism. Cultural identities and legal citizenship constitute the "immaterial" elements of global capitalism (Hardt and Negri 2000) and therefore can also provide the sites for active forms of political resistance. In the same political spirit, Donna Haraway stresses the quasi-monopoly exercised upon our cultures by: "the status of bio-technology in the transition from the economics and the biology of the Cold War era to the New World Order's secular theology of enhanced competitiveness and ineluctable market forces" (Haraway 1997:90).

Nothing expresses this cultural climate of political restoration better than the media's insistence on celebrating, with an insuppressible glee, "the end of ideologies." For the last twenty years I have sat through regular waves of celebration of the multiple deaths of every available "ideology." So much so that I am almost tempted to define ideologies as movements that never cease to end. When will a new one actually be born? The empathic reiteration of the decline of "ideology" finds its latest incarnation in the 1989 fall of the Berlin Wall. It inevitably translates into a one-way political message, namely, that all programs of change have failed, especially Marxism, communism, socialism, and feminism—hence people can now relax and carry on with the normal task of minding their own business. A hasty, and, in my opinion, fallacious dismissal of radicalism results in reasserting the banality of self-interest as a lesser and necessary evil. This moral apathy is the necessary component of neoconservative political liberalism.

This position finds a popular counterpart in academic discourse, in a generalized fatigue with "high theory." On the right of the political spectrum, this translates into downright anti-intellectualism, and the antitheoretical edge of "politics as usual" results in neopositivism, neorealism, and rampant political conservatism. In what's left of the left, however, it produces slightly more resentment-orientated reactions.[1] In the present intellectual climate of post-theory, former adepts of left-wing politics argue that the time of high speculative theories is over and we need to return to "real" concrete politics and even to direct action. This assumes that high theory today just adds an extra layer of complications that is optional rather than necessary and, in any case, redundant in the present context.

Equally problematic for feminists is the fact that "difference" is confined to the past: all differences are flattened out in a shift of perspective that encourages us to move beyond race, gender, and sexuality to construct a future beyond difference. In response, nomadic theory stresses difference as the principle of not-one, so as to remind us that difference is not a concept but a process. It, moreover, is not a simple additive, or something you can join, but rather a permanent fracture, a split form within: not a utopian future world awaiting our engagement, but a people we are missing right here and now.

Paradoxes, however, multiply all along the way. The same postindustrial culture that triumphantly asserts the end of ideology, defined as the desire for social justice, simultaneously frustrates and defeats the very conservative dreams that it so perversely aroused. For instance, the much-celebrated phenomenon of globalization and of its technologies accomplishes a magician's trick: it combines the euphoric celebration of *new* technologies, *new* economy, *new* life styles, *new* generations of both human and technological gadgets, *new* wars, *new* biogenetic patents, and *new* weapons with the utter social rejection of change and transformation. In a totally schizophrenic double pull, the consumerist and socially enhanced faith in the "new" is supposed not only to fit in with but also actively to induce the rejection of in-depth changes. The potentially innovative, deterritorializing impact of the new technologies is hampered and turned down by being indexed to the gravitational pull of traditional and dominant values.

As I stated in the earlier part of this volume, the other complex feature of these new master narratives is the ability to take "differences" into a spin, making them proliferate with an aim to ensure maximum profit (Hardt and Negri 2000). Advanced capitalism is a difference engine—a multiplier of de-territorialized differences that are packaged and marketed under the labels of "new, hybrid and multiple or multicultural identities." It is important to explore how this logic triggers a vampiric consumption of "others," in contemporary social and cultural practice. From fusion cooking to "world music," the consumption of "differences" is a dominant cultural practice. Jackie Stacey, in her analysis of the new organic food industry (Franklin, Lury, and Stacey 2000), argues that we literally eat the global economy. Paul Gilroy reminds us that we also wear it, listen to it and watch it on our many screens, on a daily basis (Gilroy 2000).

Fortunately (as I argued in chapters 1–4), otherness remains firmly grounded also as the site of production of countersubjectivities. Feminist, postcolonial, black, youth, gay, lesbian, and transgender countercultures are positive examples of these emergent subjectivities, which are "other" only in relation to an assumed and implicit "same." How to develop a transformative politics by disengaging difference or otherness from the dialectics of Sameness is therefore the challenge. The sexualized bodies of women, gays, lesbians, and transsexuals; the racialized bodies of ethnics or native others, and the naturalized bodies of animals, insects are the interconnected facets of that "constitutive difference" which is currently being restructured in the internally contradictory or schizoid ways of biogenetic capitalism.

The historical era of globalization is the meeting ground on which sameness and otherness or center and periphery confront each other and redefine their interrelation. The changing roles of the former "others" of modernity, namely, women, natives, and natural or earth others, has turned them into powerful sites of social and discursive transformation. Let us remember, with Foucault (1977b), that power is a multilayered concept, which covers both negative or confining methods (potestas) as well as empowering or affirmative technologies (potentia). This means that the paths of transformation engendered by the "difference engine" of advanced capitalism are neither straight nor predictable. They rather compose a zigzagging line of paradoxical options. Thus human bodies caught in the spinning machine of multiple differences at the end of postmodernity become simultaneously disposable commodities to be vampirized and also decisive agents for political and ethical transformation. How to tell the difference between the two modes of "becoming other" is the task of cultural and political theory and practice.

This relocation of "nature" within the opportunistic logic of technologically mediated capitalism also impacts on the public debates about the secular, especially in environmental discourses and practices. For instance, in his conversations with then Cardinal Ratzinger and in his Lodz lecture of April 2005 Habermas displayed clear signs of postsecular anxiety. A sort of cognitive and moral panic has seized the humanistic community under the pressure of the clash of civilizations and the current political economy of fear and terror, on the one hand, and nostalgia and melancholia, on the other (Massumi 1992). Part of this panic is the result of contemporary biotechnological advances. Seldom has the future of human "nature" been the subject of such concern and in-depth discussions by our wise public intellectuals as in our globalized times. Habermas coined the term "postsecular societies" to signal as well the urgency of a critical reconsideration of the function of scientific belief systems in the world today. Fear of genetic manipulations, which Habermas (2003) shares with champions of liberalism like Fukuyama (2002), implicitly endorses one of the axioms of all monotheistic religions, namely, the sacred nature of human life and procreation. This technophobic reaction to our biotechnological progress has led to a return to Kantian moral universalism. This is quite influential in feminist theory, notably through the work of Martha Nussbaum (1999, 2006) and Seyla Benhabib (2002). Much as I welcome the "ethical turn" of these theories, I do not share their liberal individualistic premises and the neo-universalism of their ethical values. I advocate critical distance both on theoretical and political grounds from the ethnocentrism of their position and also the technophobic fear it expresses (Braidotti 2002a, 2006).

Another crucial aspect of the historical contest in which these master narratives circulate is clearly the end of the cold war in the sense of the historical defeat of communism. The impact of this world-historical event on the issue of secularism was enormous and manifold. For one thing, the former Eastern European Churches—from the Orthodox to the Catholic under double leadership of the Polish trade union movement Solidarity and the Polish-born Pope John Paul II played a crucial role in bringing down the iron curtain. This alone shifts the balance of political power between church and state in former Eastern Europe and contributes to a reappraisal of the political relevance of religiously based activism.

Even further, however, what comes under serious questioning is the militant atheism of the Marxist tradition. Resting on Hegel's philosophy of history, Karl Marx saw the dismissal of religion by dialectical reason's unfolding upon human history as an inevitable aspect of human progress and emancipation. Nature and religion, need and superstition are part of the oppressive legacy we need to leave behind. Marx supports the working of reason against "the opium of the masses" as a necessary component of the political project of human liberation. Simone de Beauvoir and the core of European feminism will follow suit.

Incidentally, one of the other giants of European modernity—Sigmund Freud—was equally dismissive of religion. Freud's 1927 classic *The Future of an Illusion* stresses the national, delusional aspects of religious faith. Convinced that some of the more fanatical aspects of religious belief are perpetuated with suspicious vehemence by scientists and members of the research community, Freud warns us against all kinds of fundamentalist faith—be it in religion or in scientific rationality. The father of psychoanalysis advocates the lucid and sobering dismissal of all fanaticism in favor of a more balanced, intellectually pessimistic but morally optimistic approach to the improvement of human affairs.

It is significant, therefore, to note that both Marx and Freud—the two master thinkers of critical theory, are confirmed atheists, convinced of the fact that the historical unfolding of human progress will necessarily eliminate religious faith (Marx) and that humanity will necessarily be better off without it (Freud). The end of the cold war and the defeat of the communist political experiment cast serious doubts over these certainties. The postsecular predicament therefore is also a post-Marxist one and is tied to the post–cold war condition.

NEOLIBERAL POSTFEMINISM

In such a political context, gender politics is in a spin. In institutional settings, feminist activism was replaced by the less confrontational policy of gender mainstreaming, which is a combination of equal opportunities politics as a strategy and of basic feminist empiricism as a method. In society at large, the "postfeminist" wave gives way to neoconservatism in gender relations. The new generations of corporate-minded businesswomen and show business icons disavow any debt or allegiance to the collective struggles of the rest of their sex while the differences in status, access, and entitlement among women are increasing proportionally. Even in the so-called advanced world, women are the losers in the current technological revolutions and the multiple waves of economic upheavals they have engendered.

Postfeminist neoliberalism is a dominant motif; it is a variation on the theme of historical amnesia in that it expresses the rejection of a common connection to other women. Its defining features are the following: firstly it considers financial success or status as the sole indicator of the status of women. Social failure is accordingly perceived as a lack of emancipation, as money alone is taken as the means of freedom. Secondly, it celebrates the global value of profit as the motor of women's progress, in keeping with neoliberal principles. This implies that even the most basic social democratic principle of solidarity is misconstrued as old-fashioned welfare support and dismissed accordingly.

Thirdly, postfeminist liberal individualism is profoundly ethnocentric: it takes the form of a contradictory and racist position, which argues along civilization or ethnic lines (Huntington 1996). It is complicitous with a neoliberal discourse about white supremacy, namely that our women (Western, Christian, mostly white or "whitened" and raised in the tradition of secular Enlightenment) are already liberated and thus do not need any more social incentives or emancipatory policies. "Their women," however (non-Western, non-Christian, mostly not white and not whitened as well as alien to the Enlightenment tradition), are still backward and need to be targeted for special emancipatory social actions or even more belligerent forms of enforced "liberation." This simplistic position, defended by people as different as Cherie Blair in Britain and Ayaan Hirsi Ali in the Netherlands, to name but a few, re-instates a worldview based on colonial lines of demarcation. It fails to see the great gray areas in between the pretentious claim that feminism has already succeeded in the West and the equally false statement that feminism is nonexistent outside this geopolitical region. As far as I am concerned, those in-between degrees of complexity are the only ones that matter, and they should be put at the center of the agenda. This position fails to take into account, for instance, the precious, patient, and pragmatic work accomplished by the women's movements in the world over the last thirty years, also and especially in the non-Western world, such as the Revolutionary Association of Women of Afghanistan (RAWA).

Neoliberal ethnocentrism entails some formidable lapses of memory, which take the form of ignorance of the history of women's struggles and of feminist genealogies. This is expressed, for instance, in the transformation into feminist heroines of women who had explicitly chosen to keep distant from the women's movements in the radical years. This approach has its creative moments, when a posteriori feminist credentials are granted to strong individual personalities, mostly women artists, like Louise Bourgeois, Yoko Ono, or, for that matter, Madonna. It can also empower public figures who happen to be women, like Madeleine Albright, Benhazir Bhutto, or Princess Diana. I would draw the line at Mother Teresa, but some feminist friends have reprimanded me for this lapse into old-fashioned secularism.

The tendency to fabricate new feminist heroines becomes more problematic, however, when it flattens out all other political considerations in order to stress the individual value of women like Margaret Thatcher or Condoleezza Rice independently of their politics and values. In other words, the postfeminist master narrative of neoliberalism has reintroduced the syndrome of "the exceptional woman," which was a recognized topos before the women's movement introduced more egalitarian principles of interconnection, solidarity, and teamwork. The pernicious part of this syndrome is that it not only denies the collective history of women's struggles, but it also fosters a new sense of isolation among women and hence new forms of vulnerability.

Even more problematic is the next step in this process, when the quest for strong and exceptional figureheads stretches back in time, causing revisionist rewriting of history. Right-wing women like Eva Peron are being reformatted as feminist heroines in contemporary popular culture. The most blatant case to date is the reappraisal of the German Nazi supporter and filmmaker Leni Riefenstal and the attempts to pass her off as a model of emancipation. A convinced and unrepentant Nazi, but also a film director and artist of great talent, after the fall of the Nazis, Riefenstal was singled out for the denazification program and her work was banned. She was made to pay for her mistakes far more than Martin Heidegger, Karl Jung, and other Nazi supporters. Nevertheless, I feel moral repulsion and strong political opposition to a single-minded reappraisal of this character solely on the ground of gender politics. Riefenstahl's Nazi sympathies, her personal bond to Hitler, her refusal to acknowledge or apologize for her responsibilities as the main image maker of the Third Reich, and her use of concentration camp prisoners as stand-ins in some of her lighter entertainment features are objectionable on all accounts. Moreover, the current reappraisal of Riefenstal and her fascist aesthetics perpetuates both the myth and the practice of white supremacy under the spurious guise of the emancipation of European women (Sontag 2003; Gilroy 2000). To disconnect feminist politics and genealogies from the practices of racism, anti-Semitism, xenophobia, domination, exclusion, and murderous violence is complicitous with the crimes of the totalitarian regime that women like Riefenstal helped to create. Individualism pushed to such extremes breeds horror.

Not surprisingly, neoliberal postfeminism is oblivious to the structural injustices that are built into the globalization process. It thus contributes to the polarized geopolitical situation of women. This can be rendered through the caricature of world politics today in the shape of, on the one hand, an allegedly "feminised," aging, secular, and feminist Western world—the emblem of which is the European Union, with a more masculine United States of America counterpart to supervise this "clash of civilizations" through its military power and its supreme contempt of international law. In this stereotypical framework, opposition to the West is represented as the allegedly more virile, youthful, masculine, and religious-minded non-Western world, of which Islamic culture is the standard-bearer. Such a clash of civilizations is postulated and fought out on women's bodies as bearers of authentic ethnic identity. Religion and secularism are constructed as opposites in this confrontational discourse, and this opposition, projected upon the bodies of women, gets both sexualized and racialized within a neo-imperial discourse of triumphant sovereignty.

One of the recent emblems of this situation is the burka-clad body of the Afghan woman, in defense of whom so anti-abortionist, archconservative, and antifeminist a president as George W. Bush claimed to launch one of his many commercially driven wars of conquest. What cynic would believe the claim that the war was fought to help out the poor oppressed masses of Islamic women? And why reduce Muslim women to the position of emblems of oppression? And yet this is the political discourse that circulates in the global economical world disorder: one in which reductive sexual difference defined as the specificity of women's marginalized condition is again the terrain on which power politics is postulated.

In the Islamophobic context of the European Union today, in a global climate of economic recession, perpetual war, and anxiety about security, discourses about the emancipation of women, gays, lesbians, and transsexuals have become key political issues. The public debates on these issues tend to focus on Islam and result in the criminalization of Muslims residents and citizens in a way that is reminiscent of the most sinister chapters of European colonial and fascist history. Right-wing politicians in Europe, like Sarkozy in France and Wilders in the Netherlands, have also targeted women's bodies—through the veil, headscarf, and burka debates—as major political issues. This overemphasis on religious and cultural identity allows them to conceal and ignore more grounded and concrete concerns about the social inequality and economic marginalization suffered by Muslim migrants in the European Union today, as Tariq Ramadan rightly points out (Ramadan 2003).

The new wars of the third millennium are also religious crusades that pitch religious fundamentalism as a non-Western, mostly Muslim problem against secular democracy as the defining feature of the Western world in a mutually exclusive and confrontational discourse. This belligerent program is postulated on the bodies of women, gays, lesbians, and transsexuals in that it inscribes sexual emancipation into a nationalist script that asserts Western exceptionalism and its superior standards of governmentality. Both authentic autochthonous femininity and the legal and social emancipation of gays, lesbians, and transsexuals have thus turned into markers of civilizational standards. They get racialized and nationalized within a neo-imperial discourse of triumphant Western sovereignty. This calls for prompt and effective political resistance.

THE POSTSECULAR CONDITION

Originally coined by Jurgen Habermas, the term *postsecular* has been adopted in a broad range of intellectual traditions. Nemoianu (2006) points out that university curricula were quick in picking up and institutionalizing the term. An explicit interest in the spiritual dimension of critical thought was, however, quite noticeable in some strands of the postmodernist tradition, notably in Vattimo's work (2005) and in the late Derrida (2002), influenced by Lévinas's thought on Judaism and alterity. Political philosophy reflects this mood, rediscovering with Derrida the mystical foundations of the law and of political authority or turning toward Schmidt's emphasis on political theology. Explicit references to Saint Paul and the Christian legacy of critical theory have also been made of late by Lyotard (1998), Badiou (1998), Žižek (2000 and 2003), and others.

Another important debate that is implied here concerns Foucault's unfinished work on the construction of ethical subject relations (Foucault 1976, 1984a, b), and I regret being unable to assess it fully. Suffice it to say that the emphasis on political spirituality, which marks a turn in Foucault's work on the technologies of the self and resulted in a reappraisal of pre- and early Christian rituals, protocols, and aesthetics of existence, was prompted by the 1979 Iranian Revolution (Afary and Anderson 2005). Foucault's enthusiastic support for the new political spirituality exemplified by the revolutionary Islamic government of Iran took many by surprise and distressed the feminists at the time, including Beauvoir and Millett. As Foucault never quite took the trouble to address his androcentric bias, this issue remains a problematic knot in Foucault's unresolved relationship to feminism (Diamond and Quinby 1988; Braidotti 1991; McNay 1992). Again, I shall not discuss this further here, but the point is taken.

On the other hand, loyal to his civic republicanism and Kantian/universalistic framework, Jurgen Habermas defends the right of all religious discourses to play a role in public life, provided they are expressed in secular terms and concepts. Habermas thus attempts to strike a middle ground between militant or idealized secularism and religious dogmatism. Nonetheless, the point of consensus between Habermas and the Catholic Church is that the fundamental European concepts of universalistic egalitarianism, civic responsibility, and democracy are directly indebted to Christianity.

That secularism is Christianity's great gift to mankind is the notion that has acquired the status of a new consensus among critical Western intellectuals today. Best expressed in Charles Taylor's idea that we now live in a "secular age," this notion spells the end of the modernity-driven equation between the advance of science and democracy and the retreat of religion into the private sphere (Taylor 2007). A strong and civic-minded believer, Taylor repudiates "exclusive humanism" and wants religious faith restored to a central position in Western societies. In passing, he takes several swipes

at an unnamed group of "postmodernist philosophers" who follow Nietzsche in proclaiming the death of God and a fall into the most predictable
form of moral and cognitive relativism. Arguing that secularism spells a disenchantment with the process of modernization and Western science, Taylor pleads for the reenchantment of our being in the world and the renewal
of our social nexus. Fully predicated on Christian ontology, and supported
by a Hegelian teleology of world history as the linear progression of *the* idea
of man, based on liberal humanism, history proceeds for Taylor by fashion-
ing social imaginaries. These collectively held representations of our shared
value system constitute a background to the explicit expression of beliefs. In
this mindset the social imaginary of secularism is a form of disenchantment.
Taylor's position is a warning call for Westerners to reassess the role they are
willing to give to faith in their social life.

To unveil the Christian roots of what we have uncritically called secularism is for Taylor an urgent political and moral priority. The only reason why this statement is at all newsworthy is that it exposes and provokes
the century-old European habit of open hostility toward religions. One of
the lasting legacies of the Enlightenment, in fact, is to equate religion with
superstition—as Voltaire recommended—and piety with bigotry. Secular
humanism has developed a strong connection to atheism, and our current
practice of secularism sits uncomfortably within this tense legacy. The postsecular predicament marks a crisis of this paradigm, which turned Western
rationalism into a universalistic secular model for the rest of the world. We
are now in a position to take into serious consideration Talal Asad's suggestion (2003) that there may be several quite different definitions and practices
of secularity. By extension, this means that the idealized Western notion of
the secular has to be questioned. A postsecular predicament therefore assumes and, to a certain extent, takes for granted this historical legacy and
builds on it. Thus, Jurgen Habermas's seminal analysis of this historical
condition stresses the significance of the "return" of religion in previously
secularized countries in the Western world. The former axiom that stipu-
lated a direct correlation between the modernization of society and the secularization of its members has been reviewed quite radically.

The "postsecular turn" refers therefore to a change of consciousness,
which acknowledges not only the persistence of religious beliefs and practices but also their compatibility with processes of modernization. Habermas attributes this change of approach to three main factors: firstly, global

conflicts and the war on terror have made Europeans aware of our own relativity with the global horizon. Secondly, religions provide "communities of interpretation" to guide public opinion in difficult moral decisions—euthanasia, reproductive medicine, abortion, animal rights, climate change, etc.—which are the inevitable side effects of our technological development. Thirdly we must consider the impact of migrant communities and refugees, which create "confessional schisms" within secularized societies. In all cases, as Borradori (2003) rightly points out, fundamentalist reactions within the Christian, Islamic, Hindu, or Jewish religions should not be read as a simple return to premodern times. They rather constitute articulate responses and even resistance to the failed premises and broken promises of modernity.

Habermas astutely comments on the difficulty Europe experiences not only in assimilating resident foreigners but also, through recognition of their presence, in accepting our postcolonial status. Religious tolerance should emerge instead as a side effect of this cultural diversity and internal pluralism. The pressures of economic globalization, however, add an extra element of anxiety. As Habermas put it: "The West presents itself in a form deprived of any normative kernel as long as its concern for human rights only concerns the attempt at opening up new free markets and as long as, at home, it allows free reign to the neoconservative division of labour between religious fundamentalism and a kind of evacuating depleting secularization" (Borradori 2003:33).

The key question then becomes for Habermas: how should we see ourselves as members of a postsecular society and what should we reciprocally expect from each other? Recent events such as the assassination of Theo van Gogh in Amsterdam, the affair of the Mohammed cartoons in Denmark, the recent Swiss referendum against building mosques, and the extreme, anti-immigrant measures and deportations of President Sarkozy in France and the Italian Lega Nord are symptoms of Europe's incompetence in dealing with its internal dissonance and with the presence of foreigners in its midst. Moreover, considering the long history of xenophobic suspicion toward the East, the recurring trope of Islamic backwardness cannot be seen as new, but rather as the contemporary variation on a historically established sociocultural theme. The defining feature of the contemporary variation on this theme, however, takes the form of the postsecular return of religion in the public sphere.

The loss of the normative consensus about two interlinked notions: the uniqueness of the Western model of secularism, on the one hand, and the recognition of the Christian roots of European humanism, on the other, results in a crisis that for Habermas is productive, in that it breaks with the more strident aspects of secularism and atheist activism. A more reflexive form of religious consciousness might emerge from this new situation—one that would overcome the political opposition between radical multicultural-ism, which accepts internal diversity and religious pluralism, and "militant secularism"—or "sex-cularism"—which fights for a flat inclusion of all citizens into a common standard regardless of their multiple differences.

Whereas Habermas works with a universalistic and hence gender-neutral notion of citizenship, Joan Scott focuses on the consequences of the projection of the debate on secularism upon the status of Muslim women. The simultaneous sexualization and racialization of this debate emerges as the central problem. Scott's analysis of the controversy over the veil in France (Scott 2007) raises the crucial issue about feminist politics: why so much divisive, obsessive, and aggressive attention to the headscarf? What is it about the headscarf that makes it an abject site of controversy and aberration? The political context accounts for a great deal of these negative political passions. As argued earlier, the clash of civilizations has turned the Islamic veil into a global symbol of patriarchal oppression and cultural and social underdevelopment in the eyes of the West. Scott points out a number of crucial issues that seem forgotten in the debate, namely, only a minority of Muslim women in Europe actually wears the headscarf, the vast majority having assimilated into Western societies and values. Secondly, analogous garments worn by Islamic men (beards, loose clothing) do not seem to evoke as much political rage—and behavior. Thirdly, the headscarf is a contemporary phenomenon, linked to global migration and to the coercive imposition of a Western model of modernization (Roy 1999), and hence it qualifies as "modern" to all ends and purposes. Fourthly, religious behavior and ostentatious display of religious affiliations by Christian groups across Europe do not seem to score as much as a mention in this secularist crusade. To date, Susan Harding (2000) remains a pioneer of feminist criticism of Christian Evangelical fundamentalism.

As a consequence, the facile binary schemes of oppositions offered by the secularists do not suffice: traditional versus modern, fundamentalism versus secularism, church versus state, private versus public, particular versus universal, group versus individual, cultural pluralism versus national unity, identity versus equality. These dichotomies do not capture the complexities of either Islam or "the West." Rather, they are polemics that in fact create their own reality: incompatible cultures, a clash of civilizations, and rising xenophobia.

According to Scott, the real function of the headscarf debate is to provide an oppositional answer to the identity questions thrown open in Europe by economic globalization, the project of European unification, and world migration. These phenomena have eroded the basis of cultural homogeneity and sovereignty on which the European nation-states used to rest and opened a dramatic crisis for Europe's self-representation. In this context, the negative construction of the public figure of the Muslim fundamentalist fulfills a specular function and thus confirms the Europeans in their alleged cultural and social superiority. The body and the status of women is the terrain on which this civilization battle is being fought.

FEMINIST DILEMMAS

I have argued so far that one of the major features of the globalized world is that religion is back with a vengeance. Nietzsche's claim rings hollow across the spectrum of contemporary global politics: God is not dead at all. The monotheistic view of the Divine Being merely slipped out the back window during the passionately secularized second half of the twentieth century, only to return through the front door, with the failed promises of modernization and the clash of civilizations in the third millennium. To present the postsecular turn as a challenge for feminism consequently reveals a number of implicit assumptions about the feminist project itself. Let me explore these feminist dilemmas further, in the hope both of broadening our understanding of the postsecular predicament and of mapping its intersections with feminist politics.

The bulk of European feminism is justified in claiming to be secular in the structural and historical sense of the term. Like other emancipatory philosophies and political practices, the feminist struggle for women's rights in Europe has historically produced an agnostic, if not downright atheist, position. Historically, it descends from the Enlightenment critique of religious dogma and clerical authority. The massive influence exercised by existentialist feminism (Beauvoir 1973) and Marxist or socialist feminisms (Firestone 1970; Rowbotham 1973; Mitchell 1974; Barrett 1980; Davis 1981; Coward 1983; Delphy 1984) on the second feminist wave also accounts for a perpetuation of this position. As the secular and rebellious daughters of the Enlightenment, feminists were raised in rational argumentation and detached self-irony. The feminist belief system is accordingly civic, not theistic and viscerally opposed to authoritarianism and orthodoxy. Feminist politics is also, and at the same time, however, a double-edged vision (Kelly 1979) that combines rational arguments with political passions and creates alternative social blueprints.

Feminists, however, tend to have major paradoxes to offer, as Joan Scott (1996) so eloquently put it. Not the least of these paradoxes is the mixed legacy of the vision of political subjectivity and, more specifically, of the sexual liberation revolution of the 1970s. Not only did this sexual revolution *not* translate into equality across the board of society and culture, but it also had many different historical sources than the second wave of the women's movement. Joan Scott argues that we need multiple genealogies of the sexual liberation movement, for instance, the social factors, birthrate and demography, advances in science, medicine, and technology, economic factors, and postcolonial issues. More importantly, argues Scott, we need to play these multiple and often complex narratives against the dominant teleological tale of emancipation through secularism. This can also help feminists in resisting the hyperbolical rhetoric of the clash of civilization.

My argument builds from this to state that the postsecular turn challenges European political theory in general and feminism in particular because it challenges the axiom that equates secularism with emancipation. A postsecular approach makes manifest the notion that agency, or political subjectivity, can actually be conveyed through and supported by religious piety and may even involve significant amounts of spirituality. This statement has an important corollary—namely, that political agency need not be critical in the negative sense of oppositional and thus may not be aimed solely or primarily at the production of countersubjectivities. Subjectivity is rather a process ontology of autopoiesis, or self-styling, which involves complex and continuous negotiations with dominant norms and values and hence also multiple forms of accountability. This position is defended within feminism by a variety of different thinkers ranging from Harding (2000) to Mahmood

(2005). The double challenge of linking subjectivity to religious agency and of disengaging both from oppositional consciousness and critique defined as negativity is one of the main issues I will address in the rest of this essay. In the conclusion I will raise the issue of the affirmative power of critical theory, to which I will return also in chapter 11.

The corollary of the axiom that equates secularism with emancipation is the belief that women's emancipation is directly indexed upon sexual freedom, in keeping with the European liberal tradition of individual rights and self-autonomy. This is a crucial point, which again stresses the importance of sexuality as the major axis of subject formation in European culture and in its philosophies. Precisely because of the historical importance of sexuality, sexual difference is such a central axis in the formation of identity and of social relations, as I argued in the first few chapters of this book. As Joan Scott recently argued (2007), however, this historically specific model cannot be universalized, and it is the basic fault of contemporary European politicians that they enforce this model and insist on its homogeneity in spite of rising evidence of its contingent and hence partial applicability.

The postsecular predicament forces if not a complete revision, at least a relativization of the dominant European paradigm that equates emancipation with sexual liberation. Scott (2009) subjects to serious historical analysis the common assumption that secularism automatically encourages the sexual self-expression of women and therefore supports their struggle against oppression. At the core of this assumption, argues Joan Scott, is the belief that secularism automatically or by logical necessity produces individual autonomy and by extension it also fosters women's rights. This teleological conviction, however, can be easily refuted by history. Historically—whether we take the French Revolution or the many movements of national liberations, there is no evidence that a concern for the equal status of women was a priority for those who acted to separate church from state. High secularism is essentially a political doctrine of the separation of powers, which has even historically consolidated in Europe as a social consensus about the necessity of separating church from state in matters of religious faith, moral values, and spiritual norms and practices. This vision of secularism has moreover been questioned, and other plausible definitions of the term have been offered, for instance, by anthropology and sociology. The doctrine of separation of powers, however, is prominent in political theory, and I adopt it as such.[2] Furthermore, this tradition of secularism actually introduces a new polarization between religion and citizenship, which is socially enacted in a new partition between a private belief system and a public political sphere. This private/public distinction is gendered and also socialized.

It is an equally clean historical fact that women in Europe have been assigned to both the private domain and to the realm of faith and religion. This traditional attribution of religious faith to women—in opposition to allowing them full political citizenship—grants them a higher entitlement to engage in religious activity than to participate in public affairs. This apparent privilege, however, immediately pales into political insignificance in view of the entrenched sexism of monotheistic religions and their shared conviction of the need to exclude women from the ministry and the administering of women of sacred functions. Furthermore, Scott comments on this historical association of women's religion to point out some more inner contradictions. All the secular contact achieved is a new, reinforced distinction between emotions or unreason (faith, religion, the private sphere) and reason or rational citizenship (the public sphere). Because, in this polarized scheme, women were assigned with distressing regularity to the pole of unreason, passions, and emotions, including religion, these compounded reasons combined to actually reenforce the oppression of women and keep them excluded from the public sphere of citizenship. Therefore, at the historical moment of origin of European secularism, women were not even considered the political equals of men. Hence the necessity to question the "idealized secular" and its political manipulations by politicians and populists today. Most prominent among the questions left unresolved by militant, idealized secularism is "How does secularism posit the relationship between equality and difference? And what are we to make of the fact that, both logically and historically, one does not at all guarantee the other?"

I think there are sobering and important warnings. Considering the binary system that controls the production of gender identities and the constant confinement of women to passion, body, and the unreason, it is crucial to reassert the importance of sexual difference as the principle of not-one (see chapter 2). This means that one single narrative can never suffice to account for sexual difference as a process of sexual differing, which acts, for Scott, as a perennial source of psychic anxiety and, for me, as a permanent internal fracture. The debate over secularism is forcefully being imposed over this complex and unresolved issue through self-congratulatory tales of

European egalitarianism, on the one hand, or warmongering narratives of civilizational crusades on the other. A responsible postsecular feminist position needs to question both those lines. .

CONTEMPORARY POLITICAL TENSIONS

One key aspect of the legacy of feminist European secularism that should be cleared at the start of a new possible dialogue on the postsecular predicament is the issue of anticlericalism. The critique of the church as an institution of power (potestas) has been a persistent feature of the European left and of the emancipatory movements it has supported since the eighteenth century. Voltaire's rallying cry *écrasez l'infame* still sounds credible to most agnostic European ears, especially in relation to the dogmatic and patriarchal attitude of the Catholic Church. The memoirs of the grand old ladies of European feminism are explicit statements of this position (Beauvoir 1992, 1993; Rossanda 2005). I concur with Scott about the established historical connection between the oppression of women and the persistence of religious practices in European history. Feminism has accordingly been secularist by necessity as well as by conviction. There are, however, some major political problems with these ideas in the global context today. All the problems come down to the political context. Because "the clash of civilizations" is Islamophobic in character and has triggered a wave of anti-Muslim intolerance in the flat sense of the return of religion across Europe and the world, public discussions on the postsecular condition tend to concentrate almost exclusively on Islam, making it the most targeted of monotheistic religions. This reduction of the postsecular condition to the "Muslim issue," in a context of a war on terror that results in the militarization of the social space, means that any unreflective brand of normative secularism runs the risk of complicity with anti-Islam racism and xenophobia. What is needed, therefore, is a more balanced kind of analysis and diversified approach that includes all the monotheistic religions and contextualizes them within shifting global power relations.

Moreover, because of the sexual nationalism of the current European debates about Islam and the extent to which the status of women, gays, lesbians, and transsexuals and the degrees of their emancipation has become part of the geopolitical "clash of civilizations," feminists and queer activists cannot be simply secular or be secular in a simple or self-evident sense. More complexity is needed in the debate about women's, gays', lesbians', and transsexuals' self-determination and agency. The lessons imparted by postcolonial and race studies are crucial to this discussion, and their intersection with feminist politics absolutely necessary. Similarly, the European dimension of the debate is paramount, including the shifting structures of European Union–based citizenship (Balibar 2001).

In this context a reductive and ethnocentric secularist position was often taken up by significant European feminists, such as Elizabeth Badinter (2002) in France, public figures like Ciska Dresselhuys and Ayaan Hirsi Ali in the Netherlands and Oriana Fallaci in Italy (2004), often striking a strident and aggressive note. This is an objectionable position not only because it is racist but also in terms of its failure to acknowledge the historical specificity of the phenomenon of postsecularism in the world today. This means that some feminists' visceral reaction against the postsecular turn is a serious misreading. It is as if some of them had fallen into bad dreams of their own, as if they were reliving the memories of their struggles against the Christian and mostly Catholic Church on the back of the Muslim headscarves debate or the never-ending discussions about the veil. By contrast, the rising popularity of the Christian-backed new virginity and sexual abstinence movements in the Western world seems to evoke less anxiety among vintage feminists.[3] It is urgent therefore to develop more accurate cartographies of the specific postsecular conjuncture they are currently caught in.

Religious extremism and the politically conservative return of God is a feature of all monotheistic religions today. This multilayered process encompasses policy making at the global level, including the UN organizations; widespread and capillary social networks of religious activism at grassroot levels throughout the world, also in the so-called advanced world (Harding 2000); and the use of violence, both military and guerrilla. In other words, the crisis of secularism amidst both second- and third-generation descendants of Muslim immigrants and amidst born-again and born-that-way Christians is a phenomenon that takes place within the social and political horizon of late globalized postmodernity, not in premodern times. It is of here and now. Even Sam Huntington (1996) recognizes this important aspect.

This is clearly evidenced by the comeback of Christian and religious militantism all over the world, in the public arena, beyond the boundaries of the private spiritual domain. When he was still only Cardinal Ratzinger, Pope Benedict the Sixteenth had already declared Nietzsche his own personal enemy. Today, he joins forces with the Evangelical Protestants' "born-again" fanaticism in leveling the charge of moral and cognitive relativism against any project that challenges the traditional, Christian, and humanistic view of the moral subject. This *doxa* or common belief stresses the necessity of strong foundations, like an unequivocally binary gender system, as the basic points of reference that guarantee human decency, moral and political agency, and ethical probity.

Solidified in these beliefs, the religious hard-line offensive operates a number of disjunctions: it separates women from mothers and rewards the latter, but also subjugates them to the rights of the embryo and the child. It also separates gays from humanity, depriving them of the right to have rights—which is the basic definition of human rights. The forceful collapse of human sexuality with reproduction demonizes all forms of homo- and transsexuality, while campaigning against contraception, family planning, and nonmarital sex of all kinds. It also produces the absurd proposal that abstinence is the cure for the HIV epidemic, which is spreading not only in sub-Saharan Africa, as everyone knows—but also in former Eastern Europe and especially the Baltic states, as most choose to ignore. Finally, Christian and other religious militants attack contemporary science on two fronts, biogenetics, or genetic technologies, and evolutionary theories, to which they oppose contemporary variations on the theme of creationism and obscurantism.

As a result of this radicalization of global politics in an age of constant warfare, aggressively polarized sexual difference has returned to the world stage in a fundamentalist and reactionary version, reinstating a worldview based on colonial lines of demarcation. This produces the dominant dichotomy I analyzed before between "our women"—Western, Christian, white or "whitened" and raised in the tradition of secular Enlightenment—who are already liberated and "their women"—non-Western, non-Christian, and alien to the Enlightenment tradition—who need help to liberate themselves.

The manipulative exploration of the status of women as markers of lines of civilizational distinctions is, paradoxically enough, reiterated with distressing regularity by the non-Western opponents of advanced capitalism. This type of polarization results in mutual and respective claims about authentic and unitary female identity on the part of the allegedly "liberated"

West and of its traditionalist opponents. They are mirror images of each other, and each fails to take into account the productive and pragmatic work accomplished by the women's movements over the last thirty years, also in the non-Western world. Both delete the feminist political agendas.

The manipulation of feminist and gay rights by right-wing politicians in Europe today is reinforced by the anti-intellectualism of the present political context. On the aftermath of the attacks on the World Trade Center, the U.S. government wasted no time in declaring that academics are the "weak link" in the war against terror. Being suspected of disloyalty to their culture and lack of patriotism is not new for critical thinkers, feminists, and antiracists, though the recent campaign does leave the century-old tradition of "academic freedom" in tatters. In such a context, academic debates have become simultaneously less relevant to the public sphere and infinitely more important as a statement of freethinking. They also constitute a political gesture of resistance, considering the militarization of the social space I have already mentioned and the subsequent erosion of civil liberties and democratic accountability. Feminist academic debates on the postsecular are no exception, but their impact is seriously hampered today.

There are also internal problems: one of the most problematic aspects of the current academic debates is the systematic sidelining of feminist scholarship in the discussions about globalization, the war on terror, and religious extremism. The extent of antifeminism in academic discourse today is surprising, and it deserves more specific analysis. It is made all the more paradoxical by the fact that gender and sexual difference issues are so central to global politics and contemporary forms of nationalism (Yuval-Davis and Anthias 1989).

THE CONCEPTUAL PARADOXES

Two main questions are left begging in the previous section: firstly, how secular has European feminism been, historically? Secondly, what counts as "European" for the sake of this debate? Let us consider the counterarguments.

Developing alongside but in antagonism to the mainstream secularist line, other feminist traditions have been thriving. Various schools of feminist spirituality and alternative spiritual practices have a long and established history in Europe and elsewhere. Major writers in the feminist tradition, especially in the U.S., notably Audre Lorde (1984), Alice Walker (1984), and Adrienne Rich (1987), acknowledge the importance of the spiritual dimension of women's struggle for equality and symbolic recognition. The work of Mary Daly (1973), Elizabeth Schussler Fiorenza (1983), and Luce Irigaray (1990), to name but a few, highlights a specific feminist tradition of nonmale-centered spiritual and religious practices.

Feminist theology in the Christian (Keller 1998), Muslim (Wadud 1999; Tayyab 1998), and Jewish(Adler 1998) traditions has produced well-established communities of both critical resistance and affirmation of creative alternatives. Across the great monotheistic religions, feminist theologians have produced taxonomy of core issues for their field, including a critique of the holy laws, a hermeneutics of the sexism in the holy texts, and a call for new rituals and ceremonies. Among these, the witches' movement, currently best exemplified by Starhawk (1999) and ·reclaimed by the epistemologist Stengers (1997), stresses the importance of countertheological heresy, blasphemy, and sacrilege as part of the feminist project. In our technologically mediated world, neopagan elements have also emerged in cyberculture and various brands of posthuman techno-asceticism (Halberstam and Livingston 1995; Epps 1996; Braidotti 2002a).

All the nonsecularists stress the deep spiritual renewal that is carried by and implicit in the feminist cause, insisting that it can be of benefit to the whole of mankind and not only to the females of the species (Russell 1974). This humanist spiritual aspiration is ecumenical in nature and universalist in scope.

Black and postcolonial theories have never been loudly secular. In the very religious context of the U.S., African American women's literature is filled with references to Christianity; black feminist and critical theory have been postsecular for a long time, as bell hooks (1990) and Cornell West (1994) demonstrate. Furthermore, postcolonial and critical race theories today have developed nontheistic brands of situated neohumanism. Examples are Paul Gilroy's planetary cosmopolitanism (2000), Avtar Brah's diasporic ethics (1996), Edouard Glissant's poetics of relations (1990), Ernesto Laclau's micro-universal claims (1995), Homi Bhabha's "subaltern secularism" (1994), Vandana Shiva's antiglobal neohumanism (1997), as well as the rising wave of interest in African humanism or Ubuntu, from Patricia Hill Collins (1991) to Drucilla Cornell (2004).

Edward Said (1978) was among the first to alert critical theorists in the Western tradition to the need to develop a reasoned account of Enlightenment-based secular humanism, which would weigh the colonial experience, its violent abuses and structural injustice, as well as postcolonial existence (Bhabha 1994). French poststructuralist philosophers, while upholding philosophical distance from religious orthodoxy, also argued that, in the aftermath of colonialism, Auschwitz, Hiroshima, and the Gulag—to mention but a few of the horrors of modern history—Europeans need to develop a critique of Europe's delusion of grandeur in positing themselves as the moral guardian of the world and as the motor of human spiritual and technological evolution. This line is pursued in philosophy by Deleuze's rejection of the transcendental vision of the subject (1968) and emphasis on radical immanence, Irigaray's decentering of phallologocentrism (1974); Foucault's critique of European humanism (1975), Derrida's deconstruction of the center (1997), and Glissant's critique of Eurocentrism (1990).

Consequently we can detect several intersecting lines of questioning the secular legacy of European culture and philosophy. The antihumanism of some social and cultural critics within a Western poststructuralist perspective can be read alongside the cosmopolitan neohumanism of contemporary race, postcolonial, and non-Western critics. Both these positions, all other differences notwithstanding, produce inclusive alternatives to humanist individualism and uncritical secularism. Without wishing to flatten out structural differences, nor to draw easy analogies between them, there is much to be gained by trying to synchronize their critical efforts and respective political aims and reground claims to connections and transversal alliances among different postsecular constituencies. A minimum line of questioning should be the one I indicated earlier: "how secular have we been?" And also: "is the model of secularism derived from Christianity the only, let alone, the best one?"

There is another conceptual angle to this discussion and it concerns the residual spirituality of critical theory. Let us start by returning to the idea I presented at the start of this chapter as a sort of new consensus—defended by Habermas and Taylor that the dominant notion of secularism defined as contractual agreement or respect for the Law is in fact a secular distillation of Judeo-Christian precepts. Instead of following the conservative postsecularist position that argues that—as a consequence—respect for human rights, equality, and democracy, which lie at the core of European modernity and its emancipatory projects are implicitly religious, albeit by negation—other possible lines of thought emerge. One of them, based on nomadic immanence, is that the value system of European secular humanism needs not—either by logical or social necessity—be coupled to a unitary vision of the autonomous subject of literal humanism. On the contrary, a nomadic vision of the subject as a transversal assemblage and a nonteleological vision of human evolution shifts the debate in very innovate ways.

Firstly, it exposes the hegemonic power of the idea that secularism is an indirect offshoot of Christianity. It is rather the case that, as William Connolly (1999) astutely remarked, this specific brand of secularized humanism has passed itself off as the embodiment of universalism, thus achieving paradigmatic value and absolute moral authority as well as the social status of a dominant norm. This paradigm is now being challenged, and we can rightfully speak of three interrelated consequences. The first is that the Christian-derived notion of secularism is not only very culture specific and not universal or unique. The second is that it is linked both historically and conceptually to the vicissitudes of Western modernity and the models of citizenship and subjectivity it engendered. Thirdly, this is not the only model of modernization. We need to acknowledge the partiality of secular frames of mind, both in classical philosophy and in contemporary critical theory.

The second innovative force of a nomadic postsecular position concerns the need to acknowledge the residual spirituality that animates the very project of thinking and to create new cartographies suited to the complexities of our times. This can be achieved by avoiding reverse dialectical thinking. For instance—the axiom that Western secularism is predicated on the rational distinction between faith and reason, institutionalized in the separation of church from state and the division of powers between the judiciary, the legislative, and the religious authorities. It need not lead to the conclusion that a negation is still a powerful mode of relation and that therefore many Westerners are secular by default. What can also follow from exactly the same premise is that we need to acknowledge not only the persistence of emotional, irrational, spiritual elements in thinkers of all political persuasion but also their fundamentally productive nature.

In the absence of such acknowledgment, the debate is caught in an oppositional logic of negation. The Eurocentric argument runs like this: without Judeo-Christian tradition there is no progressive emancipation and therefore no secularism and hence no postsecular condition. A double negation engenders the inevitable positivity of the excluded term. This line of reasoning would consequently leave Islam in the singular position of being the one monotheistic religion positing subjectivity without the need for secularist distinctions. By extension, Islam would then have no claim to modernity, emancipation, or human rights. This, as Gellner noted (1992), is not only far from unproblematic but also historically false.

Thirdly, the feminist dilemmas can get framed differently, in a political approach that starts from nonunitary subject positions, on the one hand, and the proliferation of processes of sexualization/racialization/naturalization, on the other. The general question then can best be stated as a constructive paradox: how to explain that some of the most pertinent critiques of advanced capitalism today and of the structural injustices of globalization are voiced by religiously driven social movements? The feminist issue is even more complex: in the allegedly civilization debates I reported earlier, conservative Western politicians depicted a self-congratulatory view of the status of women, gays, and lesbians in the Western world in order to justify their manipulative politics of polarization and neo-imperial warfare against the Muslim world. This depiction is deficient and misleading in terms of the history of women's struggle for citizenship rights in Europe and elsewhere in the Western world, let alone on the global scale. In fact, issues related to women's political participation and full citizenship remains unresolved and highly controversial: did European women have Enlightenment? Did the universal declaration of human rights apply to women and other minorities? Or is it rather the case that feminist struggles to achieve basic rights constitute the undercurrent of European modernity? That to feminists since Wollstonecraft the promise of Liberty, Equality, and Fraternity sounds rather hollow, even though the process of secularization prompted by the Enlightenment liberated public space for women to participate as active citizens? Such participation was never granted willingly and had to be wrenched violently through organized struggle and resistance. The struggle is still ongoing and very much unfinished even among mainstream Europeans. To deny it would be adding insult to injury.

How are feminists and gay activists to react to the foregrounding of women and gays in a postsecular civilizational debate that is really about the social/sexual contract (Pateman 1988) and the limits of a certain practice of citizenship? The following steps need to be reasserted in order to recast this debate about the public sphere in less ethnocentric and reductive terms. Firstly, that the modernization processes and the emancipation of women is still in process in the West. Secondly, and as a result, that no simple polarizations can be made between an allegedly progressive Judeo-Christian tradition and the allegedly backward Muslim one. Thirdly, the notion has to be considered that the Western modernization model may not be the only or the best one: multiple modernities are actually at stake (Eisenstadt 2000). Therefore, and in conclusion, that different form of secularism may be engendered by multiple models of modernity. This allows us to venture the idea that the postsecular condition is quite diverse and internally differentiated. Incidentally, I want to suggest that we adopt this multiethnic and complex notion of diversity as the standard definition of what counts as European today (Braidotti 2006).

Fourthly, the vitalist approach of matter-realism I have been defending in this book, with its reliance on a monistic ontology and the notion of intelligent and self-organizing or autopoietic matter, supports a nonessentialist and nontheistic reappraisal of the spiritual as a generative factor for critical theory. Contrary to those who dismiss this approach as neomystical (Žižek 2004; Hallward 2006), I will argue forcefully for its materialist or rather "matter-realist" structure as radical immanence and perpetual becoming. Let me expand on this next, by taking a detour away from nomadic subjectivity, but only in order to return to it with fresher arguments.

SECULARISM AND ITS DISCONTENTS

One way we can register the postsecular dimension of critical theory is to look for the missing links between political subjectivity, religion, and active citizenship. I want to suggest that one of these missing links is provided by psychoanalytic theory. Much has been written about Freud's atheism, anticlericalism, and the very pertinent analysis he makes of religion in *The Future of an Illusion* (1927). As I suggested earlier in this chapter, the secularist approach of Freudian psychoanalysis rests on deep skepticism about the delusional aspects of all belief systems, compounded by a scientific form of criticism. At the same time, however, psychoanalysis stresses two aspects of psychic life that point seriously in the postsecular direction: the first concerns the vitality of drives, including the all-powerful death drive whose entropic force is central to human desire. The second deals with the crucial importance of totemic and iconic figures as fundamental structures of psychic order and social cohesion. In his metapsychology period, Freud explores the material bases of human psychic and spiritual life, drawing attention to the violent and disruptive forces that both sustain and threaten the social/sexual contract. Foremost among them is exogamy, the exchange of women, as a pillar of patriarchal monotheism.

The main psychoanalytic insight concerns therefore the importance of the emotional layering of the process of subject formation. This refers to the affective, unconscious, and visceral elements of our allegedly rational and discursive belief system (Connolly 1999). To put it bluntly: psychoanalysis demonstrates that the political does not equate the rational and the religious is not the same as the irrational. Religion may well be the opium of some masses, but politics is no less intoxicating and science is the favorite addiction of many others. Die-hard champions of the equation of reason with atheism, like Dawkins (2006) and other "Enlightenment fundamentalists" are symptomatic of this axiom, being as extreme and intolerant as the religious forces they are allegedly opposing.

The legacy of psychoanalysis allows us to challenge received ideas about the rationality of political subjectivity. Let us take a simple notion, such as faith in social progress and the self-correcting powers of democratic governance. In a psychoanalytic perspective, the operational concept here is faith itself. Psychoanalysis is a sober reminder of our historically cumulated contradictions: we are confronting today a postsecular realization that all beliefs are acts of faith, regardless of their propositional content. Even or especially when they invoke the superiority of reason, science, and technology. All belief systems contain a hard core of spiritual hope—as Lacan put it: if you believe in grammar, you believe in God.

This insight can be compounded by another set of considerations, borrowed from media and cultural studies, about the social imaginary and its unconscious interpellations. Much has been written on the power of identification and the mass appeal triggered by images and representations of dominant icons—ranging from the ubiquitous face of Che Guevara or the young Angela Davis to the images of Nelson Mandela and other secular saints. Whereas their totemic function is religious in the sacrificial sense of the term ("they suffered so that we may be better off"), their iconic value is clearly inscribed in the market economy. It can be understood as the process of hyperindividualistic branding of the faces of celebrities. This phenomenon is border crossing and includes Elvis Presley and Princess Diana in some quarters and resistance or guerrilla fighters and suicide bombers in others. Again, the residues of religious worship practices are evident here: the images of transgressive and iconoclastic female saints or inspiring icons, ranging from Saint Teresa of Avila, or Joan of Arc to Anne Frank to Mother Teresa of Calcutta, have played a significant role in the collective cultural imaginary.

Contemporary technoculture has intensified this trend. Madonna, known in her Judaic (con) version as Esther, has a standing dialogue and stage act as/with Jesus Christ. Evelyn Fox Keller (1983), in her seminal work on feminist epistemology, recognizes the importance of Buddhism in the making of contemporary microbiologist McClintock's Nobel-prize winning discoveries. Henrietta Moore's recent anthropological research on sexuality in Kenya (2007) argues that, considering the impact of grassroots religious organizations, being white is less of a problem in the field today than being a failed Christian. Recently, however, Donna Haraway came out as a failed secularist (2006); while Helen Cixous (2004) saw it fit to write a book entitled: "Jacques Derrida as a Young Jewish Saint." Now, how nonsecular is all this?

The mystical elements of mass popular culture have been commented upon by critical theorists as diverse as Adorno and Horkheimer, and Deleuze and Guattari. In the age of digital saturation of our social sphere by fast-circulating visualization technologies, the mystical overtones of global icons and the semireligious cult and following they evoke have become permanent features of our culture. The relative decline of psychoanalysis as a hermeneutical tool of social and cultural critique in academic circles, however, prevents a more coherent reading of the links that neoliberal societies have established between visual culture, global icons, and a postsecular social imaginary that fetishizes them into the "sacred monsters" of global consumption.

A possible alternative to psychoanalysis has been offered by a shift of emphasis in contemporary political ontology toward a Spinozist rather than Freudian-Hegelian framework. Such a shift of paradigm toward nomadic immanence means, among others, that less emphasis is placed on dialectics of consciousness and more attention is paid to issues of empowerment, positivity, and the critique of the negative (see chapter 10). It also affects the feminist understandings of the postsecular predicament. The Freudian theory of the libido harnessed the drives back onto a system that equates desire with a dialectical structure of recognition and sameness. This inscribes alterity—the structural presence of others—as a limit or negation at the core of the desiring subject. Desire is deployed along an entropic curve for Freud and is equated with lack in Lacan. Nomadic theory unlinks them because of the new forms of interrelationality that have been enabled by global technological developments. Contemporary technologies allow for forms of social interaction by desiring subjects, which are nomadic, not unitary; multirelational, not phallocentric; connective, not dialectical; simulated, not specular; affirmative, not melancholy; and relatively disengaged from a linguistically mediated system of signification (Braidotti 2006). If we look at recent figurations of major theorists and thinkers, they all attest to multilayered relationality: Deleuze's rhizomes (1976), Guattari's molecular politics (1986), Hardt and Negri's multitudes (2004), feminist critiques of scattered hegemonies by Grewal and Kaplan (1994), diasporic belongings by Avtar Brah (1996), Haraway's cyborgs (1985), queer subjectivity (Butler 1991), and my nomadic subject (2006).

This shift of paradigm from classical psychoanalytic hermeneutics to more multilayered neomaterialist approaches, however, should not be allowed to obscure the relevance of psychoanalysis to the discussion about the postsecular predicament.

NOMADIC SPIRITUALITY

One area where residual traces of spirituality can be clearly seen is in the contemporary rise of neovitalist thought. As I have argued in chapter 5, social theory since poststructuralism has emphasized the materially grounded transformative processes of becoming, complexity in network societies or biopower in the sense of vital politics. The return to vitalism, and the turn to "matter-realism" redefined through technological flows of complex information systems, is itself a symptom of the postsecular turn in political theory. Classical vitalism is a problematic notion, considering its dramatic history of holism and complicity with fascism. Contemporary neovitalism as a philosophy of flows and flux, however, presupposes and benefits from the philosophical monism that is central to a materialist and nonunitary vision of subjectivity.

As a neovitalist notion immanence expresses the residual spiritual values of great intimacy and a sense of belonging to the world as process of perpetual becoming (Bataille 1988). Moreover, it is the case that, theoretically and politically, vitalism stands against the emphasis on political theology that, adapted from Carl Schmitt (1996), shaped the thinking of Leo Strauss and the American neocons through the Bush Jr. years (Derrida 2002; Norton 2004). The difference between the two is that political theology in its classical enunciation as well as in the contemporary interpretation by Agamben (1998) reduces modern political theories to the secularized version of theological concepts. This fundamentally authoritarian reduction overemphasizes the ruthlessly dichotomous ("friend or enemy") and polarizing nature ("you are with us or against us") of the political relation. By stressing this dimension as what is specific about politics, this theory ends up in a confrontation with death and mortality as well as in an indictment of modernity as being structurally violent.

Neovitalist feminist thought, on the other hand, pursues a very different line of political reasoning, which stresses the creative potential of social phenomena that may appear negative at first. The theoretical advantage of this approach is the ability to account for the fluid workings of power in advanced capitalism by grounding them in immanent relations and hence resist them by the same means. What is postsecular about this is *amor fati*: a deep love of the world and of its often pathetic and almost always dramatic vicissitudes and a profound engagement in the task of collectively constructing socially sustainable horizons of hope. For now, let me illustrate this trend with reference to more holistic and integrated ways of discussing subjectivity as flows of interrelationality. This trend has emerged as a feature of contemporary matter-realist postsecular feminist theory in a number of areas.

Feminism has moved away from Beauvoir's intransigent repudiation of religious beliefs and the subsequent reassertion of classical transcendence as a feminist strategy. This philosophical position was challenged by the notion of nonhierarchical or horizontal transcendence (Irigaray 1984) and by the idea of radical immanence in Deleuzian feminism (Braidotti 1991; Colebrook 2000a, 2002; Grosz 2004).

Third-wave feminism (Henry 2004) has voiced anti-oedipal philosophical and methodological claims about feminist time lines that redesign possible futures in affirmative ways. The renewed interest in authors like Darwin (Grosz 1999a) echoes in the rise of multiple micropolitical investigations of 'life itself' (Parisi 2004). This transversal convergence between philosophical antifoundationalism and feminist epistemology results in a posthuman wave that radicalizes the premises of science studies beyond anything envisaged by classical postmodernist feminism (Wilson 1998; Bryld and Lykke 1999; Franklin, Lury, and Stacy 2000). Feminist cultural studies of science attempt to disengage biology from the structural functionalism of DNA-driven linearity and to veer it instead toward more creative patterns of evolutionary development (Halberstam and Livingston 1995). The result is a nonessentialist brand of vital neoholistic thought that points explicitly to a spiritual dimension, best exemplified by the growing number of references to Bergson (Fraser, Kember, and Lury 2006; Grosz 2004).

Posthuman feminism, in the neovitalist mode (Haraway 1997, 2003; Hayles 1999; Guattari 1995) is a fast-growing new intersectional alliance that offers hybrid and transdisciplinary approaches. It gathers the remains of poststructuralist antihumanism and joins them with feminist reappraisals of contemporary technoculture in a nondeterministic frame. Posthumanism has also some inhumane aspects; Vandana Shiva (1997) stresses, for example, the extent to which the bodies of the empirical subjects who signify difference (woman/native/earth or natural others) have become the disposable bodies of the global economy. Contemporary capitalism is "biopolitical" in that it aims at controlling all that lives: it has already turned into a form of biopiracy in that it aims at exploiting the generative powers of women, animals, plants, genes, and cells. Because the self-replicating vitality of living matter is targeted for consumption and commercial exploitation of biogenetic culture, environmentalism has evolved into a new global alliance for sustainable futures. Haraway recognizes this trend and pays tribute to the martyrized body of OncoMouse (Haraway 1997) as the farming ground for the new genetic revolution and manufacturer of spare parts for other species.

These trends indicate that the postsecular turn has been taken within feminist theory, though it may not always bear that name. The residual spirituality of much contemporary feminist theory demonstrates the compatibility of political subjectivity with issues that do not fall easily within the boundaries of the secular tradition in feminism, as defined in the first section of this essay. The new agenda includes straightforward religious matters, questions of neovital politics, environmental holism and deep ecology, the biopolitical management of life and the quest for suitable resistance in the era of biogenetic capitalism, or what ethical values best suit the respect for ethnic and cultural diversity. Each of these deserves more specific analysis than I can grant it here.

Postsecular nomadic theory stresses the generative power of the self-styling of alternative ethical relations of both intimacy and experimentation with multiple human and nonhuman others. I shall explore these more systematically in chapter 11, so for the moment let us stay focused on the postsecular dimension only. The shift of perspective away from dialectical oppositions toward a subtler understanding of the multiple workings of power puts to active use the residual spirituality that sustains a political project based on affirmation.

My position resonates with Connolly's call for a form of postsecularism different from the nonexclusive humanist kind that preoccupies Charles Taylor. Connolly urges us to come to terms with a world without either divine providence or a natural predisposition to human mastery (2008) and to turn this new condition into strength, via a Deleuzian politics of immanence. In his important statement against militant secularism, moreover, Connolly (1999) questions the stability as well as the oversimplifications of this position. He also argues that vehement secularists hinder an adequate understanding of "the layered density of political thinking and judgment in the eve of globalization." Connolly wants to replace this limited view with "an ethos of engagement" that allows for affect, viscerality, and wider modes of connections than those allowed by Western rationalism. Careful to avoid binary reversals, and thus refusing to assert a God-centered worldview, Connolly aims to refashion secularism as a model of thinking and of organizing public life. In this respect, Connolly offers the figuration of the rhizome as an alternative: an "asecular" conception of social life that allows for "the visceral register of intersubjectivity, an ethic of cultivation, and the politics of becoming" (1999:11). He also calls it: "a minor post-secular tradition" (2008).

Answering Taylor obliquely but unequivocally, Connolly argues, with Deleuze, that "despite Nietzsche's aristocratic proclivities, this enchantment with the pluriformity of being is highly pertinent to a democratic ethos of generosity and forbearance" (1999:16). Connolly's "politics of becoming"—adapted from Deleuze's vitalist philosophy—aims at the production of alternative subject positions "out of the energies, sufferings, and lines of flight available to culturally defined differences in a particular institutional constellation" (1999:57). Connolly relies on nomadic thought to the extent that he posits a nontheistic, postsecular ethics, in the recognition of the fragility of the ethical bond to Otherness and in critical generosity. The background to this postsecular ethics is what Deleuze would call "the virtual," that is to say, the awareness that we "inhabit a world where the admirable possibilities of being outstrip the time and corporeal capacity of any particular individual or achieve to embody them all" (1999:55). An ethics of engagement combines "multidimensional plurality" (1999:154) with different moral sources, quantitative proliferation of beliefs with a qualitative theft in the practice of becoming-democratic. It inscribes diversity on the ontological level.

In my own nomadic thought, Deleuze's neovitalist ecophilosophical intervention in favor of a transversal and dynamic vision of subjectivity pursues this project and radicalizes it further. As a result, political consciousness cannot be left where the Enlightenment project had originally located: on the side of rationality, autonomy, teleology of progress, and emancipation. Given the complex and weblike structure of contemporary power, political resistance has to be conceptualized accordingly. Biocentered egalitarianism has a planetary dimension, which acknowledges the importance of cosmic resonances and rhythms. These are postsecular notions, but not in any simple apolitical manner. On the contrary, they stress that political subjectivity consists of multiple micropolitical practices of daily activism or interaction in a world we inhabit for ourselves and for future generations. As Rich put it in her recent essays, the political activist has to think "in spite of the times" and hence "out of my time," thus creating the analytics—the conditions of possibility—of the future (2001:159). Critical theory occurs somewhere between the no longer and the not yet, not looking for easy reassurances but for evidence that others are struggling with the same questions. Consequently, "we" are in *this* together.

■ ■ ■

My argument has shown that there is no logical necessity to assume that the Western model of emancipation, based on secularism and the equation of liberation with sexual freedom, is the only, let alone the best paradigm for feminist activism. A plurality of other models—both of secularity and of women's emancipation—is both feasible and desirable. Lest this be mistaken for cultural relativism, let me reiterate again the point about the feminist politics of location as both a methodology and a strategy. The link between political subjectivity and oppositional consciousness and the tendency to reduce the latter to negativity also need to be reviewed. Critical theory can be just as and more persuasively theoretical if it embraces philosophical monism, nomadic subjectivity and vital politics, and disengages the process of consciousness-raising from the logic of negativity, connecting it instead to creative affirmation. The corollary of this shift is twofold: firstly, it proves that political subjectivity or agency need not be aimed solely at the production of radical countersubjectivities. It is not a destructive oppositional strategy that aims at storming the Bastille of phallocentrism or undoing the winter palace of gender. It rather involves negotiations with dominant norms or technologies of the self. Secondly, it argues that political subjectivity rests on an ethics of otherness that values reciprocity as mutual specification or creation, but not as the recognition of sameness.

The political economy of subjectivity I have been arguing for does not condition the emergence of the subject on negation but on creative affirmation, not on loss but on vital generative forces. This shift is central to the postsecular turn in feminist theory, which imagines a subject whose existence, ethics, and politics are not indexed on negativity and hence on the horizon of alterity and melancholia. The nomadic subject is looking for the ways in which otherness prompts, mobilizes, and allows for the affirmation of what is not contained in the present conditions.

This has implications for the link between sexuality, politics, and desire. Nomadic vitalist politics stresses the need to return to sexuality as an ontological, polymorphous, and complex force and consequently to disengage it from both identity issues and all dualistic oppositions. Feminist and gay activists may want to look for subversion not in counteridentity formations and all the embattled identity politics that goes with it—but rather in deterritorialization of all identities indexed on sex. This means by extension that sexuality is to be approached as a force, or constitutive element, that is capable of deterritorializing gender identity and institutions.

A renewed emphasis on sexuality, as opposed to classical feminist or queer theories of sex and gender, emerges from this shift of perspective, as I argued in chapter 6. I would reappraise the radical critique Foucault developed of the overemphasis our culture places on sex-gender as an indicator of identities and inner truths about ourselves. As an operator of power, a conveyor of major social regulations, and a tool for consumerism, sex-indexed identities are a trap from which we need to liberate ourselves. Foucault's notorious criticism of feminist theories of sexual liberation, in the first volume of his history of sexuality, reiterates the point that there is no possible liberation through but only from sex-gender. By extension, the idea that sexual liberation is central to a political project of liberation or emancipation—which is constitutive of Western feminism and integral to its secular bias—paradoxically reiterates the Christian notion that desire is integral to the constitution of subjectivity.

Foucault's project challenges this bias by proclaiming the "end of the monarchy of sex" as being in congruence with the de-regulation of sexual repression and the commercial exploitation of marginal or dissident sexualities. The only credible subversive move, according to Foucault, is the refusal of all identities based on sex-gender and not only of a dominant heterosexual model or of its binary homosexual counterpart. Even more crucial is the effort to undertake serious experimentations with alternative modes of relation that are not mediated via sex and therefore escape both commercial commodification and the social normativity that accompanies it. This experimental sexual pragmatics also accomplishes the creative task of returning sexuality to its original complexity as a force of intensity, intimacy, and relationality. The centrality of desire is accordingly displaced by experimenting with modes of ethical subjectivity (for the later Foucault) and transversal collective assemblages (for Deleuze and Guattari) that free the subject from the dictatorship of sex as a term that indexes access to identity formations and their respective power entitlements. Nomadic neo-asceticism (Braidotti 2006) emerges as a resource, with renewed emphasis on a political spirituality that labors to free the subject from constituted identities and experiment with new modes of relation.

This nomadic vision of desire is crucial to the postsecular turn I mentioned above. Desire is located transversally, in the specific singularity of immanent interrelations among subjects collectively engaged in the expression and actualization of their power of becoming or potentia. The model of alternative ethics proposed by philosophies of nomadism implies a nonhierarchical idea of transcendence and a nonbinary model of interrelation.

Desire is never a given. Rather, like a long shadow projected from the past, it is a forward-moving horizon that lies ahead and toward which one moves.

Between the no longer and the not yet, desire traces the possible patterns of becoming. These intersect with and mobilize sexuality, but never stop there—identity is a black hole also and especially when it is indexed on the parameters of a gender system that today more than ever combines redemptive emancipatory benevolence with violent militarized coercion into the Western neo-imperial project. Against the platitudes of sex as conspicuous consumption and the arrogance of nationalist projects of enforced liberation of non-Westerners, we may want to rethink sexuality beyond genders, as the ontological drive to pure becoming. Desire sketches the conditions for intersubjective encounters, through the unavoidable accident of an insight, a flush of sudden acceleration that marks a point of no return. Accepting this risk and that challenge may rescue contemporary sexual politics from the paradoxical mix of commercialized banalities and perennial counteridentity claims, on the one hand, and belligerent and racist forms of neocolonial civilizationism, on the other.

NOMADIC CITIZENSHIP

PART THREE

8

COMPLEXITY AGAINST
METHODOLOGICAL NATIONALISM

Something in the world forces us to think.

—DELEUZE AND GUATTARI, *WHAT IS PHILOSOPHY?*

THE SUBJECT AS MULTIPLICITY, PROCESS, AND BECOMING

As I have been arguing so far, nomadic theory rests on a nonunitary philosophy of the subject. This has important implications for both the
social construction and the public perception of the scientist as the
prototype of "the man of reason" (Lloyd 1984). This humanistic subject
of Western science claimed to be structured and ordained along the axes
of self-reflexive individualism and rationality, which are the legacy of the
European Enlightenment and are indexed on a linear and progressive temporal line. Nomadic theory, on the contrary, moves beyond these categories
and rests on a process ontology that challenges the traditional equation of
subjectivity with rational consciousness, resisting the reduction of both to
a linear vision of progress. Thus, instead of deference to the authority of
the past, nomad thought proposes the fleeting copresence of multiple time
zones, in a time continuum that activates and deterritorializes stable identities. It also offers a very dynamic vision of the time sequences of memory

(see chapter 1). This vision of the subject enlists the creative resources of the imagination to the task of enacting transformative relations and actions in the present. This ontological nonlinearity rests on a Spinozist ethics of affirmation and becoming that predicates the positivity of difference (I will return to this in chapter 11).

The nomadic vision of the subject as a time continuum and a collective assemblage implies a double commitment, on the one hand, to processes of change and, on the other, to a strong ethics of the ecosophical sense of community—of "our" being in *this* together. Our copresence, that is to say, the simultaneity of our being in the world together, sets the tune for the ethics of our interaction with both human and nonhuman others. An ethical relation based on biocentered egalitarianism requires us to synchronize the perception and anticipation of togetherness, of our shared, common condition. A collectively distributed consciousness emerges from this—i.e., a transversal form of nonsynthetic understanding of the relational bond that connects us. This places the relation and the notion of complexity at the center of both the ethics and the epistemic structures and strategies of the subject.

This vision of a collectively assembled, externally related, and multilayered subject that acts in a time continuum breaks frontally with the established view of the European subject of knowledge. Following the critical premises of poststructuralist critiques of humanism by Foucault (1966), Deleuze and Guattari (1972, 1980), Derrida (1991), and Irigaray (1977), nomadic thought questions also the classical vision of the philosophical subject as the quintessential European citizen. "Europe" stands in this discussion for a tacit consensus about the self-evidence of the universalizing powers of self-reflexive and self-correcting reason. This flattering rendition of philosophical "Europeanness" transforms Europe from a concrete geopolitical location, and a specifically grounded history, into an abstract concept and a normative ideal that can be implemented across space and time, provided the right preconditions are met. Europe as the symbol of universal self-consciousness posits itself as the site of origin of reason and designates itself as the motor of the world-historical unfolding of the philosophical *ratio*. This titanic sense of entitlement rests structurally on the claim to universality and also on a hierarchical and dialectical vision of Otherness or difference. It also inscribed an entrenched form of methodological nationalism at the heart of the accepted vision of science as simultaneously the distillation of rationality and the quintessence of the European culture.

Nomadic thought consists in the rejection of the unitary vision of the subject as a self-regulating rationalist entity and of the traditional image of thought and of the scientific practices that rest upon it. This view has important implications for the production of scientific knowledge. The dominant vision of the scientific enterprise—which Deleuze aptly calls "royal science"—is based on the institutional implementation of a number of laws that discipline the practice of scientific research and police the thematic and methodological borders of what counts as respectable, acceptable, and fundable science. In so doing, the laws of scientific practice regulate what a mind is allowed to do, and thus they control the structures of our thinking. Foucault's archaeology of knowledge (1966) is a foundational text and a crucial point of origin for a critique of this intrinsically normative image of thought at work within the allegedly "objective" practice of science.

The deeply entrenched antihumanism of poststructuralist thought becomes radicalized in Deleuze and Guattari's conceptual redefinition of the practice of thinking and hence also of scientific reason. Nomadic subjectivity moves beyond the mere critique of both the identitarian category of a sovereign self and dominant subject position, on the one hand, and the image of thought that equates subjectivity with rational consciousness on the other. The linear, Enlightenment-based vision of human progress as the effect of a deployment of scientific reason upon the theater of the world historical experience of humans is accordingly abandoned. An alternative vision is proposed of both the thinking subject, of his or her evolution on the planetary stage and the structure of thinking. I will develop this insight in two parallel directions: the first is a sociopolitical critique of the allegedly universal subject of knowledge that attacks conceptual Eurocentrism. The second is a more conceptual critique of the rationalist frame of subjectivity, but also of what it means to think at all. Both converge on the rejection of methodological nationalism, though not of science as such.

Let us start with the critique of universalism. Social criticism of science, following the insights of feminist (Lloyd 1984; Irigaray 1997; Harding 1986; Haraway 1992b), postcolonial (Spivak 1999), and race theorists (Gilroy 2000), takes the universalist claim of "the knowing subject of science" to task and exposes the cluster of vested interests and particularities that actually sustain its claims. A binary logic of self-other opposition is at work in this falsely universalistic model, which results in reducing "difference" to pejoration, disqualification, and exclusion (Braidotti 1991, 1994a). Subjectivity is postulated on the basis of sameness, i.e., as coinciding with the dominant image of thought and representation of the subject as a rational essence. Deleuze and Guattari offer the perfect synthesis of this dominant image of the subject as masculine/white/heterosexual/speaking a standard language/property-owning/urbanized. This paradigm equates the subject with rationality, consciousness, moral and cognitive universalism. This vision of the "knowing subject"—or the "man" of humanism—constructs itself as much by what it includes within the circle of his entitlements as in what it excludes. Otherness is excluded by definition, which makes the others into structural and constitutive elements of the subject, albeit by negation (as I argued in chapters 1 through 4). Throughout Western philosophy, Otherness has been constructed with distressing regularity along intertwined axes of sexualization, racialization, and naturalization (Braidotti 2002b, 2006). The others—women or sexual minorities; natives, indigenous and non-Europeans, and earth or animal others—have been marginalized, excluded, exploited, and disposed of accordingly. The epistemic and world-historical violence engendered by the claim to universalism and by the oppositional view of consciousness lies at the heart of the conceptual Euro-centrism that Deleuze and Guattari are attacking.

Insofar as rhizomatic subjectivity and nomadic thought challenge the methodological Eurocentrism of epistemology, they also critique the complicity between this discipline of thought and nationalism. It becomes not only feasible but even imperative to question the habit of thought that reiterates the Eurocentric character of philosophy. The question of what is European about Continental philosophy, for instance, can and should be raised as a way of suspending the assimilation of philosophy into a hegemonic vision of European consciousness (Bernasconi and Cook 2003).

I am very keen to stress this aspect of nomadic theory and to add a note of concern at the relative neglect suffered by the methodological implications of nomadic thought for contemporary science and for epistemology. Especially in the last few years, there has been increasing compartmentalization in the reception of Deleuze's thought. Thus scholarship about the "political" Deleuze is often distinct from that on the "cultural" or the "epistemological" aspects of Deleuze and Guattari's complex corpus. This is a problematic tendency, which projects spurious distinctions over a thinker whose rhizomatic rigor and rejection of traditional dividing lines is—or should be—beyond dispute.

Contrary to the ongoing recompartmentalization of Deleuze's thought, I want to stress the practical implications of his philosophy for today's world as well as its methodological innovations. Deleuze's critique of capitalist power relations, for instance, is an integral part of his reconceptualization of the specific domain and responsibility of science and of scientific labor. I would argue, in other words, for a multilayered unity of thought and a nomadic kind of rigor within the Deleuzian rhizomatic universe and to call accordingly for a more multifaceted reception of his work by his admirers and his critics alike. The point of Deleuze and Guattari's work is to empower us to think differently about the analytic and historical preconditions for new forms of materialist and complex subjectivity. This transformative ethics provides the inner cohesion of their work and the core of their methodological innovation.

The second direction in which I deploy Deleuze's insights is conceptual. Deleuze and Guattari's defense of the parallelism between philosophy, science, and the arts is not to be mistaken for a flattening out of the differences between these different genres of intellectual pursuit. There is no easy isomorphism, but rather an ontological unity among the three branches of knowledge. Deleuze and Guattari take care to stress the differences between the distinctive styles of intelligence that these practices embody, but these qualitative differentiations are possible only because they are indexed on a common plane of intensive self-transforming life energy. This continuum sustains the ontology of becoming that is the conceptual motor of nomadic thought. Insofar as science has to come to terms with the real physical processes of an actualized and defined world, it is less open to the processes of becoming or differentiation that characterize Deleuze's monistic ontology. Philosophy is a subtler tool for the probing intellect, one that is more attuned to the virtual plane of immanence, to the generative force of a generative universe, or "chaosmosis," which is nonhuman and in constant flux.

Deleuze calls the radical alterity of a mind-independent reality "Chaos" and defines it positively as the virtual formation of all possible forms. The generative force of "Chaos" is the source of its vital elemental powers of renewal and transformation—through endless processes of actualization of determinate forms. The key elements of this conceptual operation are the notion of a deep vitalist interrelation between ourselves and the world, in an ecophilosophical move that binds us to the living organism that is the cosmos as a whole. By extension, for philosophers, this leads to a redefinition of the activity of thinking away from the rationalist paradigm to a more intensive and empathic, ecosophical mode. Thinking is the conceptual counterpart of the ability to enter modes of relation, to affect and be affected, sustaining qualitative shifts and creative tensions accordingly. Manuel De Landa (2002) analyzes brilliantly the intensive mode of Deleuzian science and stresses the crucial importance of processes of actualization over and above universal essence and linear realisations. De Landa stresses that, apart from the antiessentialism, intensive nomad science also aims to avoid typological thinking, "that style of thought in which individuation is achieved through the creation of classifications and of formal criteria for membership in those classifications" (De Landa 2002:41). The ruling principle of resemblance, identity, analogy, and opposition has to be avoided in thinking about the virtual and intensive becomings. Deleuze demands "that we give an account of that which allows making such judgements or establishing those relations" (De Landa 2002:42).

Secondly, there is the shift away from an epistemological theory of representation to an ontology of becoming. By way of comparison, Lacan—and Derrida with him—define Chaos epistemologically as that which precedes form, structure, and language. Confined to the unrepresentable, this post-Hegelian vision reduces "Chaos" to that which is incomprehensible. For Deleuze, however, following Spinoza, Bergson, and Leibniz, Chaos en-/unfolds the virtual copresence of any forms. This produces a number of significant shifts: from negative dialectics to affirmative affects, from entropic to generative notions of desire, from a focus on the constitutive outsides that frame subjectivity to a geometry of assemblages that require mutual actualization and temporary synchronization, from an oppositional and split to an open-ended and relational vision of the subject, from the epistemological to the ontological turn in philosophy.

Thirdly, the important aspect of nomadic vitalism is that it is neither organicist nor essentialist but rather pragmatic and immanent. There is no overarching concept of life, just practices and flows of becoming, complex assemblages and heterogeneous relations—no idealised transcendental, but virtual multiplicities. The monistic ontology that sustains this vision of life as vitalist, self-organizing matter also allows it to reunite the different branches of the sciences in a new deal. Bonta and Protevi (2004) stress that Deleuze's "geo-philosophy" encourages the humanities and social sciences to engage with contemporary biology and physics in very creative ways. The emphasis falls on complexity in distinguishing between actualized states and virtual becomingson the basis of a vision of matter as autopoietic. The former constitute the object of "royal science," the latter the frame for "minor science"; both are necessary at different points in time, but only "minor science" is ethically transformative and not bound to the economic imperatives of advanced capitalism and its cognitive excursions into living matter.

As a consequence, one can venture the preliminary conclusion that the main implication of nomadic theory for the practice of science is that the scientific laws need to be retuned according to a view of the subject of knowledge as a complex singularity, an affective assemblage, and a relational vitalist entity. This could also be described as a metamethodological shift away from the methodological nationalism implicit in the rationalist view of the humanist subject of knowledge.

CARTOGRAPHIES AND ACCOUNTABILITY

Nomadic theory has targeted the oppositional logic of universalistic reason for criticism and calls it to accountability. Radical epistemologies such as feminism, environmentalism, postcolonial, race, and critical legal theories formulate a response to concrete world historical events, such as the oppression of women and sexual minorities, colonialism, fascism, the Holocaust, communist totalitarianism, and human right abuses. These last exemplify some of the crimes that were committed in the name of Europe's alleged universal civilizing mission and its self-proclaimed monopoly over scientific rationality. These historical events are set off against the self-aggrandizing narratives of rational, cosmopolitan universalism. The juxtaposition highlights the need for new critical and creative modes of addressing subjectivity and ethics, and, more specifically, it aims to debunk methodological nationalism.

Both the critique of ahistorical Eurocentrism and the quest for alternative genealogies of European universalism express a form of ethical and political accountability that requires adequate understandings of one's specific location, that is to say, one's embedded and embodied perspectives. Michel Foucault's cartographies of power (1977a) provide a conceptual and methodological example of this approach, as does Deleuze's concept of radical immanence (1995) and the intrusive science it produces (De Landa 2002).

The feminist method of the politics of location is also central to this debate, in that it provides both the means to explore and the creative force to experiment with alternative representations of the knowing subject.

The politics of location, first developed (Rich 1985) as a way of making sense of diversity among women within the category of sexual difference, became the cornerstone of feminist situated epistemologies (Haraway 1988). In its nomadic variable, it can be extended into a cartographic method of accounting for multiple differences within any subject position (Braidotti 1994a). These degrees of differentiation are explored and rendered as analyses of power locations and power relations. This method aims at achieving epistemological and political accountability by unveiling the power locations one inevitably inhabits as the site of one's subject position. A cartography is a theoretically based and politically informed reading of the present. As such it responds to my two main requirements: namely, to account for one's locations in terms both of space (the geopolitical or ecological dimension) and time (the historical and genealogical dimension) and to provide alternative figurations or schemes of representation for these locations in terms of power as restrictive (potestas) but also empowering or affirmative (potentia). I consider this cartographic gesture to be the first methodological move toward a vision of subjectivity as ethically accountable and politically empowering.

The practice of accountability for one's embodied and embedded locations, as a relational, collective activity of undoing power differentials, is linked to two crucial notions: memory and narratives. (I have already introduced the notion of nomadic memory in chapter 1 and shall return to it in chapters 11 and 12.) Nomadic consciousness activates the process of bringing into discursive representation that which by definition escapes self-representation and can only be disclosed by the active intervention of others. The accounts of these "politics of locations" are cartographies of power that go beyond genealogical self-narratives and express a view of subjectivity that is relational and outside directed. In nomadic thought this vision is expressed through *conceptual personae* or figurations. These are ways of situating and framing the subject position, and its political and epistemological practices, so as to produce an array of creative counterimages of the subject. Examples are feminist/womanist/queer/cyborg/diasporic/native/nomadic—as figurations of the feminist subject positions. These are figurations for specific geopolitical and historical locations. To mistake them for mere metaphors would be to miss the point altogether (Braidotti 2011).

Figurations are forms of literal expression of the politics of location that bring into representation that which the dominant system had declared off-limits. They are situated practices that require the awareness of the limitations as well as the specificity of one's locations. A figuration renders our image of thought in terms of a decentered and multilayered vision of the subject as a dynamic and changing entity; as such it can be taken as a dramatization of the processes of becoming. This process assumes that identity takes place in between nature/technology, male/female, black/white, local/global, present/past—in the spaces that flow and connect such seeming binaries. We live in permanent processes of transition, hybridization, and nomadization. And these in-between states and stages defy the established modes of theoretical representation, precisely because they are zigzagging, not linear and process oriented, not concept driven. Critique and creation strike a new deal in actualizing the practice of *conceptual personae* or figuration as the active pursuit of affirmative alternatives to the dominant vision of the subject.

In this critical perspective, to stress the situated structure of philosophical discourse—and thus reject universalism—also means to recognize the partial or limited nature of all claims to knowledge. This has both ethical and methodological consequences in that it requires specific forms of accountability for the production of knowledge. The critiques of both universalism and of liberal individualism are fundamental starting points to rethink the interconnection between the self and society in an accountable manner that would actualize the becoming-minor of science.

To apply this to the issue of methodological nationalism: a new agenda needs to be set, no longer that of European or Eurocentric universal, rational subjectivity, but rather a radical transformation in a process of rupture from Europe's imperial, fascistic, and undemocratic tendencies. Leading sociologist Ulrich Beck (2007) concurs with this view and even emphasizes the need to go beyond methodological nationalism to develop a genuinely cosmopolitan critical theory that would redefine socially relevant science for the third millennium.

Less prone to overarching generalizations, nomadic thought strikes a more cautious note. If the fundamental question, as Deleuze teaches us, is not about who we are but rather about what we are capable of becoming, then methodological nationalism must give way to self-criticism and nomadic transformations on the basis of accountability for our complex history. As Balibar (2001) and Bauman (2004) have argued recently, contemporary European subjects of knowledge must meet the ethical obligation to be accountable for their past history and the long shadow it casts on their present-day politics. In a nomadic perspective, the new mission that Europe has to embrace entails the criticism of narrow-minded self-interests, intolerance, and xenophobic rejection of otherness. Symbolic of this closure of the European mind is the fate of migrants, refugees, and asylum seekers who bear the brunt of racism in contemporary Europe. Multiple counterdefinitions of cosmopolitan values constitute the site of resistance to this mind-set and a forum for ongoing discussion.

This process-oriented vision of the subject is capable of a universalistic reach, though it rejects moral and cognitive universalism. It expresses a grounded, partial form of accountability, based on a strong sense of collectivity and relationality. The fact that "we" are in *this* together results in a renewed claim to community and belonging by singular subjects. This results in a proliferation of locally situated micro-universalist claims, which Genevieve Lloyd calls: "a collaborative morality" (Lloyd 1996:74).

One evident and illuminating example of this alternative approach is the situated neohumanist cosmopolitanism that has emerged as a powerful ethical claim in the work of postcolonial and race theorists as well as in feminist theories. Examples are Paul Gilroy's planetary cosmopolitanism (2000), Avtar Brah's diasporic ethics (1996), Edouard Glissant's politics of relations (1990), Ernesto Laclau's micro-universal claims (1995), Homi Bhabha's "subaltern secularism" (1994), Vandana Shiva's antiglobal neohumanism (1997), African American spirituality, as bell hooks (1990) and Cornell West (1994) demonstrate, as well as the rising wave of interest in African humanism, or Ubuntu, from Patricia Hill Collins (1991) to Drucilla Cornell (2002).

Thus the antihumanism of social and cultural critics within a Western poststructuralist perspective can be read alongside the neohumanism of contemporary race, postcolonial, and non-Western critics. Both these positions, all other differences notwithstanding, produce inclusive alternatives—locations and figurations—that enlarge and go beyond humanist individualism. Without wishing to flatten out structural differences, nor draw easy analogies between them, I want to stress the resonances between their efforts and respective political aims and passions. Western posthumanism, on the one hand, and non-Western neohumanism, on the other, transpose hybridity, nomadism, diasporas, creolization processes into means of regrounding claims to connections and alliances between different constituencies. They bring strong evidence to support the claim that methodological nationalism and theoretical Eurocentrism are of hindrance, rather than assistance, in trying to redefine the cosmopolitan and interconnected nature of the contemporary subject. This alternative vision of the subject combines critical elements, like the rejection of Euro-universalism, with creative elements, like the recomposition of a new ethical sense of panhumanity. In both cases the transformative element is of crucial importance.

DEFAMILIARIZATION: TOWARD ANTI-OEDIPAL SCIENCE

Transformative projects involve a radical repositioning on the part of the knowing subject, which is neither self-evident nor free of pain. No process of consciousness-raising ever is. In poststructuralist feminism the "alternative science project" (Harding 1986) has also been implemented methodologically through the practice of disidentification from familiar and hence comforting values and identities (De Lauretis 1986; Braidotti 1994a).

Disidentification involves the loss of cherished habits of thought and representation, a move that can also produce fear, sense of insecurity, and nostalgia. Change is certainly a painful process, but this does not equate it with suffering (see chapter 11), nor does it warrant the politically conservative position that chastises all change as dangerous. The point in stressing the difficulties and pain involved in the quest for transformative processes is rather to raise an awareness of both the complexities involved, the paradoxes that lie in store, and develop a nomadic "ethics of compassion" (Connolly 1999).

Changes that affect one's sense of identity are especially delicate. Given that identifications constitute an inner scaffolding that supports one's sense of identity, shifting our imaginary identifications is not as simple as casting away a used garment. Psychoanalysis taught us that imaginary relocations are complex and as time-consuming as shedding an old skin. Moreover, changes of this qualitative kind happen more easily at the molecular or subjective level, and their translation into a public discourse and shared social experiences is a complex and risk-ridden affair. In a more positive vein, Spinozist feminist political thinkers like Moira Gatens and Genevieve Lloyd (1999) argue that such socially embedded and historically grounded changes are the result of "collective imaginings"—a shared desire for certain transformations to be actualized as a collaborative effort. They are transversal assemblages aimed at the production of affirmative politics and ethical relations.

Let me give you a series of concrete examples of how disidentifications from dominant models of subject formation can be productive and creative. First of all, feminist theory is based on a radical disengagement from the dominant institutions and representations of femininity and masculinity to entering the process of becoming-minoritarian or of transforming gender. In so doing feminism combines critique with creation of alternative ways of embodying and experiencing our sexualized selves.

Secondly, in race discourse the awareness of the persistence of racial discrimination and of white privilege has led to serious disruptions of our accepted views of what constitutes a subject. This has resulted, on the one hand, in the critical reappraisal of blackness (Gilroy 2000; Hill Collins 1991) and, on the other, to radical relocations of whiteness (Ware 1992; Griffin and Braidotti 2002). Specifically, I would like to refer to Edgar Morin's account of how he relinquished Marxist cosmopolitanism to embrace a more "humble" perspective as a European (Morin 1987). This process includes both positive and negative affects: disappointment with the unfulfilled promises of Marxism is matched by compassion for the uneasy, struggling, and marginal position of postwar Europe, squashed between the U.S. and the USSR. This produces a renewed sense of care and accountability that leads Morin to embrace a postnationalistic redefinition of Europe as the site of mediation and transformation of it own history, which I have previously discussed.

All these disidentifications occur along the axes of becoming-woman (sexualization) and becoming-other (racialization) and hence remain within the confines of anthropomorphism. A more radical shift is needed therefore to break from the latter and develop postanthropocentric forms of identification. Donna Haraway's work is fundamental in actualizing this shift. Nomadic theory's vital geocentrism—the love of zoe—is a parallel effort in the same direction. Becoming-earth or becoming-imperceptible are more radical breaks with established patterns of thought (naturalization) and introduce a radically imminent planetary dimension. This anthropological exodus, however, is especially difficult emotionally as well as methodologically.

The positive benefits aspects of this disidentification are epistemological but extend beyond; they include a more adequate cartography of our real-life conditions and hence less pathos-ridden accounts. Becoming free of the topos that equates the struggle for identity changes with suffering results in a more adequate level of self-knowledge. It therefore clears the ground for more adequate and sustainable relations to the others who are crucial to the transformative project itself.

On the methodological front, de-oedipalizing the relationship to the non-human others, becoming-earth, is a form of radical pacifism that sets strong ethical requirements upon the philosophical subject. It requires a form of disidentification from a century-old habit of anthropocentric thought and humanist arrogance, which is likely to test the ability and willingness of the humanities to question what exactly is "human" about them and to dis-engage the human from banal anthropocentrism. The "hard" or experimental sciences, of course, have accomplished this move long ago and with relative ease. It may be worth considering the hypothesis therefore that the humanities' development toward complexity may be hampered by the anthropocentrism that underscores their Euro-centric bias. Nomadic thought, on the other hand, points to rich and complex posthumanities to come.

Defamiliarization is a sobering process by which the knowing subject evolves from the normative vision of the self he or she had become accustomed to. The frame of reference becomes the open-ended, interrelational, multisexed, and transspecies flow of becoming by interaction with multiple others. A subject thus constituted explodes the boundaries of humanism at skin level.

For example, the Deleuzian unorganic body is delinked from the codes of phallologocentric functional identity (Deleuze and Guattari 1980). The "body without organs" sings the praise of anomalies. It also introduces a sort of joyful insurrection of the senses, a vitalist and pan-erotic approach to the body. It is recomposed so as to induce creative disjunctions in this system, freeing organs from their indexation to certain prerequisite functions. This also includes the brain, whose function is extended beyond the mind to encompass multiple other forms of perception, cognition, and affectivity. This calls for a generalized recoding of the normative political anatomy and its assigned bodily functions as a way of scrambling the old metaphysical master code and loosening its power over the constitution of subjectivity. It actualized the embodiment of mind, as well as the "embrainment of the body" (Marks 1998). The subject is recast in the nomadic mode of collective assemblages. The aim of deterritorializing the functionalist norm also supports the process of becoming-animal/woman/minoritarian/nomadic.

Nonhuman others are no longer the signifying system that props up the humans' self-projections and moral aspirations. Nor are they the gatekeepers that trace the liminal positions in between species. They have rather started to function quite literally in a code system of their own. This neoliteral approach to otherness goes beyond the masters of modernity's insights about the inhuman structures of subjectivity. Both Freud and Darwin connect the human to time lines that stretch across generations and species and yet endure in the embodied and embedded memory of the community. Evolutionary theory acknowledges the accumulated memory of the species and thus installs a time line that connects us intergenerationally to the prehuman and prepersonal layers of our existence. Whereas psychoanalysis propels the instance of the unconscious into a critique of rationality and logocentrism, evolutionary theory, on the other hand, pushes the line of inquiry outside the frame of anthropocentrism. Pushed even further with nomad theory (Braidotti 2006), the metaphorical dimension of the human interaction with others is replaced by a neoliteral approach based on the vitalist immanence of life.

This deeply "matter-realist" approach has important ethical implications. In terms of the human-animal interaction, as I argued in chapter 3, the ego-saturated, oedipal familiarity of the past is replaced by the recognition of a deep bioegalitarianism, namely, that "we" are in *this* together. The bond between "us" is a vital connection based on sharing this territory or environment in terms that are no longer hierarchical or self-evident. They are rather fast-evolving and need to be renegotiated accordingly. Gilles Deleuze and Felix Guattari's theory of "becoming" expresses this profound and vital interconnection by positing a qualitative shift of the relationship away from speciesism and toward an ethical appreciation of what bodies (human, animal, others) can do. An ethology of forces emerges as the ethical code that can reconnect humans to nonhumans. De-oedipalizing the relationship to nonhuman others is a method of defamilarization that expresses a posthuman bodily materialism and lays the grounds for bioegalitarian ethics (Ansell-Pearson 1997).

DECENTERING ANTHROPOCENTRISM

One of the great innovations of Deleuze's philosophy is the rigorous brand of methodological nonaggression that animates it. The monistic ontology that he adapts from Spinoza, to which he adds the Bergsonian time continuum, situates the researcher—be it the philosopher, the scientist, or the artist—in a situation of great intimacy with the world. There is no violent rupture or separation between the subject and the object of her or her inquiry, no predatory gaze of the cold clinician (Braidotti 2011) intent on unveiling the secrets of nature (Jordanova 1993). An elemental ontological unity structures the debate. This nonessentialist vitalist position calls for more complexity and diversity in defining the processes of scientific inquiry and its methodology.

As a result of the conceptual shifts introduced by Deleuze and Guattari, the burden of responsibility is placed on the practitioners to develop new tools of analysis for the subtler degrees of differentiation and variations of intensity that characterize the formation of the "knowing" subject. The decentering of anthropocentrism is one of the effects of the scientific advances of today—from biogenetics to evolutionary theories. This means that the naturalized, animals, or "earth-others"—in fact, the planet as a whole—have ceased to be the boundary markers of the metaphysical uniqueness of the human subject. As I suggested earlier, scientific inquiry and exploration has been historically an outward-looking enterprise, framed by the dominant human masculine habit of taking for granted free access to and consumption of the bodies of others. As a mode of relation, negative difference is oedipalized in that it is both hierarchical, and hence structurally violent, and saturated with projections, identifications, and fantasies. These are centered on the dialectics of fear and desire, which is the trademark of the Western subject's relation to his "others." They are also the expression of his sense of entitlement to knowledge—the systematic "curiosity" that, from Odysseus on, has been the emblem of applied intelligence and scientific inquiry in our culture. Desire and fear are the motor of the scientific quest for knowledge about, and control over, the others.

Scientific disciplines have historically developed specific practices and methods, which also implement the self-styling of the scientist as the rational subject par excellence. Foucault teaches us that disciplines of control are coextensive with the making of scientific discourses and institutions. These technologies of control of natural or other forces are both genderized and racialized to a very high degree, and historically they have harped with distressing regularity on the disposable bodies of "others."

The challenge today is how to transform, deterritorialize, or nomadize the human-nonhuman interaction in philosophical practice so as to bypass the metaphysics of substance and its corollary, the dialectics of otherness, secularizing, accordingly, the concept of human nature and the life that animates it. With Deleuze and Guattari, I would speak of a generic becoming-minoritarian/animal as a figuration for the humanoid hybrids we are in the process of becoming. It is clear that our science—bio-genetics and informatics—can deal with this postanthropocentric shift, but can philosophy and the humanities rise to the occasion?

The answer lies in the ethical underpinnings of the nomadic vision of philosophical thinking. The displacement of anthropocentrism and recognition of transspecies solidarity are based on the awareness of "our" being in *this* together; that is to say, environmentally based, embodied, and embedded, in symbiosis with each other. Biocentered egalitarianism is a philosophy of radical immanence and affirmative becoming that activates a nomadic subject into sustainable processes of transformation. Becoming-animal/nonhuman consequently is a process of redefinition of one's sense of attachment and connection to a shared world, a territorial space. It expresses multiple ecologies of belonging, while it enacts the transformation of one's sensorial and perceptual coordinates in order to acknowledge the collective nature and outward-bound direction of what we call the self. The subject is fully immersed in and immanent to a network of nonhuman (animal, vegetable, viral) relations. My code word for this relentless elemental vitality of Life itself is *zoe*. The zoe-centered embodied subject is shot through with relational linkages of the symbiotic, contaminating/viral kind that interconnect it to a variety of others, starting from the environmental or ecoothers. This nonessentialist brand of vitalism reduces the hubris of rational consciousness, which, far from being an act of vertical transcendence, is rather recast as a downward push, a grounding exercise. It is the act of an unfolding of the self onto the world and the enfolding within of the world.

TRANSPOSITIONS

The postanthropocentric shift entails a number of important theoretical and methodological implications for the practice of science. Deleuze's nomadic vision of the subject does not necessarily preclude the position in which the subject is placed by scientific methods of inquiry, but displaces it in a number of structural and productive ways. The more obvious innovations are methodological: nomadic thought requires less linearity and more rhizomatic and dynamic thinking processes. A commitment to process ontology and to tracking the qualitative variations in the actualization of forces, forms, and relations forces some creativity on the usually sedate and conformist community of academic philosophers and institutional scientists.

The basis for this practical method is that of affirmative differences, or creative repetitions, i.e., retelling, reconfiguring, and revisiting the concept, phenomenon, event, or location from different angles. This is the application of the key concept of Spinoza's perspectivism, but it also infuses it with a nomadic tendency that establishes multiple connections and lines of interaction. Central to this is the notion of repetition as the internal return of difference, not of sameness. It is creative mimesis, not static repetition. Revisiting the same idea or project or location from different angles is therefore not merely a quantitative multiplication of options, but rather a qualitative leap of perspective. This leap takes the form of a hybrid mixture of codes, genres, or modes of apprehension of the idea, event, or phenomenon in question. The researcher must consequently become accountable for these transpositions through intensive, or affective cartographies of the relations that empower and sustain them. Hence the switch to a process-oriented method, as opposed to system-driven classifications.

The key methodological feature that emerges from this is an intensive form of interdisciplinarity, transversality, and boundary crossings among a range of discourses. More specifically, nomadic transpositions constitute a way of reworking the interrelation between axes of difference: sexualization, racialization, naturalization. All these share a passionate commitment to dislodge "difference" from its hegemonic position as an instrument of world-historical systems of domination, exclusion, and disqualification, as I argued before (chapters 1–4). Deleuze's wide-ranging reading habits offer a perfect example of this approach: references to modernist literature and music coexist peacefully alongside comments on contemporary mathematics and physics. This transdisciplinary approach enacts a rhizomatic embrace of diversity in scholarship that can only be sustained by a double talent: enormous erudition and a rigorous structure of thought. No wonder most academics flee from the challenge of Deleuze's texts, arguing that they are either too complex or too "unfocused" for their liking. Nomadic texts are not written for those who confuse thinking with the mere exercise of sedentary protocols of institutional reason. Deleuze brings transdisciplinarity to bear in the actual methods of thought, thus making conceptual diversity into a core issue.

I have also defined this methodological approach as "transpositions." This is a situated method of tracking the qualitative shifts or ontological leaps from generative chaos or indeterminate forms to actualized or determinate forms, while avoiding the pitfalls of subjectivism and individualism. Theoretically, a transposition has a double genealogical source: from music and genetics. In both cases it indicates an intertextual, cross-boundary or transversal transfer of codes, in the sense of a leap from one code, field, or axis into another. These leaps are not to be understood merely in the quantitative mode of plural multiplications, but rather in the qualitative sense of complex multiplicities. In other words, it is not just a matter of weaving together different strands, variations on a theme (textual or musical), but rather of playing the positivity of difference as an ontological force and of setting up adequate frames of resonance for their specific rhythms of becoming. As a term in music, transposition indicates variations and shifts of scale in a discontinuous but harmonious pattern. It is thus created as an in-between space of zigzagging and of crossing: nonlinear and chaotic, but in the productive sense of unfolding virtual spaces. Nomadic, yet accountable and committed; creative and hence affective, relational, and cognitively driven; discursive and also materially embedded—it is coherent without falling into the logocentric inflexibility of instrumental rationality.

In genetics, *transposition* refers to processes of mutation, or the transferral of genetic information, that occur in a nonlinear manner, which is nonetheless neither random nor arbitrary (Keller 1983). This is set in opposition to the mainstream scientific vision that tends to define the gene as a steady entity that transmits fixed units of heredity in an autonomous and self-sufficient manner and genetic variation as random events. Transposable moves appear to proceed by leaps and bounds and are ruled by chance, but they are not deprived of their logic or coherence. Central to genetic transpositions is the notion of material embodiment and the decisive role played by the organism in framing and affecting the rate and the frequency of the mutations. Transpositions occur by a carefully regulated dissociation of the bonds that would normally maintain cohesiveness between the genes, which are laid out in a linear manner on the chromosome. Nobel Prize–winning geneticist Barbara McClintock shows that, as a result of the dissociative impact, a mutation occurs that splits the chromosome into two detached segments. The rate of the mutation of these "jumping genes" is internally determined by the elements of the cell itself and is thus not prewritten in the gene. The notion of transposition emphasizes the flexibility of the genome itself. This implies that the key to understanding genetics is the process itself, the sequence of the organized system. This can be traced a posteriori as the effect of the dissociative shifts or leaps, but these controlling agents remain immanent to the process itself and are contingent upon the rearrangements of the elements. In other words, genetics information is contained in the sequence of the elements, which in turn means that the function and the organization of the genetic elements are mutable and interdependent.[1]

Consequently, our genetic system does not operate under the law of evolution defined as selection and aggressive struggle for survival. Rather, it proceeds by variations and adaptations—that is to say, by qualitative changes and structural transformations of the nonlinear and antiteleological kind. Consequently, as Hilary Rose put it ever so wittily: "DNA, far from being the stable macho molecule of the 1962 Watson-Crick prize story, becomes a structure of complex dynamic equilibrium" (Rose 2001:61) No body and no particle of matter is independent and self-propelled in nature as in the social. Ultimately, genetic changes are under the control of the organisms, which, under the influence of environmental factors, are capable of influencing the reprogramming of the genetic sequence itself.

Further, the notion of transposition describes the connection between the text and its social and historical context in the material and discursive sense of the term. The passion that animates all scientific and philosophical endeavors for nomadic thought is a concern for our historical situation, in so-called advanced, postindustrial cultures at the start of the third millennium. In my work this has become an emphasis on *amor fati*, not as fatalism, but rather in the pragmatic mode of the cartographer. In other words, my working definition of a nomadic scientific method in the human and social sciences (the "subtle sciences"), as well as in genetics, molecular biology, and evolutionary theory (the "hard sciences"), cannot be dissociated from an ethics of inquiry that is adequate to and respectful of the complexities of the real-life world we are living in. I am committed to start my critical work from this complexity, not from a nostalgic reinvention of an all-inclusive holistic ideal.

NONLINEAR TIME

Linearity is especially problematic on the methodological front for radical epistemologies and marginal discourses. Their challenge is how to implement a coherent but nonhierarchical system of transmission for the cultural and political memory of minorities. How to keep alive a past that is often not recognized by official institutional culture? Foucault's early work on genealogies as countermemories of resistance is again foundational. Deleuze expands this pioneering effort into a conceptual critique of the powers of dominant memory systems over the human and social sciences. Deleuze's favorite example is the ravages accomplished by the teaching of the history of philosophy as a normative canonical discipline that kills theoretical creativity and turns philosophy into an intimidating oedipal machine.

Radical epistemologies addressed the same methodological issue—how to intervene creatively upon a canonized corpus of texts—so as to enable the transmission of the cultural and political capital of centuries-old political movements such as socialism, pacifism, or feminism. Linearity is the dominant time of Chronos, not the dynamic time of becoming, or Aion, and as such it is a very inadequate way of accounting for intergenerational relations among political subjects of a countercultural movement: for instance, women who belong to different historical phases of the women's movement or youth that was born after the end of communism. Nowadays, with a third feminist wave in full swing (Henry 2004), it is difficult to avoid both the hierarchical oedipal narrative of mothers and daughters of the feminist revolution and the negative passions that inevitably accompany such narratives. The best antidote is an anti-oedipal approach to the question of intergenerational ethics. It results in the need to find adequate accounts for the zigzagging nature of feminist intellectual and cultural memories as well as their respective political genealogies. Both rest, however, on a nomadic vision of memory as becoming.

This raises methodological issues of how to account for a different notion of time, focused on Aion, the dynamic and internally contradictory or circular time of becoming. Thus, instead of deference to the authority of the past, we have the fleeting copresence of multiple time zones in a continuum that activates and deterritorializes stable identities. This dynamic vision of the subject enlists the creative resources of the imagination to the task of enacting transformative relations and actions in the present: an ontological nonlinearity that rests on Spinoza's ethics of affirmation and becoming and predicates the positivity of difference. A nomadic methodology needs flows of empowering desire that mobilize the scientific subject and activate her out of the gravitational pull of envy, rivalry, and ego-indexed claims to recognition. This project requires a serious critique of institutional structures and modes of oedipalized, competitive, and negative interaction.

Remembering in the nomadic mode is the active reinvention of a self that is joyfully discontinuous, as opposed to being mournfully consistent, as programmed by phallogocentric culture. It destabilizes the sanctity of the past and the authority of experience. This is the tense of a virtual sense of potential. Memories need the imagination to empower the actualization of virtual possibilities in the subject. They allow the subject to differ from oneself as much as possible while remaining faithful to oneself or, in other words, enduring. Becoming is molecular in that it requires a singular overthrowing of the internalized simulacra of the self, consolidated by habits and flat repetitions. The dynamic vision of the subject as assemblage is central to a vitalist yet antiessentialist theory of desire, which also prompts a new practice of ethics.

Desire is the propelling and compelling force that is driven by self-affirmation or the transformation of negative into positive passions. This is a desire not to preserve, but to change: it is a deep yearning for transformation or a process of affirmation. Empathy and compassion are key features of this nomadic yearning for in-depth transformation. Proximity, attraction, or intellectual sympathy is both a topological and qualitative notion: it is a question of ethical temperature. It calls for an affective framing for the becoming of subjects as sensible or intelligent matter. The affectivity of the imagination is the motor for these encounters and of the conceptual creativity they trigger.

One of the ways in which this can be accounted for is through an intensive or affective mapping of how each of us relates to and interacts with the ideas/events/codes as processes. I shall return to the affective element later. Ethically, each researcher or writer has to negotiate the often dramatic shifts of perspective and location that are required for the implementation of a process-oriented—as opposed to concept-based and system-driven—thought. In other words, we need to rise to the challenge of more conceptual creativity.

Methodologically, this vision allows us to replace linearity with a more rhizomatic and dynamic style of thinking. The basic method is that of creative repetitions, i.e., retelling, reconfiguring, and revisiting the concept, phenomenon, event, or location from different angles, so as to infuse it with a nomadic spin that establishes multiple connections and lines of interaction.

This method supports the project of actualizing a nomadic redefinition of the subject and the quest for a balancing act between past traditions and present transformations through the method of disidentification from dominant images of thought. The relationship between creativity and critique is renegotiated through a balance between the creative experimentations with "minor science" and the necessary dose of negative criticism that is constitutive of oppositional consciousness. Nomadic thought aims at recasting critique as affirmation. I shall return to this in chapter 11.

SOCIAL SUSTAINABILITY

The concept of social sustainability is particularly relevant to this methodological debate. It has two reference points: sustainability as a temporal notion (time duration of life as bios) and endurance as an intensive notion (the ability to sustain intensities or zoe). It brings together both the duration of life and the intensities of encounters. This is for me the most direct consequence of the relational vitality and elemental complexity that mark Deleuze's thought: life is not a teleological notion, and thus it doesn't seek or want to express itself. Life, simply by being life, expresses itself. This is why I defend the idea of amor fati. To accept amor fati in its radical immanence is to change one's relation to life and, in doing so, perhaps change life itself—allow it expressive intensities it would not otherwise possess.

This complex task is facilitated by adopting a nonunitary vision of nomadic subjectivity, which, coupled with the idea of desire as plenitude and not as lack, produces a more transformative approach to the ethics of thinking. The stated criteria for this new ethics include nonprofit; emphasis on the collective; acceptance of relationality and of viral contaminations; and a link between theory and practice, including the importance of creation. They are not moral injunctions, but frames for an ongoing experiment.

They need to be enacted collectively, so as to produce effective cartographies of how much bodies can take, which I also call thresholds of sustainability. They also aim to create collective bonds, a new affective community or polity.

This project must include an evaluation of the costs involved in pursuing active processes of change and orecognition of the pain and difficulty these entail. The problem of the costs within the schizoid logic of our times concerns mostly potestas, the quantitative, not potentia, or incorporeal intensities. Creation, or the invention of the new, can only emerge from the qualitative intensities and thus cannot apply to a notion that measures the tolerance of bodies as actualized systems. Hence again another aspect of the ethical question: if, in the name of encouraging (prehuman or individual) life (zoe), we value the incorporeal invention of quality and primarily affect and precept; if (again, following Deleuze) we insist on the incorporeal emphasis on affects and precepts or becoming (as distinguished from affected bodies and perceptions of entities), then how can we use a concept of sustainability to argue against the cost of fidelity to the concept or the precept? That would involve a corporeal criterion to the incorporeal. This is a conceptual double bind and a true ethical dilemma.

How can we combine sustainability with intensity? One line I would propose is to hold everyone, not only exceptional people like writers or thinkers but just anyone (*homo tantum*), accountable for the ethical effort to be worthy of the production of affect and precept. It is a noble ethics of overcoming the self and stretching the boundaries of how much a body can take; it involves compassion for pain, but also an active desire to work through it and find a way across it (more in chapter 12). The challenge is therefore to reconcile the absolute difference (or différend) between incorporeal affects, or the capacity to experiment with thresholds of sustainability, with our corporeal fate as such and such an affected body. What methodological and ethical criteria can we create in the context of this difference? How can one (simultaneously?) increase affectivities as the capacity to invent or capture affect and look after the affected bodies? What kind of synchronized effort could achieve this aim? In other words, what is the "cost" of the capacity to be affected that allows us to be the vehicle of creation? What would a qualitative concept of cost be? These are the core criteria for a nomadic ethics agenda for an experimental becoming-minor of science.

AFFECT, MEMORY, AND THE IMAGINATION

Nomadic methodology works by empowering creative alternatives. This philosophical creativity operates a shift of paradigm toward a positive appraisal of differences, multiplicity, and complexity not as an end in themselves but as steps in a process of recomposition of the coordinates of subjectivity. This has some important methodological implications for the role and function of memory and the imagination. The cartographic accounts of the subject of complexity and becoming, which I've described previously, entail a sort of affective mapping of the thinker's/reader's interaction with others: texts, ideas, concepts, or artworks. This perceptive and conceptual engagement with bodies of work bypasses classical binary thought.

All radical pedagogies stress the crucial role played by the memory in the formation of politically active and ethically conscious subjects. Remembering the wound, the pain, the injustice—bearing witness to the missing people—to those who never managed to gain powers of discursive representation is central to the radical ethics and politics of philosophical nomadism. Another important use of memory is connected to the affective dimension. Let me illustrate it with an example: what exactly is involved in "working from memory" when one is writing commentaries on the history of philosophy or on other theoretical texts? The most notorious statement to this effect concerns Deleuze's two-volume study of cinema, in which he states that he did not watch again any of the movies he was to discuss. He just wrote from the memory of the first time he watched those films, which often was years before. Most of his literary citations, however, bear the same style: they are rarely verbatim repetitions of the original texts. Nor are they "close textual readings," following the dominant mode of teaching philosophy in the academic world today, where the repetition of "his master's voice" is the name of the game. "Faithfulness" here equates flat repetition or the replication of sameness.

Writing from memory or "by heart" involves a number of precise methodological steps. Firstly, it means that one is exempted from checking against the original, at least during the process of writing the actual commentary. This expresses the conviction that the "truth" of a text is somehow never really "written." Neither is it contained within the signifying space of the book, nor is it about the authority of a proper noun, a signature, a tradition, a canon, let alone the prestige of a discipline. The authoritativeness of citation is discarded for an altogether different kind of accuracy. The "truth" of a text resides rather in the affects, i.e., the kind of outward-bound interconnections or relations that it enables, provokes, engenders, and sustains. Thus a text is a relay point between different moments in space and time, as well as different levels, degrees, forms, and configurations of the thinking process. Thinking, like breathing, is not held into the mold of linearity, or the confines of the printed page, but it happens outside, out of bounds, in webs of encounters with ideas, others, texts. The linguistic signifier is merely one of the points in a chain of effects, not its center or its endgame.

Secondly, and as a consequence of what I've just described, "working from memory" implies respecting the specific, nonlinear temporality of this intensive process of thinking. The notion of "duration" is of crucial importance here. The active, minoritarian, or nomadic memory triggers molecular becomings and thus works toward affirmation. In order to do so, however, it constantly reconnects to the virtual totality of a continuously recomposing block of past and present moments. In a synchronization exercise, moments in time coincide in the "here and now" of actualizing processes of heightened intensity or becoming.

When applied to the reading of theoretical, social, and cultural texts, this means that one starts working from oral traces and affective imprints, i.e., more viscerally. The focus is not on representation or citation, but on the affective traces, on what is left over, what remains, what has somehow caught and stuck around, the drags and the sediments of the reading and the cognitive process. This assumes that the focus does not fall on textual interiority and a detailed reproduction of the text's intentions, meanings, and conceptual structures. Equally inadequate is the weight of oedipal tradition and the veneration of the authority of the past as a support mechanism for the habit of faithful textual commentaries.

I prefer to think of this way of relating to memory in terms of nomadic transpositions, that is to say, as creative and highly generative interconnections that mix and match, mingle and multiply possibilities of expansion and growth among different units or entities. Transpositions require precision in terms of the coordinate of the encounters, but also a high charge of imaginative force. They may appear as random association to the naked eye, but in fact they are a specific and accurate topology of forces of attraction, which find their own modes of selection, combination, and recomposition.

Musical scores function by transpositions, much as the transmission of genetic information (Keller 1983): they proceed by leaps and bounds, but this is neither anarchical nor chaotic. The coherence of this system is the result of the affinity and empathy that allowed for the preliminary selection to be made in the first place, resulting in the storage of the data in/as memory. There is no spontaneity at work here, but rather a careful dosage of forces, a process of selective affinities.

The model for this is the quick glance of the painter that captures the "essence" of a landscape, or the precise quality of the light upon it, in a fleeting moment, which is wrongly rendered in terms of "insight." It has nothing whatsoever to do with interiority, however, nor with inscrutable depths. It is rather related to external forces, their irresistible energy and mobility. Just as travelers can capture the "essential lines" of a landscape or a place in the speed of crossing it, this is not superficiality, but a way of framing the longitudinal and latitudinal forces that structure a certain spatiotemporal "moment."

These multilayered levels of affectivity are the building blocks for creative transpositions, which compose a plane of actualization of relations, that is to say, points of contact between self and surroundings. They are the mark of immanent, embodied, and embedded relations. Capturing such forces is not dependent on the supervising control of a conscious subject who centralizes and ordains the information according to a hierarchy of sensorial and cognitive data.

Moments like that—when the self is emptied out, dissolving into rawer and more elementary sensations—mark heightened levels of awareness and receptivity. In spiritual practices like meditation, what is labeled as concentration is represented by a deep vacuum. You look through reality to focus elsewhere. In fact, you are focussing on the ever-receding horizon of elsewhereness itself, that is, infinity. An intransitive gaze that marks the intensive state of becoming. What looks like absent-mindedness, on closer scrutiny, reveals itself to be a qualitative leap toward a more focused, more precise, more accurate perception of one's own potentia, which is one's capacity to "take in" the world, to encounter it, to go toward it. It is about respecting a creative void without forcefully imposing a form that corresponds to the author's own intentions or desires—it is an opening-out toward the geophilosophical or planetary dimension of "chaosmosis" (Guattari 1995). The form, or the discursive event, rather emerges from the creative encounter of the doer and the deed or from the active process of becoming. This amounts to turning the self into the threshold of gratuitous (principle of non-profit), aimless (principle of mobility or flow) acts that express the vital energy of transformative becomings.

If the activity of thinking is represented along these lines, it then follows that the more self-reflexive a posteriori process of theorizing this activity requires methodological skills other than the ones usually praised, rewarded, and perpetuated in academic circles. Notably, the key habit of "faithfulness to the text" and of citation as repetition of the author's intended meaning gets displaced. Instead what comes to the fore is the creative capacity that consists in being able to render the more striking lines, forces, or affective charges of any given text or author. To do so, what one needs to be loyal to is neither the spurious depth of the text nor the author's latent or manifest intentionality and even less to the sovereignty of the phallic master. Loyalty is instead required to the intensity of the affective forces that compose a text or a concept so as to account for what a text can do, what it has done, how it has impacted on one according to the affective coordinates I have outlined. Accounting backward for the affective impact of various items or data on oneself is the process of remembering. In Bergson, as in Deleuze, it has as much to do with the imagination, that is to say, creative reworking, as with the passive repetition of chronologically prior, recorded, and hence retrievable experiences. Memory is ongoing and forward-looking precisely because it is a singular yet complex subject that is always already in motion and in process. This memory has to do with the capacity to endure, to "sustain" the process of change or transformation. Duration and endurance are also ethical categories to do with sustainability, not just an aesthetic one. Sustainability emerges (again) as the guiding principle of these intensive methods of analysis.

Creativity is a nomadic process in that it entails the active displacement of dominant formations of identity, memory, and identification. Becoming has to do with emptying out the self, opening it out to possible encounters with the "outside." As Roy puts is: "the pragmatic purpose was to introduce a 'swerve' or deviation in the plane of taken-for-granted assumptions by means of which a new experiment of thought could be inserted in the interstices that might help teachers get an insight into the generative possibilities of the situation" (Roy 2003:2)

Remembering in the nomadic mode is the active reinvention of a self that is joyfully discontinuous, in contrast to being mournfully consistent, as programmed by phallogocentric culture. It destabilizes the sanctity of the past and the authority of experience. This is the tense of a virtual sense of potential. Memories need the imagination to empower the actualization of virtual possibilities in the subject. They allow the subject to differ from oneself as much as possible while remaining faithful to oneself or, in other words, enduring.

Desire as plenitude rather challenges the matrix of having and lacking access to recognition by Self and Other as transcendent categories. Becoming is molecular in that it requires singular overthrowing of the internalized simulacra of the self, consolidated by habits and flat repetitions. The dynamic vision of the subject as assemblage is central to a vitalist yet antiessentialist theory of desire, which also prompts a new practice of sustainable ethics that aims "to open up the fastness in which thought takes refuge, provoking by that same parting novel, nonhumanist stirrings" (Roy 2003:1). Desire is the propelling and compelling force that is driven by self-affirmation or the transformation of negative into positive passions. This is a desire not to preserve but to change: it is a deep yearning for transformation or a process of affirmation. Empathy and compassion are key features of this nomadic yearning for in-depth transformation. Proximity, attraction, or intellectual sympathy is both a topological and qualitative notion: it is a question of ethical temperature. It is an affective framing for the becoming of subjects as sensible or intelligent matter. The affectivity of the imagination is the motor for these encounters and the conceptual creativity they trigger. It is a transformative force that propels multiple, heterogeneous "becomings" of the subject.

CONCLUSION: AFFIRMATIVE VISIONS

As I argued earlier, the conditions for renewed political and ethical agency cannot be drawn from the immediate context or current state of the terrain. They have to be generated affirmatively and creatively by efforts geared to creating possible futures, by mobilizing resources and visions that have been left untapped, and by actualizing them in daily practices of interconnection with others.

This project requires more visionary power or prophetic energy, qualities that are neither especially in fashion in academic circles nor highly valued scientifically in these times of commercial globalization. Yet the call for more vision is emerging from many quarters in critical theory. Feminists have a long and rich genealogy in terms of pleading for increased visionary insight. From the very early days, Joan Kelly (1979) typified feminist theory as a double-edged vision, with a strong critical and an equally strong creative function. Faith in the creative powers of the imagination is an integral part of feminists' appraisal of lived embodied experience and the bodily roots of subjectivity, which would express the complex singularities that feminist women have become. Donna Haraway's work (1997, 2003) provides the best example of this kind of respect for a dimension where creativity is unimaginable without some visionary fuel.

Prophetic or visionary minds are thinkers of the future. The future as an active object of desire propels us forth and motivates us to be active in the here and now of a continuous present that calls for resistance. The yearning for sustainable futures can construct a livable present. This is not a leap of faith, but an active transposition, a transformation at the in-depth level (Braidotti 2006). A prophetic or visionary dimension is necessary in order to secure an affirmative hold over the present as the launching pad for sustainable becoming or qualitative transformations. The future is the virtual unfolding of the affirmative aspect of the present, which honors our obligations to the generations to come.

The pursuit of practices of hope, rooted in the ordinary micropractices of everyday life, is a simple strategy to hold, sustain, and map out sustainable transformations. The motivation for the social construction of hope is grounded in a profound sense of responsibility and accountability. A fundamental gratuitousness and a profound sense of hope is part of it. Hope, as I will argue in chapter 10, is a way of dreaming up possible futures: an anticipatory virtue that permeates our lives and activates them. It is a powerful motivating force grounded not only in projects that aim at reconstructing the social imaginary but also in the political economy of desires, affects, and creativity. Contemporary nomadic practices of subjectivity—both in pedagogy and other areas of thought—work toward a more affirmative approach to critical theory.

Beyond unitary visions of the self and teleological renditions of the processes of subject formation, a nomadic philosophy can sustain contemporary subjects in the effort to synchronize themselves with the changing world in which they try to make a positive difference. Against the established tradition of methodological nationalism, a different image of thought can be activated that rejects Euro-universalism and trusts instead in the powers of diversity. It also enlists affectivity, memory, and the imagination to the crucial task of inventing new figurations and new ways of representing the complex subjects we have become. The key method is an ethics of respect for complexity that produces cosynchronizations of nomadic selves and thus constitutes communities across multiple locations and generations. Science is socially inscribed and ecologically integrated not along a nationalistic axis but in a rhizomic web of planetary connections that enable "us" to be in *this* together.

9

NOMADIC EUROPEAN CITIZENSHIP

One broaches the subject of the European Union with a lot of hesitation these days.

Whatever hopes and aspirations this project may have aroused in the past; it is at present a source of global concern, both for those who live within its boundaries and for the rest of the world. The project of construction of a "new" European identity as a multicultural social democratic space within the framework of the European Union is controversial, to say the least. The current political context of increasing Euroskepticism coupled with growing xenophobia highlights the inner tensions of the European political project. In spite of the successful introduction of the euro as the common currency, the global financial crisis, exemplified in the "Greek case," casts doubts on the sustainability of the European project. The EU is positioned simultaneously as a major player within the global economy and as an alternative social space not deprived of progressive elements. The transformative potential of this project not only counteracts the aggressive aspects of neoliberalism on a number of key issues (privacy, telecommunication, genetically modified food, and the environment) but also stresses the need to reflect back on the dangers of Eurocentrism (Balibar 2001).

In the rest of this chapter I will emphasize the progressive potential of the EU in terms of the becoming-nomadic of Europe. This political project entails the redefinition not only of the interrelation of the member states but also of the power relations within them. These processes of revision of identity triggers contradictory reactions. Not the least contradictory is the simultaneous celebration of transnational spaces, on the one hand, and the resurgence of hypernationalisms at the microlevel. The global city and Fortress Europe stand both face-to-face and as two sides of the same coin (Sassen 1995). In relation to this, I want to defend a process of the "becoming-minoritarian" of Europe (Deleuze and Guattari 1980) as a way of both bypassing the binary global-local and of destabilizing the established definitions of European identity. My position rests on the assumption of the decline of Eurocentrism as a historical event, which represents a qualitative shift of perspective in our collective sense of identity. Several political movements today, from the Green Party to the European Social Forum, give top priority to a post-Eurocentric vision of the European Union. Some progressive thinkers, including feminist and postcolonial scholars, are also critiquing nationalism as a necessary step toward the construction of a new European—as in EU—citizenship.

The nomadic vision of a collectively assembled, externally related, and multilayered subject that acts in a time continuum clashes frontally with the established view of the European subject of knowledge. Following the critical premises of poststructuralist critiques of humanism by Foucault (1966), Deleuze and Guattari (1972, 1980), Derrida (1991), and Irigaray (1977), nomadic thought questions the classical vision of the philosophical subject as the quintessential European citizen. As I argued in the previous chapter, "Europe" stands in this discussion for a tacit consensus about the self-evidence of the self-reflexive and self-correcting powers of reason. "Europeanness," in other words, is not a specific geopolitical location with a political history, but rather a universal and abstract concept. Europe as the symbol of universal self-consciousness posits itself as the site of origin of reason and self-designates itself as the motor of the world-historical unfolding of rationality, reducing difference to a structural position of pejoration. The epistemic and world-historical violence engendered by the claim to universalism and by the oppositional view of consciousness lies at the heart of a methodological nationalism or conceptual Eurocentrism, which I analyzed in the previous chapter.

Nomadic theory rejects nationalism and takes another route: it practices philosophy as the art of connection making. I follow both Foucault's redefinition of the philosopher as a technician of practical knowledge and the feminist commitment to produce relevant knowledge claims that reflect the lived experience of women and of other marginal subjects. This philosophical practice is enacted through cartographic analyses of specific problem areas. As a materialist cartographic practice, nomadic theory is well suited to the task of mapping out complex interactions among many structures, subjects, and social relations. These cartographies are accountable mappings of materially grounded and historically specific embedded and embodied locations. The point of these accounts is to generate the conditions for transformative or affirmative engagements with the present. By stressing these interrelated elements, I hope to take forward the discussion on the progressive and critical possibilities of the "new" Europe.

FROM EUROCENTRISM TO THE BECOMING-MINOR OF EUROPE

Continental philosophy—prior to and including poststructuralism—is historically connected to the issue of European identity and "civilization." Since the end of the nineteenth century and the early decades of the twentieth century, the "crisis" of European philosophy has both reflected and highlighted larger sociopolitical issues linked to the geopolitical status of Europe and to the growing sense of crisis about European hegemony. Nietzsche and Freud, then Husserl and Fanon, and later Adorno and the Frankfurt school are evidence of this trend. According to the poststructuralist generation, the crisis of philosophical humanism coincides historically with the decline of Europe as an imperial world power, especially after the Second World War. Nowadays, wise old men like Habermas and Derrida and progressive spirits like Balibar have taken the lead in the public debate by stressing the advantages of a postnationalist sense of the European Union.

Insofar as Continental philosophy carries a built-in question about European identity, philosophical self-reflexivity has a unique contribution to make to the debate on Europe. Nomadic theory in particular can help to desegregate intellectual debates, which tend to stay confined within set political groups or discursive communities. Philosophical reflection assesses and often resets theoretical lines of demarcation and thus can produce discursive interconnections along areas or questions of common concern. Let us start by taking seriously the novel contest of the European Union.

My argument is about the "becoming-minor" of the European Union in the sense of a postnationalist European space. I rest this project on two sets of arguments: one political, the other historical. Politically, on the Continent, the opposition to the European Union is led by the authoritarian right, which is nationalist and xenophobic. As Stuart Hall put it (Hall 1987, 1990), the great resistance to the European Union, as well as the American suspicion of it, is a defensive response to a process that aims at overcoming the idea of European nation-states. The short-range effect of this process is a nationalist wave of paranoia and xenophobic fears, which is simultaneously anti-European and racist. I have argued that late postmodernity (Braidotti 2002a, b) functions through the paradox of simultaneous globalization and fragmentation. It is as if the law of the "excluded middle" did not hold, and one thing and its opposite can simultaneously be the case (Appadurai 1994). Thus the expansion of European boundaries coincides with the resurgence of micronationalist borders at all levels in Europe today. Unification coexists with the closing down of borders; the common European citizenship and the common currency coexist with increasing internal fragmentation and regionalism; a new, allegedly postnationalist, identity coexists with the return of xenophobia, racism, and anti-Semitism (Benhabib 1999a). The disappearance of the Soviet empire simultaneously marks the triumph of the advanced market economy and the return of tribal ethnic wars of the most archaic kind. Globalization means both homogenization and extreme power differences (Eisenstein 1998).

Strong opposition to the EU is also voiced, however, by the nostalgic left, which seems to miss the topological foundations for international working-class solidarity. The cosmopolitan tradition of socialism militates against the European dimension: solidarity with the third world always carries a politically correct consensus, whereas an interest in European matters is often dismissed as being vain and self-obsessive. Speaking as a left-wing feminist intellectual, I must say that the left has often been unable to react with energy and vision to the historical evidence of the dislocation of European supremacy and the coming of the American empire (Hardt and Negri 2000). The left has also been slow to understand the nondialectical and schizophrenic nature of advanced capitalism (Deleuze and Guattari 1972, 1980). In this light, the feminist, pacifist, and antiracist movements can be of great inspiration in drawing more lucid and relevant political cartographies of contemporary power relations.

Historically, the project of the European Union originates in the defeat of fascism and Nazism after World War II. The moral and political bankruptcy of European "civilization" was exemplified by the holocaust perpetuated against the Jewish and Roma populations as well as the persecution of homosexuals and communists by the Nazi and fascist regimes. The life and work of one of the initiators of the project of European federation—Altiero Spinelli (Spinelli 1992; Spinelli and Rossi 1998)—testifies to this, as does that of his wife Ursula Hirschman (Spinelli 1979; Hirschman 1993) and Ursula's brother Albert Hirschman (Hirschman 1945, 1994). The project of the EU is consequently grounded in antifascism, antinationalism, and antimilitarism (Spinelli and Rossi 1998). It was imposed on the European nation-states as a punishment for two Franco-German wars that spilled over into global wars. In the context of the cold war, the new European community, as a showcase of Western superiority, also played the role of streamlining the reconstruction of Europe's war-torn economy.

The two branches of my argument—the political and the historical—converge upon a single conclusion: that "the European Union" as a progressive project means a site of possible political resistance against nationalism, xenophobia, and racism, bad habits that are endemic to the old imperial Europe. It follows therefore that the question of the European Union no longer coincides with European identity, but rather constitutes a rupture from it and a transformation. The scholarship reflects this double track: there is far more work on European identity, as such, than on the European Union. Critical theory, including feminism, is especially notable for the silence on the postnationalist political project of the EU and is prone to anti-Europeanism. This view of Europe as a postnationalist project, however, should be appealing to these critiques of power since it rejects the idea of Europe as a world power driven by a form of universalism that has implied the exclusion or consumption of others.

Both historically and politically, the project of European unification involves a process of consciousness-raising, which in turn expresses a critique of the self-appointed missionary role of Europe as the alleged center of the world. In an argument that runs parallel to feminist theory, this progressive and nomadic vision of Europe promotes a regrounding of this pretentious and false universalism into a more situated, local perspective. As the work of feminist philosophers like Genevieve Lloyd (1985) has pointed out, universalistic claims are actually highly particular and partial. Feminist epistemologists, especially Sandra Harding (1991) and Donna Haraway (1992a), have produced some of the most significant critiques of the false universalism of the European subject of knowledge. They have also offered powerful alternative accounts of both subjectivity and of an enlarged sense of scientific objectivity. This process of epistemological revision runs parallel to new theorizations of the subject. While it does not always result in such new theorizations, it does, however, amount to a revision of the ethnocentrism implicit in a universalistic posture that positions Europe as the center of the knowing subject: science as the white man's burden (Harding 1993). Such a dislocation of pseudo-scientific assertions of white superiority amounts to a regrounding of Europe, no longer as the center but as one of the many peripheries in the world today. This process of consciousness-raising is a sober awakening to the concrete particularity of the European situation.

A range of new, alternative subjectivities has indeed emerged in the shifting landscapes of advanced capitalism and its global diasporas. They are contested, multilayered, and internally contradictory subject positions, all of which does not make them any less ridden with power relations. Hybrid and in between, traditional descriptions in terms of sociological categories such as "marginals," "migrants," or "minorities" are, as Saskia Sassen (1995) suggests, grossly inadequate. From the angle of "different constitutive others," this inflationary production of different differences simultaneously expresses the logic of capitalist proliferation and exploitation but also the emerging subjectivities of positive and self-defined others. It all depends on one's locations or situated perspectives. Far from seeing this as a form of relativism, I see it as an embedded and embodied form of enfleshed materialism. It is important to resist the uncritical reproduction of Sameness on a molecular, global, or planetary scale by approaching differences in a nondialectical and multilayered framework that stresses their subversive potential.

The work on power, difference, and the politics of location offered by postcolonial and antiracist feminist thinkers who are familiar with the European situation—among them notably Spivak (1987), Hall (1992), Brah (1993), and Gilroy (1987)—helps us to illuminate the paradoxes of the present. One of the most significant effects of late postmodernity in Europe is the phenomenon of transculturality in a pluriethnic or multicultural European social space. World migration—a huge movement of population from periphery to center, working on a worldwide scale of "scattered hegemonies" (Grewal and Kaplan 1994), has challenged the claim to an alleged cultural homogeneity of European nation-states and of the struggling European Union. Present-day Europe is struggling with multiculturalism at a time of increasing racism and xenophobia. The paradoxes, power dissymmetry, and fragmentations of the present historical context rather require that we shift the political debates from the issue of differences between cultures to differences *within* the same culture. These are the shifting grounds on which periphery and center confront each other, with a new level of complexity that defies dualistic or oppositional thinking.

Nomadic theory argues, if a sociocultural mutation is taking place in the direction of a multiethnic, multimedia society, that the transformation cannot affect only the pole of "the others." It must equally dislocate the position and the prerogative of "the same," the former center. In other words, what is changing is not merely the terminology or metaphorical representation of the subjects, but the very structure of subjectivity, the social relations, and the social imaginary that support it. It is the syntax of social relations, as well as their symbolic representation, that is in upheaval. The customary standard-bearers of Eurocentric phallocentrism no longer hold in a civil society that is, amongst others, sexed female *and* male, multicultural, and not inevitably Christian or secular. More than ever, the question of social transformation begs that of representation: what can the male, white, Christian monotheistic symbolic do for emerging subjects-in-process? The challenges as well as the anxieties evoked by them mark patterns of becoming that require new forms of expression and representation, that is to say, socially mediated forms, which need to be assessed critically. Feminist theory is a relevant and useful navigational tool in these stormy times of locally enacted, global phenomena, i.e., "G-local" changes.[1]

GLOBAL DIASPORAS

The point of the matter is, as I stated at the start of the chapter, that we live in a world that is organized along multiple axes of mobility, circulation, flows of people and commodities (Cresswell 1997). Displacement is a central feature of the postmodern era, as critics like Probyn have also pointed out (1990). Moreover, as Ernesto Laclau (1995) has argued, the point is that processes of hybridization and nomadic identities are neither marginal nor self-chosen phenomena. It is rather the case, as Dahrendorf (1990) has argued, that advanced capitalism itself functions by organizing constant flows and displacements in such a way as to erode its own foundations. The crisis of the nation-state in the age of transnational capital flow is a significant example of this (Mouffe 1994), and contemporary technologies are contributing to accelerate this trend (Castells 1996).

The globalized world is defined as a transnational space of mobility, borders, transitions, and flows. It expresses "the overlapping and non-linear contact zones between natures and cultures: border, travel, creolization, transculturation, hybridity and diaspora" (Clifford 1994:303). In her seminal work on the cartographies of diasporic social spaces, Avtar Brah argues that they are sites of transition and exchange of people, information, cultures, commodities, and capital. The diaspora affects as much the roots of indigenous people as the routes of itinerant subjects in the postcolonial world order.

Greek in origin, the term *diaspora* was first used to describe the experience of the Jews, and now provides a non-normative description of the uprooting and dispersion of a great deal of populations: the Armenian, Turkish, Palestinian, Cuban, Greek, Chinese, Hungarian, and Chilean, to name but a few. Clifford comments: "In the late twentieth century, all or most communities have diasporic dimensions (moments, tactics, practices, articulations). Some are more diasporic than others" (Clifford 1994:310), Robin Cohen (1997) subjects Clifford's notion of "travelling cultures" to detailed analysis. While resisting the metaphorization of diasporic subject positions as some icon of postmodernity, Cohen inscribes them at the heart of the historical condition of globalization. The diasporic subject position is not only negative but also productive of two-way processes of cultural signification, especially in terms of antinationalism. Cohen comments: "Diasporas are positioned somewhere between nation-states and 'travelling cultures'" (Cohen 1997:135). Avtar Brah confirms that diasporic space is made of relationality and that it inscribes "a homing desire while simultaneously critiquing discourses of fixed origins" (Brah 1996:193).

The global diaspora has enormous implications for a world economy linked by a thick web of transnational flows of capital and labor. Such a system is marked by internal processes of migration implying mobility, flexibility or precariousness of work conditions, transience and impermanent settlements. Last but not least, globalization is about a deterritorialization of social identity that challenges the hegemony of nation-states and their claim to exclusive citizenship (Cohen 1997). This proliferation of ethnic and racialized differences produces the stratification of layers of multiple controls in a political economy of "scattered hegemonies" (Grewal and Kaplan

1994). This is a system of centerless but constant surveillance and manipulation, which pitches the center against the many peripheries in a complex logic that operates not only between the geopolitical blocks but also
within them.

Massive concentrations of infrastructures exist alongside complex, worldwide dissemination of goods. The technologically driven advanced culture
that prides itself in being called the information society is, in reality, a concrete, material infrastructure that is concentrated on the sedentary global
city. Sassen defines global economies as: "the location of transnational
spaces within national territories" (Sassen 1994:xiii). Translated to the language of philosophical nomadism, global migration is a molar line of seg-
mentation or reterritorialization that controls access to different forms of
mobility and immobility. The global city and the refugee camp are not dialectical or moral opposites: they are two sides of the same global coin. They
express the schizoid political economy of our times. The point of nomadic
subjectivity is to identify a line of flight, that is to say, a creative alternative space of becoming that would fall not between the mobile/immobile,
the resident/foreigner, but within these categories. The point is to neither
dismiss nor glorify the status of marginal, alien others, but to find a more
accurate, complex location for a transformation of the terms of this political interaction.

Let me therefore make one point perfectly clear: I would never want to
argue that rootlessness and homelessness or constant mobility and displacement are universal features, although they have taken place, to different ex-
tents, in all periods of history. On the contrary, I do take shifts, mutations,
and processes of change as key features of the particular historical period
we are going through. Precisely because of this, social critics need to be very
situated in their approach to any analysis of the new subject positions that
have become available in postindustrial times. The differences in degrees,
types, kinds, and modes of mobility and—even more significantly—of non-
mobility need to be mapped out with precision and sensitivity. This cartographic accuracy is made necessary by the fact that nonunitary subject
positions, migrants, hybrids, nomads, and cyborgs are key elements of our
historicity. They function as generic terms for the indexation of different
degrees of access and entitlement to subject positions in the historical era of
postmodernity. They situate subjects in one of the many polylocated centers
that weave together the global economy. Power is the key issue, and *mobil-*

ity is a term that indexes access to it. As such, power relations are internally contradictory, and they require suitable politically invested cartographies that account for them.

James Clifford (1994), who is more sympathetic to metaphors of travel and displacement than to nomadism, makes careful distinctions between different kinds of travel from the colonial exploration or bourgeois "tour" to the itineraries of immigrant or indentured laborers. Zygmunt Bauman, in his analysis of postmodern ethics (1993), juxtaposes the figuration of the pilgrim to that of the tourist and the nomad and gives them diametrically opposed ethical codings. These differences need to be accounted for in such a way as to make the power differences explicit. These accounts are narratives of the diaspora, which, at the end of this millennium, concern most communities, though to various degrees. The different narratives, however, have to be embedded in specific histories and geographies, thus preventing hasty metaphorizations (Braidotti 2011). This goal echoes the aims of the feminist cartographic and materialist philosophies of the subject that I am defending. It is a way of avoiding universalistic generalizations and grounding critical practice so as to make it accountable. At both the micro- and the macrolevels of the constitution of subjectivity, we need more complexities both in terms of genders and across ethnicities, class, and age. This is the social agenda that needs to be addressed in the framework of the new European Union.

I therefore want to propose an alliance between two parallel but distinct projects and lines of argumentation, which also correspond to different forms of consciousness. They are, on the one hand, the deconstruction of the unitary idea of Europe as the "cradle" of civilization—with its corollary implications of rational citizenship, liberal individualism, and universalism. On the other, the deconstruction of the unitary idea of gendered identities, fixed in the essentialist opposition masculine/feminine. In the same way that feminist theories after poststructuralism promote a split, multiple, hybrid, diasporic, and nomadic vision of the subject-in-process, I see the new European Union as a framework for the transformation of Europe in the sense of becoming-minoritarian.

This dual deconstructive strategy keeps the two axes of gendered and European subjectivities parallel but quite distinct and perhaps even asymmetrical to each other. I think such distinctions are important because femi-

nism and European consciousness are grounded in different political movements: the former on the many world-historical women's movements, the
latter on the progressive potential of the project of European unification.
Distinctions between these two parallel lines are important also on another
score: these two discourses—feminism and Europe—are separate at the institutional level, and they suffer from an excessive segregation of discursive
competences. European discussions on citizenship and feminist debates do
not intersect easily, and they seldom cross-reference each other. As a result,
EU discussions on the social role of women and on gender mainstreaming
hardly draw on the rather impressive amount of research compiled by feminists over the last twenty years on the question of alternative forms of political subjectivity. A new alliance is therefore needed between, on the one hand,
a postnationalist vision of European subjectivity based on the critique of
Eurocentrism and, on the other, multiple visions of the subject-as-process,
which stem from the rejection of feminine essentialism within feminism.
This is an attempt to come to terms with the paradoxes and internal contradictions of our own historical predicament as "post-Europe Europeans,"
just as gender theory has had to deal with the fragments, the deconstruction
and reconstruction of the "post-Woman women" in the feminist processes
of transformation (Braidotti 1994a, 2002a).

REROUTING EUROPE

The European Union as a nomadic project has to do with the sobering experience of taking stock of our specific location and, following the feminist
politics of location, adopting embedded and embodied perspectives. This
is the opposite of the grandiose and aggressive universalism of the past: it
is a situated and accountable perspective. It's about turning our collective
memory to the service of a new political and ethical project, which is forward-looking and not nostalgic. Daniel Cohn-Bendit recently stated that if
we want to make this European project work, we really must start from the
assumption that Europe is the specific periphery where we live and that we
must take responsibility for it (1995). Imagining anything else would be a
repetition of that flight into abstraction for which our culture is (in)famous:
at best, it may procure us the benefits of escapism, at worst, the luxury of

guilt. We have to start from where we are. This is a plea for lucidity and for accountability. We need both political strategies and imaginary figurations that are adequate to our historicity.

This is, however, only one side of the paradoxical coin of European deconstruction in the age of the European Union. The other side, simultaneously true and yet absolutely contradictory, is the danger of recreating a sovereign center through the new European federation. That the two are simultaneously the case makes European identity one of the most contested areas of political and social philosophy in our world at the moment. This reactive tendency toward a sovereign sense of the Union is also known as the "Fortress Europe" syndrome and has been extensively criticized by feminists and antiracists. They warn us against the danger of replacing the former Eurocentrism with a new "Europ-ism" (Essed 1991), i.e., the belief in an ethnically pure Europe. The question of ethnic purity is crucial and it is, of course, the germ of Eurofascism.

One concrete way to combine the politics of nomadic becoming with the political analysis of Europe is by singling out the issue of whiteness. Let me explain. For people who inherit the European region, the condition of economic and cultural globalization translates concretely into the end of the myth of cultural homogeneity. As Michael Walzer (1992) has argued, this is the foundational political myth in Europe, as much as multiculturalism is the central myth in the United States. Of course, European history at any point in time provides ample evidence to the contrary: waves of migrations from the East and the South make a mockery of any claim to ethnic or cultural homogeneity in Europe, while the persistent presence of Jewish and Muslim citizens challenges the identification of Europe with Christianity. Nonetheless, the myth of cultural homogeneity is crucial to the tale of European nationalism.

In our era, these myths are being exposed and exploded into questions related to entitlement and agency. Thus the European Union is faced with the issue: can one be European and black or Muslim? Paul Gilroy's work on black British subjectivity (1987) is indicative of the problem of how European citizenship and blackness emerge as contested issues. However, I want to argue that whiteness is also called into play. One of the radical implications of the project of the European Union is the possibility of giving a specific location, and consequently historical embeddedness or memory, to antiracist whites. It can, finally, racialize our location, which is quite a feat because, until recently in Europe, only white supremacists, Nazi skins, and other fascists actually had a theory about the qualities that are inherent to white people. Like all fascists, all these groups are biological and cultural essentialists. Apart from this, whiteness was, quite simply, invisible, just not seen, at least not by whites. It took the work of black writers and thinkers to expose whiteness as a political issue. Located in the lily-white purity of our universalistic fantasy, disembodied and disembedded, we actually thought we had no color. Then Toni Morrison (1992) and bell hooks (1994) came along and painted us in, forcing white feminists to take race into account. But whiteness as such was already a political issue, as it had been criticized for providing the cornerstone of European and Anglo-American political, cultural, and economic hegemony.

In his analysis of the representation of whiteness as an ethnic category in mainstream films, Richard Dyer (1993) defines it as "emptiness, absence, denial or even a kind of death". Being the norm, it is invisible, as if natural, inevitable, or the ordinary way to do things (Ware 1992). The source of the representational power of white is its propensity to be everything and nothing, whereas black, of course, is always marked off as *a* color. The effect of this structured invisibility, and of the process of the naturalization of whiteness, is that it masks itself off into a "colorless multicoloredness." White contains all other colors. This insight is strengthened philosophically by the work of Michel Foucault on the Panopticon (Foucault 1975)—the void that lies at the heart of the system and defines the contour of both social and symbolic visibility (Young 1990). Deleuze and Guattari (1972, 1980) also comment on the fact that any dominant notion—such as masculinity or race—has no positive definition: the prerogative of being dominant means that a concept gets defined oppositionally, by casting outward upon others the marks of oppression or marginalization. Virginia Woolf (1938) had already commented on this aspect of the logic of domination when she asserted that what matters is not so much that He, the male, should be superior, so long as She, the Other is clearly defined as inferior. There is no dominant concept other than that which acts as a term to index and patrol access and participation to entitlements and powers. Thus the invisibility of the dominant concepts is also the expression of their insubstantiality— which makes them all the more effective in their murderous intents toward the many others on whose structural exclusion they rest their vampirelike powers.

Now the immediate consequence of this process of naturalization or invisibility is not only political but also methodological, namely, that whiteness is very difficult to analyze critically. It tends to break down into subcategories of whiteness: Irishness, Italianness, Jewishness, etc. It follows therefore that nonwhites have a much clearer perception of whiteness than whites. Just think of bell hooks's important work on whiteness as terror and as a death-giving force and of feminist critiques of whiteness in mythology and fairy tales like Snow White (hooks 1995). The reverse, however, is not the case: black and other ethnic minorities do not need this specular logic in order to have a location of their own.

The experience of white European immigrants tends to confirm the lethal insubstantiality of whiteness. As cultural identity is external and retrospective, it is defined for Europeans in the confrontation with other—usually black—peoples. This was the experience of Irish, Italian, and Jewish immigrants in countries like the U.S., Canada, and Australia. Their "whiteness" emerged oppositionally, as a distancing factor from the natives and blacks. Feminist critics like Frankenberg (1994) and Brodkin Sacks (1994) have analyzed this phenomenon of a "whitening" process by which Euro-immigrants—especially Jews and Italians—were constructed as "whitened" citizens in the U.S. The extent to which this kind of "whitened" identity is illusory as it is racist, can be seen by how divided the diasporic Euro-immigrant communities actually are: they are all in their respective ghettos, antagonistic toward each other and locked in mutual suspicion. But all are equally "whitened" by the gaze of the colonizer, bent on pitching them against the black population. By learning to view their subject positions as racialized white people, we can work toward antiracist forms of whiteness or at least antiracist strategies to rework whiteness. This strategy has interesting new potential with respect to women from the east of Europe today. Comparable dynamics are also operating within the EU, which result in a new racialized hierarchy that polices access to full EU citizenship. Thus, for peoples from the Balkans, or the southwestern regions of Europe, insofar as they are not yet "good Europeans," they are also not quite as "white" as others. The whitening process expands with the new frontiers of the EU pushing out the "illegal others." An oriental or Eastern ethnic divide is operating, which equates EU citizenship with whiteness and Christianity, casting shadows of suspicion on all "others." Joanna Regulska (1998) is one of the feminist scholars who have adapted the methodology of postcolonial theory to the study of Eastern European women.

My political strategy in this regard is to support the claim of European identity as an open and multilayered project, not as a fixed or given essence. A cultural identity of this kind confronts historical contradictions in order to turn them into spaces of critical resistance to hegemonic identities of all kinds. My own choice to rework whiteness in the era of advanced capitalism involves, firstly, situating it, in the geohistorical space of Europe and within the political project of the European Union. This amounts to historicizing it and demystifying its allegedly "natural" locations. The next step, following the method of a feminist politics of location, is to analyze it critically, to revisit it by successive deconstructive repetitions that aim at emptying out the different layers of this complex identity, excavating it till it opens out to the new.

The third step consists in trying to reroute European identity, so as to undo its hegemonic tendencies. I refer to this kind of identity as "nomadic." Being a nomadic European subject means being in transit within different identity formations, but, at the same time, being sufficiently anchored to a historical position to accept responsibility for it. The key words are *accountability* and the *strategic relocation of whiteness*. It is also a way of positing the "becoming-minoritarian of Europe" by dispelling the privilege of invisibility that was conferred on Europe as an alleged center of the world. By assuming full responsibility for the partial perspective of its own location, a minoritarian European space opens up a possible political strategy for those who inhabit this particular center of power in a globalized world marked by scattered hegemonies and hence no longer dominated by European power alone.

The emphasis I place on a situated politics of location echoes and supports the nonunitary structure of the subject. Locations are historicized and grounded contingent foundations that structure one's being-in-the-world, one's social modes of belonging and not belonging. In other words, being diasporic, nomadic, hybrid, in-between are not the same. They translate sociologically into different structural locations in relation to language, culture, class, and labor, access to and participation in power in the broadest sense of the term. The *post* in *postindustrialism* is not the same as the *post* in *postcolonialism* or *postcommunism*. Historically, however, these *post* conditions resonate with each other, and, politically, they are quite often mixed together and coincide on a number of targets and goals. The task of the social critic—and of this project—is to make relevant distinctions among these different locations, but also to map the points of intersection so as to contribute to a politically invested cartography of the common grounds and moments that can be shared by multiply located subjects who are committed to reconstructing subjectivities and not merely to deconstruction for its own sake. I call this the new materialism of posthumanistic subjects who are embedded, embodied, accountable but not unitary.

FLEXIBLE CITIZENSHIP

I have argued so far that ideas of identity as multiple, mobile, and nomadic are by now the most accurate way to describe our historical condition. It is also the case, however, that they cause waves of collective cultural and political anxiety. In such a context I want to defend the thesis that there is much to be gained by adopting a nonunitary and multilayered vision of identity; linking it to new practices of flexible citizenship and refusing to give in to fear or anxiety.

The effects of the global trend upon the notion and practice of citizenship are indeed enormous. The classical model that links citizenship to belonging to a territory, an ethnicity, and a nation-state and opposes it to a condition of statelessness is no longer adequate. The phenomenon globally known as flexible citizenship describes the unlinking of the three basic units that used to compose citizenship: one's ethnic origin or place of birth, the nationality or bond to a nation-state, and the legal structure of actual citizenship rights and obligations. These three factors are disaggregated and disarticulated from each other and become rearranged in a number of interesting ways. Most of us today have some direct experience of this kind of deterritorialization, including European higher education marked by the flow of international students and colleagues. The university has historically been an itinerant institution; medieval students traveled from one study center to the other; in the global era this feature of our history intensifies and becomes quite dominant. Starting from this premise, let us look at three different models of flexible citizenship and hence of nonunitary identity. The first consists of the effects of neoliberal deregulation of the labor market, the second of world migration and population flows, and the third revolves around the specific case of the EU. These three cases represent different configurations of the central problem I am discussing and shape specific legal and ethical aspects of citizenship practices today.

Neoliberalism

Displacement is a central feature of advanced capitalism itself, as I have argued throughout this book. As Dahrendorf (1990) suggested, processes of hybridization and nomadic identities are neither marginal nor self-chosen phenomena. Deregulated capitalism itself functions by organizing constant flows and displacements of capital, people, and resources in such a way as to erode its own foundations. Transnational capital flow erodes the nation-state (Mouffe 1994), and contemporary technologies accelerate this trend (Castells 1996) by setting up cybernetworks of surrogate digital citizenship or mediated belonging. These accounts are narratives of the globalized diaspora, which, at the end of this millennium, concern most communities, though in different degrees. Aihwa Ong, who coined the term *flexible citizenship*, put it succinctly: "I can live anywhere," he stated, "so long as it is close to an airport!" (Ong 1993).

Clearly, some basic distinctions are called for here. The differences between the social positions are crucial. Between, for instance, expatriate entrepreneurs, the jet-setting media star, the mobile sportsman or top athlete or soccer players, on the one hand, and the global chain of care, illegal migrant workers, and asylum seekers, on the other. An effective way to account for the power differences among these positions is to analyze the effect of the globalized labor market on issues of citizenship. The unlinking of ethnicity and of nationality from citizenship is one of the most obvious impacts of the neoliberal world order and of the forms of mobility it instigates.

In the neoliberal model, having or not having citizenship is being replaced by opportunities created by transnational market conditions and access to technological know-how; formal, legalistic citizenship is replaced and repackaged in benefits and entitlements—such as legal residency and dual nationality—that are structured and supported by global capital. Flexible citizenship here describes the moves of subjects structured opportunistically across market conditions, but positioned differently across them. The free movers of this biased system follow the jobs, wherever they may take them—with some surprising twists. Just think where David Beckham ended up, albeit temporarily.

World Migration

The second case has already been mentioned in the former. Saying that we now live in a world organized along multiple axes of mobility, circulation, flows of people and commodities amounts to saying that we live in ethnically mixed worlds. Europe is ill-equipped to confront the phenomenon of mass migration. The phenomenon of a pluriethnic or multicultural European social space is controversial, to say the least. World-migration—a huge movement of population from periphery to center, working on a worldwide scale of "scattered hegemonies" (Grewal and Kaplan 1994)—has challenged the claim to an alleged cultural homogeneity of European nation-states and of the European Union. It also goes deeper and further than a mere pluralistic proliferation of minorities and minority rights, to paraphrase Kymlicka's idea of multicultural citizenship (1995).

Avtar Brah's analysis (1996) of the new diasporic and hybrid identities is indicative of the qualitative shift at stake in these discussions. Brah stresses that the sheer scale of the global diaspora challenges any assumption of monoculturalism in the new Europe and hence, by extension, even a critique of the notion of minority rights, because if there is no majority there cannot be a minority. There are no margins if the center is being differentiated internally under the spin of global forces.

Diaspora is a space of transition and exchange that defines the indigenous peoples as much as the nomadic subjects of the post/colonial world order. Cross-referring to Gilroy, Brah defines diasporic identities as being both about roots and routes; that is to say, they are "processes of multi-locationality across geographical, cultural and psychic boundaries" (Brah 1996:194). These are accentuated under the impact of the new information technologies, which dislocate the relationship between the local and the global and thus complicate the idea of multilocality. World migration as an internally differentiated pattern of human flow redistributes citizenship accordingly.

The paradoxes, power dissymmetry, and fragmentations of the present historical context require that we shift the political debates from the issue of differences between cultures to differences *within* the same culture. These are the shifting grounds on which periphery and center confront each other, with a new level of complexity that defies dualistic or oppositional thinking. If it is the case that a sociocultural mutation is taking place in the direction of a multiethnic, multimedia society, as feminist theory argues, then the implication is that the transformation cannot affect only the pole of "the others"; it must equally dislocate the position and the prerogative of "the same," the former center. No identity is to be taken for granted anymore, certainly not the national ones and the modes of citizenship that sustain them. The recognition of this new situation has prompted liberal thinkers like Kymlicka (1995) and Benhabib (2004) to defend a multicultural vision of citizenship. This is based on respect for cultural diversity and the conviction that the liberal notion of individual rights allows for the extension of citizenship to all ethnic minorities as well as refugees and alien "others." This is a mode of recognition and acceptance. Nomadic thought starts from very different conceptual premises about subjectivity as relation and dynamic interaction. Having rejected the model of liberal individualism, in the form of a nonunitary and vitalist vision of the subject, nomadic theory does not enhance multiculturalism, which positions "others" as minorities to be tolerated at best. The emphasis falls instead on the necessity to relocate the center—the dominant subject position—in a process of becoming-minoritarian that also repositions the center-margin relationship. A becoming-minor of Europe.

The European Dimension

In relation to the two other models, I want to defend a process of the "becoming-minor" of Europe (Deleuze and Guattari 1980) as a way of both bypassing the binary global-local and of destabilizing the established definitions of European identity. This represents a qualitative shift of perspective in our collective sense of identity; more importantly, it supports the becoming-nomadic or minoritarian of European citizenship.

A radical restructuring of European identity as postnationalistic can be pragmatically implemented into a nomadic variation of flexible citizenship. This would allow all "others"—all kinds of hybrid citizens—to partake of the rights and duties of active participation and legal status in what would otherwise deserve the label "Fortress Europe." This postnationalistic sense of identity is linked to the political notion of flexible citizenship within the framework of the "new" European Union (Ferreira, Tavares, and Portugal 1998). A disaggregated idea of citizenship emerges in fact from the current EU situation—as a bundle of rights and benefits that can accommodate both native citizens and migrants: an attempt to accommodate cultural diversity without undermining European liberal democracies and the universal idea of individual human rights.

The postnationalistic definition of European identity can in fact be concretely translated into a set of "flexible forms of citizenship" that would allow for all "others"—all kinds of hybrid citizens—to acquire legal status in what would otherwise deserve the label of Fortress Europe. For instance Habermas calls for a serious European constitution, that is to say, Europe as a political project would involve the consolidation of a European public sphere that might strengthen the shared political culture of European democracies and welfare states.

This model of nomadic flexible citizenship would involve dismantling the us/them binary in such a way as to account for the undoing of a strong and fixed notion of European citizenship in favor of a functionally differentiated network of affiliations and loyalties. For the citizens of the member states of the European Union the new EU citizenship rests on the disconnection of the three elements I have discussed: nationality, citizenship, national identity. According to Ulrich Preuss, such a European notion of citizenship, disengaged from national foundations, lays the ground for a new kind of civil society beyond the boundaries of any single nation-state. Because such a notion of "alienage" (Preuss 1996:551) would become an integral part of citizenship in the European Union, Preuss argues that all European citizens would end up being "privileged foreigners." In other words, they would function together without reference to a centralized and homogeneous sphere of political power (Preuss 1995:280). Potentially, this notion of citizenship could therefore lead to a new concept of politics, which would no longer be bound to the nation-state. Of course, this notion of European citizenship is only a potential one and is highly contested at the national level, by both reactionary nostalgic forces and third-world-obsessed leftist political groups. I, however, see it as the most honest and pragmatic way to develop the progressive potential of the European Union and also of accounting for the effects of globalization upon us all. These effects boil down to one central idea: the end of pure and steady identities and a consequent emphasis on creolization, hybridization, a multicultural Europe within which "new" Europeans can take their place alongside others (Bhavnani 1992).

In her recent work on European citizenship, Benhabib (2002) interrogates critically the disjunction between the concepts of nation, the state, and cultural identity. Solidly grounded in her theory of communicative ethics, Benhabib works toward the elaboration of new rules of global democracy within a multicultural horizon. A self-professed Kantian cosmopolitan, Benhabib argues forcefully that "democratic citizenship can be exercised across national boundaries and in transnational contexts" (2002:183). She is especially keen to demonstrate that the distinction between national minority and ethnic group does very little to determine whether an identity/difference-driven movement is "democratic, liberal, inclusive and universalist" (2002:65). Benhabib also examines the extent to which the medieval charts of rights of cities can be activated against the nation-state, especially in the case of asylum laws.

Within the specific location of Europe, important work has been done on analyzing the ongoing political process of the European Union, both as a player in the global economy and as an attempt to move beyond the traditional grounds on which European nationalism has prospered, namely, essentialist identities. Of great importance in this respect is the work of Etienne Balibar (2001, 2002) on Europe as a transnational space of mediation and exchange. This new European identity is internally differentiated and hence nonunitary and committed to transcultural hybrid exchanges. It is a situated perspective based on multiple border crossings, on confrontations with shifting frontiers and borders, and on a deep commitment to pacifism and human rights. I have stressed elsewhere (Braidotti 2002b, 2003a, 2003b) the relevance of this vision of the European Union for the feminist project of situating the critique of gender and power in the lived reality of our present geopolitical locations. We need situated European perspectives on gender, feminist politics, and social theory. This is a way of thinking locally and taking full accountability for the new transnational European space. Becoming-Europeans in this critical mode is a process of actively regrounding citizenship according to a more flexible model, which is related to claiming social rights on the European level.

CONCLUSION: COLLECTIVE IMAGINING

New images and representations of Europe, however, do not readily appear out of thin air. To produce a new imaginary requires the means of revisiting it, acknowledging it, and understanding the complicity between "difference" and "exclusion" in the European mind-set. Repetitions are the road to creating positive redefinitions in a progress of creative deconstruction. Communities are also imaginary institutions made of affects and desires (Anderson 1983). Homi Bhabha, for instance (1990, 1994), stresses the fact that common ideas of "nation" are, to a large extent, imaginary tales, which project a reassuring but nonetheless illusory sense of unity over the disjointed, fragmented, and often incoherent range of internal regional and cultural differences that make up a national identity. Poststructuralist and antiracist feminists have, moreover, developed a skeptical attitude toward the idea of unitary identity. We have also become painfully aware of the extent to which the legitimating tales of nationhood in the West have been constructed over the body of women as well as in the crucible of imperial and colonial masculinity.

The project of developing a new kind of postnationalist identity is related to the process of disidentification from established, nation-bound identities. This dis-location can lead to a positive and affirmative relocation of European identities. I have stressed both the need for an adequate European social imaginary for this kind of subject position and the difficulties involved in developing this. There is no denying that such an enterprise involves a large sense of loss and is not without pain. No process of consciousness-raising can ever be painless. Migrants know this very well. Home is lived both at the material and at the imaginary level where it might be a destination or something that is repeatedly deferred. It is not necessarily a place of "origin," but can also mean belonging in multiple locations. In addition, my own experience in Australia has taught me to what extent the process of disidentification is linked to the pain of loss. This is not, however, the pathetic expression of a nostalgic yearning for a return to the past, but rather a mature, sobering experience, similar to the loss of illusions and of self-delusions of classical Greek tragedies (Braidotti 2011).

A postnationalist sense of European identity and of flexible citizenship does not come easily and in some ways is even a counterintuitive idea. It requires an extra effort in order to come into being, as it raises the question of how to change deeply embedded habits of our imagination. How can such in-depth transformation be enacted? This question is made all the more urgent by the extent to which we are already living in postnationalist ways and in a postnationalist social space. This is partly due to the obvious effects of globalization and the conformism and homogenezation of cultures brought about by telecommunication. It is also related, however, to the impact of the European Union on the legal, economic, and cultural structures in which most dwellers in Europe function nowadays. The impact of educational, scientific, and cultural exchanges is very significant in this respect, and the implementation of the common currency has done the rest. I think that it is precisely the rather large role played by these postnationalist instances in our social life that has generated the reaction against them in the form of various types of nostalgic identity claims that are proliferating across Europe today.

What we are lacking is a social imaginary that adequately reflects the social realities we already experience of a postnationalist sense of European identity. We have failed to develop adequate, positive representations of the new trans-European condition we are inhabiting on this continent. This lack of the social imaginary both feeds upon and supports the political timidity and resistances that are being moved against the European political project. More work is needed on the role of contemporary global media in both colonizing and stimulating the social imaginary of global cultures (Hall 1992; Shohat and Stam 1994; Gilroy 2000; Braidotti 2002a).

At least some of the difficulty involved is due to the lack of a specifically European—in the sense of European Union—public debate, as Habermas (1992) put it in his critique of the absence of a European public sphere. This is reflected in the rather staggering absence of what I would call a European social imaginary. Thinkers as varied as Passerini (1998), Mény (2000), and Morin (1987) all signal this problem in different ways. Passerini laments the lack of an emotional attachment to the European dimension on the part of the citizens of the social space that is Europe. Elsewhere she has developed hypotheses on a possible critical innovation of what a "love for Europe" could mean (Passerini 2003). For Mény the problem is rather the lack of imagination and visionary force on the part of those in charge of politically propelling the European Union. For Morin Europe is ill-loved and somewhat unwanted, "une pauvre vieille petite chose" (Morin 1987:23).

My question therefore becomes: how do you develop such a new European social imaginary? I think that such a notion is a project and not a given.
Nonetheless, this does not make it utopian in the sense of being overideal-
istic. Even the contrary: it is a virtual social reality that can be actualized by
a joint endeavor on the part of active, conscious, and desiring citizens. If it
is utopian at all, it is only in the positive sense of utopia: the necessary dose
of dreamlike vision without which no social project can take off and gather
support.

Something along these lines is expressed with great passion by Edgar
Morin when he describes his becoming-European as the awakening of his
consciousness about the new peripheral role of Europe in the post–World
War II era, after his years of indifference to Europe in the tradition of Marxist cosmopolitanism and international proletarian solidarity. By his own
admission, Edgar Morin overcame his own mistrust for the European dimension of both thinking and political activity in the late 1970s, when, like
most of his generation, he took his distance from the unfulfilled promises
of the Marxist utopia. This sobering experience made him see to what an
extent the new worldwide binary opposition USSR/USA had dramatically
dislocated the sources of planetary power away from Europe (Morin 1987).

The concrete result of this new consciousness-raising was that Morin
started taking seriously the scholarly work connected to the research of European roots as both a cultural and political specificity. This is the paradox
that lies at the heart of the quest for a new, postnationalist redefinition of
European identity: it becomes thinkable as an entity at the exact historical
time when it has ceased to be operational as a social or symbolic reality. The
process of becoming-Europeans entails the end of fixed Eurocentric identities, and it thus parallels the becoming-nomadic of subjectivity.

The liberatory potential of this process is equally proportional to the
imaginary and political efforts it requires of us all. The recognition of the
new multilayered, transcultural, and postnationalist idea of Europe in this
case would only be the premise for the collective development of a new sense
of accountability for the specific slice of world periphery that we happen to
inhabit.

Let me make it perfectly clear, however, that this very definition of nomadic subjects is spoken from and speaks of the specific location I have
chosen to make myself accountable for. It is an embedded European account of my own traditions or genealogies. In other words, it is only one of

many possible locations that may apply to some of the people who situate themselves—in terms of genealogical consciousness and related forms of accountability—with respect to the kind of power relations that go with the continent of Europe. This is neither the only, nor is it the best of all possible locations. It merely happens to be the cartography that I acquired and chose to be accountable for. I want to present this kind of embodied genealogical accountability as my contribution to our discussions on gender and power. Through the pain of loss and disenchantment, just as "post-Woman women" have moved away from compulsory gender dichotomies toward a redefinition of being-gendered-in-the-world, "post-Eurocentric Europeans" may be able to find enough creativity and moral stamina to grab this historical chance to become just Europeans in the postnationalist sense of the term. This would be a gesture toward in-depth transformation.

The sobering experience—the humble and productive recognition of loss, limitations, and shortcomings—has to do with self-representations. Established mental habits, images, and terminology railroad us back toward established ways of thinking about ourselves. Traditional modes of representation are legal forms of addiction. To change them is not unlike undertaking a detoxification cure. A great deal of courage and creativity is needed to develop forms of representation that do justice to the complexities of the kind of subjects we have already become.

As I argued in the previous chapter, the project of changing the social imaginary requires intense personal and collective investments, which I read in the direction of a collective aspiration toward becoming-minoritarian. The assemblage formed by a body of individuals devoted to this process is both historically grounded and socially embedded. It is not, however, dependent upon state powers and structures and hence on permissions or official support. It is the community itself that decides—in a gesture of affirmation that engenders the constitution of what was till then a "missing people." This project mobilizes the collective imaginings as well as other cognitive and rational resources.

Collectively, we can empower some of these alternative becoming. This process is collective and affective: it is driven by a desire for change that is sustained by some, if not many. The European postnationalist identity is such a project: political at heart, it has a strong ethical pull made of convictions, vision, and desire. It does require labor-intensive efforts on the part of all and thus is risky. As a project, it also requires active participation and enjoyment: a new virtual love that targets less what we are than what we are capable of becoming. This liberatory potential is directly proportional to the desire and collective affects it mobilizes. The recognition of Europe as a postnationalist entity is the premise underlying the creation of a sense of accountability for the specific margin of the planet that Europeans occupy. The becoming-minoritarian of Europe enacts this reconfiguration as an active experiment with different ways of inhabiting this social space.

I want to describe the project of a postnationalist understanding of European identity as a great historical chance for Europeans to become more knowledgeable of our own history and more self-critical in a productive sense. Nietzsche argued early on in the twentieth century that many Europeans no longer feel at home in Europe (Nietzsche 1966). At the start of the third millennium, many want to argue that those who do not identify with Europe in the sense of the center—the dominant and heroic reading of Europe—are ideally suited to the task of reframing Europe, by making it accountable for a history in which fascism, imperialism, and domination have played a central role. In nomadic European subjects lie the postnationalist foundations for a multilayered and flexible practice of European citizenship in the frame of the new European Union.

The project of flexible citizenship as part of the becoming-minor of Europe is an ethical transformation by a former center that chooses the path of immanent changes. Through the pain of loss and disenchantment, "postnationalist Europeans" may be able to find enough self-respect to become the subjects of multiple ecologies of belonging and go out into the world, among many others, free of white men's burden, free of fear of not being in charge—nomadic, disenchanted, but ethically vibrant, in love with complexities—nomadic citizens of the third millennium.

POWERS OF AFFIRMATION

PART FOUR

10

POWERS OF AFFIRMATION

A certain fragility has been discovered in the very bedrock of existence even, and perhaps above all, in those aspects of it that are most familiar, most solid and most intimately related to our bodies and to our everyday behaviour. But together with this sense of instability . . . one in fact discovers something that perhaps was not initially foreseen, something one might describe as precisely the inhibiting effect of global, totalitarian theories.

—MICHEL FOUCAULT, *POWER/KNOWLEDGE*

This chapter addresses one of the paradoxes that has become central to my work: how to engage in affirmative politics, which entails the creation of sustainable alternatives geared to the construction of social horizons of hope, while at the same time doing critical theory, which implies resistance to the present. This is one of the issues Deleuze and Guattari discuss at length, notably in *What Is Philosophy?* (1992): the relationship between creation and critique. It is, however, a problem that has confronted all activists and critical theorists: how to balance the creative potential of critical thought with the dose of negative criticism and oppositional consciousness that such a stance necessarily entails.

Central to this debate is the question of how to resist the present, more specifically the injustice, violence, and vulgarity of the times, while being worthy of our times, so as to engage with them in a productive, albeit it oppositional and affirmative manner. I shall return to this issue in the final section of this chapter. There is a contextual and a conceptual side to this problem, and I will discuss each one of these and then examine some of their implications.

ON PUTTING THE ACTIVE BACK INTO ACTIVISM

Both by personal disposition and by philosophical training, I consider political activism to be the fundamental political passion as well as a sort of moral obligation for my generation. In defining activism as the process of becoming-political, Deleuze speaks of the European left of the 1960s and 1970s in terms of a specific sensibility, which he connects to a creative imaginary about possible futures. This desire for change clashes constitutionally with the guardians of the status quo: the judges and managers of truths and the clarity fetishists.[1] As eyewitnesses to the immediate events of the cold war in Europe and more specifically the Hungarian uprising of 1956 and the Czech and the Paris Spring revolt of 1968, Foucault and Deleuze (1972) distance themselves from the nefarious illusion of revolutionary purity, which engenders armed violence and repression. They are therefore critical of the universalist utopian element of Marxism, which inflated intellectuals to the role of representatives of the masses. They were equally suspicious, however, of the universalist humanistic assumptions and the claim to human rights or the self-correcting validity of human reason. They stress instead the need for a change of scale to unveil power relations where they are most effective and invisible: in the specific locations of one's own intellectual and social practice. One has to start from micro-instances of embodied and embedded self and the complex web of social relations that compose the self.

This leads to an increased awareness of the vulnerability of embodied subjects, which, however, results in subtler and more effective analyses of how power works in and through the body. This double emphasis on fragility, on the one hand, and despotic power relations, on the other, is crucial to a nomadic approach to the political. Activism as a frame of mind consists in connecting philosophy not so much to "LA politique" (organized or Majoritarian politics) as to "LE politique" (the political movement in its diffuse, nomadic, and rhizomic forms of becoming).

This distinction between politics and the political is of crucial importance; in the work of Michel Foucault it is postulated along the double axis of power as restrictive or coercive (potestas) and as empowering and productive (potentia). The former focuses on the management of civil society and its institutions, the latter on the transformative experimentation with new arts of existence and ethical relations. Politics is made of progressive emancipatory measures predicated on chronological continuity, whereas the political is the radical self-styling that requires the circular time of critical praxis.

In an even more grounded and ascetic tone, Deleuze and Guattari set the desire for transformations or becomings at the center of the agenda. The crucial distinction for nomadic theory is that of the axes of time and the form of affectivity they sustain. Politics is postulated on Chronos—the necessarily linear time of institutional deployment of norms and protocols. It is a reactive and majority-bound enterprise that is often made of flat repetitions and predictable reversals that may alter the balance but leave the structure of power basically untouched.

The political, on the other hand, is postulated on the axis of Aion—the time of becoming and of affirmative critical practice. It is minoritarian and it aims at the counteractualization of alternative states of affairs in relation to the present. Based on the principle that we do not know what a body can do (see chapter 12), the becoming-political ultimately aims at transformations in the very structures of subjectivity. It is about engendering and sustaining processes of "becoming-minoritarian." This specific sensibility combines a strong historical memory with consciousness and the desire for resistance. It rejects the sanctimonious, dogmatic tone of dominant ideologies, left or right of the political spectrum, in favor of the production of joyful acts of transformation. The spontaneous and creative aspects of this practice combine with a profound form of asceticism, that is to say, with an ethics of nonprofit to build upon micropolitical instances of activism, avoiding overarching generalizations. This humble yet experimental approach to changing our collective modes of relation to the environment, social and other, our cultural norms and values, our social imaginary, our bodies, ourselves, is the most pragmatic manifestation of the politics of radical immanence.

This philosophical critique of political subjectivity rests on two ideas I have addressed throughout this book. The first is the emphasis on the embodied and embedded nature of the subject, which results in unlimited confidence in lived experience. This translates into the politics of everyday life and renewed interest in the present. One has to think global, but act local. The second key argument is a focus on the dynamic interaction of Sameness and Difference. "Difference" is not a neutral category, but a term that indexes exclusion from entitlements to subjectivity. The equation of difference with pejoration is built into the tradition that defines the Subject as coinciding with/being the same as consciousness, rationality, and self-regulating ethical behavior. As I argued elsewhere in this volume, this results in making an entire section of living beings into marginal and disposable bodies: these are the sexualized, racialized, and naturalized others (Braidotti 2006).

The idea of the political produces a renewed concern for the fragility of existence and hence for multiple forms of human vulnerability, which is coupled with increased subtlety in the analysis of and resistance to power. This breaks with a Marxist tradition of taking some doses of revolutionary violence for granted and expresses renewed theoretical interest in processes and social practices of otherness, marginality, and exclusion. The negative charge attributed to difference marks both world-historical events such as European colonialism and fascism and also discursive events internal to the history of philosophy itself. This radically immanent materialist politics is no longer orthodox Marxist, but rather focused on embodiment and lived experience. It takes seriously affects, sexuality, pacifism, human rights, environmental isssues, and sustainable futures. The clearest expression of this politics is less the joyful insurrection of May '68 than the more reflexive biopolitical ethos of new activist movements that were initiated in its wake, like Amnesty International, S.O.S. Racism, and Médecins sans frontieres.

By extension, what is central to a nomadic theory of the political is the critique of the inertia, the repressive tolerance, and the deeply seated conservatism of the institutions that are officially in charge of knowledge production, especially the university, but also the media and the corporate sector. Foucault explicitly singles out for criticism the pretension of classical philosophy to be a master discipline that surveys and organizes other discourses. In his archaeological and later genealogical work, Foucault (1977b) opposes to this abstract and universalistic understanding the function of philosophy as a toolbox, a very pragmatic and localized analysis of power relations within the exercise of philosophical reason. The philosopher becomes no more than a provider of analytic services: a technician of knowledge.

Deleuze (1953, 1962) redefines philosophy in the "problematic" mode as the constant questioning of the humanistic "image of thought" at work in most of our ideas with the aim to destabilize them in the "nomadic" mode. Arguing against its metadiscursive tendency, Deleuze redefines philosophy instead as a radical form of immanence. Thinking in the critical mode proposed by the French poststructuralists consists in locating the affects and especially the political passions that sustain the theoretical process. Both Foucault and Deleuze are critical of rationality as the dominant vision of the subject and as a human ideal, but they also reject the pitfall of cognitive and moral relativism by stressing that the crisis of classical subjectivity is not a catastrophe, but rather the expression of the irrepressible vitality of thought. Rejecting both the plaintive mode of nostalgia and the glorification of the aporetic, Deleuze proposes instead a radical redefinition of thinking as the activity that consists in the act of creation of new forms of thought and of collective experiments with ways of actualizing them.

This engagement with the present—and the spirit of the times—sets the political agenda in a variety of realms, ranging from sexuality and kinship system to religious and discursive practices. The analyses of these themes are transmitted through narratives—mythologies or fictions, which I have renamed as "figurations" (Braidotti 2002a, 2006) or cartographies of the present. A cartography is a politically informed map of one's historical and social locations, enabling the analysis of situated formations of power and hence the elaboration of adequate forms of resistance. Michel Foucault (1975) worked extensively on the notion of genealogy or countermemories as a tool to draw the "diagrams of the present" in his analysis of the microphysics of power in postindustrial societies. Gilles Deleuze and Felix Guattari (1980) also stressed the importance of immanent analyses of the singular actualizations of concrete power formations.

Feminism also pioneered the practice of the politics of locations (Rich 1985) as a method for grounding activism. It also perfected the strategy of positive renaming and resignification of the subject. A location is an embedded and embodied memory: it is a set of countermemories, which are activated by resisting thinkers against the grain of the dominant social representations of subjectivity. A location is a materialist temporal and spatial site of coproduction of subjects in their diversity. Accounting for this complexity is, therefore, anything but an instance of relativism. Locations provide the ground for political and ethical accountability. Remembrance, cartographies of locations, political (dis)identifications, and strategic reconfigurations are the tools for consciousness-raising that were devised by transformative epistemologies such as feminism and race theory (Passerini 1988; Haraway 1989; West 1994).

Both my practice and my concept of the political therefore pay tribute to this tradition of radical politics at a point in history where the general tendency is to dismiss it or deride it as a failed historical experiment. The main thesis I want to defend is that one of the most significant theoretical innovations it introduced is what later became known as "radical immanence" (Deleuze 1980). This includes the notions of political passions, affirmative ethics, and the rigorous vision of affectivity they entail.

ON POLITICAL PASSIONS

The emphasis on the politics of affectivity is therefore central to the conceptual structure of nomadic thought. Contrary to its detractors, to whom I shall return later, I see poststructuralist philosophies as building upon but also moving beyond the spirit of the 1970s and laying the foundations for future projects by opposing all totalitarian ideologies as well as the totalizing power of theories. This translates into two interrelated notions: the first is a general suspicion of the political class and of the state apparatus. The second is the theoretically daring notion that politics and the process of becoming-political neither require nor especially benefit from the existence of the state. Nomadic theory trusts autonomous but mutually connected communities or groups-multitudes (Hardt and Negri 2000) or complex singularities (Deleuze and Guattari 1986) engaged in the project of constituting aternative structures. These aim to become better attuned to resistance against the political economy of schizoid, difference-minded, commodifying advanced capitalism. This stateless condition is not a form of exile and nonbelonging, but rather an active experiment with the composition of sustainable communities, capable of sharing a common life and values, in the absence of a binding state structure. Let me explore this point further.

The poststructuralist generation made subjectivity into a real issue, which became all the more poignant and ethically urgent as a way of accounting for the moral and political bankruptcy of recent events in European history. The first was the Second World War and the long shadow of fascism and widespread collaboration. Nazism also marked a violent disruption in the history of philosophy: it chased away, or brutally murdered, the thinkers who had developed critical theory, notably Marxists, psychoanalysts, and other opponents of Western supremacy. France in the 1970s marks the return of critical theories to a continent that had savagely eradicated them.

A second aspect of European history that deeply affected the critical spirit of radical philosophies was colonialism. The self-aggrandizing and ethnocentric mystifications that surrounded French colonial history had been criticized by Fanon, Genet, Sartre, and Beauvoir—the postwar generation of critical thinkers. There is no question that the May '68 generation came of age politically during the Algerian liberation war and first experienced political violence in the anticolonialism movements (Hamon and Rotman 1988a). The persistence of the postcolonial question in the work of the poststructuralists is strong, as expressed in Julia Kristeva's idea of becoming "strangers to ourselves" (1991). This deconstructed vision of the European subject is active also in Irigaray's thought about Eastern philosophy (1997) and in Cixous's reappraisal of her Algerian Jewish roots (1997). Gayatri Spivak's vocal advocacy (1993) of new postcolonial subjects asserts the noncentrality of European hegemony, as did Foucault's enthusiastic reaction to the Iranian revolution. The work of Jacques Derrida (1997), Massimo Cacciari (1994), and Gilles Deleuze and Felix Guattari (1980) points strongly in this direction as well.

The third world-historical manifestation of European domination that haunted the thinkers of May '68 was obviously Marxism, as I mentioned before. The generation that came of age politically in 1968 introduced—with Althusser—a radical critique of the orthodoxy of Marxism, upheld by the (Western) European communist parties that acted as the moral guardians of the legacy of antifascism. With Lacan, they also challenged the authority of the International Psychoanalytic Association, which managed Freud's legacy with great rigidity. The new forms of philosophical radicalism developed in France in the late 1960s are a vocal critique of the dogmatic structure of communist and psychoanalytic thought and practice. The generation of the poststructuralists appealed directly to the subversive potential of the texts of Marxism and psychoanalysis so as to recover their anti-institutional critical stance.

They did not reject the bulk of Marx and Freud, but rather endeavored to recover and develop the radical core. In their view, the crux of the problem was the theory of the subject, which is implicit in these theories: under the cover of the unconscious, or the bulk of historical materialism, the subject of critical European theory preserved a unitary, hegemonic, and royal place as the motor of human history. This is the implicit humanism that triggered the criticism of thinkers like Foucault and Deleuze. The rejection of humanistic assumptions therefore took the form of unhinging the subject, freeing it respectively from the dictatorship of a libido dominated by oedipal jealousy and from the linearity of a historical telos that had married reason to the revolution.

The philosophical generation that proclaimed the "death of man" was simultaneously antifascist, anticolonialist, postcommunist, and posthumanist. Moreover, they rejected Eurocentrism and the classical definition of European identity in terms of humanism, rationality, and the universal.

A POLITICAL ECONOMY OF AFFECT

Considering the extent to which the post-1989 world order has resulted in the dismissal of radical politics, some reflection is needed on the nature of public representations of the political today. I have argued throughout this book that the contemporary form of globalized capitalism both harps upon affective and emotional layers, cultural memories and aspirations of subjects that are essentially constructed as consumers of identity-bound pleasures. Moods and yearnings are both publicly expressed and commodified, mostly for the sake of biopolitical governance and adequate consumption, which entails a significant amount of distortion and even of willful ignorance of the actual historical events. This calculated ignorance is also due to the perverse temporality at work in our globalized world: advanced capitalism is an unsustainable "future eater" (Flannery 1994), driven by all-consuming entropic energy. Devoid of the capacity for critical self-reflexion and genuine creativity, global capital merely promotes the recycling of spent hopes, repackaged in the rhetorical frame of the "new" and wrapped up in persistent anxiety about the future. In a schizophrenic double pull of euphoria and paranoia, which confirms Deleuze and Guattari's analyses (1972, 1980), the consumerist and socially enhanced faith in the new manages to coexist alongside the complete social rejection of subversive change and radical transformations. The potential for creating alternative practices of subjectivity clashes with the reterritorialization of desires through the gravitational pull of established values bent on short-term profit. This achieves a disastrous double effect: it reasserts individualism as the norm while reducing it to consumerism.

The collective memories of the radical politics of the 1970s are inscribed in this social context and consequently partake of its perverse political economy. An example of the schizoid double pull is the contemporary popularity of images of 1970s icons in popular culture, cinema, fashion music, and the media. They range from the ubiquitous face of Che Guevara or the young Angela Davis, to the images of Marilyn Monroe, JFK, Martin Luther King, Baader-Meinhof and the Red Army Faction, and other political immortals. Their totemic function is sacred or at least postsecular in the sacrificial sense of the term ("they suffered so that we may be better off"). Their symbolic value, however, is clearly inscribed in the current market economy as the commodification of radical political culture through the hyperindividualistic branding of the faces of its celebrities. This phenomenon is postideological and border crossing: nowadays it also includes Nelson Mandela and Princess Diana in some quarters and resistance or guerrilla fighters and Islamist suicide bombers in others.

Following the schizoid social climate of our times, however, the fashionable currency of radical popular culture heroes coexists with endless celebrations of "the end of ideologies," especially those of the radical left of the 1960s. Since the fall of the Berlin wall, the public debate around the events of '68 has grown more heated and polemical. This has been especially acrimonious among French intellectuals, most of whom have seen it fit to replace their youthful radicalism with age-worn conservatism. Ranging from the revisionist style (Ferry and Renault 1985), to media-savvy glamour (Lévy 1977) to decent neohumanism (Todorov 2002). This movement, known as les nouveaux philosophes, peaked in Andre Glucksmann's (1976), Alain Finkielkraut's (1987) and Ferry and Renault's (1985) indictment of the events of 1968 as a symbol of left-wing authoritarianism. Adding insult to injury, they accused all poststructuralist philosophies of complicity with terror and mass murder.

Deleuze was one of the first to comment on this hasty and fallacious historical dismissal of critical radicalism in both politics and philosophy—

and a reduction of both to the events of 1968. Targeting the fame-seeking narcissism of the *nouveaux philosophes*, Deleuze (2002)—stressed its political conservatism, which results in the reassertion of the banality of individualistic self-interest as a lesser and necessary evil. This moral apathy is constitutive of the neoconservative political liberalism of our era and of the arrogance with which it proclaimed the "end of history" (Fukuyama 1992). Against the vanity of these media stars, Deleuze instead stressed how critical philosophers have tried to avoid this pitfall: "we've been trying to uncover creative functions which would no longer require an author-function for them to be active" (2002:139). Other leading figures of philosophical poststructuralism like Lyotard (1986) and Hocquenghem (1986) also take a clear stand against the trivialization and self-serving dismissal of the spirit of 1968.

The political movement that best exemplifies the affirmative spirit of nomadic politics is feminism. The second feminist wave of the 1970s was based not only on a critique of the false universality of the liberal democratic system and the failed promises of its exclusionary humanism. It also interrogated the entrenched masculinism of the allegedly radical left and its leaders. Of all the social movements of that period, the women's movement in particular illustrates the self-organizing capacity, the organizational energy, and the visionary force of a leaderless structure. Propelled by collectively shared aspirations to freedom, respect for diversity, desire for social and symbolic justice, and a "politics of everyday life," feminism was a passionate, humorous, and politically rigorous movement. Disrepectful of dominant norms, but aware of its responsibility for the masses of women whose rage and vision it embodied, the collective endeavor of the women's movement is one of the most succesful political experiments of the twentieth century.

I consequently find it difficult to understand why the radical experiment of feminism is seldom quoted or even mentioned in contemporary debates about the political. The deletion of the women's movement and the subsequent dismissal of feminism as a merely cultural phenomenon is mistaken on several accounts. Firstly, it does not do justice to the vast body of scholarship produced by the feminists themselves—which has been so influential as to change the disciplinary contours of many political debates, especially on citizenship and subjectivity. Secondly, it misunderstands the feminist politics of experience—summarized in the slogan: "The personal is the political." The 1970s feminism is build on the politics of desire as the positive affirmation of a collectively shared longing for plenitude and the actualization of one's politics, regardless of sex, race, class, or sexual preferences. A political form of felicity, this radical aspiration to freedom aimed to confront and demolish the established, institutionalized form of gender identities and the power relations they actualize.

Furthermore, the emphasis on the politics of happiness or of feeling at home in one's culture—far from being a regression into narcissism—is an incisive comment on the mindless confrontation of dominant morality and social order. As such it encourages the counteractualization of different political economies of affect and desire. The pursuit of political felicity is collective, not individualistic, and free of profit motives, being elevated to the gratuitous task of constructing social horizons of hope.

This combination of critical acumen and creative potency is what I value most in the post-'68 philosophies. Feminism put it clearly by voicing the need for a "double-edged vision" of critique and creativity (Kelly 1979) that goes beyond complaint and denunciation to offer empowering alternatives. Lenin's world-shattering slogan "what's to be done?" mirrors a lost world when the social consensus—at least in the political left—was that the philosopher's task had always been to interpret the world, but that point now was to change it. Much has happened to the world and to people's desire for change since such an imperative saw the red light of day. In the climate of fear and anxiety that marks the postindustrial societies of the global era since the end of the cold war in 1989, the question "what is to be done?" tends to acquire a far less imperial and definitely more pathetic tone. What can we do to cope with the fast rate of changes? With the crumbling of established certainties and values? The evaporation of dear and cherished habits? How far can we go in taking the changes? How far are we capable of stretching ourselves? Or, to paraphrase the neo-Spinozist teachings of Deleuze: how much can our bodies—our embodied and embedded selves—actually take?

The ethical lesson of May '68 is that there is no logical necessity to link political subjectivity to oppositional consciousness and reduce them both to negativity. Political activism can be all the more effective if it disengages the process of consciousness-raising from negativity and connects it instead to creative affirmation. In terms of the crucial relationship to sameness and difference, this means that the dialectical opposition is replaced by the recognition of the ways in which otherness prompts, mobilizes, and engenders actualization of virtual potentials. These are by definition not contained in the present conditions and cannot emerge from them. They have to be brought about or generated creatively by a qualitative leap of the collective imaginary.

Because of the emphasis on the positivity of desire, it is impossible to understand the specific political economy of affects of nomadic political theory without reference to psychoanalytic politics. The main psychoanalytic insight concerns the importance of the emotional layering of the process of subject formation. This refers to the affective, unconscious, and visceral elements of our allegedly rational and discursive belief system (Connolly 1999). To put it bluntly: the political does not equate the rational and the revolution is not the same as the irrational. Religion may well be the opium of some masses, but politics is no less intoxicating, and science is the favorite addiction of many others.

The poststructuralist approach builds on the psychoanalytic notion of an open-ended or nonunitary subject activated by desire. Deleuze and Guattari especially take the instance of the unconscious not as the black box, or obscure god, of some guilt-ridden subject of Lack, but rather as a receptor and activator of gratuitous forms of unprogrammed orientations and interconnections. This situates sensuality, affectivity, empathy, and desire as core values in the discussion about the politics of contemporary nonunitary subjects. Equally central to this generation of philosophers is the focus on power as both restrictive (potestas) and productive (potentia) force. It also means that power formations are both monuments and documents, in that they are expressed in social institutions and in systems of representation, narratives, and modes of identification. These are neither coherent nor rational, and their makeshift nature, far from diminishing their effectiveness, is crucial to their hegemonic power. The awareness of unconscious processes translates into a recognition of the instability and lack of coherence of the narratives that compose the social text. Far from resulting in a suspension of political and moral action, this political sensibility becomes for the poststructuralists the starting point to elaborate sites of political resistance suited to the paradoxes of this historical condition.

THE CURRENT CONTEXT

As I have suggested before, the public debate on social and cultural theory over the last ten years shows a decline of interest in politics, whereas discourses about ethics, religious norms, and values have become dominant. Some master narratives circulate, which reiterate familiar themes: one is the inevitability of capitalist market economies as the alleged historical apex of human progress (Fukuyama 1992, 2002). Another is a contemporary brand of biological essentialism, which exacerbates aggressive individualism under the cover of "the selfish gene" (Dawkins 1976) and new evolutionary psychology. Another resonant refrain is that God is not dead. Nietzsche's claim rings hollows across the spectrum of contemporary global politics, dominated by the clash of religiously defined civilizations and widespread xenophobia (see chapter 7).

The biopolitical concerns that fuel identity politics and the perennial warfare of our times also introduce a political economy of negative passions in our social context. This negative affective economy expresses our actual condition: we now live in a militarized social space, under pressure of increased security enforcement and escalating states of emergency. The binary oppositions of the cold war era have been replaced by all-pervasive paranoia: the constant threat of the impending catastrophe. From environmental disaster to terrorist attack, accidents are imminent and certain to materialize: it is only a question of time.

In this context a passion for political activism has been replaced by rituals of public collective mourning. Melancholia has become a dominant mood and mode of relation. There is, of course, much to be mournful about, given the pathos of our global politics: our social horizon is war ridden and death bound. The promises of globalization turned out to be deceitful, and their financial rewards disappointing. We live in a culture where religious-minded people kill in the name of "the right to life" and where mighty nations wage war for "humanitarian" reasons. The question of what exactly counts as the "human" and what constitutes the basic unit of reference for the human in the globalized world is more urgent than ever. Depression and burnout are constant features of our most "advanced" societies. Psychopharmaceutical management of the population results in widespread use of legal and illegal drugs, a narcotic subtext that is understudied. Bodily vulnerability is increased by the great epidemics: some new ones, like HIV, Ebola, SARS, or avian flu; others more traditional, like TB and malaria. Health has become more than a public policy issue: it is a human rights, immigration, and a national defense concern.

While new age remedies and lifelong coaching of all sorts proliferate, our political sensibility has become accustomed to daily doses of horror:

we have taken a "forensic" turn (Braidotti, Colebrook, and Hanafin 2009). Pushing this insight to its conceptual extreme, Giorgio Agamben (1998) argues that the reduction of some categories of humans to the status of "bare life" is the end result of the project of Western modernity. As a political ontology, it marks the liminal grounds of human destitution—calculated degrees of dying (more on this in chapter 13). At the same time developed cultures are obsessed with youth and longevity, as testified by the popularity of antiaging treatments and plastic surgery.

Among all these paradoxes, melancholia rules. Hal Foster (1996) describes our schizoid cultural politics in terms of "traumatic realism"—an obsession with wounds, pain, and suffering combined with the irresistible urge to display them in public. Proliferating medical panopticons produce a global pathography (Seltzer 1999): we go on television talk shows to make a public spectacle of our pain. This is almost a parodic confirmation of the diagnosis Michel Foucault made of the Western world's sexual and emotional impoverishment. In the first volume of his *History of Sexuality*, Foucault analyzes the paradox of a culture that verbalizes and visualizes to the utmost of its ability—the claim that it is sexually oppressed, miserable, and frustrated. We scream our pain at the top of our voices and publicly claim the right to be liberated from the invisible chains of our repression. Foucault's political program unfolds from this ironic premise into a full-scale critique of the theory and practice of sexual liberation. Arguing that there is no freedom to be gained through but only *from* sexuality, Foucault's work explores the possibility of developing different forms and relations of intimacy. How to undo the sovereignty of phallocentric sex in favor of multiple other connections is the ethical impulse that sustains Foucault's work on the technologies of self-other relations (Braidotti 2011). It is in this tradition of thought that I want to argue the case for the politics of affirmation.

In the same vein, nomadic theory argues that no freedom is possible within capitalism because the axiom of money and profit knows no limit. The system functions axiomatically, which means, as Toscano (2006) pointed out, that it refuses to provide definitions of the terms it works with, but prefers to order certain domains into existence with the addition or subtraction of certain norms or commands. Axioms operate by emptying flows of their specific meaning in their coded context and thus by decoding them. As Protevi puts it (Protevi and Patton 2003), through processes of overcoding preexistent regimes of signs are decoded and subjected to the aims of a centralizing hierarchical machine that turns activity into labor, territories into land, and surplus value into profit. Axioms simply need not be explained, and its terms of relation need not be defined, their objects being treated as purely functional—note the emphasis on the "new" and "the next generation of gadgets". Being fundamentally meaningless, the decoded flows of capitalism are purely operational modes of regulation. They can get attached to any type of social organization—slave plantations as well as factories—and to different state structures—socialism as well as liberal democracies.

As such, the axioms of capitalism are extremely adaptable, capable of great internal variation and structured around a perverse sort of opportunism. Such flexibility and multiple realizability constitute a formidable apparatus of domination or capture. As Eugene Holland points out (2006), however, there is an entropic and self-destructive element to advanced capitalism in that it exposes and endangers the very sources of its wealth and power, which previous systems kept hidden or protected. Advanced capitalism operates on contemporary decoded or deterritorialized flows of change and reterritorializes or stratifies them for the sake of profit. Royal science is the epistemic counterpart of this same political economy of stratification and systemic containment or consistency. Epistemologically, minor science opposes royal science by insisting on the problematic mode and the opening of the scientific field to what Manuel De Landa (2002) calls the intensive force of science.

Advanced capitalism never attains absolute deterritorializations and always engenders social subjection. Nomadic theory opposes to the axiom the diagrammatic process of schizoid becoming, which encourages flows without the insertion of axioms. Nomadic thought focuses on an ethological approach to analyze the ways in which capitalism axiomizes and captures subjectivity in order to subject it to the imperatives of surplus value. Political praxis focuses therefore on the construction of alternative models of subjectivity.

THE NEW BODILY MATERIALISM; OR, THE EMPIRICAL TRANSCENDENTAL

Throughout the different phases of his extraordinarily cohesive body of work, Deleuze never ceases to emphasize the empowering force of affirmative passions and thus redefines the embodied subject as an empirical transcendental entity.

In so doing, Deleuze goes further than any social constructivist attack on the "myth" of human nature, while also moving beyond the ways in which psychoanalysis "sacralizes" the sexual body. Deleuze's philosophy aims instead at replacing both these views with what I would call a high-tech brand of vitalism, the respect for bio-organisms and also for biodiversity. This also engenders the "intensive" style of writing that is his trademark, to which I will return in a later section. This results in a project that aims at alternative figurations of human subjectivity and of its political and aesthetic expressions. Rhizomes, bodies-without-organs, nomads, processes of becoming, flows, intensities, and folds are part of this rainbow of alternative figurations that Deleuze throws our way.

For Deleuze thought is made of sense and value: it is the force, or level of intensity, that fixes the value of an idea, not its adequation to a preestablished normative model. An idea is a line of intensity marking a certain degree or variation in intensity. An idea is an active state of very high intensity, which opens up hitherto unsuspected possibilities of life and action. Thinking carries the affirmative power of life to a higher degree. The force of this notion is that it puts a stop to the traditional search for ideas or lines that are "just" (in theory and politics alike). For if ideas are projectiles launched into time they can be neither "just" nor "false." Or, rather, they can be either "just" or false depending on the degree and levels of intensity of the forces, affects, or passions that sustain them. Philosophy as critique of negative, reactive values is also the critique of the dogmatic image of thought they sustain. It expresses the thinking process in terms of a typology of forces (Nietzsche) or an ethology of passions (Spinoza). In other words, Deleuze's rhizomatic style brings to the fore the affective foundations of the thinking process. Thinking, in other words, is to a very large extent nonconscious, in that it expresses the desire to know, and this desire is that which cannot be adequately expressed in language, simply because it is that which sustains it. Through this intensive structure of the thinking process, Deleuze points to the prephilosophical foundations of philosophy: its embodied, fleshy starting block.

We are faced here with the problem of what is ontologically there but propositionally excluded by necessity in the philosophical utterance. There is the unspoken and the unspeakable desire for thought, the passion for thinking, the epistemophilic substratum on which philosophy later erects its discursive monuments. This affective stratum makes it possible for Deleuze to speak of a prediscursive moment of thinking. Pursuing this insight in a Spinozist mode, Deleuze rejects the phantoms of negation, putting thought at the service of creation. In this perspective, we shall call philosophy all that expresses and enriches the positivity of the subject as an intensive, affective thinking entity.

Deleuze's analysis of thinking (especially in *Nietzsche and Philosophy* and *Difference and Repetition*) point in fact to a sort of structural aporia in philosophical discourse. Philosophy is both logophilic and logophobic, as Foucault had already astutely remarked (Foucault 1977a). Discourse— the production of ideas, knowledge, texts, and sciences—is something that philosophy relates to and rests upon in order to codify it and systematize it; philosophy is therefore logophilic. Discourse being, however, a complex network of interrelated truth effects, it far exceeds philosophy's power of codification. So philosophy has to "run after" all sorts of new discourses, such as women, postcolonial subjects, the audiovisual media, and other new technologies, etc., in order to incorporate them into its way of thinking; in this respect philosophy is logophobic. It is thus doomed to accept processes of becoming or to perish.

The strength of this philosophy of immanence lies in its social and historical relevance. It assumes that the overcoming of dialectics of negativity is historically and politically necessary in the framework of a polycentered, posthumanist, and postindustrial world. I would also like to add that it is conceptually necessary to get over the built-in pessimism of a philosophy of eternal returns that does not trigger any margins of empowering difference. Whereas Derrida, confronted with the same challenges, ends up glorifying the aporetic circle of undecidability and endless reiteration; whereas Irigaray invests in the feminine as the sole force that can break the eternal return of the Same and its classical Others, rhizomatic thinking empowers subjectivity as a multiplicity and along multiple axes. Only such a qualitative leap can accomplish that creative overturning of the melancholia of negativity, bad conscience, law, and lack. This brand of vitalistic pragmatism is an instigation to empower positively the difference nomadic subjects can make. It has nothing to do with voluntarism and all to do with a shift of grounds, a change of rhythms, a different set of conceptual relations and affective colors. Resonances, harmonies, and hues intermingle to paint an altogether different landscape of a self that, not being One, functions as a relay point for many sets of intensive intersections and encounters with multiple others. Moreover, not being burdened by being One, such a subject can envisage forms of resistance and political agency that are multilayered and complex. It is an empirical transcendental site of becoming.

Resting on Spinoza, whom he decidedly recasts out of the Hegelian mold, Deleuze opens a whole dimension to the debate about the politics of desire and the desirability of an enfleshed subject who may actually yearn for change and transformation. Not happy with accommodation, and well beyond the libidinal economy of compensation, this subject that is not one actively desires processes of metamorphosis of the self, society, and of its modes of cultural representation. This project of undoing the Hegelian trap that consists in associating desire with lack and negativity results in a radical new ethics of enfleshed, sustainable subjects.

The point about virtuality is that it aims at actualizations through radical forms of empirical pragmatism. The force of the virtual is to stress that the "real," and hence the grounds for the political, does not coincide with present conditions but rather with the virtual dimension of incorporeal events. The virtual itself can bring about actualizations but never just coincide with them. Cosmos is another term for this self-ordering and emergence-producing capacity of the universe (Protevi and Patton 2003).

Chaos is formless but not undifferentiated: infinite speed linked to the eternal return that selects simulacra for their divergence. This infinite speed constitutes the outside of philosophy, and it is both a threat and a resource to philosophical thought, which has to strike a balance between the infinite speed and some sort of consistency. According to Deleuze, this is achieved through drawing the planes of immanence, the invention of conceptual personae, and the creation of concepts. In this respect nomadic theory can be described as an ethics of chaos or of virtual creativity.

Boundas (2007b) stresses that the virtual strikes a time line of its own, which is neither the immemorial past nor the apocalyptic or messianic future. We need to think the time of becoming, without reifying either the past or the future, so as to safeguard nondetermining and antiteleological tendencies. In other words, the virtual is the "untimely"—the impassive and dynamic aspects of multiplicities in the process of actualization. The political needs to be attached to the untimely as well. This is accomplished through a series of balancing acts or assemblages—to be out of joint but also engaged with the times, to be vowed to the future but active in the here and now, and to actualize sustainable systems while staying tuned and loyal to the force of the virtual.

OPPOSITIONAL CONSCIOUSNESS

The conceptual case of my argument rests on the rejection of the traditional equation between political subjectivity and critical oppositional consciousness and the reduction of both to negativity, as I argued in the previous chapter. There is an implicit assumption that political subjectivity or agency is about resistance, and that resistance means the negation of the negativity of the present. A positive is supposed to be engendered by this double negative. Being against implies a belligerent act of negation, the erasure of present conditions.

This assumption shares in a long-constituted history of thought, which in Continental philosophy is best exemplified by Hegel. The legacy of Hegelian-Marxist dialectics of consciousness is such that it positions negativity as a necessary structural element of thought. This means that the rejection of conditions or premises that are considered unsatisfactory, unfair, or offensive—on either ethical or political grounds—is the necessary precondition for their critique. A paradoxical concomitance is thus posited between the conditions one rejects and the discursive practice of critical philosophy and subsequent actions. This paradox results in establishing negativity as a productive moment in the dialectical scheme, which fundamentally aims at overturning the conditions that produced it in the first place. Thus, critical theory banks on negativity and, in a perverse way, even requires it. The corollary of this assumption is that the same material and discursive conditions that create the negative moment—the experience of oppression, marginality, injury, or trauma—are also the condition of their overturning. The material that damages is also that which engenders positive resistance, counteraction, or transcendence (Foucault 1977a). The process of consciousness-raising is crucial to the process of overturning or overcoding the negative instance. What triggers and at the same time is engendered by the process of resistance is collective oppositional consciousness. There is consequently a political necessity to elaborate adequate understandings and suitable representations of our real-life conditions. The negative experience can be turned into the matter that critical theory has to engage with. In this process, it turns into the productive source of countertruths and values, which aim at overcoding the original negative instance. Epistemology therefore clears the ground for the ethical transformation that sustains political action.

This process is too often rendered in purely functional terms as the equation of political creativity/agency with negativity or unhappy consciousness. I want to suggest, however, that much is to be gained by adopting a non-Hegelian analysis that foregrounds instead the creative or affirmative elements of this process. This shift of perspective assumes philosophical monism and the recognition of an ethical and affective component of subjectivity; it is thus both an antidualistic and antirationalist position. A subject's ethical core is not his/her moral intentionality so much as the effects of power (as repressive—potestas—and positive—potentia) her actions are likely to have upon the world. It is a process of engendering empowering modes of becoming (Deleuze 1968). Given that, in this neovitalist view, the ethical good is equated with radical relationality aiming at affirmative empowerment, the ethical ideal is to increase one's ability to enter into modes of relation with multiple others. Oppositional consciousness and the political subjectivity or agency it engenders are processes or assemblages that actualize this ethical urge. This position is affirmative in the sense that it actively works toward the creation of alternatives by working through the negative instance and cultivating relations that are conducive to the ethical transmutation of values.

What this means practically is that the conditions for political and ethical agency are not dependent on the current state of the terrain. They are not oppositional and thus not tied to the present by negation; instead they are affirmative and geared to creating possible futures. Ethical and political relations create possible worlds by mobilizing resources that have been left untapped, including our desires and imagination. The work of critique must focus on creating the conditions for overturning of negativity precisely because they are not immediately available in the present. Moving beyond the dialectical scheme of thought means abandoning oppositional thinking so as to index activity in the present on the task of sustainable possible futures. The sustainability of the future rests on our ability to mobilize, actualize, and deploy cognitive, affective, and ethical forces that had not been activated thus far. These driving forces concretize in actual, material relations and can thus constitute a network, web, or rhizome of interconnection with others. We have to learn to think differently about ourselves. To think means to create new conceptual tools that may enable us to both come to terms and actively interact with empowering others. The ethical gesture is the actualization of our increased ability to act and interact in the world.

To disengage the process of subject formation from negativity to attach it to affirmative otherness means that reciprocity is redefined not as mutual recognition but rather as mutual definition or specification. We are in *this* together in a vital political economy of becoming that is both trans-subjective in structure and transhuman in force. Such a nomadic vision of the subject, moreover, does not restrict the ethical instance within the limits of human otherness, but also opens it up to interrelations with nonhuman, posthuman, and inhuman forces. The emphasis on nonhuman ethical relations can also be described as a geopolitics or an ecophilosophy in that it values one's reliance on the environment in the broadest sense of the term. Felix Guattari's idea of the three ecologies: the social, the psychic, and the environmental, is very relevant to this discussion. I discussed this in chapter 4. Considering the extent of our technological development, emphasis on the ecophilosophical aspects is not to be mistaken for biological determinism. It rather posits a nature-culture continuum (Haraway 1997; Guattari 1995, 2000) within which subjects cultivate and construct multiple ethical relations. The concepts of immanence, multiple ecologies, and oneo-vital politics become relevant here.

I have argued so far that oppositional consciousness is central to political subjectivity, but it is not the same as negativity, and that, as a consequence, critical theory is about strategies and relations of affirmation. Political subjectivity or agency therefore consists of multiple micropolitical practices of daily activism or interventions in and on the world we inhabit for ourselves and for future generations. As Rich put it in her recent essays, the political activist has to think "in spite of the times" and hence "out of my time," thus creating the analytics—the conditions of possibility—of the future (2001:159). Critical theory occurs somewhere between the no longer and the not yet, not looking for easy reassurances but for evidence that others are struggling with the same questions. Consequently, "we" are in *this* together indeed.

WHAT IS AFFIRMATION?

In order to understand the kind of transmutation of values I am defending here, it is important to depsychologize this discussion about positivity, negativity, and affirmation and approach it instead in more conceptual terms. We can then see how common and familiar this transmutation of values actually is. The distinction between good and evil is replaced by that between affirmation and negation or positive and negative affects.

What is positive in the ethics of affirmation is the belief that negative affects can be transformed. This implies a dynamic view of all affects, even those that freeze us in pain, horror, or mourning. The slightly depersonalizing effect of the negative or traumatic event involves a loss of ego-indexes perception, which allows for energetic forms of reaction. Clinical psychological research on trauma testifies to this, but I cannot pursue this angle here. Diasporic subjects of all kinds express the same insight. Multilocality is the affirmative translation of this negative sense of loss. Following Glissant (1990), the becoming-nomadic marks the process of positive transformation of the pain of loss into the active production of multiple forms of belonging and complex allegiances. Every event contains within it the potential for being overcome and overtaken—its negative charge can be transposed. The moment of actualization is also the moment of its neutralization. The ethical subject is the one with the ability to grasp the freedom to depersonalize the event and transform its negative charge. Affirmative ethics puts the motion back into emotion and the active back into activism, introducing movement, process, becoming. This shift makes all the difference to the patterns of repetition of negative emotions. It also reopens the debate on secularity in that it actually promotes an act of faith in our collective capacity to endure and to transform.

What is negative about negative affects is not a normative value judgment but rather the effect of arrest, blockage, rigidification, that comes as a result of a blow, a shock, an act of violence, betrayal, trauma, or just intense boredom. Negative passions do not merely destroy the self but also harm the self's capacity to relate to others—both human and nonhuman others—and thus to grow in and through others. Negative affects diminish our capacity to express the high levels of interdependence, the vital reliance on others that is key to both a nonunitary vision of the subject and to affirmative ethics. Again, the vitalist notion of life as zoe is important here because it stresses that the life I inhabit is not mine, it does not bear my name—it is a generative force of becoming, of individuation and differentiation: apersonal, indifferent, and generative. What is negated by negative passions is the power of life itself—its potentia—as dynamic force, vital flows of connections, and becoming. And this is why they should neither be encouraged, nor should we be rewarded for lingering around them too long. Negative passions are black holes.

This is an antithesis of the Kantian moral imperative to avoid pain or to view pain as the obstacle to moral behavior. It displaces the grounds on which Kantian negotiations of limits can take place. The imperative not to do onto others what you would not want done to you is not rejected as much as enlarged. In affirmative ethics, the harm you do to others is immediately reflected in the harm you do to yourself, in terms of loss of potentia, positivity, capacity to relate, and hence freedom. Affirmative ethics is not about the avoidance of pain, but rather about transcending the resignation and passivity that ensue from being hurt, lost, and dispossessed. One has to become ethical, as opposed to applying moral rules and protocols as a form of self-protection: one has to endure.

Endurance is the Spinozist code word for this process. Endurance has a spatial side to do with the space of the body as an enfleshed field of actualization of passions or forces. It evolves affectivity and joy, as in the capacity for being affected by these forces to the point of pain or extreme pleasure. Endurance points to the struggle to sustain the pain without being annihilated by it. Endurance also has a temporal dimension about duration in time. This is linked to memory: intense pain, a wrong, a betrayal, a wound are hard to forget. The traumatic impact of painful events fixes them in a rigid eternal present tense out of which it is difficult to emerge. This is the eternal return of that which precisely cannot be endured and, as such, returns precisely in the mode of the unwanted, the untimely, the unassimilated, or inappropriate/d. They are also, however, paradoxically difficult to remember, insofar as re-membering entails retrieval and repetition of the pain itself.

Psychoanalysis, of course, has been here before (Laplanche 1976). The notion of the return of the repressed is the key to the logic of unconscious remembrance, but it is a secret and somewhat invisible key: it condenses space into the spasm of the symptom and time into a short-circuit that mines the very thinkability of the present. Kristeva's notion of the abject (1982) expresses clearly the temporality involved in psychoanalysis—by stressing the structural function played by the negative, by the incomprehensible, the unthinkable, the other of understandable knowledge. Later Kristeva (1991) describes this as a form of structural dissociation within the self that makes us strangers to ourselves.

Deleuze calls this alterity Chaos and defines it positively as the virtual formation of all possible form. Lacan, on the other hand—and Derrida with him, I would argue—defines Chaos epistemologically as that which precedes form, structure, language. This makes for two radically divergent conceptions of time and—more importantly for me here—of negativity. That which is incomprehensible for Lacan—following Hegel—is the virtual for Deleuze, following Spinoza, Bergson, and Leibniz. This produces a number of significant shifts: from negative to affirmative affects, from entropic to generative desire, from incomprehensible to virtual events to be actualized, from constitutive outsides to a geometry of affects that require mutual actualization and synchronization, from a melancholy and split to an open-ended weblike subject, from the epistemological to the ontological turn in philosophy.

Nietzsche has also been here before. The eternal return in Nietzsche is the repetition, not in the compulsive mode of neurosis, nor in the negative erasure that marks the traumatic event. It is the eternal return of and as positivity. In a nomadic, Deleuzian-Nietzschean perspective, ethics is essentially about transformation of negative into positive passions, i.e., moving beyond the pain. This does not mean denying the pain, but rather activating it, working it through. Again, the positivity here is not supposed to indicate a facile optimism or a careless dismissal of human suffering. It involves compassionate witnessing of the pain of others, as Zygmunt Bauman (1993) and Susan Sontag (2003) point out—in the mode of empathic copresence. More on this in the next chapter.

The emphasis on the pursuit and actualization of positive relations and the ethical value attributed to affirmation do not imply any avoidance or disavowal of conflict. The rather simplistic charge of pacifism pushed to the extremes of passivity is often made against Spinozist nomadic thought and its Deleuzian spin-offs (Hallward 2006; Žižek 2003). Nothing could be further from the truth than these charges of apolitical holism. Two crucial points need to be raised here: firstly, that amor fati is not passive fatalism, but pragmatic and labile engagement with the present in order to collectively construct conditions that transform and empower our capacity to act ethically and produce social horizons of hope or sustainable futures.

Secondly, the ethical cultivation of positivity does not exclude, either logically or practically, situations of antagonism or conflict. Starting from the premise that we are dealing with a postidentitarian politics need to depsychologize the discussion about positivity and posit it instead in terms of an ethnology of forces, it follows that some of the positive relations may well be of the antagonistic kind. What matters—and this is the shift of perspective introduced by affirmative ethics—is to resist the habit of inscribing antagonistic relations in a logic of dialectical negativity. The transcendence of dialectics, in other words, has to be enacted in the inner structure of relations—of the interpersonal as well as the nonhuman kind. Antagonism need not be inscribed in the lethal logic of the struggle of consciousness, which we have inherited from Hegel via Sartre, Beauvoir, and even Lacan—through Kojève. This habit of thought needs to be resisted and recoded away from the emphasis it places on the need for recognition by the other and hence the necessity of establishing negativity as the precondition for the process of subject -formation and the emergence of the Self.

Provided this conceptual shift is enacted, it becomes feasible, and for nomadic theory desirable, to engage in antagonistic relations within the framework of affirmative politics. Positivity does not imply mindless acceptance or acritical passivity. It rathers prioritizes the construction of frames for the transformation of negative passions and forces in the here and now of concrete relations. It is in this respect that Boundas defends Deleuze's notion of amor fati against the tendentious change of mystical surrender made by Peter Hallward. Boundas stresses the rigorous pragmatism of Deleuze's ethical position. He firmly rejects messianic deferrals of action, with clear emphasis placed on the ethical urgency to enact actualizations, and more especially counteractualizations, so as to defeat the pull of negativity.

BEING WORTHY OF WHAT HAPPENS TO US

One of the reasons negative associations linked to pain, especially in relation to political processes of change, are ideologically laden has to do with the force of habit. Starting from the assumption that a subject is a molar aggregate, that is to say, a sedimentation of established habits, these can be seen as patterns of repetitions that consolidate modes of relation and forces of interaction. Habits are the frame within which nonunitary or complex subjects get reterritorialized, albeit temporarily. One of the established habits in our culture is to frame "pain" within a discourse and social practice of suffering that requires rightful compensation. Equally strong is the urge to understand and empathize with pain. People go to great lengths in order to ease all pain. Great distress follows from not knowing or not being able to articulate the source of one's suffering or from knowing it all too well, all the time. The yearning for solace, closure, and justice is understandable and worthy of respect.

This ethical dilemma was already posed by J. F. Lyotard (1983) and, much earlier, by Primo Levi (1958) about the survivors of Nazi concentration camps. Namely, that the kind of vulnerability we humans experience in the face of events on the scale of small or high horror is something for which no adequate compensation is even thinkable. It is just incommensurable: a hurt, or wound, beyond repair. This means that the notion of justice in the sense of a logic of rights and reparation is not applicable. For the poststructuralist Lyotard, ethics consists in accepting the impossibility of adequate compensation—and living with the open wound.

This is the road to an ethics of affirmation, which respects the pain but suspends the quest for both claims and compensation and resists the logic of retribution of rights. This is achieved through a sort of depersonalization of the event, which is the ultimate ethical challenge. The displacement of the zoe-indexed reaction reveals the fundamental meaninglessness of the hurt, the injustice, or the injury one has suffered. "Why me?" is the refrain most commonly heard in a situation of extreme distress. This expresses rage as well as anguish at one's ill fate. The answer is plain: actually, for no reason at all. Examples of this are the banality of evil in large-scale genocides like the Holocaust (Arendt 1963), the randomness of surviving them. There is something intrinsically senseless about the pain, hurt, or injustice: lives are lost or saved for all reasons and for no reason at all. Why did some go to work in the WTC on 9/11 while others missed the train? Why did Frida Kahlo take that tram, which crashed so that she was impaled by a metal rod, and not the next one? For no reason at all. Reason has nothing to do with it. That's precisely the point. We need to unlink pain from the epistemological obsession that results in the quest for meaning and move beyond, to the next stage. That is the path to transformation of negative into positive passions.

This is not fatalism, and even less resignation, but rather a Nietzschean ethics of overturning the negative. Let us call it amor fati; we have to be worthy of what happens to us and rework it within an ethics of relation. Of course, repugnant and unbearable events do happen. Ethics consists, however, in reworking these events in the direction of positive relations. This is not carelessness or lack of compassion, but rather a form of lucidity that acknowledges the meaninglessness of pain and the futility of compensation. It also reasserts that the ethical instance is not one of retaliation or compensation but rather rests on active transformation of the negative.

Genevieve Lloyd (2008) provides a most illuminating account of the contrast between two different approaches to the nature of human freedom: "Descartes' account of the will as the locus of freedom and Spinoza's rival treatment of freedom as involving the capacity to shape a life in accordance with the recognition of necessity" (2008:1). Necessity is not passivity, but rather the creative acceptance of the potential of underlying tendencies that are already present. The convergence of freedom and necessity is the conceptual core of Spinozist ethics: "the joyful acceptance and appropriation of what must be" (Lloyd 2008:200).

This is related to the idea that, as humans, we are all part of nature and both animated and limited "by the causal determination exerted on us by the rest of the whole" (Lloyd 2008:213). This ontology of immanence is central to Spinoza's materialism; Deleuze develops it into a whole ethical system by stressing that we must not use the existing properties of actualized strata and conditions to predict what a body can do—the virtual multiplicities that sustain those strata or assemblages. This is the source of the nondeterministic vitalism of nomadic theory.

Paul Patton (2000) also stresses this affective dimension of the core of an ethic of critical human freedom that aims at transgressing the limits of what one is capable of becoming. For Constantin Boundas (2007b), the ability for individuation that is implied in this ontology of freedom connects it to the powers of the virtual : "Becoming worthy of the event . . . requires the ascesis of the counter-actualisation of the accidents that fill our lives and as a result our participation in the intensive, virtual event" (Boundas 2007:132b). In other words, the "worthiness" of an event—that which ethically compels us to engage with it—is not its intrinsic or explicit value according to given standards of moral or political evaluation, but rather the extent to which it contributes to conditions of becoming. It is a vital force to move beyond the negative.

Protevi argues (Protevi and Patton 2003) that, in this nomadic view, the political is the nonreactive and nonhabitual response of reactive engagement with the events of one's life that can reshape one's becoming. A sort of creative disorganization of the negative that aims at keeping life immanent, nonunitary, and nonreified according to dominant codes and hegemonic traditions of both life and thought.

This requires a double shift. Firstly, the affect itself moves from the frozen or reactive effect of pain to proactive affirmation of its generative potential. Secondly, the line of questioning also shifts from the quest for the origin or source to a process of elaboration of the questions that express and enhance a subject's capacity to achieve freedom through the understanding of its limits.

What is an adequate ethical question? One that is capable of sustaining the subject in his quest for more interrelations with others, i.e., more "Life," motion, change, and transformation. The adequate ethical question provides the subject with a frame for interaction and change, growth and movement. It affirms life as difference-at-work and as endurance. An ethical question has to be adequate in relation to how much a body can take. How much can an embodied entity take in the mode of interrelations and connections, i.e., how much freedom of action can we endure? Affirmative ethics assumes, following Nietzsche, that humanity does not stem from freedom but rather that freedom is extracted from the awareness of limitations. Affirmation is about freedom from the burden of negativity, freedom through the understanding of our bondage.

CONCLUSION: IN SPITE OF THE TIMES

The real issue is conceptual: how do we develop a new postunitary vision of the subject, of ourselves, and how do we adopt a social imaginary that does justice to the complexity? Shifting an imaginary is not like casting away a used garment, but more like shedding an old skin. How do changes of this magnitude take place? It happens often enough at the molecular level, but in the social it is a painful experience, given that identifications constitute an inner scaffolding that supports one's sense of identity. Part of the answer lies in the formulation of the project: "we" are in *this* together. This is a collective activity, a group project that connects active, conscious, and desiring citizens. It points toward a virtual destination: postunitary nomadic identities, floating foundations, etc., but it is not utopian. As a project, it is historically grounded, socially embedded, and already partly actualized in the joint endeavor, that is, the community, of those who are actively working toward it. If this be utopian, it is only in the sense of the positive affects that are mobilized in the process: the necessary dose of imagination, dreamlike vision, and bonding without which no social project can take off.

The ethical process of transforming negative into positive passions engenders a politics of affirmation in the sense of creating the conditions for endurance and hence for a sustainable future. Virtual futures grow out of sustainable presents and vice versa. Transformative politics takes on the future as the shared collective imagining that endures in processes of becoming. The ethical-political concept here is the necessity to think with the times and in spite of the times, not in a belligerent mode of oppositional consciousness, but as a humble and empowering gesture of coconstruction of social horizons of hope.

Several social critics (Massumi 1997; Bourke 2005) have pointed out that the political economy of advanced capitalism is one of fear, terror, and manic-depressive moods of alternating apocalyptic gloom and euphoria.[2] A culture of guilt and apathy has settled into a society that acts as if it was traumatized. The climate of international terror and warfare provides the opportunity to indulge in self-idealization, a process Gilroy describes as "post-colonial melancholia." Global terrorism has turned us all into victims, made suddenly and violently aware of our vulnerability. This excessive psychologization of historical traumas results in the incapacity to replace collective social action and active political imagination with the psychology of mourning and the logic of guilt, retaliation, and compensation. In opposition to this, nomadic theory proposes the powers of affirmation of a culture of ethical responsibility and activated historical memory. Hence the importance of vigilance and critical scrutiny and the analysis of the workings of the state and the government. This is in keeping with the Spinozist political ontology of ethics as the extraction of freedom from a clear understanding of our limitations.

The final aspect of affirmative politics I want to spell out is that of generational time lines, in the sense of the construction of social horizons of hope, that is, of sustainable futures. Modernity, as an ideology of progress, postulated boundless faith in the future as the ultimate destination of the human. Zygmunt Bauman quotes one of my favorite writers, Diderot, when stating that modern man is in love with posterity. Postmodernity, on the other hand, is death bound and sets as its horizon the globalization process in terms of technological and economic interdependence. Capitalism had no built-in teleological purpose, historical logic, or structure, but is a self-imploding system that would not stop at anything in order to fulfill its aim: profit. This inherently self-destructive system feeds on, and thus destroys, the very conditions of its survival: it is omnivorous, and what it ultimately eats is the future itself. Being nothing more than this all-consuming entropic energy, capitalism lacks the ability to create anything new: it can merely promote the recycling of spent hopes, repackaged in the rhetorical frame of the "next generation of gadgets." Affirmative ethics expresses the desire to endure in time and thus clashes with the deadly spin of the present.

The future today is no longer the self-projection of the modernist subject, as I indicated in chapter 8. It is a basic and rather humble act of faith in the possibility of endurance (as duration or continuity) that honors our obligation to the generations to come. It involves the virtual unfolding of the affirmative aspect of what we manage to actualize in the here and now. Virtual futures grow out of sustainable presents and vice versa. This is how qualitative transformations can be actualized and transmitted along the genetic/time line. Transformative postsecular ethics takes on the future affirmatively, as the shared collective imagining that is a continual process of becoming, to effect multiple modes of interaction with heterogeneous others. This is what futurity is made of. It is a nonlinear evolution: an ethics that moves away from the paradigm of reciprocity and the logic of recognition and installs a rhizomatic relation of mutual affirmation.

Sustainability expresses the desire to endure in both space and time. In Spinozist-Deleuzian political terms, this sustainable idea of endurance is linked to the construction of possible futures, insofar as the future is the virtual unfolding of the affirmative aspect of the present. An equation is therefore drawn between the radical politics of disidentification, the formation of alternative subject positions, and the construction of social hope in the future. This equation rests on the strategy of transformation of negative passions into affirmative and empowering modes of relation to the conditions of our historicity.

In order to appreciate the full impact of this idea, we need to think back to the perverse temporality of advanced capitalism with which I started this essay. Insofar as the axioms of capitalism destroy sustainable futures, resistance entails the collective endeavor to construct social horizons of endurance, which is to say of hope and sustainability. It is a political practice of resistance to the present, which activates the past in producing the hope of change and the energy to actualize it. In so doing, it processes negative forces and enlists them to the empowering task of engaging with possible futures. Hope is an anticipatory virtue that activates powerful motivating forces: countermemories, imagination, dream work, religion, desire, and art. Hope constructs the future in that it opens the spaces onto which to project active desires; it gives us the force to process the negativity and emancipate ourselves from the inertia of everyday routines. It is a qualitative leap that carves out active trajectories of becoming and thus can respond to anxieties and uncertainties in a productive manner and negotiate transitions to sustainable futures.

By targeting those who come after us as the rightful ethical interlocutors and assessors of our own actions, we take seriously the implications of our own situated position. This form of intergenerational justice is crucial. This point about intragenerational fairness need not, however, be expressed or conceptualized in the social imaginary as an oedipal narrative. To be concerned about the future should not necessarily result in linearity, i.e., in restating the unity of space and time as the horizon of subjectivity. On the contrary, nonlinear genealogical models of intragenerational decency offer up one way of displacing the oedipal hierarchy. These models involve a becoming-minoritarian of the elderly, the senior, and the parental, but also a de-oedipalization of the bond of the young to those who preceded them. It calls for new ways of addressing and solving intergenerational conflicts— other than envy and rivalry—joining forces across the generational divide by working together toward sustainable futures. By practicing an ethics of nonreciprocity in the pursuit of affirmation.

An example: older feminists may feel the cruel pinch of aging, but some young ones suffer from 1970s envy. Middle-aged survivors of the second wave may feel like war veterans, but some of generation Y, as Iris van der Tuin taught me, call themselves "born-again baby boomers!" So who's envying whom?

"We" are in *this* together, indeed. Those who go through life under the sign of the desire for change need accelerations that jolt them out of set habits; political thinkers of the postsecular era need to be visionary, prophetic, and upbeat—insofar as they are passionately committed to writing the prehistory of the future. That is to say: to introduce change in the present so as to affect multiple modes of belonging through complex and heterogeneous relations. This is the horizon of sustainable futures.

Hope is a sort of "dreaming forward" that permeates our lives and activates them. It is a powerful motivating force grounded in our collective imaginings. They express very grounded concerns for the multitude of "anybody" that composes the human community. Lest our greed and selfishness destroy or diminish it for generations to come. Given that posterity per definition can never pay us back, this gesture is perfectly gratuitous.

Against the general lethargy, the rhetoric of selfish genes and possessive individualism, on the one hand, and the dominant ideology of melancholic lament, on the other, hope rests with an affirmative ethics of sustainable futures. A deep and careless generosity, the ethics of nonprofit at an ontological level. Why should one pursue this project? For no reason at all. Reason has nothing to do with this. Let's just do it for the hell of it—to be worthy of our times while resisting the times and for love of the world.

11

SUSTAINABLE ETHICS AND THE BODY IN PAIN

INTRODUCTION: AGAINST MORAL UNIVERSALISM

The fact that, in the climate of political restoration that marks our global context, interest in politics is in decline, whereas ethics triumphs in the public debate, is not necessarily an advantage. The charge of moral and cognitive relativism is in fact made against any project that shows a concerted effort at challenging or decentering the traditional, humanistic view of the moral subject. This overdefensive attitude asserts the belief in the necessity of strong foundations such as those that a classical liberal view of the rationalist subject can guarantee. Doxic consensus is set: without steady identities resting on firm grounds, basic elements of human decency, moral and political agency, and ethical probity are threatened. In opposition to this belief, which has little more than long-standing habits and the inertia of tradition on its side, I want to argue that a posthumanistic and nomadic vision of the subject is best suited to provide an alternative foundation for ethical and political subjectivity that respects the complexity of our times.

This argument is framed by a larger dispute, which I will not explore at length here—that of the thorny relationship between poststructuralist ethics in Continental philosophy, on the one hand, and the dominant, mostly Anglo-American traditions of moral philosophy, on the other. Todd May (1995) argued persuasively that moral philosophy as a discipline does not score highly in poststructuralist philosophy or in French philosophy as a whole. This is no reason, however, to move against it the lazy charges of moral relativism and nihilism. One only has to look across the field of French philosophy—Deleuze's ethics of immanence (Deleuze and Guattari 1972, 1980), Irigaray's ethics of sexual difference (1984), Foucault's attempt to self-style the ethical relationship, Derrida's and Lévinas's emphasis on the receding horizons of alterity—to be fully immersed in ethical concerns. It is the case that ethics in poststructuralist philosophy is not confined to the realm of rights, distributive justice, or the law; it rather bears close links with the notion of political agency, freedom, and the management of power and power relations. Issues of responsibility are dealt with in terms of alterity or the relationship to others. This implies accountability, situatedness, and cartographic accuracy. A poststructuralist position, therefore, far from thinking that a liberal individual definition of the subject is the necessary precondition for ethics, argues that liberalism at present hinders the development of new modes of ethical behavior.

In other words, for nomadic thought, the proper object of ethical inquiry is not the subject's universalistic or individual core—his/her moral intentionality, or rational consciousness, as much as the effects of truth and power that his/her actions are likely to have upon others in the world. This is a kind of ethical pragmatism, which defines ethics as the practice that cultivates affirmative modes of relation, active forces, and values. It is also conceptually linked to the notion of embodied materialism and to a nonunitary vision of the subject. Ethics is therefore the discourse about forces, desires, and values that act as empowering modes of becoming, whereas morality is the implementation of established protocols and sets of rules (Deleuze 1968). Philosophical nomadism shares Nietzsche's distaste for morality as sets of negative, resentful emotions and life-denying reactive passions. Deleuze joins this up with Spinoza's ethics of affirmation to produce a very accountable and concrete ethical line about joyful affirmation.

There is no logical reason therefore why Kantians should have a monopoly on moral thinking. In moral philosophy, however, one touches Kantian moral universalism at one's peril. From the Habermasian school and its American branch—Benhabib (2002), Fraser (1996)—to the humanist Kantianism of Martha Nussbaum (1999), a rejection of poststructuralist theories in general and ethics in particular has taken place. Sabine Lovibond (1994), for instance, expresses her concern with the loss of moral authority that is entailed by a nonunitary vision of the subject and reasserts the necessity of a Kantian agenda as the only source of salvation after the debacle of postmodernism.

I want to take the opposite road and attempt to read poststructuralist philosophy in its own terms rather than reduce it to the standards of a system of thought—in this case the Kantian tradition—that shares so few of its premises. There are serious advantages to the antirepresentational slant of contemporary poststructuralist philosophy, in that it entails the critique of liberal individualism and its replacement by an intensive view of subjectivity. The ethics of nomadic subjectivity rejects moral universalism and works toward a different idea of ethical accountability in the sense of a fundamental reconfiguration of our being in a world that is ethnically diverse, technologically and globally mediated, and fast changing. One of the most pointed paradoxes of our era is precisely the clash between the urgency of finding new and alternative modes of political and ethical agency, on the one hand, and the inertia or self-interest of neoconservative thought on the other. It is urgent to explore and experiment with more adequate forms of nonunitary, nomadic, and yet accountable modes of envisaging both subjectivity and democratic, ethical interaction.

Two crucial issues arise: the first is that, contrary to the panic-stricken universalists, an ethics worthy of the complexities of our times requires a fundamental redefinition of our understanding of the subject in his/her contemporary location and not a mere return and nostalgic appeal to canonical and rigid philosophical tradition. Second, an alternative ethical stance based on radical immanence and becoming is capable of a universalistic reach, if not a universalistic aspiration. It just so happens to be a grounded, partial form of accountability, based on a strong sense of collectivity and community building. In what follows I want to argue for the relevance of a nomadic approach to this urgent ethical project.

The wealth and variety of ethical positions created by poststructuralist philosophies calls for at least some synoptical overview. The following discursive alignments can be seen at present in poststructuralist ethical thought. Besides the classical Kantians (see Habermas's recent work on human nature, 2003), we have a Kantian-Foucauldian coalition that stresses the role of moral accountability as a form of biopolitical citizenship. Best represented by Nicholas Rose (2001) and Paul Rabinow (2003), this group works with the notion of "Life" as bios, that is to say, as an instance of governmentality that is as empowering as it is confining. This school of thought locates the ethical moment in the rational and self-regulating accountability of a bio-ethical subject and results in the radicalization of the project of modernity.

A second grouping takes its lead from Heidegger and is best exemplified by Agamben (1998). It defines bios as the result of the intervention of sovereign power, as that which is capable of reducing the subject to "bare life," that is to say, zoe. The latter is, however, contiguous with Thanatos or death. The being-alive-ness of the subject (zoe) is identified with its perishability, its propensity and vulnerability to death and extinction. Biopower here means Thanatos-politics and results in the indictment of the project of modernity.

Another important cluster in this brief cartography of new ethical discourses includes the Lévinas-Derrida tradition of ethics, which is centered on the relationship between the subject and Otherness in the mode of indebtedness, vulnerability, and mourning (Critchley 1992). I have enormous respect for this school of thought, but the project I want to pursue takes as the point of reference bios-zoe power defined as the nonhuman, vitalistic, or postanthropocentric dimension of subjectivity. This is an affirmative project that stresses positivity and not mourning.

The last discursive coalition, to which this project belongs, is inspired by the neovitalism of Deleuze, with reference to Nietzsche and Spinoza (Ansell-Pearson 1997, 1999). Biopower is only the starting point of a reflection about the politics of life itself as a relentlessly generative force. Contrary to the Heideggerians, the emphasis here is on generation, vital forces, and natality. Contrary to the Kantians, the ethical instance is not located within the confines of a self-regulating subject of moral agency, but rather in a set of interrelations with both human and inhuman forces. These forces can be rendered in terms of relationality (Spinoza), duration (Bergson), immanence (Deleuze), and, in my own terms, ethical sustainability. The notion of the nonhuman, inhuman, or posthuman emerges therefore as the defining trait of nomadic ethical subjectivity.

TRANSFORMATIVE ETHICS AND THE RELOCATION OF OTHERNESS

At the core of this ethical project is a positive vision of the subject as a radically immanent, intensive body, that is, an assemblage of forces or flows, intensities, and passions that solidify in space and consolidate in time within the singular configuration commonly known as an "individual" self. This intensive and dynamic entity is rather a portion of forces that is stable enough to sustain and undergo constant though nondestructive fluxes of transformation. It is the body's degrees and levels of affectivity that determine the modes of differentiation. Joyful or positive passions and the transcendence of reactive affects are the desirable mode. The emphasis on "existence" implies a commitment to duration and conversely a rejection of self-destruction. Positivity is built into this program through the idea of thresholds of sustainability. Thus an ethically empowering option increases one's potentia and creates joyful energy in the process. The conditions that can encourage such a quest are not only historical; they concern processes of transformation or self-fashioning in the direction of affirming positivity. Because all subjects share in this common nature, there is a common ground on which to negotiate the interests and the eventual conflicts.

It is important to see that this fundamentally positive vision of the ethical subject does not deny conflicts, tension, or even violent disagreements between different subjects. The legacy of Hegel's critique of Spinoza is still looming large here, notably the criticism that a Spinozist approach lacks a theory of negativity that may adequately account for the complex logistics of interaction with others. It is simply not the case that the positivity of desire cancels or denies the tensions of conflicting interests. It merely displaces the grounds on which the negotiations take place. The Kantian imperative of not doing to others what you would not want done to you is not rejected as much as enlarged. In terms of the ethics of conatus, in fact, the harm that you do to others is immediately reflected in the harm you do to yourself, in terms of loss of potentia, positivity, self-awareness, and inner freedom. Moreover, the "others" in question are nonanthropomorphic and include planetary forces. This move away from the Kantian vision of an ethics that obliges people, and especially women, natives, and others, to act morally in the name of a transcendent standard or universal rule is not a simple one. I defend it as a forceful answer to the complexities of our historical situation; it is a move toward radical immanence against all Platonist paradigms and classical humanist denials of embodiment, matter, and the flesh.

What is at stake, however, in nomadic ethics is the notion of containment of the other. This is expressed by a number of moral thinkers in the Continental tradition, such as Jessica Benjamin (1988) in her radicalization of

Irigaray's horizontal transcendence, Lyotard in the "differend" (1983) and his notion of the "unattuned," and Butler (2004a) in her emphasis on "precarious life." They stress that moral reasoning locates the constitution of subjectivity in the interrelation to others, which is a form of exposure, availability, and vulnerability. This recognition entails the necessity of containing the other, the suffering and the enjoyment of others in the expression of the intensity of our affective streams. Nomadic theory embraces this ethical concern but proposes an alternative answer: an embodied and connecting form of relation over and against the hierarchical forms of containment implied by Kantian forms of universal morality.

Traditional moral reasoning locates the constitution of subjectivity in the interrelation to others, which is a form of exposure, availability, and vulnerability. This recognition entails the necessity of containing the other, the suffering and enjoyment of others. I want to argue instead that an embodied and connecting relation to others as an ethical category can also emerge from the radical redefinition of the same-other relation by the vital politics of life itself. This includes external and nonhuman forces: cells, as Franklin et al. (2000) argue; viruses and bacteria, as Parisi (2004) points out; and earth others, as Haraway has been arguing for a long time. This posthuman ethics rests on a multilayered form of relationality. It assumes as the point of reference not the individual but the relation. This means openness to others, in the positive sense of affecting and being affected by others, through couples and mutually dependent corealities. Containment of the other occurs through interrelational affectivity and the construction of common planes of actualization of alternative subjects, projects, and communities.

The nomadic ethics of affirmation is all the more original if set alongside another poststructuralist tradition of ethical thought. In the Lévinas-Derrida school, currently pursued by Butler, Critchley, and others, the emphasis falls on vulnerability as the defining feature of the human. The potential capacity to be wounded and hence to require the care, solidarity and love of others becomes, by extension, the major ethical requirement. In this perspective, sovereign power is defined as the political force that is capable of inflicting pain and to decide on issues of life and death, survival and extinction, as we shall also see in the next chapter. Ethics consequently calls into question the foundational violence of such a system.

Spinozist ethics and its nomadic variation, on the other hand, choose a different emphasis, not so much on vulnerability as on the body's capacity to express multiple forms of empowerment. This implies the ability and the commitment to the production of conditions that transform the negative instance, including hurt and pain. The precondition for the constitution of an ethical subject is therefore, for nomadic theory, the body as the threshold of virtual becomings and collective assemblages that actualize alternative projects. I shall return to this point later on in the chapter.

The objection that a Spinozist ethics fails to account for the interaction with the Other is predictable, and it is connected, on the one hand, to the issue of negotiations of boundaries, limits, and costs and, on the other, to affectivity and compassion. The nomadic view of ethics takes place within a monistic ontology that sees subjects as modes of individuation within a common flow of zoe. Consequently, there is no self-other distinction in the traditional mode, but variations of intensities, assemblages set by affinities, and complex synchronizations. Biocentered egalitarianism breaks the expectation of mutual reciprocity that is central to liberal individualism. Accepting the impossibility of mutual recognition and replacing it with one of mutual specification and mutual codependence is what is at stake in a nomadic ethics of sustainability. This is against both the moral philosophy of rights and the humanistic tradition of making the anthropocentric Other into the privileged site and inescapable horizon of otherness.

In other words, Otherness is approached as the expression of a productive limit, or generative threshold, that calls for an always already compromised set of negotiations. This is the function of the other's face in Lévinas (1999) and, by extension, Derrida's ethics. It is also the position defended both by Simon Critchley (2007) on the infinite demand of the Other and the non-negotiable nature of "justice" and "hospitality." Nomadic theory prefers to look instead for the ways in which otherness prompts, mobilizes, and allows for flows of affirmation of values and forces that are not yet sustained by the current conditions. This is affirmative ethics.

I should add, for the sake of scholarly accuracy, that Lévinas's case is complex, as there are significant resonances between his notion of passivity and Deleuze's affirmation. Lévinas's brand of immanence, however, differs considerably from Deleuze's life-oriented philosophy of becoming. Lévinas—like Irigaray—inscribes the totality of the Self's reliance on the other as a structural necessity that transcends the "I" but remains internal to it. Deleuze's immanence, on the other hand, firmly locates affirmation in the exteriority, the cruel, messy outsideness of Life itself. Creative chaos is not chaotic—it is the virtual formation of all possible forms (Deleuze 1969). Life is not an a priori that gets individuated in single instances, but it is imma-nent to and thus coincides with its multiple material actualizations. It is the site of birth and emergence of the new—life itself. I refer to this generative force as zoe, which is the opposite therefore of Agamben's "bare life"—in that it is a creative force that constructs possible futures.

BECOMING ETHICAL: ON SUSTAINABILITY

What is, then, the subject of ethical affirmation? It is a slice of living, sen-sible matter activated by a fundamental drive to life: a potentia (rather than potestas)—neither by the will of God, nor the secret encryption of the ge-netic code—and yet this subject is embedded in the corporeal materiality of the self. The enfleshed intensive or nomadic subject is rather a transversal entity: a folding in of external influences and a simultaneous unfolding out of affects. A mobile unit in space and time, and therefore an enfleshed kind of memory, this subject is not only in process but is also capable of lasting through sets of discontinuous variations while remaining extraordinarily faithful to itself.

This idea of the "faithfulness" of the subject is important, and it builds on the rejection of liberal individualism. This may appear counterintuitive to Anglo-American readers and require of them an effort of the imagina-tion. Allow me to plead for the short-term benefits that will flow, however, from this stretching exercise and for the dividends it will return in terms of added understanding. This "faithfulness to oneself," consequently, is not to be understood in the mode of the psychological or sentimental attachment to a personal "identity" that often is little more than a social security num-ber and a set of photo albums. Nor is it the mark of authenticity of a self ("me, myself, and I") that is a clearinghouse for narcissism and paranoia— the great pillars on which Western identity predicates itself. It is rather the faithfulness of mutual sets of interdependence and interconnections, that is to say, sets of relations and encounters. It is a play of complexity that en-compasses all levels of one's multilayered subjectivity, binding the cognitive to the emotional, the intellectual to the affective, and connecting them all to a socially embedded ethics of sustainability. Thus the faithfulness that is at stake in nomadic ethics coincides with the awareness of one's condition of interaction with others, that is to say, one's capacity to affect and to be affected. Translated into a temporal scale, this is the faithfulness of duration, the expression of one's continuing attachment to certain dynamic spatiotemporal coordinates.

In a philosophy of temporally inscribed radical immanence, subjects differ. But they differ along materially embedded coordinates because they come in different mileages, temperatures, and beats. One can and does change gears and move across these coordinates, but cannot claim all of them all of the time. The latitudinal and longitudinal forces that structure the subject have limits of sustainability. By latitudinal forces Deleuze means the affects a subject is capable of, following the degrees of intensity or potency: how intensely they run. By longitude is meant the span of extension: how far they can go. Sustainability is about how much of it a subject can take.

In other words, sustainable subjectivity reinscribes the singularity of the self, while challenging the anthropocentrism of Western philosophy's understanding of the subject and of the attributes usually reserved for "agency." This sense of limits is extremely important to ensure productive synchronizations and prevent nihilistic self-destruction. To be active, intensive, or nomadic does not mean that one is limitless. That would be the kind of delirious expression of megalomania that you find in the new master narratives of the cyberculture of today, ready and willing to "dissolve the bodily self into the matrix." On the contrary, to make sense of this intensive, materially embedded vision of the subject, we need a sustainability threshold or frame. The containment of the intensities or enfleshed passions, so as to ensure their duration, is a crucial prerequisite to allow them to do their job, which consists in shooting through the humanistic frame of the subject, exploding it outward. The dosage of the threshold of intensity is both crucial and inherent to the process of becoming, insofar as the subject is embodied and hence set in a spatiotemporal frame.

What is this threshold of sustainability, then, and how does it get fixed? A radically immanent intensive body is an assemblage of forces or flows, intensities, and passions that solidify in space and consolidate in time within the singular configuration commonly known as an "individual" self. This intensive and dynamic entity—it's worth stressing it again—does not coincide with the enumeration of inner rationalist laws, nor is it merely the unfolding of genetic data and information. It is rather a portion of forces that is stable enough to sustain and to undergo constant, though nondestructive, fluxes of transformation. D. W. Smith argues that there are three essential questions about immanent ethics: "How is a mode of existence determined? How are modes of existence to be evaluated? What are the conditions for the creation of new modes of existence?" (Smith 1998:259). On all three scores, it is the body's degrees and levels of affectivity that determine the modes of differentiation. Joyful or positive passions and the transcendence of reactive affects are the desirable mode. The emphasis on "existence" implies a commitment to duration and conversely a rejection of self-destruction. Positivity is built into this program through the idea of thresholds of sustainability.

Thus an ethically empowering option increases one's potentia and creates joyful energy in the process. The conditions that can encourage such a quest are not only historical; they all concern processes of self-transformation or self-fashioning in the direction of affirming positivity. Because all subjects share in this common nature, there is a common ground on which to negotiate the interests and the eventual conflicts. It is important to see in fact that this fundamentally positive vision of the ethical subject does not deny conflicts, tension, or even violent disagreements between different subjects. This move away from the Kantian vision of an ethics that obliges people, and especially women, natives and others, to act morally in the name of a transcendent standard or a universal moral rule is not a simple one. I defend it as a forceful answer to the complexities of our historical situation: it is a move toward radical immanence against all Platonist and classical humanistic denials of embodiment, matter, and the flesh. They stress that moral reasoning locates the constitution of subjectivity in the interrelation to others, which is a form of exposure, availability and vulnerability. This recognition entails the necessity of containing the other, the suffering and the enjoyment of others in the expression of the intensity of our affective streams.

If the point of ethics is to explore how much a body can do, in the pursuit of active modes of empowerment through experimentation, how do we know when we have gone too far? How does one know if one has reached the threshold of sustainability? This is where the nonindividualistic vision of the subject as embodied and hence affective and interrelational, but also fundamentally social, is of major consequence. Your body will thus tell you if and when you have reached a threshold or limit. The warning can take the form of opposing resistance, falling ill, feeling nauseous, or it can take other somatic manifestations, like fear, anxiety, or a sense of insecurity. Whereas the semiotic-linguistic frame of psychoanalysis reduces these to symptoms awaiting interpretation, I see them as corporeal warning signals or boundary markers that express a clear message: "too much!" One of the reasons why Deleuze and Guattari are so interested in studying self-destructive or pathological modes of behaviors, such as schizophrenia, masochism, anorexia, various forms of addiction, and the black hole of murderous violence, is precisely in order to explore their function as markers of thresholds. This assumes a qualitative distinction between, on the one hand, the desire that propels the subject's expression of her conatus, which in a neo-Spinozist perspective is implicitly positive in that it expresses the essential best of the subject—and, on the other hand, the constraints imposed by society. The specific, contextually determined conditions are the forms in which the desire is actualized or actually expressed.

This is all the more salient if we consider that advanced capitalism is a system that tends to constantly stretch its limits and plays with the idea of overreaching itself, moving toward "timeless time" (Castells 1996). How shall I put it? All planes are always overbooked, and this is a fitting metaphor for the political economy of profit and its saturation of our social space. Insofar as the subject is under constant pressure to function and find points of stability within the ever-shifting limits or boundaries, capitalism is a system that actively generates schizophrenia in the sense of enhancing the value of unfixed meanings: an unlimited semiosis without fixed referents (Holland 1999). This makes the question of negotiation thresholds of sustainability all the more urgent. If the boundaries are forever being stretched and hence blurred, however, perspectival shifts are necessary in order to keep up and account for the process and thus identify points of resistance. Schizophrenia is a molecular mode of undoing the molar aggregates of the commodification system, of inducing flows into them. This avoids the consolidation and overcodification (constant control) that are characteristic of the Majority, but in return it runs the danger of fluidity to the point of self-destruction. How to find a point of balance is an ethical question.

This historical context makes it difficult to detect the thresholds of sustainability or markers of the limits. If your body will not make it manifest or if you choose to ignore the message that this is "too much!" others are likely to send out significant warning signals. The subject lies at the intersections with external, relational forces. It's about assemblages. Encountering them is almost a matter for geography, because it's a question of orientations, points of entry and exit, a constant un-folding. In this field of transformative forces, sustainability is a concrete social and ethical practice—not the abstract economic ideal that development and social planning specialists often reduce it to. It is a concrete concept about the embodied and embedded nature of the subject. The sensibility to and availability for changes or transformation are directly proportional to the subject's ability to sustain the shifts without cracking. The border, the framing or containing practices, are crucial to the whole operation; one that aims at affirmative and not nihilistic processes of becoming. In other words, joyful-becoming as potentia or a radical force of empowerment. Lloyd (1994, 1996) explains how such a vitalistic and positive vision of the subject is linked to an ethics of passion that aims at joy and not at destruction. She carefully points out the difficulties involved in approaching Spinoza's concept of ethics as "the collective powers and affinities of bodies" (Lloyd 1996:23). Lloyd stresses the advantages of approaching these potencies of embodied subjects in terms of the ethology proposed by Deleuze, insofar as it challenges the centrality of the notion of the individual to an ethical sense of values or to a socially well-functioning system.

It is the case that in the composition of the forces that propel the subject, the rhythm, speed, and sequencing of the affects as well as the selection of the constitutive elements are the key processes. It is the orchestrated repetition and recurrence of these changes that mark the steps in the process of becoming-intensive. In other words, the actualization of a field of forces is the effect of an adequate dosage, whereas it is also simultaneously the prerequisite for sustaining those same forces. This is because the subject is an affective entity, a conatus defined as a "striving" without an agent in control of it. This founding desire is a life force that intersects with all that moves and exists. Far from being the case that the individual possesses or controls such a force, it is rather the case that being a subject consists in partaking in such a striving.

The notion of the individual is enlarged to enclose a structural sense of interconnection between the singular self and the environment or totality in which it is embodied and embedded. Lloyd defines this interconnectiveness not as a synthesis, but rather as a series of "nested embeddings of individuals" (Lloyd 1994:12). According to this enlarged sense of the individual, an inward-looking understanding of the individual self is not only an error but also a cognitive and ethical misjudgment. The inward-looking individual fails to see the interconnection as part and parcel of his/her nature and is thus inhibited by an inadequate understanding of him/herself. The truth of self lies in its interrelations to others in a rhizomic manner that defies dualistic modes of opposition. Reaching out for an adequate representation of oneself includes the process of clearing up the confusion concerning one's true nature as an affective, interconnected entity. Ultimately this implies understanding the bodily structure of the self. Because of this bodily nature, the process of self-consciousness is forever ongoing and therefore incomplete or partial. This partiality is built into Spinoza's understanding of the subject.

Bodily entities, in fact, are not passive, but rather dynamic and sensitive forces forever in motion, which "form unities only through fragile synchronization of forces" (Lloyd 1994:23). This fragility concerns mostly the pitch of the synchronization efforts; the lines of demarcation between the different bodily boundaries, the borders that are the thresholds of encounter and connection with other forces, the standard term for which is *limits*. Because of his monistic understanding of the subject, Spinoza sees bodily limits as the limits of our awareness as well; this means that his theory of affectivity is connected to the physics of motion. Another word for Spinoza's conatus is therefore *self-preservation*, not in the liberal individualistic sense of the term, but rather as the actualization of one's essence, that is to say, of one's ontological drive to become. This is neither an automatic nor an intrinsically harmonious process, insofar as it involves interconnection with other forces and also, consequently, conflicts and clashes. Negotiations have to occur as stepping-stones to sustainable flows of becoming. The bodily self's interaction with her environment can either increase or decrease that body's conatus or potentia. The mind as a sensor that prompts understanding can assist by helping to discern and choose those forces that increase its power of acting and its activity in both physical and mental terms. A higher form of self-knowledge, by understanding the nature of one's affectivity, is the key to a Spinozist ethics of empowerment. It includes a more adequate understanding of the interconnections between the self and a multitude of other forces, and it thus undermines the liberal individual understanding of the subject. It also implies, however, the body's ability to comprehend and physically sustain a greater number of complex interconnections and to deal with complexity without being overburdened. Thus only an appreciation of complexity, and of increasing degrees of complexity, can guarantee freedom of mind in the awareness of its true, affective, and dynamic nature.

Thinking the unity of body and mind, sustainable ethics stresses the power (potentia) of affects (affectus). Starting from the assumption that the property of substance is to express itself, the term *expression* implies "dynamic articulation" (Lloyd 1996:31) and not merely passive reflection: "Affectus refers to the passage from one state to another in the affected body—the increase or decrease in its powers of acting" (Lloyd 1996:72). This "power of acting"—which is in fact a flow of transpositions—is expressed by Spinoza in terms of achieving freedom through an adequate understanding of our passions and consequently of our bondage. Coming into possession of freedom requires the understanding of affects or passions by a mind that is always already embodied. The desire to reach an adequate understanding of one's potentia is the human being's fundamental desire or conatus. An error of judgment is a form of misunderstanding (the true nature of the subject) that results in decreasing the power, positivity, and activity of the subject. By extension: reason is affective, embodied, dynamic: understanding the passions is our way of experiencing them—and making them work in our favor. In this respect Spinoza argues that desires arise from our passions. Because of this, they can never be excessive—given that affectivity is the power that activates our body and makes it want to act. The human being's built-in tendency is toward joy and self-expression, not toward implosion. This fundamental positivity is the key to Deleuze's attachment to Spinoza.

Lloyd argues that Spinoza's treatment of the mind as part of nature is a source of inspiration for contemporary ethics. Spinozist monism acts "as a basis for developing a broader concept of ethology, a study of relations of individual and collective and being affected" (Lloyd 1996:18). Clearly, it is a very nonmoralistic understanding of ethics that focuses on the subject's powers to act and to express their dynamic and positive essence. An ethology stresses the field of composition of forces and affects, speed and transformation. In this perspective, ethics is the pursuit of self-preservation, which assumes the dissolution of the self: what is good is what increases our power of acting, and that is what we must strive for. This results not in egotism, but in mutually embedded nests of shared interests. Lloyd calls this "a collaborative morality" (Lloyd 1996:74). Because the starting point for Spinoza is not the isolated individual, but complex and mutually depended corealities, the self-other interaction also follows a different model. To be an individual means to be open to being affected by and through others, thus undergoing transformations in such a way as to be able to sustain them and make them work toward growth. The distinction activity/passivity is far more important than that between self and other, good and bad. What binds the two is the idea of interconnection and affectivity as the defining features of the subject. An ethical life pursues that which enhances and strengthens the subject without reference to transcendental values but rather in the awareness of one's interconnection with others.

Lloyd and Deleuze can be synthesized into the concept of a sustainable, nonunitary, perspectival self that aims at endurance. Endurance has a temporal dimension. It has to do with lasting in time; hence duration and self-perpetuation (traces of Bergson here). But it also has a spatial side to do with the space of the body as an enfleshed field of actualization of passions or forces. It evolves affectivity and joy (traces of Spinoza), as in the capacity for being affected by these forces to the point of pain or extreme pleasure (which comes to the same). It may require putting up with and tolerating hardship and physical pain. It also entails the effort to move beyond, to construct affirmative interaction. Apart from providing the key to an ethology of forces, endurance is also an ethical principle of affirmation of the positivity of the intensive subject or, in other words, its joyful affirmation as potentia. The subject is a spatiotemporal compound that frames the boundaries of processes of becoming. This works by transforming negative into positive passions through the power of an understanding that is no longer indexed upon a phallogocentric set of standards, but is rather unhinged and affective.

This turning of the tide of negativity is the transformative process of achieving freedom of understanding through the awareness of our limits, of our bondage. This results in the freedom to affirm one's essence as joy, through encounters and mingling with other bodies, entities, beings, and forces. Ethics means faithfulness to this potentia or the desire to become.

Becoming is an intransitive process: it's not about becoming anything in particular—only what one is capable of and attracted to and capable of becoming; it's life on the edge, but not over it. It's not deprived of violence, but deeply compassionate. It's an ethical and political sensibility that begins with the recognition of one's limitations as the necessary counterpart of one's forces or intensive encounters with multiple others. It has to do with the adequacy of one's intensity to the modes and time of its enactment. It can only be empirically embodied and embedded, because it's interrelational and collective.

ENDURANCE AND NEGATIVE PASSIONS

An ethics of affirmation involves the transformation of negative into positive passions: resentment into affirmation, as Nietzsche put it. The practice of transforming negative into positive passions is the process of reintroducing time, movement, and transformation into a stifling enclosure saturated with unprocessed pain. It is a gesture of affirmation of hope in the sense of affirming the possibility of moving beyond the stultifying effects of the pain, the injury, the injustice. This is a gesture of displacement of the hurt, which fully contradicts the twin logic of claims and compensation. This is achieved through a sort of depersonalization of the event, which is the ultimate ethical challenge.

Moreover, the ethics of affirmation is about suspending the quest for claims and compensation, resisting the logic of retribution of rights and taking instead a different road. In order to understand this move it is important to depsychologize the discussion of affirmation. Affectivity is intrinsically understood as positive: it is the force that aims at fulfilling the subject's capacity for interaction and freedom. It is Spinoza's conatus or the notion of potentia as the affirmative aspect of power. It is joyful and pleasure prone and it is immanent in that it coincides with the terms and modes of its expression. This means concretely that ethical behavior confirms, facilitates, and enhances the subject's potentia, as the capacity to express her freedom. The positivity of this desire to express one's innermost and constitutive freedom (conatus, potentia, or becoming) is conducive to ethical behavior, however, only if the subject is capable of making it endure, thus allowing it to sustain its own impetus. Unethical behavior achieves the opposite: it denies, hinders, and diminishes that impetus or is unable to sustain it. Affirmation is therefore not naive optimism or Candide-like unrealism. It is about endurance and transformation. Endurance is self-affirmation. It is also an ethical principle of affirmation of the positivity of the intensive subject—its joyful affirmation as potentia. The subject is a spatiotemporal compound that frames the boundaries of processes of becoming. This works by transforming negative into positive passions through the power of an understanding that is no longer indexed upon a phallogocentric set of standards, but is rather unhinged and therefore affective.

This sort of turning of the tide of negativity is the transformative process of achieving freedom of understanding through the awareness of our limits, of our bondage. This results in the freedom to affirm one's essence as joy, through encounters and mingling with other bodies, entities, beings, and forces. Ethics means faithfulness to this potentia or the desire to become. Deleuze defines the latter with reference to Bergson's concept of "duration," thus proposing the notion of the subject as an entity that lasts, that endures sustainable changes and transformation and enacts them around him/herself in a community or collectivity. Affirmative ethics rests on the idea of sustainability as a principle of containment and tolerable development of a subject's resources, understood environmentally, affectively, and cognitively. A subject thus constituted inhabits a time that is the active tense of continuous "becoming." Endurance has therefore a temporal dimension: it has to do with lasting in time—hence duration and self-perpetuation. But it also has a spatial side to do with the space of the body as an enfleshed field of actualization of passions or forces. It evolves affectivity and joy, as in the capacity for being affected by these forces, to the point of pain or extreme pleasure, which come to the same; it means putting up with hardship and physical pain.

The point, however, is that extreme pleasure or extreme pain—which may score the same on a Spinozist scale of ethology of affects—are, of course, not the same. On the reactive side of the equation, endurance points to the struggle to sustain the pain without being annihilated by it. It also introduces a temporal dimension about duration in time. This is linked to memory: intense pain, a wrong, a betrayal, a wound are hard to forget. The traumatic impact of painful events fixes them in a rigid, eternal present tense out of which it is difficult to emerge. This is the eternal return of that which precisely cannot be endured and returns in the mode of the unwanted, the untimely, the unassimilated or inappropriate/d. They are also, however, paradoxically difficult to remember, insofar as re-membering entails retrieval and repetition of the pain itself.

Contrary to the traditional morality that follows a rationalist and legalistic model of possible interpretation of the wrongs one suffered to a logic of responsibility, claim, and compensation, affirmative ethics rests on the notion of the random access to the phenomena that cause pain (or pleasure). This is not fatalism, and even less resignation, but rather amor fati as we saw in the previous chapter. This is a crucial difference: we have to be worthy of what happens to us and rework it within an ethics of relation. Of course, repugnant and unbearable events do happen. Ethics consists, however, in reworking these events in the direction of positive relations. This is not carelessness or lack of compassion, but rather a form of lucidity that acknowledges the impossibility of finding an adequate answer to the question about the source, the origin, the cause of the ill fate, the painful event, the violence suffered. Acknowledging the futility of even trying to answer that question is a starting point.

The central part of this project concerns the dissolution of liberal individualism and the subject's ability to escape from herself. This is rendered by Foucault through the idea of the "limit-experience," which breaks the frame of predictable subject positions. This aspect of Foucault is influenced by Bataille and Blanchot as well as Nietzsche. It marks the point of dissolution of the subject—usually by confrontation with an extreme experience. It is also known as desubjectivation (Tobias 2005). The fragility and vulnerability of the human is revealed in this experience, which borders on self-destruction. Desubjectivation concerns both affect and cognition. As a limit experience, it marks the threshold of (un)sustainability, i.e., it prompts the awareness of fragility and the recognition of contingency. It also propels the subject to act according to this awareness. The result of the confrontation with the limit (the limit experience) is the transformation of the subject's relation to knowledge and to itself as a knowing subject. The limit experience accounts for the conversion of the subject into something else. This is the ethical moment.

The later Foucault argues, contrary, for instance, to Deleuze, that the question of the limits of the philosophical subject, which is operationalized through Bataille, was already raised by Kant's critical thought. This is expressed in both "Preface to Transgression" and in Foucault's genealogy of the human and social sciences in "The Order of Discourse." Through this reference, Foucault links the domain of ethics to knowledge and cognition in the sense of forces that activate a subject's capacity to act upon itself and others (potentia). This is self-styling or autopoiesis as productive self-creation. Ethics as praxis.

Ethics is about freedom from the weight of negativity, freedom through the understanding of our bondage. A certain amount of pain, the knowledge about vulnerability and pain, is actually useful. It forces one to think about the actual material conditions of being interconnected and thus being in the world. It frees one from the stupidity of perfect health and the full-blown sense of existential entitlement that comes with it.

Nomadic subjectivity is a field of transformative affects whose availability for changes of intensity depends firstly on the subject's ability to sustain encounters with and the impact of other forces or affects. I am defending here a radically materialist, antiessentialist vitalism attuned to the technological era, which could not be further removed from the illusion of eternal youth, perfect health, and social success marketed by contemporary culture. The genetic multiplication of virtual embodiments promised by technoculture boosts this imaginary. The nomadic, enfleshed, vitalist but not essentialist vision of the subject is a self-sustainable one that owes a great deal to the project of an ecology of the self. The rhythm, speed, and sequencing of the affects as well as the selection of the forces are crucial to the process of becoming. It is the pattern of reoccurrence of these changes that marks the successive steps in the process, thus allowing for the actualization of forces that are apt to frame and thus express the singularity of the subject. Thinking through the body, and not in a flight from it, means confronting boundaries and limitations and living with and through pain (Sobchack 1999).

What is ethics, then? Ethics is a thin barrier against the possibility of extinction. It is a mode of actualizing sustainable forms of transformation. This requires adequate assemblages or interaction: one has to pursue or actively create the kind of encounters that are likely to favor an increase in active becomings and avoid those that diminish one's potentia. It is an intensive ethics, based on the shared capacity of humans to feel empathy for, develop affinity with, and hence enter into relation with other forces, entities, beings, waves of intensity. This requires dosage, rhythms, styles of repetition and coordination, or resonance. It is a matter of unfolding out and enfolding in the complex and multilayered forces of bios-zoe as a deeply inhuman force.

In other words, potentia, in order to fulfill its inherent positivity, must be "formatted" in the direction of sustainability. Obviously, this means that it is impossible to set one standard that will suit all; a differential approach becomes necessary. What bodies are capable of doing, or not, is biologically, physically, psychically, historically, sexually, and emotionally specific: singular and hence partial. Consequently, the thresholds of sustainable becomings also mark their limits. In that respect, "I can't take it anymore" is an ethical statement, not the assertion of defeat. It is the lyrical lament of a subject-in-process who is shot through with waves of intensity, like a set of fulgurations that illuminate his self-awareness, tearing open fields of self-knowledge in the encounter of and configuration with others. Learning to recognize threshold, borders, or limits is thus crucial to the work of understanding and the process of becoming. For Lacan, limits are wounds or scars, marks of internal lacerations and irreplaceable losses as well as liberal thoughts; limits are frontiers that cannot be trespassed without the required visas or permissions. For Deleuze, however, limits are simultaneously points of passage or thresholds and markers of sustainability.

Deleuze has an almost mathematical definition of the limit as that which one never really reaches. Deleuze discusses with Claire Parnet (1977) the question of the limit in terms of addiction. Reminiscing on his own early alcoholism, Deleuze notes that the limit or frame for the alterations induced by alcohol is to be set with reference not so much to the last glass, because that is the glass that is going to kill you. What matters instead is the "second-to-last" glass, the one that has already been and thus is going to allow you to survive, to last, to endure—and consequently also to go on drinking again. A true addict stops at the second-to-last glass, one removed from the fatal sip or shot. A death-bound entity, however, usually shoots straight for the last one. That gesture prevents or denies the expression of the desire to start again tomorrow, that is to say, to repeat that "second-to-last shot" and thus endure. In fact, there is no sense of a possible tomorrow: time folds in upon itself and excavates a black hole into which the subject dissolves. No future.

ABOUT PAIN AND VULNERABILITY

But what about pain? Affirmative politics, with its emphasis on life as a generative force, may seem counterintuitive at first. And yet the urge that prompts this approach is anything but abstract. It is born of the awareness that in-depth transformations are at best demanding and at worst painful. This is not a complaint, nor is it meant as a deterrent against change. I consider melancholic states and the rhetoric of the lament to be integral to the logic of advanced capitalism and hence a dominant ideology and long for more affirmative alternatives.

As I will argue in more depth in the next chapter, in a biopolitical per-spective infused by the politics of "bare life" or perennial state of emergency, the emphasis falls on the condition of neglect, abuse, and marginalization to which large sectors of the world population are confined. It is the condition of indignity in which noncitizens are kept within the borders of "Fortress Europe" in detention camps and nonaccess zones.

There is a necropolitical side to this as well, of course, as evidenced by geopolitical disasters like Chernobyl, Hurricane Katrina in New Orleans, or other great catastrophes in what Ulrich Beck calls "global risk society." To call such events "natural" is a great deception.

Linked to this increased global vulnerability is the biopolitical manage-ment of the world population in terms of diseases and epidemics. Global health also plays a role in the medical and genetic screening of prospective migrant and asylum seekers. The ideal is the joining of a healthy migrant body to an unharmed social host so as to sustain high standards of living , i.e., citizenship as biolegitimacy.

Biowelfare has become a new social norm, whether it is in the tendentious case of the quest for weapons of mass destruction or in the fight against the new pandemics like avian, Mexican, or other forms of influenza. Last but not least in the biopolitical management of death is humanitarian aid as a form of global solidarity where health and physical survival have become the basic requirements of global citizenship.

In all these cases, citizenship is disaggregated along the new and mul-tiple axes that challenge physical integrity and bodily survival today. It is subsequently reaggregated so as to redefine what counts as a human, more especially how the human relates to the attribution of basic rights and en-titlements. Citizenship is thus deterritorialized and becomes postnational, biogenetic, and necropolitical. Dealing with these complexities requires complex and flexible models of belonging.

Neoliberalism has been quick in appropriating the radical potential of this situation and reinscribing it within a normative frame. Some thinkers, for instance, stress the role of moral accountability as a form of biopolitical citizenship, thus inserting into the ethical debates the notion of "biopower" as an instance of governmentality that is as empowering as it is confining (Rose 2001; Rabinow 2003; Esposito 2004). This school of thought locates the political moment in the relational and self-regulating accountability of a bioethical subject that takes full responsibility for her genetic existence.

The advantage of this position is that it calls for a higher degree of lucidity about one's bio-organic existence. The disadvantage of this position, however, in a political context of dismantling the welfare state and increasing privatization, is that it allows a neoliberal perversion of this notion. Bioethical citizenship indexes access to and the cost of basic social services like health care to an individual's manifest ability to act responsibly by reducing the risks and exertions linked to the wrong lifestyle. In other words, here bioethical agency means taking adequate care of one's own genetic capital. The recent campaigns against smoking, excessive drinking, and overweight constitute evidence of this neoliberal normative trend that supports hyper-individualism. Other social examples of neoliberal biocitizenship are the social drive toward eternal youth, which is linked to the suspension of time in globally mediated societies (Castells 1996) and can be juxtaposed to euthanasia and other social practices of assisted death.

The notion of the new vitalism (see chapters 1–3) and "life itself" lies at the heart of biogenetic capitalism (Parisi 2004) as a site of financial investments and potential profit. Technological interventions neither suspend nor do they automatically improve the social relations of exclusion and inclusion that have been historically predicated along the axes of class and socioeconomics as well as the sexualized and racialized lines of demarcation of "otherness." Also denounced as "bio-piracy" (Shiva 1997), the ongoing technological revolution often intensifies patterns of traditional discrimination and exploitation. We have all become the subjects of biopower, but we differ considerably in the degrees and modes of actualization of that very power.

In this context, I do not want to suggest that the politics of mourning and the political economy of melancholia are intrinsically reactive or necessarily negative. A number of critical theorists forcefully argue the case for the productive nature of melancholia and its potential for creating solidarity (Gilroy 2004; Butler 2004a). I am also convinced that melancholia expresses a form of loyalty through identification with the wounds of others and hence that it promotes ecology of belonging by upholding the collective memory of trauma or pain. My argument is rather that the politics of melancholia has become so dominant in our culture that it ends up functioning like a self-fulfilling prophecy, which leaves very small margins for alternative approaches. I thus want to argue for the need to experiment with other ethical relations as a way of producing an ethics of affirmation.

Our conservative political context, moreover, has placed undue emphasis on the risks involved in changes, playing ad nauseam the refrain about the death of transformative politics. Nothing could be further removed from my project. I simply want to issue a cautionary note: processes of change and transformation are so important, and ever so vital and necessary, that they have to be handled with care. We have to take the pain of change into account, not as an obstacle to but as a major incentive for an ethics of transformation.

Let us consider seriously the issue of pain. Pain in our culture is associated to suffering by force of habit and tradition and is given negative connotations accordingly. Supposing we look a bit more critically into this associative link, however: what does pain or suffering tell us? That our subjectivity consists of affectivity, interrelationality, and forces. The core of the subject is affect and the capacity for interrelations to affect and be affected. Let us agree to depsychologize this discussion from this moment on, not in order to deny the pain but rather to find ways of working through it.

This vision of ethics involves a radical repositioning or internal transformation on the part of subjects who want to become-minoritarian in a productive and affirmative manner. It is clear that this shift requires changes that are neither simple nor self-evident. They mobilize the affectivity of the subjects involved and can be seen as a process of transformation of negative into positive passions. Fear, anxiety, and nostalgia are clear examples of the negative emotions involved in the project of detaching ourselves from familiar and cherished forms of identity. To achieve a postidentity or nonunitary vision of the self requires disidentification from established references. Such an enterprise involves a sense of loss of cherished habits of thought and representation and thus is not free of pain. No process of consciousness-raising ever is.

The beneficial side effects of this process are unquestionable and in some way they compensate for the pain of loss. Thus the feminist questioning and in some cases rejection of gender roles triggers a process of disidentification with established forms of masculinity and femininity, which has fueled the political quest for alternative ways of inhabiting gender and embodying sexuality (Braidotti 2002a). In race discourse, the awareness of the persistence of racial discrimination and white privilege has led, on the one hand, to the critical reappraisal of blackness (Gilroy 2000; Hill Collins 1991) and, on the other, to a radical relocation of whiteness (Griffin and Braidotti 2002).

In a Spinozist vein, these are transformative processes that not only re-work the consciousness of social injustice and discrimination but also pro-duce a more adequate cartography of our real-life condition, free of delu-sions of grandeur. It is an enriching and positive experience, which, however, includes pain as an integral element. Migrants, exiles, refugees have first-hand experience of the extent to which the process of disidentification from familiar identities is linked to the pain of loss and uprooting. Diasporic sub-jects of all kinds express the same sense of injury. Multilocality is the affir-mative translation of this negative sense of loss. Following Glissant (1990), becoming-nomadic marks the process of positive transformation of the pain of loss into the active production of multiple forms of belonging and com-plex allegiances. What is lost in the sense of fixed origins is gained in an increased desire to belong, in a multiple rhizomic manner that transcends the classical bilateralism of binary identity formations.

The qualitative leap through pain, across the mournful landscapes of nostalgic yearning, is the gesture of active creation of affirmative ways of belonging. It is a fundamental reconfiguration of our way of being in the world, which acknowledges the pain of loss but moves further. This is the defining moment for the process of becoming-ethical: the move across and beyond pain, loss, and negative passions. Taking suffering into account is the starting point; the real aim of the process, however, is a quest for ways of overcoming the stultifying effects of passivity, brought about by pain. The internal disarray, fracture, and pain are the conditions of possibility for ethical transformation. Clearly, this is an antithesis of the Kantian moral imperative to avoid pain or to view pain as the obstacle to moral behavior. Nomadic ethics is not about the avoidance of pain; rather it is about tran-scending the resignation and passivity that ensue from being hurt, lost, and dispossessed. One has to become ethical, as opposed to applying moral rules and protocols as a form of self-protection. Transformations express the af-firmative power of Life as the vitalism of bios-zoe, which is the opposite of morality as a form of life insurance.

The sobering experience—the humble and productive recognition of loss, limitations, and shortcomings—has to do with self-representations. Established mental habits, images, and terminology railroad us back toward established ways of thinking about ourselves. Traditional modes of repre-sentation are legal forms of addiction. To change them is not unlike under-taking a detoxification cure. A great deal of courage and creativity is needed to develop forms of representation that do justice to the complexities of the kind of subjects we have already become. Defamiliarization is part of this process, as we saw in chapter 8. We already live and inhabit social reality in ways that surpass tradition: we move about, in the flow of current social transformations, in hybrid, multicultural, polyglot, postidentity spaces of becoming (Braidotti 2002a). We fail, however, to bring them into adequate representation. There is a shortage on the part of our social imaginary, a deficit of representational power, which underscores the political timidity of our times.

■ ■ ■

My position prioritizes complexity as a key component of this approach to alterity, and it accordingly promotes a triple shift. Firstly, it continues to emphasize a radical ethics of transformation in opposition to the moral protocols of Kantian universalism. Secondly, it shifts the focus from a unitary and rationality-driven consciousness to an ontology of process, that is to say, a vision of subjectivity that is propelled by affects and relations. Thirdly, it disengages the emergence of the subject from the logic of negation and attaches subjectivity to affirmative otherness—reciprocity as creation, not as the re-cognition of Sameness. From here onward, I will concentrate on this third aspect: affirmation or the critique of the negative. This will lead me to discuss affirmation as the politics of life itself, as the generative force of zoe.

Sustainable ethics allows us to contain the risks while pursuing the original project of transformation. This is a way to resist the dominant ethos of our conservative times, which idolizes the new as a consumerist trend while thundering against those who believe in change. Cultivating the art of living intensely in the pursuit of change is a political act. In that regard, I have insisted on the importance of endurance—in the double sense of learning to last in time, but also to put up and live with pain and suffering. Again, it is a question of dosage and of balance. Thresholds of sustainability need to be mapped out, so that a rate and speed of change can be negotiated and set that will allow each subject to endure, to go on, to stop at the second-to-last smoke, shot, drink, or book. This implies a differential type of ethics, which clashes with dominant morality. It has nothing to do with relativism either. Rather it contains clearly set limits that are activated by careful negotiations.

The embodied structure of the subject is a limit in itself. To accept differential boundaries does not condemn us to relativism, but to the necessity to negotiate each passage. In other words: we need a dialogical mode. We need future-oriented perspectives, which do not deny the traumas of the past but transform them into possibilities for the present. Not the heavenly future, but rather a more sustainable one, situated here and now.

The key features of this idea of ethical freedom are, firstly, the focus on self-determination or self-styling through the very acts of resistance or transgression. This is in contrast to the juridical conception of freedom as a set of universal rights or entitlements. Secondly, this idea of freedom emphasizes critical analysis and constant questioning. This is linked to the notion of governmentality in the sense of a general organization of knowledge and of disciplinary apparati that produce modes of subjectivity (Dumm 1996). The lesson of Spinoza about the structurally repressive function of the state in relation to the project of realizing conatus is also relevant. This tradition of thought is wary of the institutions that govern us. Thus vigilance is the price of freedom; it is the task of the critical thinkers, as analysts of power, to assess the conditions that are conducive to social change as opposed to the emphasis on unchangeable factors.

Thirdly, the issue of self-scrutiny cannot be separated from the social analysis of the conditions of domination. A micropolitics of resistance can be seen as a web of emancipatory practices. Localized and concrete ethical gestures and political activities matter more than grand overarching projects. In that respect, nomadic theory is a form of ethical pragmatism.

12

FORENSIC FUTURES

This chapter focuses on contemporary debates on the politics of life itself, with special emphasis on how a nomadic philosophy of radical immanence results in shifting the boundaries between biopower and necropolitics, life and death. This kind of vital politics is understood not only in the sense of the government of the living but also in relation to practices of dying. I will refer to the vitalist force of life itself—as zoe—so as to point to its nonhuman structure. My argument is that both the concept of life and that of death need to be approached with more complexity and that Deleuze's vital materialism is of great assistance in this task. I will use the case of environmental justice as illustration.

THE POLITICS OF LIFE AS BIOS/ZOE

My argument in this book has been that we are witnessing today a proliferation of discourses that take life as a subject and not as the object of social and discursive practices. The discussion about biopolitics and biopower can be considered as central to a number of discourses and practices, namely, the law, legal discourse and critical jurisprudence, social and political theory and policy making in areas of governance, health, the environment, and the management of diversity. Reflections of the changing structure of life, the nature-culture continuum, and especially of the notion of the human have also been the focus of several interdisciplinary areas of analysis, like cultural studies, feminist theory, new media, and science and technology studies. They have developed original tools and methods that are of relevance to social theory today.

These radical changes have induced major dislocations of the classifications among species, categories, and substances, which had been hierarchically ordained and dialectically opposed. Issues of power and power relations are consequently central to this discussion. The notion of "life itself" lies at the heart of biogenetic capitalism as a site of financial investments, scientific research, and tradable commodities (see chapters 1–3). The potential profit emerging from this web of interests is considerable. The next step of my argument, however, raises the hypothesis that these technological interventions neither suspend nor do they automatically improve the social relations of exclusion and inclusion that historically had been predicated along the axes of sexualization (women, gays and lesbians and sexual minorities), racialization (native, indigenous peoples, colonial others), and naturalization (animals, plants, and earth others). In some ways, the globally linked and technologically mediated structure of biogenetic capitalism merely reenforces and intensifies the traditional patterns of discrimination and exploitation. Also denounced as "bio-piracy" (Shiva 1997), the ongoing technological revolution targets all that lives, the planet as a whole, as the capital worthy of interest. In other words, we have all become the subjects of biopower, but we differ considerably in the degrees and modes of actualization of that very power. "We" may be in *this* together, but we differ quite radically in terms of locations and allocations of power. Neither the category "we" nor *this* project can be assumed to be monolithic or static. Accounting for these power differentials in terms of processes, flows, and complex relations is one of the challenges of contemporary critical theory.

Nomadic theory states that rising to the challenge of complexity entails a redefinition of the very grounds of subjectivity. Social theory needs to shift the emphasis from the classical and highly formalized concept of bios to zoe. I have drawn a distinction between "*zoe*," as vitalistic, prehuman, and generative life, to *bios*, as a political discourse about social and political life.

Bios, as the classical counterpart of *Logos*, traditionally referring to the self-reflexive control over discourses and practices of life, is a prerogative reserved for the humans. Given that this concept of "the human" was colonized by phallogocentrism, it has come to be identified with male, white, heterosexual, Christian, property-owning, standard language-speaking citizens (Deleuze and Guattari 1980). *Zoe* marks the outside of this vision of the subject. Nomadic philosophy establishes a conceptual alliance with the efforts of evolutionary theory to strike a new relationship to the nonhuman. Contemporary scientific practices have forced us to touch the bottom of some inhumanity that connects to the human precisely in the immanence of its bodily materialism. With the genetic revolution, we can speak of a generalized "becoming infrahuman" of zoe. The category of Life has cracked under the strain and has splintered into a web of interconnected effects.

This emphasis on life as bios-zoe opens up the ecophilosophical dimension of the problem; it inaugurates alternative ecologies of belonging and moves critical theory along the path of a geophilosophy. It also, and more importantly, marks a shift away from anthropocentrism toward a new emphasis on the inextricable entanglement of human and nonhuman, biogenetic and cultural forces in contemporary social theory. It points us toward a sort of biocentered egalitarianism, which, as Keith Ansell-Pierson suggests (1997), forces a reconsideration of the concept of subjectivity in terms of "life-forces." This distinction supports the argument that the emergence of new discourses about "life" results in the need for a shift of paradigm in political thought. This challenge calls for more social and intellectual creativity in both scientific and mainstream cultures, as Deleuze's nomadic philosophy never ceases to remind us.

To advance the last step of my argument: contemporary posthuman social and cultural theory (Hayles 1999; Wolfe 2003) is addressing the dislocation of the classical boundaries between the human and his others, stressing the importance of becoming animal, becoming other, becoming insect— trespassing the categorical metaphysical boundaries. A posthuman ecophilosophy is emerging that challenges the anthropocentrism of so much social-constructivist theory and progressive political thought.

Postanthropocentrism raises a number of questions, not the least of which is the vital politics of an enlarged sense of our environmental interconnections. Ultimately, this shift of perspective leads to a serious reconsideration of what counts as the ultimate "other" of life itself—that is to say, death as a process. Aspects of life that go by the name of death are on the social agenda as an integral part of the bios/zoe process; they introduce differentiations internal to the category of life, which add further complexity.

The postanthropocentric approach allows for a nonbinary way of positing the relationship between same and other, between different categories of living beings, and ultimately between life and death. The emphasis and hence the mark of "difference" now falls on the "other" of the living body (following its humanistic definition): *Thanatos*—the dead body, the corpse or spectral other.

BEYOND THE BIOPOLITICAL

The theoretical context for these debates rotates round the legacy of Foucault's unfinished project on contemporary governmentality in an era that marks the official end of postmodernist deconstructions. The unfinished nature of Foucault's project has been complicated by two elements in the reception of his work: the first is the split that has occurred between the so-called second Foucault, who, through the history of sexuality, defined as technologies of self-styling, posits a new model of ethical interrelation, and the earlier Foucault, who concentrated on the analysis of power formations and patterns of exclusion.

This split reception institutionalizes a new division of labor between power analyses, on the one hand, and ethical discourses, on the other. This allows for a residual type of Kantianism to emerge on Foucault's back, to so speak. It is therefore urgent to assess the state of the theoretical debates on biopower after Foucault, especially in terms of its legal, political, and ethical implications. As we saw in the previous chapter, a form of biopolitical citizenship has emerged within the ethical debates on the notion of "biopower" as an instance of governmentality that is as empowering as it is confining (Rose 2001; Rabinow 2003; Esposito 2004). This school of thought locates the political moment in the relational and self-regulating accountability of a bioethical subject that takes full responsibility for his/her genetic existence. The second problematic element in the reception of Foucault's biopower is the fast rate of progress and change undergone by contemporary biotechnologies and the challenges they throw at the human and social sciences. Here Foucault's work has been criticized, notably by Donna Haraway (1997), for relying on an outdated vision of how technology functions. It is argued that Foucault's biopower provides cartography of a world that no longer exists. Haraway suggests that we have now entered instead the age of the informatics of domination. In feminist theory—a very relevant area of scholarship that I find missing from far too much of the scholarship on biopolitics, globalization, and technology studies—this point has been taken very seriously (Barad 2003). Feminist, environmentalist, and race theorists who have addressed the shifting status of "difference" in advanced capitalism in a manner that respects the complexity of social relations and critiques liberalism while highlighting the specificity of a gender and race approach (Gilroy 2000; Butler 2004b; Braidotti 2002a; Grosz 2004).

The central piece of the discrepancy between Foucault's biopower and the contemporary structure of scientific thought concerns the issue of anthropocentrism. Contemporary technologies are not man centered but have shifted away toward a new emphasis on the mutual interdependence of material, biocultural, and symbolic forces in the making of social and political practices. The focus on life itself may encourage a sort of biocentered egalitarianism (Ansell-Pearson 1997), forcing a reconsideration of the concept of subjectivity in terms of "life forces." It dislocates but also redefines the relationship between self and other by shifting the traditional axes of difference—genderization, racialization, and naturalization—away from a binary opposition into a more complex and less oppositional mode of interaction.

Biopolitics thus opens up an ecophilosophical dimension of reflection (Braidotti 2006) and inaugurates alternative ecologies of belonging both in kinship systems and in forms of social and political participation. I would like to suggest that these "hybrid" social identities and the new modes of multiple belonging they enact may constitute the starting point for mutual and respective accountability and pave the way for an ethical regrounding of social participation and community building.

The central insight of Foucault's political anatomy, however, is that biopower concerns as much the management of dying as that of living. The question of the governance of life contains that of extinction as well. Here we do need to return to the early Foucault and not be misled by the residual Kantianism of his second phase. Conceptually, the "matter-realist" vitalism of nomadic theory, grounded in ontological monism (see chapter 5), allows us to rethink mortality as a dynamic principle and not only as a source of grief and mourning. Politically, we need to assess the advantages of the politics of vital affirmation (see chapter 10) as an antidote to the ruling ideology of melancholia. Ethically, we need to relocate compassion and care of others in this new frame.

THE RISE OF NECROPOWER

Much contemporary critical theory has engaged with this issue: Agamben with his emphasis on "bare life" (1998), Bauman and his concern for human and other "waste" (1998), Butler on pain and vulnerability (2004a), following Derrida on mourning (2002), and Simon Critchley's explicit interest on philosophers' views on death (2008). The challenge for nomad theory is to rethink ethical and political life beyond survival and mortality. To rethink forensic futures in a sustainable manner.

The sheer scale of this expansion of quantified differences alters the terms of classical biopolitical thought as postulated by Foucault, who demonstrated not only the constructed structure of what we call human nature but also its relatively recent appearance on the historical scene, which makes it coextensive with forms of social control and disciplining. Donna Haraway's analyses go further and assume that contemporary science has moved beyond Foucault's biopower and has already entered the age of "the informatics of domination," which is a different regime of visualization and control and as "a system to be managed, a field of operations constituted by scientists, artists, cartoonists, community activists, mothers, anthropologists, fathers, publishers, engineers, legislators, ethicists, industrialists, bankers, doctors, genetic counsellors, judges, insurers, priests, and all their relatives—has a very recent pedigree" (Haraway 1997:174).

This also means that the political representation of embodied subjects nowadays can no longer be understood within the visual economy of biopolitics in Foucault's (1976) sense of the term. The representation of embodied subjects is no longer visual in the sense of being scopic, as in the post-Platonic sense of the simulacrum. Nor is it specular, as in the psychoanalytic mode of redefining vision within a dialectical scheme of oppositional recognition of self and/as other. It has rather become schizoid or internally disjointed. It is spectral: the body is represented as a self-replicating system that is caught in a visual economy of endless circulation. The contemporary social imaginary is immersed in this logic of boundless circulation and thus is suspended somewhere beyond the life and death cycle of the imaged self. The social imaginary led by genetics has consequently become forensic in its quest for traces of a life that it no longer controls. Contemporary embodied subjects have to be accounted for in terms of their surplus value as genetic containers, on the one hand, and as visual commodities circulating in a global circuit of cash flow, on the other hand. Much of this information is not knowledge driven, but rather media inflated and thus indistinguishable from sheer entertainment. Today's capital is spectral, and our gaze forensic.

Nomadic theory's main contribution to this debate rests on the concepts of radical immanence and nondeterministic vitalism, which unfold onto an affirmative ethics of bioegalitarianism. The schizoid logic of biogenetic capitalism both express and exploit the simultaneously materialist and vitalist force of life itself, zoe as the generative power that flows across all species. Ansell-Pearson takes it as a prompt to "begin to map non-human becomings of life" (1997:109). The becoming-earth axis of transformation entails the displacement of anthropocentrism and the recognition of transspecies solidarity on the basis of "our" being in *this* together. That is to say: environmentally based, embodied, embedded and in symbiosis with each other. Bio-centred egalitarianism is a philosophy of radical immanence and affirmative becoming, which activates a nomadic subject into sustainable processes of transformation.

This organic or corporeal brand of materialism lays the foundations for a system of ethical values where "life" stands central. Life is not sacralized as a preestablished given, but rather posited as process, interactive and open-ended. Life is far from being codified as the exclusive property or the unalienable right of one species—the human—over all others. As I stated earlier, the old hierarchy that privileged bios—discursive, intelligent, social life—over zoe—brutal "animal" life—has to be reconsidered. Zoe as generative vitality is a major transversal force that cuts across and reconnects previously segregated domains. Biocentered egalitarianism is a materialist, secular, precise, and unsentimental response to transversal, transspecies structural reconnections.

The displacement of anthropocentrism is exposed by Deleuze and Guattari in the theory of becoming-minoritarian/becoming-animal (see chapters 2–3). This process of molecularization entails the redefinition of one's sense of attachment and connection to a shared world, a territorial space. It expresses multiple ecologies of belonging, while it enacts the transformation of human sensorial and perceptual coordinates in order to acknowledge the collective nature and outward-bound direction of what we call the self. This "self" is in fact a movable assemblage within a common life space that the subject never masters or possesses, but merely inhabits, crosses, always in a community, a pack, a group, or a cluster. Becoming-animal marks the frame of an embodied subject, which is by no means suspended in an essential distance from the habitat/environment/territory, but is rather radically immanent to it. For philosophical nomadism, the subject is fully immersed in and immanent to a network of nonhuman (animal, vegetable, viral) relations. The zoe-centered embodied subject is shot through with relational linkages of the symbiotic, contaminating/viral kind, which interconnect it to a variety of others, starting from the environmental or eco-others.

ZOE-POWER REVISITED

This has consequences for the status of social and political theory itself. Thinkers that take their lead from Heidegger, best exemplified by Agamben (1998), define "bios" as the result of the intervention of sovereign power as that which is capable of reducing the subject to "bare life," that is to say, zoe. The being-aliveness of the subject (zoe) is identified with its perishability, its propensity and vulnerability to death and extinction. Biopower here means Thanatos-politics and results, among other things, in an indictment of the project of modernity.

My understanding of "life" as a bios-zoe ethics of sustainable transformations differs considerably from what Giorgio Agamben (1998) calls bare life or the rest, after the humanized "bio-logical" wrapping is taken over. Bare life is that in you which sovereign power can kill: it is the body as disposable matter in the hands of the despotic force of power (potestas). Included as necessarily excluded, bare life inscribes fluid vitality at the heart of the mechanisms of capture of the state system. Agamben stresses that this vitality, or "aliveness," however, is all the more mortal for it. This is linked to Heidegger's theory of Being as deriving its force from the annihilation of animal life.

The position of zoe in Agamben's system is analogous to the role and the location of language in psychoanalytic theory: it is the site of constitution or "capture" of the subject. This "capture" functions by positing—as an a posteriori construction, a prelinguistic dimension of subjectivity that is apprehended as "always already" lost and out of reach. Zoe—like the prediscursive in Lacan, the *chora* of Kristeva, and the maternal feminine of Irigaray—becomes for Agamben the ever-receding horizon of an alterity that has to be included as necessarily excluded in order to sustain the framing of the subject in the first place. This introduces finitude as a constitutive element within the framework of subjectivity, which also fuels an affective political economy of loss and melancholia at the heart of the subject (Braidotti 2002a).

In his important work on the totalitarian edge of regimes of biopower, Agamben perpetuates the philosophical habit that consists in taking mortality or finitude as the transhistorical horizon for discussions of "life." This fixation on Thanatos—which Nietzsche criticized over a century ago—is still very much present in critical debates today. It often produces a gloomy and pessimistic vision not only of power but also of the technological developments that propel the regimes of biopower. I beg to differ from the habit that favors the deployment of the problem of bios-zoe on the horizon of death or of a liminal state of not-life.

I find this overemphasis on the horizons of mortality and perishability inadequate to the vital politics of our era. I therefore turn to another significant community of scholars' work within a Spinozist framework that includes Deleuze and Guattari (1972, 1980), Guattari (1995), Glissant (1990), Balibar (2002), Hardt and Negri (2000). The emphasis falls on the politics of life itself as a relentlessly generative force. This requires an interrogation of the shifting interrelations between human and nonhuman forces. The latter are defined both as in-human and as posthuman.

Speaking from the position of an embodied and embedded female subject, I find the metaphysics of finitude to be a myopic way of putting the question of the limits of what we call life. It is not because Thanatos always wins out in the end that it should enjoy such conceptual high status. Death is overrated. The ultimate subtraction is after all only another phase in a generative process. Too bad that the relentless generative powers of death require the suppression of that which is the nearest and dearest to me, namely, myself, my own vital being-there. For the narcissistic human subject, as psychoanalysis teaches us, it is unthinkable that Life should go on without my being there. The process of confronting the thinkability of a Life that may not have "me" or any "human" at the center is actually a sobering and instructive process. I see this postanthropocentric shift as the start of an ethics of sustainability that aims at shifting the focus toward the positivity of zoe.

This project aims to elaborate sets of criteria for a new social and political theory that steers a course between humanistic nostalgia and neoliberal euphoria about biocapitalism. Social and political practices that take life itself as the point of reference need not aim at the restoration of unitary norms, or the celebration of the master narrative of global profit, but rather at social cohesion, the respect for diversity and sustainable growth. At the heart of my research project lies an ethics that respects vulnerability while actively constructing social horizons of hope.

Patrick Hanafin (2010) suggests that this transversal vision of subjectivity may help us provide a political and ethical counternarrative to "the imposed bounded subject of liberal legalism." This involves a move from thinking of legal subjectivity as death bound and always already male—to thinking about singularities without identity who relate intimately to one another and the environment in which they are located. This points toward a critical politics of rights. The majoritarian masculine legal social compact is built on the desire to survive. This is not a politics of empowerment, but one of entrapment in an imagined natural order, which in our system translates into a biopolitical regime of discipline and control of bodies. What this means is that we are recognized as full citizens only through the position of victims, loss and injury, and the forms of reparation that come with it. Nomadic theory raises the question of what political theory might look like if it were not based on negative instances of wound and loss. In other words, another fundamental binary of Western philosophical thinking gets uncoupled: that of a political life qualified by death or a political philosophy that valorizes our mortal condition and creates a politics of survival.

This is, not unlike Virginia Woolf, a mode of thinking "as if already gone," that aims to think with and not against death. Hanafin argues that this may well constitute the ultimate threat to a legal system built on nec-ropolitical premises. The individual who refuses to accept law's prohibition to self-style his own death and refuses to be styled by the coercive speech of law. In self-styling one's death one is choosing to affirm one's life and the desire not to live a degraded existence.

William Connolly's "politics of becoming" (1999) argues a similar case: an "ethos of engagement" with existing social givens, which may bring about unexpected consequences and transformations. This ethics is based on the notion of propelling a new entity into being out of injury and pain. It actively constructs energy by transforming the negative charge of these experiences. The time line for this political activity is that of Aion, of becoming. This is different from working within or against the Chronos of the hegemonic political order. Hanafin quotes Blanchot on the importance of maintaining a refusal that turns into an affirmation and bringing about an affirmation that undoes existing arrangements.

ON CONTEMPORARY NECROPOLITICS

The emphasis on the politics of life itself, and especially the shifting boundaries between life and death, add a necropolitical dimension to contemporary debates on power. There are two main lines of research in this area: one that focuses on the destructive consequences of the biogenetic character of advanced capitalism (Foucault 1976, 1984a, 1984b), in terms of species extinction and environmental disasters. "Life" can be a threatening force, as evidenced by new epidemics and environmental catastrophes that blur the distinction between the natural and the cultural dimensions. "The politics of life itself" designates the extent to which the notion of biopower has emerged as an organizing principle for the proliferating discourses that make technologically mediated "life" into a contested political field (Rose 2001). Living matter itself becomes the subject and not the object of inquiry, and this shift toward a biocentered perspective affects the very structure and interaction of social relations.

These concerns have both neoliberal (Fukuyama 2002) and neo-Kantian thinkers struck by high levels of anxiety about the sheer thinkability of the human future (Habermas 2003). In opposition to this, I have defended the politics of "life itself" and approach these phenomena in a non-normative manner. The focus in this chapter, however, is on the social manifestations of the shifting relation between living and dying in the era of the politics of "life itself."

The other field of research concentrates on the brutality of the new wars and the renewed expressions of violence, which refers not only to the government of the living but also to multiple practices of dying. This explosion of discursive interest in the politics of life itself, in other words, also affects the question of death and new ways of dying. Biopower and necropolitics are two sides of the same coin, as Mbembe (2003) brilliantly argues. The post-cold war world has seen not only a dramatic increase in warfare but also a profound transformation of the war instance as such. Mbembe expands Foucault's insight in the direction of a more grounded analysis of the biopolitical management of survival. Aptly renaming it "necro-politics," he defines this power essentially as the administration of death: "the generalized instrumentalization of human existence and the material destruction of human bodies and population" (Mbembe 2003:19).

The implications of this approach to bio/necropower are radical: it is not up to the rationality of the law and the universalism of moral values to structure the exercise of power, but rather the unleashing of the unrestricted sovereign right to kill, maim, rape, and destroy the life of others. This same power, following Agamben, structures the attribution of different degrees of "humanity" according to hierarchies that are disengaged from the old dialectics and unhinged from any political rationality. They fulfill instead a more instrumental, narrow logic of opportunistic exploitation of the life in you, which is generic and not only individual. The colonial plantation as the prototype of this political economy turns the slave into the prototype of "homo sacer" (Agamben 1998) and stresses the intrinsic links between modernization and violence and terror.

Contemporary necropolitics has taken the form of the politics of death on a global regional scale. The new forms of industrial-scale warfare rest upon the commercial privatization of the army and the global reach of conflicts, which deterritorialize the use of and the rationale for armed service. Reduced to "infrastructural warfare" (Mbembe 2003), and to a large-scale logistical operation (Virilio 2002), war aims at the destruction of all the services that allow civil society to function: roads, electricity lines, airports, hospitals, and other necessities. It also aims at protecting mineral extraction and other essential geophysical resources needed by the global economy. In this respect, the "new" wars look more like guerrilla warfare and terrorist attacks than the traditional confrontation of enlisted and nationally indexed armies. Equally significant are the changes that have occurred in the political practice of bearing witness to the dead as a form of activism, from the Mothers of the Plaza de Mayo to humanitarian aid. One thinks specifically of the case of suicide bombers in the war on terror.

The old-fashioned army has now mutated into "urban militias; private armies; armies of regional lords; private security firms and state armies, all claim the right to exercise violence or to kill" (Mbembe 2003:32). As a result, as a political category, the "population" has also become disaggregated into "rebels, child soldiers, victims or refugees, or civilians incapacitated by mutilation or massacred on the model of ancient sacrifices, while the 'survivors,' after a horrific exodus, are confined to camps and zones of exception" (Mbembe 2003: 34).

Arjun Appadurai (1998) has also provided incisive analyses of the new "ethnocidal violence" of recent forms of warfare that involve friends, kinsmen, and neighbors. He is appalled by the violence of these conflicts: "associated with brutality and indignity—involving mutilation, cannibalism, rape, sexual abuse, and violence against civilian spaces and populations. Put briefly the focus here is on bodily brutality perpetrated by ordinary persons against other persons with whom they may have—or could have—previously lived in relative amity" (Appadurai 1998:907). Clearly, this exercise of violence cannot be adequately described in terms of disciplining the body, or even as the society of control—we have rather entered the era of orchestrated and instrumental massacres, a new "semiosis of killing," leading to the creation of multiple and parallel "death-worlds" (Mbembe 2003: 37).

The social reality of refugees and asylum seekers also becomes an emblem of the contemporary necropower. Diken (2004) argues that refugees are the perfect instantiation of the disposable humanity of homo sacer and thus constitutes the ultimate necropolitical subject. The proliferation of detention and high-security camps and prisons within the once civic-minded space of the European city is a further example of the loss of credibility in the rational biopolitical order. The camps—"sterilized, monofunctional enclosures" (Diken 2004:91) stand as the symbol of the indictment of Western modernity.

Duffield (2008) pushes this analysis even further and makes a distinction between developed or insured humans and underdeveloped or uninsured humans. "Developed life is sustained primarily through regimes of social insurance and bureaucratic protection historically associated with industrial capitalism and the growth of welfare states" (Duffield 2008:149). The distinction and the tensions between these two categories constitute the terrain for the "global civil war," which is Duffield's definition of globalized advanced capitalism. The link to colonialism is clear: decolonization created nation-states whose people, once enslaved, were now free to circulate globally. These people constitute the bulk of the unwanted immigrants, refugees, and asylum seekers who are contained and locked up across the developed world. In a twist not deprived of ironic force, world migration is perceived as a particular threat in Europe precisely because it endangers Europe's main infrastructure: the welfare state.

How does the necropolitical dimension intervene in the discussion about the politics of affirmation? What are its implications for the practice of critical theory? Biopower, since Foucault, led to a more sophisticated understanding of practices that latch onto "life" as the main target. But death as a concept remains simultaneously central to political theory—in the form of the horizon of mortality and the concern for human vulnerability—and unspoken. Death as a concept remains unitary and undifferentiated, while the bios-zoe horizon proliferates and diversifies. In the rest of this chapter I will attempt to think the life-death continuum within my ongoing engagement with political accounts of nomadic and often posthuman subjectivity.

It thus follows that in the regime of biogenetic globalization capitalism entails dying. The examples to prove that Life can be a threatening force abound: the revival of old and new epidemics and the spread of environmental catastrophes that blur the distinction between the natural and cultural dimensions are obvious examples. Another clear manifestation of the necropolitics folded within the biopolitical management of life is provided by novel styles of warfare, the new "intelligent" weapons, on the one hand, and the rawness of the bodies of suicide bombers, on the other. Equally significant are the changes that have occurred in the political practice of bearing witness to the dead as a form of activism, which can be summarized as the shift from the human rights stance of the Argentine Mothers of the Plaza de Mayo to the more brutal interventionism of the Chechen war widows. The dislocation of gender roles in relation to death and killing is reflected in the image of women who kill, from recent stage productions of Medea and Hecuba to Lara Croft. The extent to which the killing of children plays a role in this shift of geopolitical belligerency deserves more space than I can grant it here.

From a posthuman digital perspective comes the debate about the proliferation of viruses, from computers to humans, animals, and back. Illness is clearly not only a privilege of organic entities, but a widespread practice of mutual contamination. A rather complex relationship has emerged in our cyberuniverse: one in which the mutual dependence between the flesh and the machine is symbiotic. This engenders some significant paradoxes, namely, that the corporeal site of subjectivity is simultaneously denied, in a fantasy of escape, and reenforced. Balsamo (1996) argues that it promotes dreams of immortality and control over life and death. "And yet, such beliefs about the technological future 'life' of the body are complemented by a palpable fear of death and annihilation from uncontrollable and spectacular body-threats: antibiotic-resistant viruses, random contamination, flesh-eating bacteria" (Balsamo 1996:1–2).

Popular culture and the infotainment industry are quick to pick up the trend. Relevant cultural practices that reflect this changing status of death can be traced in the success of forensic detectives in contemporary popular culture. The corpse is a daily presence in global media and journalistic news, while it is also an object of entertainment. The currency granted to both legal (Ritalin, Prozac) and illegal drugs in contemporary culture blurs the boundaries between self-destruction and fashionable behavior and forces a reconsideration of what is the value of "life itself." Last but not least, assisted suicide and euthanasia practices are challenging the law to rest on the tacit assumption of a self-evident value attributed to Life. Social examples of this new necrotechnology of the self are current health practices and the emphasis placed on individual responsibility for the self-management of one's health and one's own lifestyle. This privatization of good health is amplified by a social drive toward eternal youth, which is linked to the suspension of time in globally mediated societies and forms the counterpart of euthanasia and other social practices of assisted death. Spiritual death is part of the picture as well; contemporary embodied social practices that are often pathologized and never addressed fully include addictions, eating disorders, and melancholia, ranging from burnout to states of apathy or disaffection. Instead of being classified as self-destructive practices, these phenomena exemplify in a non-normative manner the shifting social relations between living and dying in the era of the politics of "life itself."

In other words, the new practices of life mobilize not only generative forces but also new and subtler degrees of extinction. This type of vitality, unconcerned by clear-cut distinctions between living and dying, composes the notion of zoe as a nonhuman yet affirmative life force. This vitalist materialism has nothing in common with postmodern moral relativism, resting solidly on a neo-Spinozist political ontology of monism and radical immanence.

NOMADIC THEORY AND DEATH

In opposition to the nostalgic trend that is so dominant in contemporary politics and also to a tendency to melancholia on the part of the progressive left (Butler 2004a), I want to argue that the emphasis on life itself can engender affirmative politics. For one thing it produces a more adequate cartography of our real-life conditions: it focuses with greater accuracy on the complexities of contemporary technologically mediated bodies and on social practices of human embodiment. Furthermore, this type of vitality, unconcerned by clear-cut distinctions between living and dying, composes the notion of zoe as a nonhuman yet affirmative life force. This vitalist materialism, inspired by Deleuze's philosophy, has nothing in common with the postmodern emphasis on the inorganic and the aesthetics of fake, pastiche, and camp simulation. It also moves beyond "high" cyber studies (Hayles 1999) into postcyber materialism (Haraway 2003).

Life is cosmic energy, simultaneously empty chaos, and absolute speed or movement. It is impersonal and inhuman in the monstrous, animal sense of radical alterity: zoe in all its powers. Zoe, or life as absolute vitality, however, is not above negativity, and it can hurt. It is always too much for the specific slab of enfleshed existence that single subjects actualize. It is a constant challenge for us to rise to the occasion, to practice amor fati, to catch the wave of life's intensities and ride it, exposing the boundaries or limits as we transgress them. We often crack in the process and just cannot take it anymore. Death is the ultimate transposition, though it is not final. Zoe carries on, relentlessly.

Death is a conceptual excess: the unrepresentable, the unthinkable, the unproductive black hole that we all fear and also a creative synthesis of flows, energies, and perpetual becomings. This unconventional approach rests on a preliminary and fundamental distinction between personal and impersonal death. The former is linked to the suppression of the individualized ego; the latter is beyond the ego: a death that is always ahead of me. It is the extreme form of my power to become other or something else. In other words, in a nomadic philosophical perspective the emphasis on the impersonality of life is echoed by an analogous reflection on death. Because humans are mortal, death, or the transience of life, is written at our core: it is the event that structures our time lines and frames our time zones. Insofar as it is ever present in our psychic and somatic landscapes, it is the event that has always already happened. Death as a constitutive event is behind us, it has already taken place as a virtual potential that constructs everything we are. The full blast of the awareness of the transitory nature of all that lives is the defining moment in our existence. It structures our becoming-subjects and the process of acquiring moral awareness. Being mortal, we all are "have beens": the spectacle of our death is written obliquely into the script of our temporality.

For nomadic theory—not unlike Hannah Arendt—the political is linked to politics as an open space of interaction and communication between singular entities and collective assemblages. We all belong to and represent multiple and contradictory communities and ecologies of belonging and, in a feminist perspective, are accountable to them.

This is not utopian, but very actual, situated here and now in the continuous present of the processes of becoming that I have been analyzing throughout this book. This is politics as an ethics of becoming other than what we were defined and programmed to be.

What would a nomadic necropolitics look like? How would a vitalist and materialist understanding of death work? We should start by itemizing the different socially distributed and organized ways of dying: violence, diseases, poverty; accidents; wars, and catastrophes. Then we may proceed by looking at internally produced and self-run ways of dying: suicide, burnout, depression, and other psychosomatic pathologies. At a more theoretical level, the idea of death as righteous killing needs to be looked at, especially in political theory where since Machiavelli it has played a central and constitutive role. Last but not least we may want to consider how philosophers have dealt with death, following Simon Critchley (2008) and the importance of death as a spiritual threshold.

What do we gain through this new approach? Firstly a fuller understanding of how biopolitics actually works in the contemporary context marked by the war on terror and by scattered acts of mass killing. This would produce a more accurate cartography of how contemporary embodied subjects are interacting and interkilling. This in turn offers new analytical tools for an ethics that respects the complexity of our times and attempts to deal with it productively. A new ethics of compassion would thus develop from a nonunitary vision of the subject and a secular spiritual commitment to the collective construction of social horizons of hope. More importantly, a nomadic zoe-centered approach connects human to nonhuman extinction so as to develop a comprehensive ecophilosophy of becoming. Postanthropocentrism thus generates new perspectives that go beyond panic and mourning and produce a more workable platform.

The key point for me is a nomadic democratic politics that disengages the political from the dialectical scheme of opposition and recognition and stresses the notion that political activity is not contingent upon present conditions but aims at constructing alternatives that are not tied to the present by negation. This gets applied concretely in the task of composing new political subjects in the form of nomadic complex assemblages. These take their departure from existing bounded identities (individual and communitarian), but activate or nomadize them in the direction of becoming-minor. This is a much grounded and totally nonmessianic (Boundas 2007a) becoming, geared to the creation of possible futures here and now: sustainable scenarios for proactive action. The time frame of this activity is the future anterior: "it will have been a progress," resisting the present while being worthy of it.

SELF-STYLING ONE'S DEATH

Practices that are commonly regarded as self-destructive, such as anorexia and bulimia, drugs, alcoholism, masochism, etc, are important for my ethics of affirmation, though not in a moralistic or even normative mode. They rather express the built-in paradoxes of nomadic embodiment. By depathologizing these allegedly "extreme" clinical cases, we can approach them not so much as indicators of disorder but as markers of a standard condition, namely, the human subjects' enfleshed exposure to the irrepressible and at times hurtful vitality of life (zoe) and hence also the familiarity with or proximity to the crack, the line of unsustainability.

On a more positive note, they also express the subject's propensity for affective interaction and involvement with others. This is a complex issue, which connects states of heightened intensity to both thresholds of sustainability and the quest for adequate forms of expression. It is the very intensity of affectivity that often makes us implode into the black hole of negative, ego-indexed forces, which are likely to hurt the embodied entity. This is where drug users, alcoholics, anorexics, and workaholics implode and self-destroy.

Deleuze discusses his own addiction to drinking extensively in *The Logic of Sense* with a praiseworthy degree of lucidity and unsentimentality. He also tracks examples and accounts of addictions through "high" cultural products, mostly literary works by Zola, Artaud, and Blanchot. He rests on Blanchot's double structure of death as both personal and impersonal.

In *The Instant of My Death,* Blanchot (2002) addresses the paradox of the impersonality of death. Death is implacable in its presence and immanent to every human life; we start dying from the word *go.*

This does not mean, however, that life unfolds on the horizon of death. This classical notion is central to the metaphysics of finitude that, especially in the Heideggerian tradition, sacralizes death as the defining feature of human consciousness. I want to stress instead the productive differential nature of zoe, which means the productive aspect of bios/zoe. This is in opposition to Agamben, who refers to bare life as the negative limit of modernity and the abyss of totalitarianism that constructs conditions of human passivity. Instead of entering the rhetoric of endless listing of the atrocities, why not be relieved that this phase of modernity is over at last and see to what extent naked life itself is productive power, a wealth of possibilities? This point can be made all the more explicit if one compares Agamben's line on the horrors of modernity to the far more productive position taken by Edouard Glissant on this very same topic, starting from the transposition of the experience of slavery. The ethics of productive affirmation are quite a different way of handling the issue of how to operate in situations that are no less extreme, while bringing out the generative force of Zoe.

Nothing could be further removed from the affirmative position of philosophical nomadism. In this perspective, death is not the teleological destination of life, a sort of ontological magnet that propels us forward: death is rather behind us. Death is the event that has always already taken place at the level of consciousness. As an individual occurrence, it will come in the form of the physical extinction of the body, but, as event, in the sense of the awareness of finitude, of the interrupted flow of my being-there, death has already taken place. We are all synchronized with death—death is the same thing as the time of our living, insofar as we all live on borrowed time. The time of death as event is the impersonal ever-present Aion, not the individualized Chronos. It is the time span of death as time itself, the totality of time.

This means that what we all fear the most, our being dead, the source of anguish, terror, and fear, does not lie ahead but is already behind us, it has been. This death that pertains to a past that is forever present is not individual but impersonal; it is the precondition of our existence, of the future. This proximity to death is a close and intimate friendship that calls for endurance, in the double sense of temporal duration or continuity and spatial suffering or sustainability. Making friends with the impersonal necessity of death is an ethical way of installing oneself in life as a transient, slightly wounded visitor. We build our house on the crack, so to speak. We live to recover from the shocking awareness that this game is over even before it started. The proximity to death suspends life not into transcendence but rather into the radical immanence of just a life, here and now, for as long as we can and as much as we take.

Death frees us into life. Each of us is always already a "has-been": we are mortal beings. Desire (as potentia) seduces us into going on living. Living just a life, therefore, is a project, not a given. If sustained long enough, it becomes a habit; if the habit becomes self-fulfilling; life becomes addictive, which is the opposite of necessary or self-evident or even pleasurable. Life is beyond pleasure and pain—it is a process of becoming, of stretching the boundaries of endurance. There is nothing self-evident or automatic about life. It is not a habit, though it can become an addiction. One has to "jump-start" into life each and every day; the electromagnetic charge needs to be renewed constantly. There is nothing natural or given about it.

"Life," in other words, is an acquired taste, an addiction like any other, an open-ended project. One has to work at it. Life is passing, and we do not own it, we just inhabit it, as a time-share location. I live in a world where some people kill in the name of the "right to life." Thus, in contrast to the mixture of apathy and hypocrisy that marks the habits of thought that sacralize "life," I would like to cross-refer to a somewhat "darker" but more lucid tradition of thought that does not start from the assumption of the inherent, self-evident, and intrinsic worth of "life." On the contrary, I would like to stress the traumatic elements of life in their often unnoticed familiarity.

THE CRACK

Paradoxically enough, it is those who have already cracked up a bit, those who have suffered pain and injury, that are better placed to take the lead in the process of ethical transformation. Their "better quality" consists not in the fact of having been wounded but of having gone through the pain. Because they are already on the other side of some existential divide, they are anomalous in some way—but in a positive way. They are a site of transposition of values. Marxist epistemology and postcolonial and feminist theory have always acknowledged the privileged knowing position of those in the "margins." The figure of Nelson Mandela—a contemporary secular saint—comes to mind, as does the world-historical phenomenon that is the Truth and Reconciliation Commission in postapartheid South Africa. This is a case of repetition that engenders difference and does not install the eternal return of revenge and negative affects; it is a massive exercise in the trans-formation of negativity into something more sustainable, more life enhanc-ing. Endurance is the Spinozist code word for this process. Endurance has a spatial side that has to do with the space of the body as an enfleshed field of actualization of passions and/or forces. It evolves affectivity and joy, as in the capacity for being affected by these forces, to the point of pain or extreme pleasure. Endurance points to the struggle to sustain the pain without being annihilated by it.

Endurance also has a temporal dimension, a quality of duration in time. This dimension is linked to memory: intense pain, a wrong, a betrayal, a wound are hard to forget. The traumatic impact of painful events fixes them in a rigidly eternal present tense out of which it is difficult to emerge. This is the eternal return of that which cannot be endured and, as such, returns precisely in the mode of the unwanted, the untimely, the unassimilated, or inappropriate/d. These modes are also, however, paradoxically difficult to remember, insofar as re-membering entails retrieval and repetition of the pain itself.

Deleuze connects the double structure of death to the crack, the line of addiction to the incorporeal, or becoming, but also to the thick material-ity of a body that perishes. This generates an ethical line of reasoning that involves two elements. Firstly, a transposition of the issue of ethics in terms of what a body can do. This entails a reflection on the limits and thresh-olds of the processes of becoming, defined as actualizations of incorporeal or virtual possibilities. Secondly, this process displaces the subject of the ethical relation by making him/her an active participant in a process, not an evaluator of human failings. This requirement is all the more stringent for the philosopher who rejects the Kantian model of the judge or priest and replaces it with that of nomadic interaction with fellow others. Deleuze ad-dresses this ethical dilemma in relation to the problem of alcoholism, which he shares fully.

It is not a search for pleasure, but an escape from it, which induces a hard-ening of the present: the memories of the sober life turn into the "outside" of the alcoholic state. The hard past becomes the soft core of an unbearable present: "the alcoholic does not live at all in the imperfect or the future; the alcoholic has only a past perfect—albeit a very special one." He has loved, he has lived, he is and has been (1990:158). More importantly, he has drunk. This convergence of a hard past and a soft present totalizes the alcoholic's experience of time into a manic sense of omnipotence: "the present has become a circle of crystal or of granite, formed about a soft core, a core of lava, of liquid or viscous glass" (Deleuze 1990:158).

This tension also swallows the act itself. The alcoholic "has drunk" always in the past perfect mode. He experiences his condition as the effect of an effect, always already lost. The present escapes the alcoholic and defies the imaginary identifications with his actual state. The past has fled or is rather suspended in a fast-fading present and "in the new rigidity of this new present in an expanding desert" (1990:159). The present perfect expresses the infinite distance between the present (I have) and the effect of the flight of the past (drunk). This results in the loss of the object itself, in every sense and direction. This loss is at the heart of the depressive mood of alcoholism. Whereas, in the affirmative ethical stance, the awareness that death has already occurred triggers the desire to live and make friends with the abyss, in negative states the horizon of time gets frozen in fear, anxiety, and despair. The present perfect engenders no possible future, but rather implodes into a black hole. Every drink is the second to last—and the next one never comes in the mode of presence. It can only be given as a has-been. This effect goes on till the end, till death. Death is the last drink. That drink which coincides with the act and the perception of the act: that is, the instant when death as event coincides with your being dead, with physical extinction.

This is why alcoholism is an addiction to life, not the courting of death: it determines the need to drink anew and drink again. Or rather "of having drunk anew" (Deleuze 1990:160) in order to triumph over the present that only signifies and subsists in death. The present is experienced as having been, as perpetual loss. It is a process of orchestrated demolition of the self—a long deep crack. The ethical position with relation to alcoholism, as in other similar states of self-destruction, is to take equal distance from two related pitfalls. One is the moralistic condemnation in the name of a belief in the intrinsic value of life. The other is the altruistic compassion for what is perceived as the alcoholic's inability to make something of himself. Both miss the point that states of alleged self-destruction are a subject's way of coping with life; they are modes of living. This assumes that life is defined as zoe and hence as a state of negotiations with the line of cracking up. A nomadic ethics of sustainable becomings acknowledges this state and makes a powerful case for positive or affirmative states. However, it avoids both normative injunctions and empathic condescension. It affirms with calm rigor that there's nothing compelling or necessary about life and staying alive, while strongly urging the subject to cultivate the kind of relations that can help us to develop sustainable paths of becoming or possible futures.

The point for Deleuze is that poor health or a dose of cracking up is actually necessary for both ethical relations and the process of serious thinking. Thought is the shield against and the surfing board that rides the crest of the cracking wave. Marguerite Duras, a lifelong alcoholic, knows this well in her prose. The message is clear: "better death than the health which we are given" (Deleuze 1990:160). This is not self-destruction; this is a way of honoring and enduring life in its often unbearable intensity.

The ethical position is affirmative: we must endure the longest and not lose sight of the "great health," which is not a question of survival (survival is a basic and minimal condition and hence cannot form the basis for an ethical relation). Ethics is rather a question of expanding the threshold of what we can endure and hence sustain, while not avoiding the effects of the crack upon the surface of our embodied selves. The crack is for Deleuze the indicator of poor health: the pain that necessarily accompanies the process of living under the overwhelming intensity of Life. Great(er) health would be the process of going to the extreme limit, without dying, but exploding the boundaries of the self to the uttermost limit. This point of evanescence of the self is also the experience of eternity within time or becoming imperceptible.

The event is inscribed in the flesh, which is the thermometer of becoming. We must therefore labor toward the counteractualization of painful events—zoe leaves its scars. "We must accompany ourselves—first, in order to survive, but then even when we die" (Deleuze 1990:161). This is a form of experimentation: "It is to give to the crack the chance of flying over its own incorporeal surface area, without stopping at the bursting within each body; it is, finally, to give us the chance to go farther than we would have believed possible" (Deleuze 1990:161). Ethics is about new incorporeal becoming, not new "revelations," but the stretching of the thresholds of sustainability. Ethics is a matter of experimentation, not of control by social techniques of alienation.

The crack designates the generative emptiness of Death, as part of zoe and the swarming possibilities it expresses. The overcoming of Death as silence by an active frequentation of the line of cracking up is, for Deleuze, the work of thought. We think to infinity, against the terror of insanity, through the horror of the void, in the wilderness of mental landscapes fit only for werewolves. We think with the shadow of death dangling in front of our eyes. Thought, however, is a gesture of affirmation and hope for sustainability and endurance not in the mode of liberal moderation but rather as a radical experiment with thresholds of sustainability. This reiterates the necessity to acknowledge and feel compassion for pain and those who suffer it, but also to work through it. Moving beyond the paralyzing effects of pain on self and others, working across it, is the key to nomadic sustainable ethics. It does not aim at mastery, but at the transformation of negative into positive passions. I do like putting the *active* back into *activism* as an ethical as well as a political project.

IMPLICATIONS FOR PERSONAL DEATH

We think to infinity, against the horror of the void, in the wilderness of nonhuman mental landscapes, with the shadow of death dangling in front of our eyes. Thought, however, is also a gesture of affirmation and hope for sustainability and endurance, of immanent relations and time-bound consistency. Moving beyond the paralyzing effects of suspicion and pain, working across them, is the key to ethics. It did not aim at mastery, but at the transformation of negative into positive passions.

Because life is desire, which essentially aims at expressing and hence extinguishing itself, by reaching its aim and then dissolving, the wish to die can consequently be seen as another way to express the desire to live intensely. The corollary is even more cheerful: not only is there no dialectical tension between Eros and Thanatos, these two entities are really just one life force that aims at reaching its own fulfillment. "Life," or zoe, aims essentially at self-perpetuation and then, after it has achieved its aim, at dissolution. It can be argued therefore that it also encompasses what we call death. As a result, what we humans most deeply aspire to is not so much to disappear, but rather to do so in the space of our own life and in our own way (Phillips 1999). It is as if each of us wishes to die only in our own fashion. Our innermost desire is for a self-fashioned, a self-styled death. We thus pursue what we are ultimately trying to avoid, we are existential suicides not from nihilism but because it is our nature to die.

Of course it is a paradox: while at the conscious level all of us struggle for survival, at some deeper level of our unconscious structures, all we long for is to lie silently and let time wash over us in the stillness of nonlife. Self-styling one's death is an act of affirmation; it means cultivating an approach, a "style" of life that progressively and continuously fixes the modalities and the stage for the final act, leaving nothing unattended. Pursuing a sort of seduction into immortality, the ethical life is life as virtual suicide. Life as virtual suicide is life as constant creation. Life lived so as to break the cycles of inert repetitions that usher in banality. Lest we delude ourselves with narcissistic pretenses, we need to cultivate endurance, immortality within time, that is to say, death in life.

Moreover, the generative capacity of this "life" cannot be bound or confined to the single, human individual. It rather transversally trespasses all boundaries in the pursuit of its aim, which is the expression of its potency. It connects us transindividually, transgenerationally, and ecophilosophically. What we humans truly yearn for is to disappear by merging into this eternal flow of becomings, the precondition for which is the loss, disappearance, and disruption of the atomized, individual self. The ideal would be to take only memories and to leave behind only footsteps. What we most truly desire is to surrender the self, preferably in the agony of ecstasy, thus choosing our own way of disappearing, our way of dying to and as our self. This can be described also as the moment of ascetic dissolution of the subject; the moment of its merging with the web of nonhuman forces that frame him/her—the cosmos as a whole. Call it death, it has rather to do with radical immanence, with the totality of the moment in which we finally coincide completely with our body in becoming at last what we will have been all along: a virtual corpse.

This is no Christian affirmation of life or transcendental delegation of the meaning and value system to categories higher than the embodied self. Quite on the contrary, it is the intelligence of radically immanent flesh that states with every single breath that the life in you is not marked by any master signifier, and it most certainly does not bear your name. The awareness of the absolute difference between intensive or incorporeal affects and the specific affected bodies that one happens to be is crucial to the ethics of choosing for death. Death is the unsustainable, but it is also virtual in that it has the generative capacity to engender the actual. Consequently, death is but an obvious manifestation of principles that are active in every aspect of life, namely, the preindividual or impersonal power of potentia; the affirmation of multiplicity and not of one-sidedness, and the interconnection with an "outside" of cosmic dimension and infinite.

It is a temporal brand of vitalism that could not be further removed from the idea of death as the inanimate and indifferent state of matter, the entropic state to which the body is supposed to "return." It is desire as plenitude and overflowing, not as lack, following the entropic model built into psychoanalytic theory. Death, on the contrary, is the becoming-imperceptible of the nomadic subject, and as such it is part of the cycles of becoming, yet another form of interconnectedness, a vital relationship that links one with other, multiple forces. The impersonal is life and death as bios/zoe in us—the ultimate outside as the frontier of the incorporeal.

The paradox of affirming life as potentia, energy, even in and through the suppression of the specific slice of life that "I" inhabits, is a way of pushing antihumanism to the point of implosion. It dissolves death into ever-shifting processual changes and thus disintegrates the ego, with its capital of narcissism, paranoia, and negativity. Death from the specific and highly restricted viewpoint of the ego is of no significance whatsoever. This vision of death as process is linked to Deleuze's philosophy of time understood as endurance and sustainability and is indebted to Nietzsche as to Spinoza.

The generative capacity of bios/zoe, in other words, cannot be bound or confined to the single, human individual. It rather transversally trespasses such boundaries in the pursuit of its aim, which is self-perpetuation. "Life" is understood here as aiming essentially at self-perpetuation and then, after it has achieved its aim, at dissolution; it can be argued that it also encompasses what we usually call death. Just as the life in me is not mine in the appropriative sense espoused by liberal individualism, but is rather a time-sharing device, so the death in me is not mine, except in a very circumscribed sense of the term. In both cases, all "I" can hope for is to craft both my life and my death in a mode, at a speed and fashion which are sustainable and adequate: "I" can self-style them autopoietically, thus expressing my essential entity as the constitutive desire to endure (potentia).

This, however, needs to be related to chaos as productive multiplicity, not to the technologies of the Self of the second Foucault. No residual Kantianism here, but rather Nietzschean affirmation. On this point Deleuze and Foucault part ways. The kind of "self" that is "styled" in and through such a process is not one, nor is it an anonymous multiplicity: it is an embedded and embodied sets of interrelations, constituted in and by the immanence of his expressions, acts, and interactions with others and held together by the powers of remembrance, i.e., by continuity in time. I refer to this process in terms of sustainability and to stress the idea of continuity that it entails. Sustainability does assume faith in a future and also a sense of responsibility for "passing on" to future generations a world that is livable and worth living in. A present that endures is a sustainable model of the future.

Death, in such a framework, is merely a point; it is not the horizon against which the human drama is played out. The center is taken by bios/zoe and their ever-recurring flows of vitality. In and through many deaths, bios/zoe lives on. Deleuze turns this also into a critique of the Heideggerian legacy, which places mortality at the center of philosophical speculation. It is against this self-glorifying image of a pretentious and egotistical narcissistic and paranoid consciousness that philosophical nomadism unleashes the multiple dynamic forces of bios/zoe that do not coincide with the human, let alone with consciousness. These are nonessentialist brands of vitalism.

IMPLICATIONS FOR ECOSOPHICAL CONCERNS

Let us take as an example environmental politics. In the era of biogenetic capitalism, the romantic idea of nature has been superseded by the urgent immanence of disappearing nature. The renaturalization of technology is especially salient and painful in the discourse about environmental catastrophes, as Protevi argues (2009). The geopolitical forces are simultaneously renaturalized and subjected to the old hierarchical power relations that let the dominant politics of the subject rule again. Dominant discourse has become simultaneously moralistic about the environment and utterly irresponsible in perpetuating anthropocentric arrogance and denial of the man-made structure of catastrophe we continue to attribute to forces beyond our collective control—the earth, the cosmos, or "nature." Our morality is simply not up to the task of the very complexities engendered by our technological advances.

This gives rise to a double ethical urgency: firstly, how to turn the mourning and loss of the natural order into effective political action. Secondly, how to ground such an action in the responsibility for future generation, in the spirit of social sustainability, which I have also explored elsewhere (Braidotti 2006). This double necessity combines positive and negative elements and focuses them in one precise direction.

Nomadic politics is based on the ethics of transformation of negative into positive passions and seeks an ethics of relation that would allow us to address the complex requirements of this situation. Based on the axiom that it is the same conditions that create the source of negativity and also the material for positive transformation, activism needs to rest on and be nurtured by conditions that don't yet exist—for instance, sustainable conditions for future generations.

We have come to the antipodes of the rationalist idea of human stewardship of nature. The environmental question of how to prevent species extinction is a biopolitical issue: which species is allowed to survive and which to die? And what are the criteria that would allow us to decide? Nomadic theory stresses the point that, in order to develop adequate criteria, we need an alternative vision of subjectivity to support this effort and make it operational.

This is zoe-based, postanthropocentric politics that potentially pitches the competitive needs of animals and plants against those of both privileged and underprivileged humans. This competition for protection and support is problematic, since it reveals the implicit anthropocentric bias of even the most progressive forms of politics. Developing a progressive environmental politics that reflects the needs of development and economic growth is an urgent challenge that concerns not only the prevention of extinction—or survival—but also the establishment of a different zoe-political order.

Nomadic ecophilosophy has addressed three interrelated issues: firstly, the new forms of reactive panhumanity engendered by shared global risk societies (Beck 1999). Secondly, the fast rate of disappearance of animal, fish, and bird species. Thirdly, the pervasive forms of technological mediation and the extent to which global communication networks and biogenetic intervention has restructured the nature-culture relation into a complex continuum.

The emphasis I have been placing on biocentered egalitarianism is a possible answer to this challenge. We need a new covenant between nature and technology, in line with the "chaosmosis" approach of becoming-one with the environment, outside oedipal sentimentality (the panda bear syndrome) and beyond the idea that environmentalism is a mere Western luxury. I outlined this process of becoming-world in chapter 4 and in my defense of the vitalist materialist assemblages of nomadic becoming in general.

The geocentered and dynamic approach calls into question what today constitutes the basic unit of reference for the human. Because of the emphasis environmentalism places on extinction, the issue of death and dying are raised. The key implication for the law of Deleuze's recasting of the life-death distinction in terms of a vital continuum based on internal differentiations is the double overturning of individualism, on the one hand—in favor of complex singularities—and of anthropocentrism, on the other—in favor of multiplicities of flows and assemblages. Poststructuralism initiated this critique of subjectivity by declaring, with Foucault, the "death of Man" defined as the humanistic subject of knowledge. Nowadays we are experiencing a further stage in this process and, as the rhizomic philosophies of Deleuze and Guattari point out, we are forced to confront the built-in anthropocentrism that prevents us from relinquishing the categorical divide between bios and zoe and thus makes us cling to the superiority of consciousness in spite of our poststructuralist skepticism toward this very notion. The monist political ontology of Spinoza can rescue us from the anthropocentric contradiction and the marginalization of nonhuman others by pushing it to the point of implosion.

As I argued earlier, through the theory of nomadic becomings or plane of immanence, Deleuze dissolves and regrounds the subject into an ecophilosophy of multiple belongings. This takes the form of a strong emphasis on the prehuman or even nonhuman elements that compose the web of forces, intensities, and encounters that contribute to the making of nomadic subjectivity. The subject for Deleuze and Guattari is an ecological entity. Guattari (1995, 2000) follows Simondon and refers to this process as a transversal form of subjectivity or "transindividuality." This mode of diffuse yet grounded subject position achieves a double aim: firstly, it critiques individualism and, secondly, it supports a notion of subjectivity in the sense of qualitative, transversal, and group-oriented agency. My point is that by adopting a different vision of the subject and with it a new notion of the nature-culture interaction, legal theory may be able to move beyond a modernist and rather reductive conception of environmental justice and environmental crime as based only on harm and reparation. As Mark Halsey put it: "Where once the sole objective was to control the insane, the young, the feminine, the vagrant and the deviant, the objective in recent times has been to arrest the nonhuman, the inorganic, the inert—in short, the so-called 'natural world'" (Halsey 2006:15).

Lest this be misunderstood for moral and cognitive anarchy, let me emphasize a number of features of this posthuman, ethicopolitcal turn. The first main point is that the legal subject of this regime of governmentality is in fact an ecological unit. This zoe-driven body is marked by interdependence with its environment through a structure of mutual flows and data transfer that is best configured by the notion of viral contamination (Ansell-Pearson 1997), a complex and intensive interconnectedness.

Secondly, this environmentally bound subject is a collective entity, moving beyond the parameters of classical humanism and anthropocentrism. The human organism is an in-between that is plugged into and connected to a variety of possible sources and forces. As such it is useful to define it as a machine, which does not mean an appliance or anything with a specifically utilitarian aim, but rather something that is simultaneously more abstract and more materially embedded. The minimalist definition of a body-machine is an embodied affective and intelligent entity that captures processes and transforms energies and forces. Being environmentally bound and territorially based, an embodied entity feeds upon, incorporates, and transforms its (natural, social, human, or technological) environment constantly. Being embodied in this high-tech ecological manner means being immersed in fields of constant flows and transformations. Not all of them are positive, of course, although in such a dynamic system this cannot be known or judged a priori. Thus we need to allow for a multiplicity of possible cartographies, ethical paths, and lines of becoming.

Thirdly, such a subject of bios-zoe power raises questions of ethical urgency. Given the acceleration of processes of change, how can we tell the difference between the different flows of changes and transformations? Lines of molarity, molecularity, and flight need to be accounted for and mapped out as a collective assemblage of possible paths of becoming. No monolithic or static model can provide an adequate answer: we need more complexity and open-endedness and a diversification of possible strategies. The starting point is the relentless generative force of bios/zoe and the specific brand of transspecies egalitarianism they establish with the human. The ecological dimension of philosophical nomadism consequently becomes manifest and, with it, its potential ethical impact. It is a matter of forces as well as of ethology.

Fourthly, the specific temporality of the subject needs to be rethought. The subject is an evolutionary engine endowed with his own embodied temporality, both in the sense of the specific timing of the genetic code and the more genealogical time of individualized memories. If the embodied subject of biopower is a complex molecular organism, a biochemical factory of steady and jumping genes, an evolutionary entity endowed with its own navigational tools and a built-in temporality, then we need a form of ethical values and political agency that reflects this high degree of complexity.

Fifthly, and last, this ethical approach cannot be dissociated from considerations of power. The bios-zoe-centered vision of the technologically mediated subject of postmodernity or advanced capitalism is fraught with internal contradictions. Accounting for them is the cartographic task of critical theory, and an integral part of this project is to account for the implications they entail for the historically situated vision of the subject (Braidotti 2002). The bios-zoe-centered egalitarianism that is potentially conveyed by current technological transformations has dire consequences for the humanistic vision of the subject. The potency of bios-zoe, in other words, displaces the phallogocentric vision of consciousness, which hinges on the sovereignty of the "I." It can no longer be safely assumed that consciousness coincides with subjectivity or that either of them is in charge of the course of historical events. Both liberal individualism and classical humanism are disrupted at their very foundations by the social and symbolic transformations induced by our historical condition. Far from being merely a crisis of values, this situation confronts us with a formidable set of new opportunities. Renewed conceptual creativity and a leap of the social imaginary are needed in order to meet the challenge. Classical humanism, with its rationalistic and anthropocentric assumptions, is of hindrance, rather than of assistance, in this process. Therefore, as one possible response to this challenge, we should consider the posthumanistic brand of nonanthropocentric vitalism propelled by nomadic theory.

CONCLUSION

PART FIVE

13

A SECULAR PRAYER

For my uncle Romano, who died on Christmas Day, 2008.

|

Because I do not hope to turn again
Because I do not hope
Because I do not hope to turn

—T. S. ELIOT, *ASH WEDNESDAY*

Although I knew, I never believed it would actually come to this. To this perfect stillness in the shade of the cypress trees I remember from my youth. Will you draw comfort from their familiar presence, I wonder ? Will their austere solemnity see you through?

Because I did not dare to hope, I did not believe you would turn to this. From one moment to the other, all warmth exited the confines of your embodied self. You turned to stone, frozen in the dead heart of a Northern Italian winter. Those who could endure came to mourn; the others just turned inward and shut their sensorial systems down. This is no country for the fainthearted, not here, not now, in the soul-wrenching stillness that lingered behind after you were gone.

This is my prayer for you, a singular and silent plea for you, from the desolate dream-crossed landscape where I now stand alone. Mine is a secular prayer, though you were a man of God. It is just a radically immanent prayer. What else could that be, but an extreme degree of attention paid to you, to your lived existence and all the affective and conceptual forces you stood for ? Nothing can ever alter what you will have been or erase the traces of all you enacted upon the world. Your deeds will endure: even dust can burst into flames.

A secular prayer, for a nomadic materialist, is an intensification of the inner and outer gaze—a renewed focus one applies to the cumulated existence, the joys and sufferings of another. It expresses a threshold of sustainable relations but also a public acknowledgment of that relation, of the bond that ties us together. Our connection was postulated on the fact that we actually did not agree on everything and needed to work at finding a common ground, a plane of consistent presence that cut across the differences of space and time and made a dialogue between us possible. Sustaining and rejoicing in that relational bond turned into a lifelong project of affirmation through joint action. A prayer is a line of flight, an outstretched hand that connects us at the speed of light across the infinitesimal distance of the heavens. Speech without word, my prayer is an acceleration that makes time stand still. The crystallization of a deep affinity, a secular prayer enacts a magical refraction of the skylight even among these frozen stones, in the growing darkness under the cypress trees. They will listen, I know, in the twilight between the no longer and the not yet. So much to say and yet, no, I never thought it would come to this.

||
—

"I meant to write about death," writes Virginia Woolf, in her diary (of February 17, 1922), "only life came breaking in as usual." Thinking is also a way of increasing the intensity of Life. The brain engineers its own acceleration, a quickening of one's perception. Thinking is like being-there with and for other entities, forces. You—a trained philosopher and an ordained priest— took your thinking seriously and did it with humility and care. The result was the same: high-intensity thinking cracks open the shield of tedium and predictability in which we wrap ourselves in order to get through the day. Philosophy-at-work gives us a measure of the possible, a taste for intensifications, a flair for the virtual: it throws you open into the generative chaos of Life.

Life is cosmic energy, simultaneously empty chaos and absolute speed or movement. It is impersonal and inhuman in the monstrous, animal sense of radical alterity: zoe in all its powers. Nomadic philosophy loves zoe and sings its praises by emphasizing active, empowering forces against all negative odds. Zoe, or life as absolute vitality, however, is not above negativity, and it can hurt. It is always too much for the specific slab of enfleshed existence that single subjects actualize. It is a constant challenge for us to rise to the occasion, to practice amor fati, to catch the wave of life's intensities and ride it out, exposing the boundaries or limits as we transgress them. We often crack in the process and just cannot take it anymore. If philosophy teaches us anything, it is that the sheer activity of thinking about such intensity is painful because it causes strain, psychic unrest, and nervous tension. It also disconnects us from others in a semi-misanthropic manner. Accelerations or increased intensities of the intellectual or other kind are, however, that which most humans of our kind are fatally attracted to. You, my teacher and mentor, showed me how to dare, but also to endure. You taught me the golden rule: brilliance requires great depths of compassion.

Death is the ultimate transposition, though it is not final. Zoe carries on, relentlessly. Death is a conceptual excess: both the unrepresentable, the unthinkable, the unproductive black hole we all fear and also a creative synthesis of flows, energies, and perpetual becomings. Because humans are mortal, death, or the transience of life, is written at our core: it is the event that structures our time lines and frames our time zones. Insofar as it is everpresent in our psychic and somatic landscapes as the event that has always already happened. Death as a constitutive event is behind us, it has already taken place as a virtual potential that constructs everything we are. The full blast of awareness of the transitory nature of all that lives is the defining moment in our existence. It structures our becoming-subjects and the process of acquiring moral awareness. Being mortal, we all are "has-beens": the spectacle of our death is written obliquely into the script of our temporality.

We think to infinity, against the horror of the void, in the wilderness of nonhuman mental landscapes, with the shadow of death dangling in front of our eyes. Thought, however, is also a gesture of affirmation and hope for sustainability and endurance, of immanent relations and time-bound consistency. Moving beyond the paralyzing effects of suspicion and pain, working across them was the key to your ethics. It did not aim at mastery, but at the transformation of negative into positive passions. This was your main ethical injunction—you taught me to put the "active" back into activism. The qualitative leap necessary to induce a positive ethics of sustainability is a creative process, a praxis, an activity. As such it simply needs to be enacted. Your order word, or maxim, was simple: "just do it!"

A maxim is just another word for a secular prayer. It is a statement or expression of our shared desire in the sense of *potentia*. It is also an act of faith in our capacity to make a difference and as such it is an expression of generosity and love of the world. It is also a plea, an open question, a reaching out, or an invitation to the cosmic dance. It is an imperative, an injunction to endure in the sense both of lasting in time and of suffering in space, but it is also a spiritual gesture, a declaration of love. It is a political act of defiance of social norms and resistance against the inertia of habits and settled conventions. More importantly, it is an act of politics as autopoiesis, or affirmative self-creation, not of an atomized self, or a separate individual, but rather as a collective, multirelational nomadic subject open to different speeds and intensities of becoming. "Do it!" is an utterance where endurance and sustainability intersect in producing an impersonal or collective mode of singularity; the stark tone cuts down the sentimentality of dominant visions of the philosopher as well as the overstated authority of the master whose dogmatism and narcissism become sources of veneration. In that respect, the ethical injunction to "just do it," to be active in the world, is the opposite of the *mots d'ordre* or the political slogan. There is no ideological assurance here of a teleologically ordained trajectory, just the humility to get on with the task, though the final destination may not be very clear. All that matter is the going, the movement.

|||
—

> Teach us to care and not to care.
> Teach us to sit still
> —T. S. ELIOT, *ASH WEDNESDAY*

At least that's what you taught me when you introduced me to philosophy, soon to become my discipline of choice. Your favorites were not always mine: you lived by Plato, Seneca, Marcus Aurelius, Saint Augustine. I , however, tended to gravitate around Spinoza, Nietzsche, and Freud—those masters of suspicion my generation fell in love with. You, on the other hand, found them wanting in generosity and power of action. Your full attention was always turned toward real-life people, and you demanded of philosophy some practical help to assist and serve others. Politics for you was multidirectional *poesis*. Ascetic and generous at the same time, you defied cynical reason by compassion and concrete action. *Vita contemplativa* was always for you nothing else than an intensified version of *vita activa*. A people's person, praxis was your prayer, unbroken and flying onward. Quick in supporting but reluctant to judge, you let the singularity of each and every one shine gently of its own true light. You had harsh things to say about the wild impatience that often inhabited me and my generation, but also taught me never to trust anybody who loudly claimed to do anything for the love of God.

On some key points, however, we agreed: vitalism and the longing for eternity, to mention just two. Our vitalism—and hence our spirituality—was respectively of the pre-Socratic and post-postmodernist kind. We agreed that because Life is desire, which essentially aims at expressing and hence extinguishing itself, by reaching its aim and then dissolving, the wish to die can consequently be seen as another way to express the desire to live intensely. The corollary is even more cheerful: not only is there no dialectical tension between Eros and Thanatos, but also these two entities are really just one life force that aims to reach its own fulfilment. "Life," or zoe, we both agreed, aims essentially at self-perpetuation and then, after it has achieved its aim, at dissolution. It can be argued, therefore, that it also encompasses what we call death. As a result, and here comes the point about eternity, what we humans most deeply aspire to is not so much to disappear, but rather to do so in the space of our own life and in our own way. It is as if each of us wishes to die only after his or her own fashion. Our innermost desire is for a self-fashioned, a self-styled death. We thus pursue what we are ultimately trying to avoid, we are existential suicides, not from nihilism, but because it is our nature to die.

Of course it is a paradox: while at the conscious level all of us struggle for survival, at some deeper level of our unconscious structures all we long for is to lie silently and let time wash over us in the stillness of nonlife. Like this perfect moment here and now, with the cypress trees casting their shady form on the frozen ground you now inhabit—at the still point of the turning wheel. Self-styling one's death is an act of affirmation; it means cultivating an approach, a "style" of life that progressively and continuously fixes the

modalities and stage for the final act, leaving nothing unattended. Pursuing
a sort of seduction into immortality, the ethical life is life as virtual suicide.
Life as virtual suicide is life as constant creation. Life lived so as to break
the cycles of inert repetitions that usher in banality. Lest we delude ourselves
with narcissistic pretenses, we need to cultivate endurance, immortality
within time, that is to say, death in life. Gently and productively.

Moreover, the generative capacity of this "Life" cannot be bound or confined to the single human individual. Rather, it transversally trespasses all
boundaries in the pursuit of its aim, which is the expression of its potency.
It connects us transindividually, transgenerationally, and ecophilosophically.
Just as the life in me is not mine or even individual, so the death in me is not
mine, except in a very circumscribed sense of the term. In both cases all "I"
can hope for is to craft both my life and my death in a mode, at a speed and
fashion that can sustain all the intensity "I" is capable of. "I" can self-style
this gesture autopoietically, thus expressing its essence as the constitutive
desire to endure. I called it *potentia*; you called it the spiritual soul.

What we humans truly yearn for is to disappear by merging into this
eternal flow of becomings, the precondition for which is the loss, disappearance, and disruption of the atomized individual self. The ideal would be to
take only memories and to leave behind only footsteps. What we most truly
desire is to surrender the self, preferably in the agony of ecstasy, thus choosing our own way of disappearing, our way of dying to and as a self. This can
also be described as the moment of ascetic dissolution of the subject; the
moment of its merging with the web of nonhuman forces that frame him/
her—the cosmos as a whole. Call it death, this point of evanescence for you
was linked to Christian transcendence. For me, it had rather to do with radical immanence, with the totality of the moment in which, we finally coincide
completely with our body in becoming at last what we will have been all
along: a virtual corpse.

For you it pointed to the resurrection of the dead in the glorious embrace of their Christian savior. The outside of the human for you was the
divine, for me, the animal or the technological other. Still, we were steering
our respective courses on parallel lines of flight. For me, at the point of
their evanescence or dissolution, subjects are enfleshed entities that are immersed in the full intensity and luminosity of becoming. Theirs, however, is
the brightness of phosphorescent worms, not the light of the eternal rays of
some monotheistic God. This, therefore, is the glorious expression of the

life force that is zoe and not the emanation of some divine essence. Radical immanence as a mode of thinking the subject, and as a philosophical style, deflates the pretense of grandiose eternity that marks the Christian religious values in which you believed so deeply. Life is eternal, but this eternity is postulated on the materialist dissolution of the self, the individual ego, as the necessary premise. That was a minimum point of consensus between us.

We ended up nonetheless sharing an ethics of joyful affirmation and becoming, opposed to the economy of loss, the logic of lack, and the moral imperative to dwell in never-ending and irresolvable states of mourning. *Vita activa* was our shared passion. We wanted to move beyond both nihilism and the tragic solemnity of traditional morality, to grow to appreciate instead that death is an affirmation of the *potentia* of that life in me which, by definition, does not bear my name: "I" just inhabits it on a time-share basis.

We were both materialist, you on the theistic side, I on the atheist one, and we remained mirror images of each other to the end. I owe my secularity to your passionate Christian convictions. We both knew, albeit in different ways, that we just do not know what an embodied human can do or become—we shared the fundamental passion of wonder at the complexity of living beings. We shared faith in human progress as well: you as the expression of our divine essence, I out of respect for the dignity of humans. Even among these frozen stones my heart warms at the thought of such affirmative power—such loveliness of values, such liveliness in action.

It is time to go. Life, this mindless force, carries on, relentless and ruthless in its overflowing *energia*, enduring endlessly. Here is my refrain, then: farewell my body-double, my corpse, my cherished other, myself—forever both more and less than one, in an endless process of becoming-other and merging with others. It is time to rest now. Because I knew that I didn't know any better, I had accepted it as evidence and cultivated the art of self-styling death as a life-form. I sat and watched and waited to see how you would do it, how you would style that last act, your final disappearing trick. I am glad I lived to tell the tale. I am ever so proud to say: you did it exceptionally well, you did it so it felt real. I was left wondering, in the cypress-lined alley, how perfect your exit had been on a sunny Christmas day. And I stood among the frozen stones, trying to reach out for words to speak this parting prayer: suffer us not to forget what we are capable of becoming, *teach us to care and not to care, teach us to sit still.*

NOTES

1. TRANSPOSING DIFFERENCES

1. Inventory, "Intent on Dissent Survey Project no. 2, 1999," Crash! exhibition, November 1999, London: Institute of Contemporary Arts.

2. META(L)MORPHOSES

1. See for instance Luke Harding, "Delhi Calling," *Guardian Weekly*, March 15–21, 2001.
2. See the *Guardian Weekly*, March 25–31, 2005, p. 17.

3. ANIMALS AND OTHER ANOMALIES

1. *Guardian Weekly*, December 27, 2001–January 2, 2002.
2. *Guardian Weekly*, August 14–20, 2003, p. 2.

6. INTENSIVE GENRE AND THE DEMISE OF GENDER

1. The distinction potestas/potentia expresses the difference between the negative or restrictive aspects of power and the positive or affirmative ones, as noted previously. This distinction has become standard in neo-Spinozist democratic political theory.

7. POSTSECULAR PARADOXES

1. I acknowledge many private conversations with Claire Colebrook on these issues.
2. See the pamphlet *The Case for Secularism: A Neutral State in an Open Society* (London: British Humanist Association, 2007). With thanks to Simon Glendinning.
3. See http://www.4abstinence.com.

8. COMPLEXITY AGAINST METHODOLOGICAL NATIONALISM

1. With thanks to my sister Gio Braidotti, Ph.D. in molecular biology.

9. NOMADIC EUROPEAN CITIZENSHIP

1. I owe this witty formulation to the discussions with my colleagues in the European Socrates Thematic Network ATHENA in 2004.

10. POWERS OF AFFIRMATION

1. With thanks to Gayatri Spivak for this formulation.
2. Joanna Bourke: "Politics of Fear Blinds Us All," *Guardian Weekly*, October 7–13, 2005, p. 13.

BIBLIOGRAPHY

Adams, Carol. 2003. *The Pornography of Meat*. New York: Continuum International.

Adler, Rachel. 1998. "Judaism." In Alison M. Jaggar and Iris M. Young, eds., *A Companion to Feminist Philosophy*, pp. 245–252. Oxford: Blackwell.

Afary, Janet, and Kevin B. Anderson. 2005. *Foucault and the Iranian Revolution: Gender and the Seduction of Islamism*. Chicago: University of Chicago Press.

Agamben, Giorgio. 1998. *Homo Sacer: Sovereign Power and Bare Life*. Stanford: Stanford University Press.

Alcoff, Linda. 2000. "Philosophy Matters: A Review of Recent Work in Feminist Philosophy." *Signs* 25, no. 3 (Spring): 841–882.

Althusser, Louis. 2005. "Du Matérialisme Aléatoire" *Multitudes,* no. 21 (Spring): 179–193.

Andermahr, Sonya, Terry Lovell, and Carol Wolkowitz. 1997. *A Concise Glossary of Feminist Theory*. London: Arnold.

Anderson, Benedict. 1983. *Imagined Communities*. New York: Verso.

Anderson, Laurie. 1984. *United States*. New York: Harper and Row.

Ansell-Pearson, Keith. 1997. *Viroid Life: Perspectives on Nietzsche and the Transhuman Condition*. New York: Routledge.

—— 1999. *Germinal Life: The Difference and Repetition of Deleuze*. New York: Routledge.

Anzaldúa, Gloria. 1987. *Borderlands/La Frontera*. San Francisco: Aunt Lute.

Appadurai, Arjun. 1994. "Disjuncture and Difference in the Global Cultural Economy." *Theory, Culture, and Society* 7:295–310.

—— 1998. "Dead Certainty: Ethnic Violence in the Era of Globalization." *Development and Change* 29:905–925.

Arendt, Hannah. 1963. *Eichmann in Jerusalem*. New York: Viking.

Asad, Talal. 2003. *Formations of the Secular: Christianity, Islam, Modernity*. Stanford: Stanford University Press.

Atkinson, Ti-Grace. 1974. *Amazon Odyssey*. Kirkwood: Putnam.

Augé, Marc. 1995. *Non-Places: Introduction to an Anthropology of Supermodernity*. London: Verso.

Badinter, Elisabeth. 2002. *Les Passions intellectuelles*, vol. 2: *L'exigence de dignité (1751–1762)*. Paris: Fayard.

Badiou, Alain. 1998. *Saint Paul: La Fondation de l'Universalisme*. Paris: Presses Universitaire de France.

Balibar, Etienne. 2001. *Nous, Citoyens de l'Europe? Les Frontiers, l'Etat, le People*. Paris: Decouverte.

—— 2002. *Politics and the Other Scene*. London: Verso.

Ballard, J. G. 1973. *Crash*. New York: Noonday.

Balsamo, Anne. 1996. *Technologies of the Gendered Body*. Durham: Duke University Press.

Barad, Karen. 2003. "Posthumanist Performativity: Toward an Understanding of How Matter Comes to Matter." *Signs* 28, no. 3 (March): 801–831.

—— 2007. *Meeting the Universe Half Way*. Durham: Duke University Press.

Barbrook, Richard. 2000. "The Holy Fools." In Patricia Pisters, ed., *Gilles Deleuze: Micropolitics of Audiovisual Culture*. Amsterdam: Amsterdam University Press.

Barker, Francis. 1984. *The Tremulous Private Body. Essays on Subjection*. London: Methuen.

Barrett, Michèle. 1980. *Women's Oppression Today*. London: Verso.

Bataille, Georges. 1988. *The Accursed Share*. New York: Zone.

Baudrillard, Jean. 1993. *Symbolic Exchange and Death*. London: Sage.

Bauman, Zygmunt. 1993. *Postmodern Ethics*. Oxford: Blackwell.

—— 1998. *Globalization: The Human Consequences*. Cambridge: Polity.

—— 2004. *Europe, an Unfinished Adventure*. Cambridge: Polity.

Beauvoir, Simone de. 1973. *The Second Sex*. New York: Bantam.

—— 1992. *The Force of Circumstance*. New York: Paragon House.

—— 1993. *All Things Said and Done*. New York: Paragon House.

Beck, Ulrich. 1999. *World Risk Society*. Cambridge: Polity.

—— 2007. "The Cosmopolitan Condition: Why Methodological Nationalism Fails." *Theory, Culture and Society* 24, nos. 7/8 (December): 286–290.

Becker, Susanne. 1999. *Gothic Forms of Feminine Fiction*. Manchester: Manchester University Press.

Beer, Gillian. 2000. *Darwin's Plots*. Cambridge: Cambridge University Press.

Benhabib, Seyla. 1999a. "Citizen, Resident, and Alien in a Changing World: Political Membership in a Global Era." *Social Research* 66, no. 3 (September): 709–744.

—— 1999b. "Sexual Difference and Collective Identities: The New Global Constellation' in *Signs* 24, no. 2 (Winter): 335–361.

———— 2002. *The Claims of Culture: Equality and Diversity in the Global Era*. Princeton: Princeton University Press.

———— 2004. *The Rights of Others: Aliens, Residents, and Citizens*. Cambridge: Cambridge University Press.

Benjamin, Jessica. 1988. *The Bonds of Love: Psychoanalysis, Feminism, and the Problem of Domination*. New York: Pantheon.

Bennett, Jane. 2001. *The Enchantment of Modern Life: Attachments, Crossings, and Ethics*. Princeton: Princeton University Press.

———— 2010. *Vibrant Matter: A Political Ecology of Things*. Durham: Duke University Press.

Bensmaia, Réda. 1994. "On the Concept of Minor Literature: From Kafka to Kateb Yacine." In Constantin V. Boundas and Dorothea Olkowski, eds., *Gilles Deleuze and the Theatre of Philosophy*, pp. 213–228. New York: Routledge.

Bernasconi, Robert, and Sybol Cook. 2003. *Race and Racism in Continental Philosophy*. Bloomington: Indiana University Press.

Bhabha, Homi K., ed. 1990. *Nation and Narration*. New York: Routledge.

———— 1994. *The Location of Culture*. New York: Routledge.

———— 1996. "Unpacking My Library: Again." In Iain Chamber and Lidia Curti, eds., *The Post-Colonial Question: Common Skies, Divided Horizons*, pp. 199–211. New York: Routledge.

Bhavnani, Kum-Kum. 1992. *Towards a Multi-Cultural Europe?* Amsterdam: Bernardijn ten Zeldam Stichting.

Blanchot, Maurice. 2002. *The Instant of My Death*. Stanford: Stanford University Press.

Bogue, Ronald. 1989. *Deleuze and Guattari*. New York: Routledge.

———— 1991. "Rhizomusocosmology." *SubStance*, no. 66, pp. 85–101.

Bonta, Mark, and John Protevi. 2004. *Deleuze and Geophilosophy: A Guide and Glossary*. Edinburgh: Edinburgh University Press.

Borradori, Giovanna. 2003. *Philosophy in a Time of Terror*. Chicago: University of Chicago Press.

Boundas, Constantin V. 1994. "Deleuze: Serialization and Subject-Formation." In Constantin V. Boundas and Dorothea Olkowski, eds., *Gilles Deleuze and the Theatre of Philosophy*, pp. 99–116. New York: Routledge.

———— 2007a. "Gilles Deleuze and His Readers: A Touch of Voluntarism and an Excess of Out-Worldliness." *Deleuze Studies* 1, no. 2 (December): 167–194.

———— 2007b. *The Companion to the Twentieth Century Philosophies*. New York: Columbia University Press.

Boundas, Constantin V., and Dorothea Olkowski, eds. *Gilles Deleuze and the Theater of Philosophy*. New York: Routledge.

Bourke, Joanna. 2005. *Fear: A Cultural History*. London: Virago.

Brah, Avtar. 1993. "Re-Framing Europe: En-Gendered Racisms, Ethnicities, and Nationalisms in Contemporary Western Europe." *Feminist Review*, no. 45 (September): 9–29.

———— 1996. *Cartographies of Diaspora—Contesting Identities*. New York: Routledge.

Braidotti, Rosi. 1991. *Patterns of Dissonance*. Cambridge: Polity.

———— 1993. "Discontinuous Becomin gs. Deleuze and the Becoming-Woman of Philosophy." *Journal of the British Society of Phenomenology* 24, no. 1: 44–55.TK

———— 1994a. *Nomadic Subjects: Embodiment and Sexual Difference in Contemporary Feminist Theory*. New York: Columbia University Press.

———— 1994b. "Of Bugs and Women: Irigaray and Deleuze on the Becoming Woman." In Carolyn Burke, Naomi Schor, and Margaret Whitford, eds., *Engaging with Irigaray*, pp. 111–137. New York: Columbia University Press.

———— 1995. "Me Tarzan and You Jane? Reconstructions of Femininity and Masculinity in Science Fiction Horror Films." In Dorrit Einersen and Ingeborg Nixon, eds., *Woman as Monster in Literature and the Media*, pp. 213–227. Copenhagen: University of Copenhagen.

———— 2002a. *Metamorphoses: Toward a Materialist Theory of Becoming*. Malden, MA: Blackwell.

———— 2002b. *Nuovi Soggetti Nomadi*. Rome: Luca Sossella.

———— 2003a. "La Pensée féministe nomade." *Multitudes* 12:27–28.

———— 2003b. "L'Europe peut-elle nous faire rêver." *Multitudes Europe Constituante?* 14:97–109.

———— 2006. *Transpositions: On Nomadic Ethics*. Cambridge: Polity.

———— 2008. "Intensive Genre and the Demise of Gender." *Angelaki* 13, no. 2 (August): 45–57.

———— 2011. *Nomadic Subjects: Embodiment and Sexual Difference in Contemporary Feminist Theory*. 2d ed. New York: Columbia University Press.

Brodkin Sacks, Karen. 1994. "How Did Jews Become White Folks?" In Steven Gregory and Roger Sanjek, eds., *Race*, pp. 78–102. New Brunswick, NJ: Rutgers University Press.

Bryld, Nette, and Nina Lykke. 1999. *Cosmodolphin: Feminist Cultural Studies of Technologies, Animals, and the Sacred*. London: Zed.

Buchanan, Ian, and Claire Colebrook, eds. 2000. *Deleuze and Feminist Theory*. Edinburgh: Edinburgh University Press.

Bukatman, Scott. 1993. *Terminal Identity. The Virtual Subject in Post-Modern Science Fiction*. Durham: Duke University Press.

———— 2003. *Matters of Gravity: Special Effects and Supermen in the Twentieth Century*. Durham:Duke University Press.

Burchill, Julie. 1998. *Diana*. London: Weidenfeld and Nicolson.

Burger, Christa. 1985. "The Reality of 'Machines': Notes on the Rhizome-Thinking." *Telos* 64 (Spring): 33–44.Butler, Judith. 1991. *Gender Trouble*. New York: Routledge.

———— 1992. "Contingent Foundations: Feminism and the Question of Postmodernism." In Judith Butler and Joan Wallach Scott, eds., *Feminists Theorize the Political*, pp. 3–21. New York: Routledge.

———— 1993. *Bodies That Matter: On the Discursive Limits of "Sex."* New York: Routledge.

———— 2004a. *Precarious Life*. New York: Verso.

———— 2004b. *Undoing Gender*. New York: Routledge.

Butler, Judith, and Joan Wallach Scott, eds. 1992. *Feminists Theorize the Political*. New York: Routledge.

Cacciari, Massimo. 1994. *The Necessary Angel*. New York: SUNY Press.

Campbell, Beatrix. 1998. *Diana, Princess of Wales: How Sexual Politics Shook the Monarchy*. London: Women's Press.

Canning, Peter. 1985. "Fluidentity." *SubStance*, no. 44, pp. 35–44.

Castells, Manuel. 1996. *The Rise of the Network Society*. Oxford: Blackwell.

Chakrabarty, Dipesh. 2000. *Provincializing Europe*. Princeton: Princeton University Press.

Cheah, Pheng. 1996. "Mattering." *Diacritics* 26, no. 1 (March): 108–139.

———— 2008. "Nondialectical Materialism." *Diacritics* 38, no. 1 (September): 143–157.

Cixous, Helene. 1997. "Mon Algeriance." *Les Inrockuptibles*, no. 115 (August): 70.

———— 2004. *Portrait of Jacques Derrida as a Young Jewish Saint*. New York: Columbia University Press.

Clifford, James. 1994. "Diasporas." *Cultural Anthropology* 9, no. 3 (August): 302–338.

Cohen, Robin. 1997. *Global Diasporas, an Introduction*. London: University College of London Press.

Cohn-Bendit, Daniel. 1995. "Transit Discussion." *Newsletter of the Institute for Human Sciences*, no. 50 (Spring): 1–4.

Colebrook, Claire. 2000a. "From Radical Representation to Corporeal Becomings: The Feminist Philosophies of Lloyd, Grost, and Gateus." *Hypatia* 15, no. 2 (April): 76–91.

———— 2000b. "Is Sexual Difference a Problem?" In Ian Buchanan and Claire Colebrook, eds., *Deleuze and Feminist Theory*, pp. 279–296. Edinburgh: Edinburgh University Press.

———— 2002. *Understanding Deleuze*. Crows Nest: Allen and Unwin.

———— 2004. "Postmodernism Is a Humanism: Deleuze and Equivocity." *Women: A Cultural Review* 15, no. 3 (Winter): 283–307.

Connolly, William. 1999. *Why Am I Not a Secularist?* Minneapolis: University of Minnesota Press.

———— 2008. *Capitalism and Christianity, American Style*. Durham: Duke University Press.

Cornell, Drucilla. 2002. Ubuntu Project with Stellenbosch University, www.fehe.org/index.php?id=281.

Coward, Rosalind. 1983. *Patriarchal Precedents*. New York: Routledge.

Creed, Barbara. 1990. "Gynesis, Postmodernism, and the Science Fiction Horror Film." In A. Kuhn, ed., *Alien Zone*, pp. 214–219. London: Verso.

———— 1993. *The Monstruous-Feminine. Film, Feminism, Psychoanalysis*. New York: Routledge.

Crenshaw, Kimberle. 1995. "Intersectionality and Identity Politics. Learning from Violence Against Women of Colour." In Kimberle Crenshaw, Neil Gotanda, Gary Peller, and Kendall Thomas, eds., *Critical Race Theory*, pp. 357–383. New York: New Press.

Cresswell, Tim. 1997. "Imagining the Nomad: Mobility and the Postmodern Primitive." In Georges Benko and Ulf Strohmayer, eds., *Space and Social Theory: Interpreting Modernity and Postmodernity*, pp. 360–382. Oxford: Blackwell.

Critchley, Simon. 1992. *The Ethics of Deconstruction*. Edinburgh: Edinburgh University Press.

———— 2007. *Infinitely Demanding: Ethics of Commitment, Politics of Resistance*. New York: Verso.

———— 2008. *The Book of Dead Philosophers*. London: Granta.

Dahrendorf, Ralf. 1990. *Reflections on the Revolution in Europe in a Letter Intended to Have Been Sent to a Gentleman in Warsaw*. London: Chatto and Windus.

Daly, Mary. 1973. *Beyond God the Father: Towards a Theory of Women's Liberation*. Boston: Beacon.

Daston, Lorraine, and Peter Galison. 2007. *Objectivity*. New York: Zone.

Davies, Jude, and Carol R. Smith. 1997. *Gender, Ethnicity, and Sexuality in Contemporary American Film*. Edinburgh: Keele University Press.

Davis, Angela. 1981. *Women, Race, and Class*. New York: Random House.

Dawkins, Richard. 1976. *The Selfish Gene*. Oxford: Oxford University Press.

———— 2006. *The God Delusion*. London: Black Swan.

De Landa, Manuel. 2002. *Intensive Science and Virtual Philosophy*. London: Continuum.

———— 2006. *A New Philosophy of Society*. New York: Continuuum.

Deleuze, Gilles. 1953. *Empirisme et subjectivité*. Paris: Presses Universitaires de France.

———— 1962. *Nietzsche et la philosophie*. Paris: Presses Universitaires de France.

———— 1966. *Le Bergsonisme*. Paris: Presses Universitaires de France.

———— 1968a. *Différence et répétition*. Paris: Presses Universitaires de France.

———— 1968b. *Spinoza et le probleme de l'expression*. Paris: Minuit.

———— 1969. *Logique du sens*. Paris: Minuit. English translation: 1990. *The Logic of Sense*. Trans. M. Lester. New York: Columbia University Press.

———— 1973. *Nietzsche aujourd'hui*. Paris: Union Generale d'Edition.

———— 1986. *Foucault*. Paris: Minuit.

———— 1988. *Le Pli*. Paris: Minuit.

———— 1995. "L'Immanence: Une vie." *Philosophie*, no. 47 (September): 3–7.

———— 2002. *Deux régimes de fous et autres textes*. Paris: Minuit.

Deleuze, Gilles, and Felix Guattari. 1972. *L'anti-Oedipe: Capitalisme et schizophrénie I*. Paris: Minuit. English translation: 1977. *Anti-Oedipus. Capitalism and Schizophrenia*. Trans. R. Hurley, M. Seem, and H. R. Lane. New York: Viking.

———— 1976. *Rhizome*. Paris: Minuit.

———— 1980. *Mille plateaux: Capitalisme et schizophrénie II*. Paris: Minuit. English translation: 1987. *A Thousand Plateaus: Capitalism and Schizophrenia*. Trans. Brian Massumi. Minneapolis: University of Minnesota Press.

———— 1986. *Nomadology: The War Machine*. New York: Semiotexte.

———— 1991. *Qu'est-ce que la philosophie?* Paris: Minuit. English translation: 1994. *What Is Philosophy?* Trans. Graham Burchell and Hugh Tomlinson. London: Verso.

Deleuze, Gilles, and Claire Parnet. 1977. *Dialogues*. Paris: Flammarion.

Delphy, Christine. 1984. *Close to Home: A Materialist Analysis of Women's Oppression*. Amherst: University of Massachusetts Press.

Derrida, Jacques. 1991. *L'Autre Cap*. Paris; Minuit.

—— 1997. *Politics of Friendship*. New York: Verso.

—— 2001. *The Work of Mourning*. Chicago: University of Chicago Press.

—— 2002. *Acts of Religion*. New York: Routledge.

—— 2006. "Is There a Philosophical Language?" In L. Thomassan. ed., *The Derrida-Habermas Reader*. Edinburgh: Edinburgh University Press.

Diamond, Irene, and Lee Quinby, eds. 1988. *Feminism and Foucault: Reflections on Resistance*. Boston: Northeastern University Press.

Diken, Bulent. 2004. "From Refugee Camps to Gated Communities: Biopolitics and the End of the City." *Citizenship Studies* 8, no. 1 (March): 83–106.

Diprose, Rosalyn. 1994. *The Bodies of Women: Ethics, Embodiment, and Sexual Difference*. London: Routledge.

Donovan, Josephine. 1990. *Gnosticism in Modern Literature: A Study of Selected Works of Camus, Sartre, Hesse, and Kafka*. New York: Garland.

Duffield, Mark. 2008. "Global Civil War: The Non-Insured, International Containment, and Post-Interventionary Society." *Journal of Refugee Studies* 21:145–165.

Dumm, Thomas. 1996. *Michel Foucault and the Politics of Freedom*, London. Sage.

Dyer, Richard. 1993. *The Matter of Images*. New York: Routledge.

—— 1997. *White*. New York: Routledge.

Einersen, Dorrit, and Ingeborg Nixon. 1995. *Woman as Monster in Literature and the Media*. Copenhagen: Copenhagen University Press.

Eisenstadt, Shmuel. 2000. "Multiple Modernities." *Daedalus* 129:1–29.

Eisenstein, Zillah. 1998. *Global Obscenities: Patriarchy, Capitalism, and the Lure of Cyberfantasy*. New York: New York University Press.

Eliot, George. 1973. *Middlemarch*. London: Penguin.

Eliot, T. S. 1930. *Ash Wednesday*. London: Faber and Faber.

Epps, Brad. 1996. "Technoasceticism and Authorial Death in Sade, Kafka, Barthes, and Foucault." *differences* 8, no. 3:79–127.

Esposito, Roberto. 2004. *Bios. Biopolitica e filosofia*, Turin: Einaudi.

Essed, Philomena. 1991. *Understanding Everyday Racism*. London: Sage.

Fallaci, Oriana. 2004. *The Force of Reason*. New York: Rizzoli.

Fausto-Sterling, Anna. 2000. *Sexing the Body: Gender Politics and the Construction of Sexuality*. New York: Basic Books.

Ferreira, Virginia, Teresa Tavares, and Silvia Portugal, eds. 1998. *Shifting Bonds, Shifting Bounds: Women, Mobility, and Citizenship in Europe*. Oeiras: Celta.

Ferry, Luc, and Alain Renault. 1985. *La Pensée 68*. Paris: Gallimard.

Finkielkraut, Alain. 1987. *La Défaite de la Pensée*. Paris: Gallimard.

Firestone, Shulamith. 1970. *The Dialectic of Sex*. New York: Bantam.

Flannery, Tim F. 1994. *The Future Eaters: An Ecological History of the Australasian Lands and People*. New York: Braziller.

Foster, Hal. 1996. *The Return of the Real*. Cambridge: MIT Press.

Foucault, Michel. 1963. *Naissance de la clinique*. Paris: Presses Universitaires de France.

—— 1966. *Les Mots et les choses*. Paris: Gallimard.

—— 1975. *Surveiller et punir*. Paris: Gallimard.

—— 1976. *Histoire de la sexualité I: Là Volontée de savoir*. Paris: Gallimard.

—— 1977a. *Language, Counter-Memory, Practice*. Ithaca: Cornell University Press.

—— 1977b. *L'Ordre du Discours*. Paris: Minuit.

—— 1980. *Power/Knowledge: Selected Interviews and Other Writings*. New York: Pantheon.

—— 1984a. *Histoire de la sexualité II: L'Usage des plaisirs*. Paris: Gallimard.

—— 1984b. *Histoire de la sexualité III: Le Souci de soi*. Paris: Gallimard.

Foucault, Michel, and Gilles Deleuze. 1972. "Les Intellectuals et le pouvoir." *L'Arc*, no. 49, pp. 3–10.

Frankenberg, Ruth. 1993. *White Women, Race Matters*. Minneapolis: University of Minnesota Press.

Franklin, Sarah. 2007. *Dolly Mixtures: The Remaking of Genealogy*. Durham: Duke University Press.

Franklin, Sarah, Celia Lury, and Jackie Stacey. 2000. *Global Nature, Global Culture*. London: Sage.

Fraser, Mariam. 2002. "What Is the Matter of Feminist Criticism?" *Economy and Society* 31, no. 4 (Winter): 606–625.

Fraser, Mariam, Sarah Kember, and Celia Lury. 2006. *Inventive Life: Approaches to the New Vitalism*. London: Sage.

Fraser, Nancy. 1996. "Multiculturalism and Gender Equity: The U.S. 'Difference' Debates Revisited." *Constellations* 3, no. 1 (April): 61–72.

Freud, Sigmund. 1927. *The Future of an Illusion*. London: Hogarth.

Fukuyama, Francis. 1992. *The End of History and the Last Man*. London: Hamilton.

—— 2002. *Our Posthuman Future: Consequences of the BioTechnological Revolution*. London: Profile.

Galison, Peter, and Lorraine Daston. 2007. *Objectivity*. Boston: Zone.

Gatens, Moira. 1991. *Feminism and Philosophy: Perspectives on Difference and Equality*. Cambridge: Polity.

Gatens, Moira, and Genevieve Lloyd. 1999. *Collective Imaginings: Spinoza, Past and Present*. New York: Routledge.

Gellner, Ernest. 1992. *Postmodernism, Reason, and Religion*. New York: Routledge.

Gilroy, Paul. 1987. *There Ain't No Black in the Union Jack*. London: Hutchinson.

—— 1993. *The Black Atlantic: Modernity and Double Consciousness*. New York:Verso.

—— 2000. *Against Race: Imaging Political Culture Beyond the Color Line*. Cambridge: Harvard University Press.

—— 2004. *After Empire: Melancholia or Convivial Culture?* New York: Routledge.

Giunta, Edvige. 2002. *Writing with an Accent: Contemporary Italian American Women Authors*. New York: Palgrave.

Glasson Deschaumes, Ghislaine, and Svetlana Slapšak, eds. *Balkan Women for Peace: Itineraries of Cross-Border Activism.* Paris: Transeuropéennes, Reseaux pour la Culture en Europe.

Glissant, Edouard. 1990. *Poetique de la relation.* Paris: Gallimard.

Glucksmann, André. 1976. *Les Maîtres penseurs.* Paris: Grasset.

Goodchild, Philip, Gilles Deleuze, and Felix Guattari. 1996. *An Introduction to the Politics of Desire.* London: Sage.

Grewal, Inderpal, and Caren Kaplan, eds. 1994. *Scattered Hegemonies: Postmodernity and Transnational Feminist Practices.* Minneapolis: University of Minnesota Press.

Griffin, Gabriele, and Rosi Braidotti. 2002. *Thinking Differently: A Reader in European Women's Studies.* London: Zed.

Griggers, Camilla. 1997. *Becoming-Woman.* Minneapolis: University of Minnesota Press.

Grossberg, Lawrence. 1997. *Bringing It All Back Home: Essays on Cultural Studies.* Durham: Duke University Press.

Grosz, Elizabeth. 1994. "A Thousand Tiny Sexes: Feminism and Rhizomatics." In Constantin V. Boundas and Dorothea Olkowski, eds., *Gilles Deleuze and the Theater of Philosophy*, pp. 187–210. New York: Routledge.

—— 1995. "Animal Sex. Libido as Desire and Death." In Elizabeth Grosz and Elspeth Probyn, eds., *Sexy Bodies: The Strange Carnalities of Feminism*, pp. 278–299. New York: Routledge.

—— 1999a. *Becomings: Explorations in Time, Memory, and Futures.* Ithaca: Cornell University.

—— 1999b. "Darwin and Feminism: Preliminary Investigations for a Possible Alliance." *Australian Feminist Studies* 14, no. 29 (April): 31–45.

—— 2004. *The Nick of Time.* Durham: Duke University Press.

—— 2005. "Bergson, Deleuze, and the Becoming of Unbecoming." *Parallax* 11, no. 2 (April-June): 4–13.

Guattari, Felix. 1995. *Chaosmosis: An Ethico-Aesthetic Paradigm.* Sydney: Power.

—— 2000. *The Three Ecologies.* London: Athlone.

Habermas, Jürgen. 1992. "Citizenshp and National Identity: Some Reflections on the Future of Europe." *Praxis International* 12:1–34.

—— 2003. *The Future of Human Nature.* Cambridge: Polity.

Halberstam, Judith, and Ira Livingston. 1995. *Post-Human Bodies.* Bloomington: Indiana University Press.

Hall, Stuart. 1987. "Minimal Selves." In *Identity: The Real Me.* London: Institute of Contemporary Arts Documents.

—— 1990. "Cultural Identity and Diaspora." In Jonathan Rutherford, ed., *Identity: Community, Culture, Difference*, pp. 435–443. London: Lawrence and Wishart.

—— 1992. "What Is This 'Black' in Black Popular Culture?" pp. 21–33. In Gina Dent, ed., *Black Popular Culture.* Seattle: Boy.

Hallward, Peter. 2006. *Out of This World: Deleuze and the Philosophy of Creation.* New York: Verso.

Halsey, Mark. 2006. *Deleuze and Environmental Damage.* London: Ashgate.

Hamon, Bervé, and Patrick Rotman. 1988. *Génération,* vol. 2: *Les Années de Poudre.* Paris: Seuil.

Hanafin, Patrick. 2010. "On Reading Transpositions: A Response to Rosi Braidotti's 'Transpositions: On Nomadic Ethics.'" *Subjectivities* 3:131–136.

Hanafin, Patrick, Claire Colebrook, and Rosi Braidotti, eds. 2009. *Deleuze and Law: Forensic Futures.* London: Palgrave MacMillan.

Haraway, Donna. 1985. "A Manifesto for Cyborgs: Science, Technology, and Socialist Feminism in the 1980s." *Socialist Review* 5, no. 2: 65–108.TK

———— 1988. "Situated Knowledges: The Science Question in Feminism as a Site of Discourse on the Privilege of Partial Perspective." *Feminist Studies* 14, no. 3 (Autumn): 575–599.

———— 1989. *Primate Visions: Gender, Race, and Nature in the World of Modern Science.* New York: Routledge.

———— 1991. *Simians, Cyborgs, and Women.* New York: Routledge.

———— 1992a. "Ecce Homo, Ain't (Ar'n't). I a Woman and Inappropriate/d Others: The Human in a Post-Humanist Landscape." In Judith Butler and Joan Scott, eds., *Feminists Theorize the Political,* pp. 86–100. New York: Routledge.

———— 1992b. "The Promises of Monsters: A Regenerative Politics for Inappropriate/d Others." In Lawrence Grossberg, Cary Nelson, and Paula Treichler, eds., *Cultural Studies,* pp. 295–337. New York: Routledge.

———— 1997. *Modest Witness.* New York: Routledge.

———— 2003. *The Companion Species Manifesto: Dogs, People, and Significant Otherness.* Chicago: Prickly Paradigm.

———— 2006. "When We Have Never Been Human, What Is to Be Done?" *Theory, Culture, and Society* 23, no. 7 and 8 (December): 135–158.

Harding, Sandra. 1986. *The Science Question in Feminism.* Ithaca: Cornell University Press.

———— 1991. *Whose Science? Whose Knowledge?* Ithaca: Cornell University Press.

———— 1993. *The "Racial" Economy of Science.* Bloomington: Indiana University Press.

———— 2000. *The Book of Jerry Falwell: Fundamentalist Language and Politics.* Princeton: Princeton University Press.

Hardt, Michael. 1992. *Gilles Deleuze: An Apprenticeship in Philosophy.* Minneapolis: University of Minnesota Press.

Hardt, Michael, and Antonio Negri. 2000. *Empire.* Cambridge: Harvard University Press.

———— 2004. *Multitude: War and Democracy in the Age of Empire.* New York: Penguin.

Hartsock, Nancy. 1987. "The Feminist Standpoint: Developing the Ground for a Specifically Feminist Historical Materialism." In Sandra Harding. ed., *Feminism and Methodology,* pp. 283–310. London: Open University Press.

Hayles, Katherine. 1999. *How We Became Posthuman: Virtual Bodies in Cybernetics, Literature, and Informatics.* Chicago: University of Chicago Press.

Hemmings, Clare. 2006. *Travelling Concepts in Feminist Pedagogy: European Perspectives.* York: Raw Nerve.

Henry, Astrid. 2004. *Not My Mother's Sister: Generational Conflict and Third-Wave Feminism*. Bloomington: Indiana University Press.

Hill Collins, Patricia. 1991. *Black Feminist Thought: Knowledge, Consciousness, and the Politics of Empowerment*. New York: Routledge.

Hirschman, Albert O. 1945. "Introduction." In Varian Fry, ed., *Assignment: Rescue: An Autobiography*. New York: Scholastic.

——— 1994. *Passaggi di Frontiera. I Luoghi e le Idee di un Percorso di Vita*. Rome: Donzelli.

Hirschmann, Ursula. 1993. *Noi Senza Patria*. Bologna: Il Mulino.

Hocquenghem, Guy. 1986. *Open Letter to Those Who Moved from Mao Collars to Rotary Wheels*. Marseilles: Agone.

Holland, Eugene W. 1999. *Deleuze and Guattari's Anti-Oedipus: Introduction to Schizo-analysis*. New York: Routledge.

——— 2006. "Nomad Citizenship and Global Democracy." In Martin Fuglsang and Bent Meier Sorensen, eds., *Gilles Deleuze and the Social: Toward a New Social Analytic*, pp. 191–206. Edinburgh: Edinburgh University Press.

hooks, bell. 1990. *Yearning: Race, Gender, and Cultural Politics*. Toronto: Between the Lines.

——— 1994. *Outlaw Culture: Resisting Representations*. New York: Routledge.

——— 1995. *Killing Rage: Ending Racism*. New York: Holt.

Huntington, Samuel. 1996. *The Clash of Civilizations and the Remaking of World Order*. New York: Simon and Schuster.

Huyssen, Andreas. 1986. *After the Great Divide: Modernism, Mass Culture, Postmodernism*. Bloomington: Indiana University Press.

Irigaray, Luce. 1974. *Speculum de l'autre femme*. Paris: Minuit. English translation: 1985. *Speculum of the Other Woman*. Trans. Gillian C. Gill. Ithaca: Cornell University Press.

——— 1977. *Ce Sexe qui n'en est pas un*. Paris: Minuit.

——— 1980. *Amante marine*. Paris: Minuit.

——— 1984. *L'Éthique de la différence sexuelle*. Paris: Minuit.

——— 1987. *Sexes et parentés*. Paris: Minuit.

——— 1989. *Le Temps de la différence*. Paris: Livre de Poche.

——— 1990. *Je, tu, nous: Pour une culture de la différence*. Paris: Grasset.

——— 1991. "Love Between Us." In Eduardo Cadava, Peter Connor, and Jean-Luc Nancy, eds., *Who Comes After the Subject?* pp. 167–177. New York: Routledge.

——— 1992. *J'Aime à toi: Esquisse d'une félicité dans l'histoire*. Paris: Grasset.

——— 1997. *To Be Two*. New York: Routledge.

Jaggar, Allison M., and Iris M. Young, eds. 1998. *A Companion to Feminist Philosophy*. Malden, MA: Blackwell.

Johnson, Richard. 1999. "Exemplary Differences. Mourning (and Not Mourning) a Princess." In Adrian Kear and L. Deborah Steinberg, eds., *Mourning Diana. Nation, Culture, and the Performance of Grief*, pp. 15–39. New York: Routledge.

Jordan, Jim. 1995. "Collective Bodies: Raving and the Politics of Gilles Deleuze and Felix Guattari." *Body and Society* 1:125–144.

Jordanova, Ludmilla. 1993. *Sexual Visions: Images of Gender in Science and Medicine Between the Eighteenth and Twentieth Centuries*. Madison: University of Wisconsin Press.

Kappelar, Susan. 1986. *The Pornography of Representation*. Cambridge: Polity.

Kavanagh, James H. 1990. "Feminism, Humanism, and Science." In Annette Kuhn, ed., *Alien Zone*, pp. 82–90. London: Verso.

Keller, Catherine. 1998. "Christianity." In Alison M. Jaggar and Iris M.Young, eds., *A Companion to Feminist Philosophy*, pp. 225–234. Oxford: Blackwell.

Keller, Evelyn Fox. 1983. *A Feeling for the Organism: The Life and Work of Barbara McClintock*. New York: Holt.

——— 2000. *The Century of the Gene*. Cambridge: Harvard University Press.

Kelly, Joan. 1979. "The Double-Edged Vision of Feminist Theory." *Feminist Studies* 5, no.1 (Spring): 216–227.

Kristeva, Julia. 1980. *Pouvoirs de l'Horreur*. Paris: Seuil.

——— 1982. *Powers of Horror: An Essay on Abjection*. New York: Columbia University Press.

——— 1991. *Strangers to Ourselves*. New York: Columbia University Press.

Kymlicka, Will. 1995. *Multicultural Citizenship*. Oxford: Clarendon.

Laclau, Ernesto. 1995. "Subjects of Politics, Politics of the Subject." *differences* 7, no. 1 (March): 146–164.

Land, Nick. 1995. "Meat: Or How to Kill Oedipus in Cyberspace." *Body and Society* 1, nos. 3 and 4 (November): 191–204.

Laplanche, Jean. 1976. *Life and Death in Psychoanalysis*. Baltimore: Johns Hopkins University Press.

Lauretis, Teresa de. 1986. *Feminist Studies/Critical Studies*. Bloomington: Indiana University Press.

——— 1987. *Technologies of Gender*. Bloomington: Indiana University Press.

——— 1990. "Eccentric Subjects: Feminist Theory and Historical Consciousness." *Feminist Studies* 6, no. 1 (Spring): 115–150.

Lazzarato, Maurizio. 1996. "Immaterial Labour." In Michael Hardt and Paolo Virno, eds., *Radical Thought in Italy: A Potential Politics*. Minneapolis: University of Minnesota Press.

——— 2004. *Les revolutions du capitalisme*. Paris: Seuil.

Lee, Hermione. 1996. *Virginia Woolf*. London: Chatto and Windus.

Levi, Primo. 1958. *Se questo è un uomo*. Turin: Einaudi.

Lévinas, Emmanuel. 1999. *Alterity and Transcendence*. London: Athlone.

Lévy, Bernard-Henri. 1977. "Response to the Master Censors." *Telos* 33 (Fall): 116–119.

Livingston, Judith, and Ira Livingston, eds. 1995. *Posthuman Bodies*. Bloomington: Indiana University Press.

Lloyd, Genevieve. 1984. *The Man of Reason: Male and Female in Western Philosophy*. London: Methuen.

——— 1994. *Part of Nature: Self-knowledge in Spinoza's Ethics*. Ithaca: Cornell University Press.

———— 1996. *Spinoza and the Ethics*. New York: Routledge.

———— 2008. *Providence Lost*. Cambridge: Harvard University Press.

Lorde, Audre. 1984. *Sister Outsider*. Trumansberg, NY: Crossing.

Lorraine, Tamsin. 1999. *Irigaray and Deleuze: Experiments in Visceral Philosophy*. Ithaca: Cornell University Press.

Lovibond, Sabina. 1994. "The End of Morality." In Kathleen Lenno and Margaret Whitford, eds., *Knowing the Difference: Feminist Perspectives in Epistemology*, pp. 63–78. New York: Routledge.

Lury, Celia. 1998. *Prosthetic Culture: Photography, Memory, and Identity*. New York: Routledge.

Lutz, Helma, Nira Yuval-Davis, and Ann Phoenix, eds. 1996. *Crossfires: Nationalism, Racism, and Gender in Europe*. London: Pluto.

Lyotard, Jean François. 1983. *Le Différend*. Paris: Minuit.

———— 1986. *Le Post-Moderne Expliqué aux Enfants*. Paris: Galilée.

———— 1988. *L'Inhumain: Causeries sur le Temps*. Paris: Galilée.

———— 1998. *La Confession d'Augustin*. Paris: Galilée.

MacCormack, Patricia. 2004. "Parabolic Philosophies: Analogue and Affect." *Theory, Culture, and Society* 21, no. 6 (December): 179–187.

———— 2008. *Cinesexualities*. London: Ashgate.

MacKinnon, Catharine. 2006. *Are Women Human? And Other International Dialogues*. Cambridge: Harvard University Press.

McNay, Lois. 1992. *Foucault and Feminism*. Cambridge: Polity.

Mahmood, Saba. 2005. *Politics of Piety: The Islamic Revival and the Feminist Subject*. Princeton: Princeton University Press.

Margulis, Lynn, and Dorion Sagan. 1995. *What Is Life?* Berkeley: University of California Press.

Marks, John. 1998. *Gilles Deleuze: Vitalism and Multiplicity*. London: Pluto.

Massumi, Brian. 1992. "Anywhere You Want to Be: An Introduction to Fear." In Joan Broadhurst, ed., *Deleuze and the Transcendental Unconscious*, pp. 175–215. Warwick: Warwick Journal of Philosophy.

———— 1997. *Deleuze, Guattari and the Philosophy of Expression*. Special issue. *Canadian Review of Comparative Literature/Revue Canadienne de Littérature Comparée* 24, no. 3 (September).

———— 1998. "Requiem for Our Prospective Dead! Toward a Participatory Critique of Capitalist Power." In Eleanor Kaufman and Kevin Jon Heller, eds., *Deleuze and Guattari: New Mappings in Politics, Philosophy, and Culture*, pp. 40–64. Minneapolis: University of Minnesota Press.

———— 2002. *Parables for the Virtual: Movement, Affect, Sensation*. Durham: Duke University Press.

Maturana, Humberto, and Francisco Varela. 1972. *Autopoiesis and Cognition: The Realization of the Living*. Dordrecht: Reidel.

May, Todd. 1995. *The Moral Theory of Poststructuralism*. University Park: Pennsylvania State University Press.

Mbembe, Achille. 2001. *On the Postcolony*. Berkeley: University of California Press.

———— 2003. "Necropolitics." *Public Culture* 15, no. 1 (January): 11–40.

Mény, Yves. 2000. *Tra Utopia e realtà: Una Costituzione per l'Europa*. Florence: Possigli.

Midgley, Mary. 1996. *Utopias, Dolphins, and Computers: Problems of Philosophical Plumbing*. New York: Routledge.

Mills Norton, Theodore. 1986. "Line of Flight: Gilles Deleuze, or Political Science Fiction." *New Political Science*, no. 15 (Summer): 77–93.

Minh-Ha, Trinh. 1989. *Woman, Native, Other*. Bloomington: Indiana University Press.

Mitchell, Juliet. 1974. *Psychoanalysis and Feminism*. New York: Pantheon.

Modleski, Tania. 1986. *Studies in Entertainment*. Bloomington: Indiana University Press.

Mohanty, Chandra. 1992. "Feminist Encounters: Locating the Politics of Experience." In Michele Barrett and Anne Phillips, eds., *Destabilizing Theory: Contemporary Feminist Debates*, pp. 254–272. Cambridge: Polity.

Moore, Henrietta. 2007. *The Subject of Anthropology*. Cambridge: Polity.

Morin, Edgar. 1987. *Penser l'Europe*. Paris: Gallimard.

Morrison, Toni. 1992. *Playing in the Dark: Whiteness and the Literary Imagination*. Cambridge: Harvard University Press.

Morton, Donald. 1999. "Birth of the Cyberqueer." In Jenny Wolmark, ed., *Cybersexualities*, pp. 55–68. Edinburgh: Edinburgh University Press.

Mouffe, Chantal. 1994. "For a Politics of Nomadic Identity." In Gorge Robertson, Melinda Mash, Lisa Tickner, Jon Bird, Barry Curtis, and Tim Putnam, eds., *Travellers' Tales: Narratives of Home and Displacement*, pp. 105–113. New York: Routledge.

Nemoianu, Virgil. 2006. "The Church and the Secular Establishment: A Philosophical Dialogue Between Joseph Ratzinger and Jürgen Habermas." *Logos* 9, no 2 (April): 17–41.

Nicolson, Nigel. ed. 1992. *Vita and Harold: The Letters of Vita Sackville-West and Harold Nicholson*. New York: Putnam's.

Nicolson, Nigel, and Joanne Trautmann, eds. 1977. *The Letters of Virginia Woolf*, vol. 3: *1923–1928*. New York: Harvest.

Nietzsche, Friedrich. 1966. *Beyond Good and Evil*. London: Vintage.

Nigianni, Chrysanthi. 2008. "Re-thinking Queer: A Film Philosophy Project." Ph.D. diss., University of East London.

Norton, Ann. 2004. *Leo Strauss and the Politics of American Empire*. New Haven: Yale University Press.

Noys, Benjamin. 2008. "The End of the Monarchy of Sex: Sexuality and Contemporary Nihilism." *Theory, Culture, and Society* 25, no. 5 (September): 104–122.

Nuhoglu Soysal, Yasemin. 1994. *Limits of Citizenship: Migrants and Postnational Membership in Europe*. Chicago: University of Chicago Press.

Nussbaum, Martha. 1999. *Cultivating Humanity*. Cambridge: Harvard University Press.

———— 2006. *Frontiers of Justice: Disability, Nationality, Species Membership*. Cambridge: Harvard University Press.

Olkowski, Dorothea. 1994. "Nietzsche's Dice Throw." In Constantin V. Boundas and Dorothea Olkowski, eds., *Gilles Deleuze and the Theater of Philosophy*, pp. 99–116. New York: Routledge.

Ong, Aihwa. 1993. "On the Edge of Empires: Flexible Citizenship Among Chinese in Diaspora." *Positions* 1, no. 3 (March): 745–778.

Parisi, Luciana. 2004. *Abstract Sex: Philosophy, Biotechnology, and the Mutation of Desire*. London: Continuum.

—— 2004. "For a Schizogenesis of Sexual Difference." *Identities* 3, no. 1 (Summer): 67–93.

Passerini, Luisa. 1988. *Autoritratto di Gruppo*. Florence: Giunti.

Passerini, Luisa, ed. 1998. *Identità Culturale Europea: Idee, Sentimenti, Relazioni*. Florence: Nuova Italia.

—— 2003. *Memoria e Utopia*. Turin: Bollati-Boringhieri.

Pateman, Carol. 1988. *The Sexual Contract*. Cambridge: Polity.

Patton, Paul. 1994. "Anti-Platonism and Art." In Constantin V. Boundas and Dorothea Olkowski, eds., *Gilles Deleuze and the Theater of Philosophy*, pp. 141–156. New York: Routledge.

—— 2000. *Deleuze and the Political*. New York: Routledge.

Phillips, Adam. 1999. *Darwin's Worms*. London: Faber and Faber.

Pisters, Patricia. 1998. "From Eye to Brain, Gilles Deleuze: Refiguring the Subject in Film Theory." Ph.diss., University of Amsterdam.

Plotnitsky, Arkady. 2002. *The Knowable and the Unknowable*. Ann Arbor: University of Michigan Press.

Preuss, Ulrich K. 1995. "Problems of a Concept of European Citizenship." *European Law Journal* 1, no. 3 (November): 267–281.

—— 1996. "Two Challenges to European Citizenship." *Political Studies* 44:534–552.

Probyn, Elspeth. 1990. "Travels in the Postmodern: Making Sense of the Local." In Linda Nicholson. ed. *Feminism/Postmodernism*, pp. 176–189. New York: Routledge.

—— 1996. *Outside Belongings*. New York: Routledge.

Protevi, John. 2009. *Political Affect: Connecting the Social and the Somatic*. Minneapolis, University of Minnesota Press.

Protevi, John, and Paul Patton, eds. 2003. *Between Derrida and Deleuze*. London: Continuum.

Rabinow, Paul. 2003. *Anthropos Today*. Princeton: Princeton University Press.

Ramadan, Tariq. 2003. *To Be a European Muslim*. Leicestershire: Islamic Foundation.

Raqs Media Collective. 2003. "'A/S/L.'" In Ursula Biemann, ed., *Geography and the Politics of Mobility*. Vienna: General Foundation.

Regulska, Joanna. 1998. "The New 'Other' European Woman.'" In Virginia Ferreira, Teresa Tavares, and Silvia Portugal, eds., *Shifting Bonds, Shifting Bounds: Women, Mobility, and Citizenship in Europe*. Oeiras: Celta.

Rich, Adrienne. 1977. *Of Woman Born: Motherhood as Experience and Institution*. London: Virago.

—— 1985. *Blood, Bread, and Poetry*. New York: Norton.

———— 2001. *Arts of the Possible*. New York: Norton.

Rose, Hilary. 2001. "Nine Decades, Nine Women, Ten Nobel Prizes: Gender Politics on the Apex of Science." In Mary Wyer, Mary Barbercheck, Donna Geisman, Hatice Orun Otzurk, and Marta Wayne, eds., *Women, Science, and Technology: A Reader in Feminist Science Studies*, pp. 53–68. New York: Routledge.

Rose, Nicholas. 2001. "The Politics of Life Itself." *Theory, Culture, and Society* 18, no. 6 (December): 1–30.

Rossanda, Rossana. 2005. *La Ragazza del Secolo Scorso*. Turin: Einaudi.

Rowbotham, Sheila. 1973. *Women, Resistance, and Revolution*. New York: Random House.

Roy, Arundhati. 2001. *Power Politics*. Cambridge: South End.

Roy, Kaustuv. 2003. *Teachers in Nomadic Spaces*. New York: Peter Lang.

Roy, Olivier. 1999. *Vers un Islam Européen*. Paris: Esprit.

Rushdie, Salman. 1997. "Crash: Was Diana's Death the Result of Sexual Assault?" *New Yorker,* September 15, pp. 68–69.

Russell, Letty M. 1974. *Human Liberation in a Feminist Perspective—A Theology*. Philadelphia: Westminster.

Said, Edward. 1978. *Orientalism*. London: Penguin.

Salvo, Louise de, and Mitchell A. Leaska, eds. 1984. *The Letters of Vita Sackville-West to Virginia Woolf*. London: Palgrave Macmillan.

Sandoval, Chela. 1999. "New Sciences: Cyborg Feminism and the Methodology of the Oppressed." In Jenny Wolmark, ed., *Cybersexualities*, pp. 247–263. Edinburgh: Edinburgh University Press.

Sassen, Saskia. 1994. *Cities in a World Economy*. Thousand Oaks, CA: Pine Forge/Sage.

———— 1995. *Losing Control. Sovereignty in an Age of Globalization*. New York: Columbia University Press.

Schmitt, Carl. 1996. *The Concept of the Political*. Chicago: University of Chicago Press.

Schussler Fiorenza, Elizabeth. 1983. *In Memory of Her: A Feminist Theological Reconstruction of Christian Origins*. New York: Crossroads.

Scott, Joan Wallach. 1996. *Only Paradoxes to Offer: French Feminism and the Rights of Man*. Cambridge: Harvard University Press.

———— 2007. *The Politics of the Veil*. Princeton: Princeton University Press.

———— 2009. "Sexularism." In *The Annual Ursula Hirschman Lecture*. Fiesole: Robert Schuman Centre for Advanced Study, European University Institute, April 23.

Seltzer, Mark. 1999. "Wound Culture: Trauma in the Pathological Public Sphere." *October* 8:3–26.

Shaviro, Steven. 1995. "Two Lessons from Burroughs." In Judith Halberstam and Ira Livingston, eds., *Posthuman Bodies*, pp. 38–54. Bloomington: Indiana University Press.

Shiva, Vandana. 1997. *Biopiracy: The Plunder of Nature and Knowledge*. Boston: South End.

Shohat, Ella, and Robert Stam. 1994. *Unthinking Eurocentrism: Multiculturalism and the Media*. New York: Routledge.

Smith, Daniel W. 1997. "'A Life of Pure Immanence': Deleuze's 'Critique et clinique' Project," In Gilles Deleuze, *Essays Critical and Clinical*, xi–liii. Trans. Daniel W. Smith and Michael A. Greco. Minneapolis: University of Minnesota Press.

Sobchack, Vivian. 1999. "Toward a Phenomenology of Non-Fictional Experience." In Michael Renov and Jane Gaines, eds., *Collecting Visible Evidence*, pp. 241–254. Minneapolis: University of Minnesota Press.

Sontag, Susan. 2003. *Regarding the Pain of Others*. New York: Picador.

Spinelli, Altiero. 1979. "La Vie Politique d'Ursula Hirschmann, Fondatrice de Femmes pour l'Europe." In *Textes et Documents*, pp. 11–15. Brussels: Ministère des Affaires Étrangères, du Commerce Extérieur et de la Coopération au Développement.

—— 1988. *Come ho Tentato di Diventare Saggio*. Bologna: Il Mulino.

—— 1992. *Diario Europeo*. Bologna: Il Mulino.

Spinelli, Altiero, and Ernesto Rossi. 1998. "Per un'Europa Libera e Unita: Progetto d'un Manifesto." In Luisa Passerini, ed., *Identità Culturale Europea: Idee, Sentimenti, Relazioni*. Florence: La Nuova Italia.

Spivak, Gayatri C. 1987. *In Other Worlds: Essays in Cultural* Politics. London: Methuen.

—— 1993. *Outside in the Teaching Machine*. New York: Routledge.

—— 1999. *A Critique of Postcolonial Reason: Toward a History of the Vanishing Present*. Cambridge: Harvard University Press.

Springer, Claudia. 1991. "The Pleasure of the Interface." In *Screen* 32, no. 3: 303–323.TK

Spurlin, William J. 1999. "Exemplary Differences: Mourning and Not Mourning a Princess." In Adrian Kear and L. Deborah Steinberg, eds., *Mourning Diana: Nation, Culture, and the Performance of Grief*, pp. 15–39. New York: Routledge.

Squier, Susan. 1995. "Reproducing the Posthuman Body: Ectogenetic Fetus, Surrogate Mother, Pregnant Man." In Judith Halberstam and Ira Livingston, eds., *Posthuman Bodies*, pp. 113–134. Bloomington: Indiana University Press.

Starhawk. 1999. *The Spiral Dance*. San Francisco: Harper.

Stengers, Isabelle. 1997. *Power and Invention: Situating Science*. Minneapolis: University of Minnesota Press.

Stimpson, Catharine R. 1988. *Where the Meanings Are*. New York: Methuen.

Stivale, Charles. 1991. "Mille/Punks/Cyber/Plateaus: Science Fiction and Deleuzo-Guattarian 'Becomings.'" *SubStance*, no. 66: 66–84.

Svevo, Italo. 1985. *La Coscienza di Zeno*. Milan: Garzanti.

Taylor, Charles. 2007. *A Secular Age*. Cambridge: Harvard University Press.

Tayyab, Basharat. 1998. "Islam." In Alison M. Jaggar and Iris M.Young, eds., *A Companion to Feminist Philosophy*, pp. 236–244. Oxford: Blackwell.

Thomas, Louis-Vincent. 1979. *Civilization and Its Divagations: Mort, Fantasmes, Science-Fiction*. Paris: Payot.

Tobias, Saul. 2005. "Foucault on Freedom and Capabilities." *Theory, Culture and Society* 22 (August): 65–85.

Todd, May. 1995. *The Moral Theory of Poststructuralism*. University Park: Pennsylvania State University Press.

Todorov, Tzvetan. 2002. *The Imperfect Garden: The Legacy of Humanism.* Princeton: Princeton University Press.

Toscano, Alberto. 2006. *The Theatre of Production: Philosophy and Individuation Between Kant and Deleuze.* Basingstoke: Palgrave.

Touraine, Alain. 2001. *Beyond Neoliberalism.* Cambridge: Polity.

Tuin, Iris van der. 2008. "Deflationary Logic: Response to Sara Ahmed's 'Imaginary Prohibitions': Some Preliminary Remarks on the Founding Gestures of the 'New Materialism.'" *European Journal of Women's Studies* 15, no. 4: 411–416.

Vattimo, Gianni. 2005. *The Future of Religion.* New York: Columbia University Press.

Verma, Jatinder. 1999. "Mourning Diana, Asian Style." In Adrian Kear and L. Deborah Steinberg, eds., *Mourning Diana: Nation, Culture, and the Performance of Grief*, pp. 120–125. New York: Routledge.

Virilio, Paul. 2002. *Desert Screen: War at the Speed of Light.* London: Continuum.

Virno, Paolo. 2004. *A Grammar of the Multitude.* New York: Semiotexte.

Wadud, Amina. 1999. *Qur'an and Woman: Rereading the Sacred Text from a Woman's Perspective.* Oxford: Oxford University Press.

Walker, Alice. 1984. *In Search of Our Mother's Gardens.* London: Women's Press.

Walkerdine, Valerie. 1999. "The Crowd in the Age of Diana: Ordinary Inventiveness and the Popular Imagination." In Adrian Kear and L. Deborah Steinberg, eds., *Mourning Diana: Nation, Culture, and the Performance of Grief*, pp. 98–107. New York: Routledge.

Walzer, Michael. 1992. *What It Means to Be an American.* New York: Marsilio.

Ware, Vron. 1992. *Beyond the Pale: White Women, Racism, and History.* New York: Verso.

West, Cornell. 1994. *Prophetic Thought in Postmodern Times.* Monroe, ME: Common Courage.

White, Eric. 1995. "They Were Men, Now They're Landcrabs: Monstrous Becomings in Evolutionist Cinema." In Judith Halberstam and Ira Livingston, eds., *Posthuman Bodies*, pp. 244–266. Bloomington: Indiana University Press.

Wiegman, Robyn. 2002. *Women's Studies on Its Own.* Durham: Duke University Press.

Wiener, Norbert. 1948. *Cybernetics; or, Control and Communication in the Animal and the Machine.* New York: Wiley.

Wilson, Elizabeth A. 1998. *Neural Geographies: Feminism and the Microstructure of Cognition.* New York: Routledge.

Wittig, Monique. 1992. *The Straight Mind and Other Essays.* Hemel Hempstead: Harvester Wheatsheaf.

Wolfe, Cary. ed. 2003. *Zoontologies.* Minneapolis: University of Minnesota Press.

Woolf, Virginia. 1938. *Three Guineas.* London: Hogarth.

—— 1977a. *Orlando.* London: Grafton.

—— 1977b. *The Waves.* London: Grafton.

—— 1980. *The Diary of Virginia Woolf,* vol. 3: *1925–1930.* New York: Harvest.

—— 1993. *Flush.* London: Penguin.

Young, Robert. 1990. *White Mythologies: Writing History and the West*. New York: Routledge.

Yuval-Davis, Nira, and Floya Anthias, eds. 1989. *Woman-Nation-State*. London: Palgrave Macmillan.

Žižek, Slavoj. 2000. *The Fragile Absolute*. London: Verso.

——— 2003. The Puppet and the Dwarf: The Perverse Core of Christianity. Cambridge: MIT Press.

——— 2004. *Iraq: The Borrowed Kettle*. London: Verso.

Zoe, Sofia. 1984. "Exterminating Fetuses: Abortion, Disarmament, and the Sexo-Semiotics of Extraterrestrialism." *Diacritics* 14, no. 2 (Summer): 47–59.

Zourabichvili, François. 2003. *Le Vocabulaire de Deleuze*. Paris: Ellipses.

INDEX

182; power relations in, 25; refugees from, 44; sameness and, 173–74; scattered hegemonies and, 137–38
"Global risk society," 319
Grossberg, Lawrence, 109–10
Grosz, Elizabeth, 111
Guattari, Felix, 5–6, 31, 37, 150, 162, 209, 222, 267, 271; on allopoietic and autopoietic systems, 115–16; on body-machine, 75; on collective, 116; on complexity dimensions, 119; ecologies of, 287; on subjectivity, 116–18

Habermas, Jurgen, 179–82
Habits, negativity and, 291–92
Hagelian dialectics, 2
Halberstam, Judith, 110
Hall, Stuart, 242
Halsey, Mark, 354
Hanafin, Patrick, 334
Happiness, politics of, 277
Haraway, Donna, 105, 122, 171, 198, 220, 237, 243, 328–30; on cyborgs, 65–66, 68–69; on "informatics of domination," 134; on OncoMouse, 92–93; on power relations, 67
Harding, Sandra, 243
Hayles, Katherine, 63; on posthuman embodiment, 75–76
Health, politics and, 279, 337
Hegel, Georg Wilhelm Friedrich, 285, 303
High theory, generalized fatigue with, 172
Hirschman, Albert, 243
Hirschman, Ursula, 243
History of Sexuality (Foucault), 280
Holocaust, 242–43, 273, 292
Homosexuality: feminist posthumanism and, 141–42; identity and, 49, 166; insects and, 111–12; postsecularism and, 195–96; Princess Diana and, 47; religion and, 190; sameness and, 166; women and, 141, 166–67
Hope: future and, 237, 297–98; motivation from, 297
Humanism, 88–89

Humanity: machines linked to, 58; Renaissance ideal of, 82; technology and evolution of, 77
Huntington, Sam, 189
Huyssen, Andreas, 57, 59

Identity: becoming and, 30–31; body-machine and, 60; changes with, 219–20; in EU, 250; in EU, postnationalist, 260–61, 263–64; EU paradoxes with, 262; EU race and, 250–54; faciality and, 48–49; faithfulness to, 306; feminism and, 14, 96; flexible citizenship and, 254–55, 257–58; in global diaspora, 246–47, 256; homosexuality and, 49, 166; memory and, 33; Princess Diana and feminist, 46–47; sexuality and, 142–43; whiteness and, 251–52; see also Becoming; Disidentification; Self
Imagination: affectivity of, 155, 229, 236; communities and, 260; memory and, 31–32, 236; of Woolf, 159; see also Creativity
Individuality, subjectivity compared to, 3–4
Industrial revolution, 56
Inequality: feminism and, 26; globalization and, 26; technology access and, 26
"Informatics of domination," 134
Insects: body and, 101; codes of, 102–3; communication of, 105–6; disease and, 111; homosexuality and, 111–12; metamorphoses of, 103–4; music of, 105–10; otherness of, 102; in popular culture, 103, 105; reproduction and, 110–12; sexuality of, 104, 110–12; see also Becoming-insect
Intensive genre: postgender and, 167–69; specificity of, 168; Woolf and, 151–56
Interconnection, of self, 310–11
Internet: brain compared to, 105; ideas accessed by, 12; see also Cyberspace
Irigaray, Luce, 15, 141–42; on Deleuze, 38
Islamophobia: in Europe, 178–79, 188–91; globalization and, 183–84; women and, 188–89

Men, becoming-minoritarian and, 36; *see also* Gender

Metamorphoses, 9–13; globalization and, 19–20; of insects, 103–4; modern existence and, 11; representation challenges with, 15; of self, 164; *see also* Becoming

Meta(l)morphoses, *see* Becoming-machine

Metaphysical cannibalism, 28

Methodological nationalism, 217–18

Metropolis, 59–60, 78

Midgley, Mary, 88–89

Mind: body unity with, 311–12; embodiment of, 2; sexuality and, 144–45

Mind-body dualism, 99–100, 144

Minorities: of becoming, 29–30; becoming-minoritarian challenges for, 41–42; negative memory and, 32; revolutions and, 32; *see also* Becoming-minoritarian

Mobility: of advanced capitalism, 25–26; of body, 311; capitalism propelling, 17–18; of creativity, 152–53; of desire, 205–6; forms of, 10; in globalization, 246; of nomadic thought, 11–12; philosophical thought and, 9–10; technology and, 12; temporality and, 12

Molar formation, 6–7; gender and, 38–39; primary function of, 34

Molar memory, 164

Moore, Henrietta, 198

Moral authority, 300–1

Moral relativism, 299–300

Morin, Edgar, 220, 262

Morrison, Toni, 251

Mortality: matter-realism and, 329; Woolf and, 334; *see also* Death

Movement, *see* Mobility

Multiplicity: in nomadic thought, 209; subject and, 209–15

Music: becoming and, 110; of birds, 106; of insects, 105–10; posthuman embodiment and, 108–9; rhizomatic, 109; technology and, 106–7; time and, 106, 109;

transpositions and, 226, 234; visualization compared to sound and, 107

Narcissism: life and, 333; sameness and, 167

Nationalism: methodological, 217–18; nomadic thought rejecting, 240–41; resurgent, 171

Necessity, freedom and, 293

Necropolitics, 335–39

Necropower, 330–32, 336

Negativity: critique of, 323; desire creating positive passions from, 229, 236, 278; desire tied to, 284; endurance and, 314–18; freedom from, 313, 315; habits and, 291–92; meaning from, 292; of minorities memory, 32; overturning, 292–93; philosophical thought and, 285; in psychoanalysis, 289–90; self destruction from, 288; subjectivity and, 287; time and, 290; zoe and, 288–89

Neoliberalism: difference and, 171; flexible citizenship and, 255–56, 319–20

Neoliberal postfeminism, 175–79; globalization and, 178–79; heroism and, 177; historical amnesia in, 176; memory lapses in, 177; racism and, 176–77; revisionist history in, 177–78

Neovitalist thought, 199–200, 302, 320; feminism and, 200

Nicholson, Harold, 160

Nomadic citizenship, 19–20; *see also* Flexible citizenship

Nomadic ecophilosophy, 352–53

Nomadic ethics, 122

Nomadic feminism, 41; power relations and, 49–50

Nomadic machines, 58–62

Nomadic spirituality, 199–203

Nomadic thought, 1; becoming-machine approach of, 76–77; becoming-minoritarian and, 34; body-machine and, 58–62; concept of, 2–3; context for, 5–8; contradictory elements in, 7;

Stacey, Jackie, 173
Stimpson, Kate, 158–59
Strauss, Leo, 200
Subject: as becoming, 209–15; as European citizen, 210–11; multiplicity and, 209–15; process-oriented vision of, 218; shifting image of, 294; striving of, 310; universalism of, 212
Subjectivity: autopoiesis and, 118; cartographic method and, 121–22; conscious agency and, 76; death and, 334; embodied, 69; empowerment and, 119; in global diaspora, 244; Guattari on, 116–18; individuality compared to, 3–4; negativity and, 287; nomadic thought and, 6, 211, 317; political, 277–78; political economy of, 204; power relations and, 4; psychoanalysis and political, 197; religion and, 186; representation and transformation of, 8–9; sameness and, 212; sustainability limits with, 307–8
Sustainability: as concrete concept, 310; endurance and, 296–97; ethics of, 162–65, 306–13; intensity combined with, 231; of memory, 235; of "plane of immanence," 161; of positive passions, 165; for potentia, 317; of relationships, 163; social, 230–31; subjectivity and limits of, 307–8; thresholds of, 323–24

Taylor, Charles, 180–81
Technology: accountability with, 87; ethics and, 80; fear of, 55–56; humanity's evolution and, 77; inequality and access to, 26; mobility and, 12; music and, 106–7; sexuality and, 78–79; women interacting with, 78–79; see also Machines
Terrorism, fear and, 295
Thanatos, 328
Thatcher, Margaret, 177
Thinking: affirmation in, 282; becoming-animal and, 84; chaosmosis and, 213–14; concept of, 2; desire for, 282–83; for life intensity, 360–61

Third wave feminism, 138, 147, 200–201
Thomas, Louis-Vincent, 103
Time: becoming and process of, 35, 284; death as, 343; music and, 106, 109; negativity and notions of, 290; nonlinear, 228–30; politics and, 31–32; timeless, 309; Woolf and dual structure of, 153–54
Touraine, Alain, 171
Transformative ethics, 302–6
Transformative politics, 295
Transindividuality, 353–54
Transpositions: context and, 227; genetic, 226–27; memory and, 233–34; music and, 226, 234; in nomadic thought, 224–28; precision of, 233
Traveling theories, 138

Universalism, 129; crimes of, 215; critique of, 211–12; ethics and, 299–302; in EU, 243–44; gender and, 133; of subject, 212

van der Tuin, Iris, 135–36
van Oldenburg, Helene, 105
Varela, Francisco, 115
Verma, Jatinder, 48
Virtual ecology, 119–20
Visualization: affirmation and, 236–38; creativity and, 237; feminism and, 72; future and, 237; music and sound compared to, 107; omnipotence of, 71–72; in popular culture, 197–98; in science, 71
Vitalism: desire and, 21; matter-realism and, 149; nomadic, 214; return to, 199–200
Vital materialism, 16
Vulnerability: global, 319; pain and, 318–23

Walkerdine, Valerie, 47
Walzer, Michael, 250
The Waves (Woolf), 155
Weaver, Sigourney, 50–51

GENDER AND CULTURE

A Series of Columbia University Press

NANCY K. MILLER AND VICTORIA ROSNER, SERIES EDITORS
CAROLYN G. HEILBRUN (1926–2003) AND NANCY K. MILLER, FOUNDING EDITORS

■ ■ ■

In Dora's Case: Freud, Hysteria, Feminism
EDITED BY CHARLES BERNHEIMER AND CLAIRE KAHANE

Breaking the Chain: Women, Theory, and French Realist Fiction
NAOMI SCHOR

Between Men: English Literature and Male Homosocial Desire
EVE KOSOFSKY SEDGWICK

Romantic Imprisonment: Women and Other Glorified Outcasts
NINA AUERBACH

The Poetics of Gender
EDITED BY NANCY K. MILLER

Reading Woman: Essays in Feminist Criticism
MARY JACOBUS

Honey-Mad Women: Emancipatory Strategies in Women's Writing
PATRICIA YAEGER

Subject to Change: Reading Feminist Writing
NANCY K. MILLER

Thinking Through the Body
JANE GALLOP

Gender and the Politics of History
JOAN WALLACH SCOTT

The Dialogic and Difference: "An/Other Woman" in Virginia Woolf and Christa Wolf
ANNE HERRMANN

Plotting Women: Gender and Representation in Mexico
JEAN FRANCO

Inspiriting Influences: Tradition, Revision, and Afro-American Women's Novels
MICHAEL AWKWARD

Hamlet's Mother and Other Women
CAROLYN G. HEILBRUN

Rape and Representation
EDITED BY LYNN A. HIGGINS AND BRENDA R. SILVER

Shifting Scenes: Interviews on Women, Writing, and Politics in Post-68 France
EDITED BY ALICE A. JARDINE AND ANNE M. MENKE

Tender Geographies: Women and the Origins of the Novel in France
JOAN DEJEAN

Unbecoming Women: British Women Writers and the Novel of Development
SUSAN FRAIMAN

The Apparitional Lesbian: Female Homosexuality and Modern Culture
TERRY CASTLE

George Sand and Idealism
NAOMI SCHOR

Becoming a Heroine: Reading About Women in Novels
RACHEL M. BROWNSTEIN

Nomadic Subjects: Embodiment and Sexual Difference in Contemporary Feminist Theory
ROSI BRAIDOTTI

Engaging with Irigaray: Feminist Philosophy and Modern European Thought
EDITED BY CAROLYN BURKE, NAOMI SCHOR, AND MARGARET WHITFORD

Second Skins: The Body Narratives of Transsexuality
JAY PROSSER

A Certain Age: Reflecting on Menopause
EDITED BY JOANNA GOLDSWORTHY

Mothers in Law: Feminist Theory and the Legal Regulation of Motherhood
EDITED BY MARTHA ALBERTSON FINEMAN AND ISABELLE KARPIN

Critical Condition: Feminism at the Turn of the Century
SUSAN GUBAR

Feminist Consequences: Theory for the New Century
EDITED BY ELISABETH BRONFEN AND MISHA KAVKA

Simone de Beauvoir, Philosophy, and Feminism
NANCY BAUER

Pursuing Privacy in Cold War America
DEBORAH NELSON

But Enough About Me: Why We Read Other People's Lives
NANCY K. MILLER

Palatable Poison: Critical Perspectives on The Well of Loneliness
EDITED BY LAURA DOAN AND JAY PROSSER

Cool Men and the Second Sex
SUSAN FRAIMAN

Modernism and the Architecture of Private Life
VICTORIA ROSNER

Virginia Woolf and the Bloomsbury Avant-Garde: War, Civilization, Modernity
CHRISTINE FROULA

The Scandal of Susan Sontag
EDITED BY BARBARA CHING AND JENNIFER A. WAGNER-LAWLOR

Mad for Foucault: Rethinking the Foundations of Queer Theory
LYNNE HUFFER

Graphic Women: Life Narrative and Contemporary Comics
HILLARY L. CHUTE

Gilbert and Sullivan: Gender, Genre, Parody
CAROLYN WILLIAMS

Nomadic Subjects: Embodiment and Sexual Difference in Contemporary Feminist Theory, 2d ed.
ROSI BRAIDOTTI

Gender and Culture Readers

Modern Feminisms: Political, Literary, Cultural
EDITED BY MAGGIE HUMM

Feminism and Sexuality: A Reader
EDITED BY STEVI JACKSON AND SUE SCOTT

Writing on the Body: Female Embodiment and Feminist Theory
EDITED BY KATIE CONBOY, NADIA MEDINA, AND SARAH STANBURY